Using Dreamweaver to Create e-Learning

A Comprehensive Guide to CourseBuilder and Learning Site

1st Edition

Garin Hess and Steven Hancock

Rapid Intake Press™
books and more for e-learning developers

www.rapidintake.com

Using Dreamweaver to Create e-Learning:
A Comprehensive Guide to CourseBuilder and Learning Site

by Garin A. Hess and Steven W. Hancock

ISBN: 0-915080-0-3

Published by Rapid Intake Press.

Rapid Intake, Inc.
1014 SE 144th CT
Vancouver, WA 98683

(360) 882-7307
FAX (360) 343-3015
www.rapidintake.com

Printing History
October 2001:   First Edition

Warning and Disclaimer
The authors and publisher of this book have made their best efforts in the preparation of this book and all the electronic examples to make them complete and as accurate as possible. The authors and publisher make no warranty, express or implied, on the information and programs in this book.

Trademarks
Numerous trademark names are used throughout this book. Every effort has been made to place indication marks on the first occurrence. The publisher cannot ensure the accuracy of this information. All trademark names have been used for the purpose of communicating the information in the book and for the benefit of the trademark owner with no intention of infringing upon that trademark.

Rapid Intake Press™
books and more for e-learning developers

http://www.rapidintake.com

About the Authors

Garin Hess is an e-learning developer with a history in instructional design and instructor-led training. With over twelve years of experience in the training and education field, his previous work includes positions as a trainer, e-learning development team leader, and training manager. He is currently CEO of Rapid Intake Inc., a firm specializing in custom e-learning design and development. Garin lives in the United States in the state of Washington with his wife and three children.

Steven Hancock is an instructional designer with a strong background in e-learning development. His instructional design and e-learning experience began at Utah State University where he worked on Dr. David M. Merrill's research and development team. He then took that experience to Brooks Air Force base in San Antonio, Texas to work with Dr. Robert Gagne to develop a prototype of an instructional design system. During the many years since that time he has worked on various projects as an Instructional Designer, Trainer, Team Leader, CBT developer, and WBT developer. He is currently the President of Rapid Intake, Inc. Steve lives in the state of Utah in the United States with his wife and seven children.

Acknowledgements

First and foremost I want to thank my wife Lynette. She has always supported me in everything I have done including the writing of this book. She is the most Christ-like person that I know.

I also need to thank Garin for asking me to join him on this adventure that we fondly call Rapid Intake. It has indeed been a joy.

I would be remiss if I didn't express my thanks to my parents. If they had not spent so many hours, sweat, and tears raising me, and my 7 siblings, right, I could not have accomplished anything in this life. They taught me how to work. They taught me how to succeed. They taught me how to be happy. They taught me how to have a balance in life. My parents truly know what is important in life and where joy is found. I am so grateful they passed that knowledge on to me.

Finally, I feel a need to thank all the professors at Utah State University who have made that Instructional Design program one of the top programs in the United States. That is really were my spark for e-learning started.

Steven Hancock

When I think of all of the people who have influenced me in writing this book, my thoughts go clear back to high school and earlier. Of course Mr. Braithwaite had no real idea that our BASIC programming class would galvanize my strong attraction to computers into a life-long love affair. And Mrs. Petersen couldn't have known that conveying her love of Robert Frost, William Shakespeare, and Joseph Conrad could possibly have had anything to do with a largely technical how-to guide to be written many years later. Yet these and so many others in my life subtly, but powerfully, shared their influence with me—their passion towards their subject, and their confidence in me.

I'm also grateful to Steve, whose down-to-earth approach to stressful situations has often brought me back to reality. I could not ask for a better business associate and friend.

But there are three people to whom I am thankful above all. My dad, whose work ethic and devotion to my mother and my brothers and sisters, and to his religion, taught me that it's possible to be successful professionally while still having a strong family and living up to your values. My mom, who encouraged excellence in all I did, often picked me up and dusted me off when I was down, and taught me I could do anything if I put my mind to it. And finally, my wife Kristin—my closest friend and ally, whose enthusiasm about what we're doing has often exceeded my own (which is tough to beat!). She is a spinning fire of life and light and I'm blessed to have her in my life.

As a final note of acknowledgement, all of these people, those mentioned and the innumerable unmentioned, represent to me the One to whom I owe all.

Garin Hess

We would both like to thank several others. Travis Fisher has been with us for several months now, and we have thoroughly abused, neglected, and sometimes (and we're sure he would agree with this) tortured him. He has been gracious enough to not run screaming out the door and has been an invaluable asset to our efforts. He is also a great CourseBuilder developer.

We need to thank our editor, Mark Brewer, for making sure we crossed our Ts and dotted our Is. He also kept us laughing through the whole process. We guarantee there is not a funnier editor anywhere.

Thanks to our reviewers (all e-learning developers) who made sure we never strayed too far off base: Alex Hogan, Bruce Duckworth, Roger Salvatore, Sharon Castillo, and Steve Wheeler.

Numerous people at Macromedia have been very helpful. Special thanks to Pat Brogan, Jean Lozano, Tom Person, and Dave Rosen. We are discovering that Macromedia produces not only awesome products, but is also an awesome company.

We would also like to thank Stefan Van As for answering questions about Learning Site Command.

Finally, we want to thank everyone on the Attain ListServ for their incredible insights, ideas, and helpful attitudes. It's fun getting to know you.

Garin Hess
Steven Hancock

Contents at a Glance

Table of Contents

Section II: Extending CourseBuilder 261

Chapter 11: Using CSS to Enhance CourseBuilder 263

Section III: Using Learning Site Command for Course Architecture 417

Chapter 17: Getting to Know Learning Site 419

Chapter 18: Defining A Learning Site 435

Chapter 19: Customizing A Learning Site 471

Section IV: Tracking Learner Data 497

Chapter 20: Using Learning Site to Track Learner Data 499

Foreword

Macromedia has long been known for its award-winning web page design and site management tools, Dreamweaver and Dreamweaver UltraDev. In 1999, Macromedia added CourseBuilder, an extension to Dreamweaver, then known as Attain Objects. At that point we had no idea how popular this extension would become among e-learning developers. Today more than 35,000 WBT developers and producers worldwide use CourseBuilder.

As CourseBuilder is limited to creating single interactive pages, Macromedia added another learning extension to Dreamweaver called Learning Site Command. This extension picks up where CourseBuilder left off, providing much needed course navigation and student data tracking tools. While Dreamweaver has been used for some time among WBT developers, Learning Site adds that integral component enabling Dreamweaver to become the popular e-learning tool that it is today.

Deciding which authoring tool to use is a tough one. We know you'll invest a considerable amount of time learning how to use it and you'll most likely have to maintain your courses for several years. At Macromedia, it is our hope that providing these two extensions to Dreamweaver, with plans for future improvement and enhancement, shows our commitment to the e-learning industry.

This year we were thrilled to have Dreamweaver UltraDev 4 awarded the Golden Seal Award for the best e-learning authoring tool. The Golden Seal Award is part of the Web-Based Training (WBT) User's Choice Awards, presented at the WBT Producer Conference and Expo.

The Gold Seal Award is given to the product in each category that accumulates the most votes in these areas:

- **Expectation.** How well the product meets the user's expectations relative to the product vendor's sales and marketing.
- **Implementation.** How well the product, when implemented, meets management objectives.
- **Impact.** How the product impacts the user's development or management efforts.
- **Satisfaction.** How the product rates overall.

By far, the most satisfying element of winning this award was knowing that this honor came not from a panel of judges but from a broad spectrum of active users of e-learning tools and technology (with over 3,200 votes cast).

However, having a good authoring tool is only half the battle—you have to know how to use it, and use it well. The single biggest message we hear from users of these extensions is "show me how to use these tools."

With this request in mind, I highly recommend *Using Dreamweaver to Create e-Learning*. Steve and Garin take you in-depth to demonstrate the potential of CourseBuilder and Learning Site. Their training experience shows through in the hands-on tutorials they provide---helping you internalize the skills required to use these tools. Moreover, throughout the book they lend helpful instructional design tips for various interactions, usability, and learner motivations. Their comprehensive approach is an absolute plus for both the novice and experienced e-learning developer.

Macromedia's tools and *Using Dreamweaver to Create e-Learning* make a winning combination. I am confident you'll be pleased with the results you achieve.

Best wishes in your e-learning development efforts,

Pat Brogan, PhD
Vice President, e-Learning
Macromedia

Introduction

Welcome to the world of e-learning. We hope you find this book useful. We have enjoyed writing it. It is the type of book we would have liked to have had when we first started creating e-learning using Dreamweaver.

We think that you will find this book useful, whether you are a newcomer to using Dreamweaver for e-learning or you have been using Coursebuilder and Learning Site for some time. In addition to step-by-step and reference information, we have included development tricks we have learned along the way. You will also find instructional design principles that we have found helpful as we've developed technology-based training.

This introduction lists prerequisite knowledge you will need, details the organization of the book, and provides basic information about using the book.

Prerequisite Knowledge

To get the most out of this book, you should have a working knowledge of Macromedia's Dreamweaver®. Although we provide information on creating e-learning using Dreamweaver, we do not teach you how to use the program.

If you are unfamiliar with Dreamweaver, there are several books on the market that you can refer to. You can also attend the course offered by Rapid Intake. To view a list of courses go to *http://www.rapidintake.com/training_courses.htm*.

We suggest that you have a working knowledge of these Dreamweaver topics:

- Planning and setting up a site
- Using Dreamweaver panels and the property inspector
- Using tables and layers to layout documents
- Using frames
- Using behaviors

How this Book is Organized

The first chapter of this book introduces e-learning and how Dreamweaver fits into that discipline. We present some advantages and disadvantages to using Dreamweaver as an e-learning authoring tool. The remaining chapters provide instruction on using CourseBuilder and Learning Site with Dreamweaver.

CourseBuilder and Learning Site are extensions to Dreamweaver. An extension is a new Dreamweaver feature that you can easily add. If you think of Dreamweaver as your web site or web page food processor, extensions are the additional choppers, grinders, etc. The functionality of the main tool doesn't change, but the add-on increases productivity as well as widens the potential of the tool.

The book is divided into four sections. Each section is described here.

Section I—Using Coursebuilder for Interactivity

This first section focuses on the basics of using the Coursebuilder extension to create interactivity. We dedicate a chapter to each of the interaction types.

If you have never used Coursebuilder before, you should spend some time in this section before moving on to other areas. If you are comfortable with Coursebuilder you can skip to section II and use section I as a reference.

Section II—Extending Coursebuilder

The second section is for the more advanced users of Coursebuilder. This section contains several chapters to help you unlock the power of the Action Manager. It also discusses using Cascading Style Sheets (CSS) styles to enhance Coursebuilder, create custom interactions, and decipher the JavaScript that Coursebuilder creates. You will want to work carefully through this section to improve your knowledge base and skill set.

Section III—Using Learning Site for Course Architecture

The third section teaches you the basics of Learning Site Command. Learning Site is the newest e-learning extension created by Macromedia. Section III will teach you how to set up your course navigation and layout. Anyone creating e-learning should discover what Learning Site has to offer.

Section IV—Tracking Learner Data

The fourth section is for those who want to use Learning Site or a Learning Management System (LMS) to track student data. In this section we simplify the student tracking process. You will need Dreamweaver® UltraDev™ if you choose to track student data using Learning Site.

Appendices

The book consists of four appendices. In Appendix A, we have included some additional information about using Dreamweaver templates for e-learning. In Appendix B, we show you how to set CourseBuilder preferences. In Appendix C, we have included some information on the limitations of different browsers. In Appendix D, we provide some instruction on using media with CourseBuilder. Every reader should be able to find something helpful in the appendices.

Do I Need Dreamweaver or UltraDev while Using this Book?

You can do most of the tasks included in this book with just Dreamweaver. There are a few chapters that require UltraDev. In this table we list each section and identify whether you need Dreamweaver or UltraDev for the tasks contained in that section.

Section	Software Needed
Section I	Dreamweaver or UltraDev

Section	Software Needed
Section II	Dreamweaver or UltraDev
Section III	Mostly Dreamweaver or UltraDev. Some tasks will require UltraDev.
Section IV	UltraDev is required for Learning Site. You can use Dreamweaver or UltraDev for communicating with an LMS.

Anyplace in this book where we refer to Dreamweaver, we are also referring to UltraDev. We will specifically refer to UltraDev during tasks that you must have UltraDev to do.

Conventions Used in this Book

In this book we have used a few conventions to make information more readily accessible.

Icons Used in this Book

There are six icons used throughout this book.

Note: The note icon is placed beside a note that contains extra information or important information about the current topic.

Caution: The exclamation point icon is placed beside a caution. Pay close attention to this information.

Tip: The light-bulb icon is placed beside a tip. The tips in this manual are practical and very helpful.

More Information: The books icon is placed beside a cross-reference. A cross-reference directs you to another place in the book or separate information altogether.

On CD: The CD icon is placed next to information that is also contained on the companion CD. You can find more information about what the CD contains in the section *What is on the CD ROM?* later in this introduction.

The hands-on icon is placed next to a section header. This icon indicates that the section contains step-by-step instructions and sample files on the CD ROM that lets you follow along. At the completion of a hands-on exercise, you will have created an interaction or made some change to an e-learning application.

Note: The visual design of any of the interactions you create in this book would need quite a bit of work before being presentable in a real course. We created them with the intention to teach functionality, not visual design. You can learn good visual design principles from any number of good books on visual design on the market today.

Typographical Conventions

This book uses a few typographical conventions that you should be aware of:

- We reference menus using an arrow between each menu option. For example, Insert → Interactive Images → Rollover Image refers to the menu option "Rollover Image" that is inside the submenu "Interactive Images" that is inside the menu "Insert".
- *Code font* indicates HTML or JavaScript code. If a lengthy piece of code is included, we set it off in its own paragraph.
- We always number step-by-step procedures. This will make it easy for you to follow.
- The instructions in this book, work in both Macintosh and Windows environments. If there is a difference, we will indicate what that difference is for the Macintosh environment.
- We indicate keyboard keys by using small caps. (For example, press the ENTER key.

What is on the CD ROM?

The CD ROM contains numerous files that are used as examples throughout the book. In the hands-on sections, you are instructed to open certain files to begin a step-by-step or to see the final results. All of these files are stored on the CD ROM. You may want to copy the files to your hard drive before you begin using them.

Caution: The sample files have been designed to work in Internet Explorer version 4.0 and later. Some sample files will not work properly in Netscape or earlier browsers due to the use of unsupported Cascading Style Sheets (CSS).

We have also included five screen movies of some of the more complex tasks. These are the movies we have included:

- **Ordered_explore.wmv**. This movie guides you through the process of creating an ordered explore interaction.
- **Multi-quest_quiz.wmv**. This movie teaches you how to create a multi-question quiz.
- **Prog_feedback.wmv**. This movie shows you how to create an interaction that provides progressive feedback.
- **Fix_LS.wmv**. This movie demonstrates what you need to do to resolve some issues that exist with Learning Site.
- **Setup_LS.wmv**. This movie shows you all the steps required to prepare Learning Site to handle data tracking.

If you are working through one of these tasks in the book, and you feel you need a little more help, use the screen movie on the CD ROM. These movies are recorded in Windows Media Player® format and can be viewed on either a Macintosh® or a Windows® machine with the Windows Media Player. To download the player go to: *http://www.microsoft.com/windows/windowsmedia*.

Finally, we have included a storyboard template that we have used in the past. We hope this will help you with your instructional design. The template is a Microsoft Word® document.

Here are the system requirements to use the files on this CD:

- **Windows**. An Intel® Pentium® processor, or equivalent, running Windows 95, 98, 2000, ME or Windows NT version 4.0 or later. You also need a minimum of 64 MB of available RAM and a CD ROM drive. To view the movies, you must have a monitor capable of 16 bit color and 1024x768 resolution.
- **Macintosh**. A Power Macintosh running Mac OS 8.6 or 9.x. You also need 64 MB of available RAM and a CD ROM drive. To view the movies, you must have a monitor capable of 16 bit color and 1024x768 resolution.

Using Dreamweaver for e-Learning

1

Let's face it. Dreamweaver was not developed for the sole purpose of creating e-learning. It is a visual HTML editor created to make the development and management of web pages and web sites much easier. However, in recent years Macromedia has developed a couple of extensions for Dreamweaver that turn it into a viable e-learning creation tool: CourseBuilder and Learning Site Command.

An extension is a new Dreamweaver feature that you can easily add to the program. If you think of Dreamweaver as your web site or web page food processor, extensions are the additional choppers, grinders, etc. The functionality of the main tool doesn't change, but the add-on increases productivity as well as widens the potential of the tool. There are many extensions available and these extensions enhance what Dreamweaver can already do.

In this chapter you will learn:

- What e-learning is and how it is used.
- How Dreamweaver fares as an e-learning development tool.
- About some additional Web technologies.
- What Coursebuilder and Learning Site are.

What is e-Learning?

There are probably as many definitions of e-learning as there are organizations that are using e-learning. The most encompassing definition that we can provide is: e-learning is using technology to promote learning.

Companies and other organizations use e-learning to describe any education initiative that includes technology. This may include WBT Web-based training (WBT), video conferencing, or something as simple as electronic documentation. These are all mediums for delivering electronic content.

In today's high-tech world it is important for companies to take advantage of quality e-learning solutions. We stress the term quality because that is what makes the difference. e-Learning delivered just because it is the latest buzzword will not solve a company problem, effectively designed e-learning will.

Many organizations assume training to be the quick-fix solution to their problems, problems that may actually exist for other reasons (i.e. organizational, managerial, economical, etc.). Having said this, if you've done your homework and you really believe that training is the issue, your effective use of e-learning will, over time, reach more employees at less cost than traditional training methods. An ineffective e-learning solution will waste your money and erode your company's trust in future e-learning opportunities.

Why Use the e-Learning Buzzword?

In many fields it is important to create new terms in order to make progress. New terms allow more discussion. For this reason, we feel that e-learning has made some important contributions to the field of instructional design.

First, e-learning has widened the scope of technology-based learning. For example, in the past you've heard about delivering training using a specific medium such as WBT or computer-based training (CBT). Since e-learning encompasses all forms of electronic learning, it forces us to think in a broader perspective. Many times a blended solution (combining different methods) is the best approach. For example,

The Importance of Instructional Design

As with any education program, quality instructional design is the key to effective e-learning. For that reason, you will find instructional design tips and techniques scattered throughout this book.

you may deliver a portion of the content over the Internet and later have the group meet via teleconference to discuss issues and concerns.

e-Learning's second contribution is that it has helped education departments get funding for educational initiatives. Buzzwords have the ability to do that. Having obtained your funding, it is very important that your final results are of the highest quality.

How does e-Learning Apply to This Book?

In this book we have focused on creating training that is delivered through a browser. Delivery may be over the Internet or through an organization's intranet. In the past this has been called WBT. Therefore, we have focused on a subset (although it is a large subset) of e-learning.

Why Use Dreamweaver to Develop e-Learning?

As we mentioned at the start of this chapter, Dreamweaver wasn't initially created with the e-learning developer in mind. So why use Dreamweaver for this purpose? For two main reasons:

- Dreamweaver is becoming a standard in IT departments.
- Macromedia (the company that creates Dreamweaver) is increasing its support for e-learning by creating learning extensions.

Dreamweaver may not be the easiest e-learning development tool, but it has quickly become one of the hottest e-learning tools in the industry. In the remainder of this section we look at some of the advantages of using Dreamweaver to create e-learning. We also take a look at some of the disadvantages.

Advantages of Using Dreamweaver

There are several advantages to using Dreamweaver for the purpose of creating and delivering e-learning, which we discuss next.

Dreamweaver is becoming a Standard in IT Departments

In the past, anything going on the Web was usually designed and developed by the IT department or outsourced to some external development company. Dreamweaver, with its close-to-WYSIWYG interface expands the possible design and development user base. Now many organizations are looking to their training departments to create e-learning. This frees the IT department for higher-level tasks. They can still interface with the training department to help make sure it fits into the overall organization's infrastructure. Some organizations have created specialized groups dedicated to e-learning initiatives combining training and IT skills. Dreamweaver serves as common ground for these sometimes disparate groups.

Moreover, in the past, on-line courses were developed using tools that no one other then the developer knew how to use. This made it impossible for anyone, other than the developer, to maintain the course. A real advantage to using Dreamweaver is that since IT departments often already have people that are familiar with it, they can help maintain the course once it is created, even if it was created by an outside organization.

How is Dreamweaver Different from Other HTML Editors?

The main advantage Dreamweaver has over other HTML editors is that Macromedia has chosen to create learning extensions for Dreamweaver. Coursebuilder and Learning Site are learning extensions. These two extensions make the creating of e-learning much easier. It can be a very difficult and tedious task to create an on-line course without these extensions.

Macromedia is Showing Support for e-Learning

Macromedia has created the two extensions that this book is primarily about: Coursebuilder and Learning Site. These extensions provide a sizeable advantage to using Dreamweaver over other visual HTML editors.

Courses Developed Using Dreamweaver Work Without Plugins

There are other tools on the market for developing learning content that you can deliver over the web. However, many of these tools require the use of a plugin in order to deliver the course. The disadvantage here is that you have to make sure everyone that wants to access the course has loaded the plugin.

Dreamweaver and its extensions produce HTML and JavaScript. Both of these languages are interpreted by the browser automatically and do not require a plugin.

 Note: Even though no plugin is required, there are differences in the way different browsers interpret JavaScript. Differences can also occur in different versions of the same browser. For that reason it is important to thoroughly test your training in different browsers and versions and then make a recommendation to those that will be using the training.

You Can Easily Incorporate Other Products

Because HTML and JavaScript are web standards, you can be pretty certain that you will be able to include learning elements in your course that are developed using other authoring tools. Product manufacturers that deliver content over the Web always provide a way to link their products into HTML files. On the down side, these products normally require plugins.

Dreamweaver also makes it a simple process to include content from other Macromedia products such as Flash® and Authorware® pieces. Dreamweaver provides tools to make this a simple process.

Disadvantages of Using Dreamweaver

Dreamweaver is not perfect. It has some limitations, as is the case with any tool.

Development Time Can be High

One disadvantage of Dreamweaver, and for that matter, any visual HTML editor, is that development time can be higher than other authoring tools. A developer who is very familiar with an Authoring tool such as ToolBook™ or Authorware could develop a course much faster.

Fortunately, CourseBuilder and Learning Site extensions really go a long way toward reducing development time and making development easier. As we have become more proficient with these tools, we can see the differences in development time leveling off. Development time should continue to decrease even more as companies create more e-learning development tools for Dreamweaver.

Browser Differences

Browser differences can be a real headache if you are required developing for multiple browsers and multiple versions of each browser. This is because different browsers and even different versions of the same browsers handle JavaScript differently. Once again, Coursebuilder and Learning Site do a good job of bridging this gap, creating pages that work in multiple browsers.

Understanding Other Web Technologies

To make the best use of Dreamweaver, you need to understand other Web technologies that are often used in conjunction with Dreamweaver. We only discuss the technologies that are mentioned in this book.

What is Dreamweaver UltraDev?

Dreamweaver and Dreamweaver UltraDev are basically the same thing with a notable difference. UltraDev includes a copy of Dreamweaver and then adds the extra power of connecting to a remote database. Connecting to a remote database lets you track learner-entered information on the server. You can also build dynamic data by responding to user-entered information.

We mainly refer to UltraDev when we are talking about tracking student data. UltraDev has other uses that can be included in an on-line course; however, database tracking is the most common use for e-learning.

 More Information: For more information about UltraDev, visit Macromedia's web site at *http://www.macromedia.com*.

What is JavaScript?

You'll read the term "JavaScript" numerous times in this book. Many of the fancy interactions that you see on a web page are created using JavaScript. JavaScript was developed by Netscape Communications® as an extension to HTML, the code used to develop Web pages. JavaScript enhances HTML and lets you accomplish more than you would be able to using just HTML.

JavaScript is a scripting language (as opposed to a programming language). This means a couple of things. First, it means that it doesn't have as much power (you can't do as much) as a programming language. Second it is an interpreted language (as opposed to a compiled language). Normally programming languages such as C or C++ must be compiled before you can see if the code you have written works. That is not true of a scripting language. JavaScript is interpreted by the browser when the page is opened. You can quickly see whether or not your code works.

Note: Since JavaScript is interpreted by the browser, it is possible to write code that works in one browser but doesn't work (or works differently) in another browser. In addition, Microsoft® has developed its own version of JavaScript called Jscript® for its browser. These languages differ slightly, so not all JavaScript is going to work the same way in all browsers. Fortunately, much of the JavaScript created using CourseBuilder and Learning Site works in multiple browsers.

Is JavaScript and Java the Same Thing?

JavaScript is not the same thing as Java. Although the names are similar the products are not the same. Java is a full-blown programming language built by Sun Microsystems®. The strength of Java is that it works on multiple operating systems.

Do I Need to Learn JavaScript?

Using Coursebuilder and Learning Site as taught in this book, lets you do a lot without learning JavaScript. However, to fully understand the pages on your site and to accomplish the most, you should at some point gain a familiarity with JavaScript.

More Information: In *Chapter 16: Behind the Scenes: Deciphering Coursebuilder's JavaScript*, we look at the JavaScript that is created by Coursebuilder and help you understand how it works.

What are ASP, CGI, JSP and ColdFusion?

ASP (Active Server Pages), CGI (Common Gateway Interface), JSP (JavaServer Pages) and ColdFusion are all technologies that allow you to send data back and forth between a server and the browser.

A normal static HTML page is simply downloaded from a server. Once that is done, the server is hands-off. However, with the aforementioned technologies it is possible to communicate with a server to record data or determine what type of page should display next. Learning Site has the ability to use ASP for data tracking.

More Information: Using Learning Site's ASP pages for student tracking is discussed in more detail in *Chapter 20: Using Learning Site to Track Learner Data.*

Introducing Coursebuilder and Learning Site

Now that you know something about Dreamweaver, we need to make one thing clear: the main focus of this book is not Dreamweaver or any of the other technologies that we just introduced. This book is about using Coursebuilder and Learning Site, the two tools you use to create e-learning.

As we have mentioned, Coursebuilder and Learning Site are extensions to Dreamweaver. You need a working knowledge of Dreamweaver is necessary, but this book does not focus on how to use Dreamweaver.

Macromedia assigns all extensions to specific categories. Coursebuilder and Learning Site are extensions in the Learning category. Currently, there are few extensions available in this category, which makes these two invaluable:

- Coursebuilder is an extension that helps you create lesson interactions. Most of these interactions are quiz questions, but other types of interactions are possible. CourseBuilder helps you create many of the individual pages included in a course

More Information: For a more complete introduction to Coursebuilder refer to *Chapter 2: Getting to Know Coursebuilder.*

- Learning Site (officially known as Learning Site Command) is an extension that helps you create the navigation and student tracking capabilities of an on-line course. Navigation can be set up with either Dreamweaver or UltraDev, but Student tracking requires the use of UltraDev. Learning Site helps you establish the course architecture (moving between pages and tracking student data).

More Information: For a more complete introduction to Learning Site see *Chapter 17: Getting to Know Learning Site.*

More Information: To find the latest extensions for Dreamweaver, use the Exchange Web site at *http://www.macromedia.com/exchange*.

Summary

e-Learning is using technology to achieve a learning objective. This book focuses on a large subset of e-learning called WBT. Dreamweaver is the industry tool of choice to create e-learning because of its broad user base and the learning extensions created by Macromedia.

In this chapter you have been introduced you to several Web technologies. In particular we have discussed two extensions that have been developed to simplify the process of creating e-learning using Dreamweaver: CourseBuilder and Learning Site.

Section I:
Using CourseBuilder for
Interactivity

Ready to get started? This section will get you off on the right foot, as well as introduce to you to some intermediate concepts and techniques you'll build on in later sections.

Getting to Know CourseBuilder **2**

Some of the most effective interactions in any e-learning course are assessment or quiz questions. In this chapter we introduce you to Macromedia CourseBuilder, one of the leading e-learning tools used to create interactive assessments and other on-line learning activities.

In this chapter you will learn:

- What CourseBuilder is.
- About the e-learning possibilities and potential CourseBuilder offers.
- To install CourseBuilder.
- To insert new interactions.
- To edit and delete existing CourseBuilder interactions.
- To create a basic interaction and become familiar with the CourseBuilder editing interface.
- How to access and use CourseBuilder's on-line help.

Macromedia has done a good job of making CourseBuilder fairly easy to use. But because CourseBuilder offers so much power and flexibility, getting started may seem overwhelming. Let's start with the basics.

What Is CourseBuilder?

CourseBuilder is an extension to Dreamweaver that lets you create interactive quiz objects with all the power of JavaScript programming, but without needing to know how to write code. It has quickly gained widespread use among WBT producers because it leverages Dreamweaver as an existing tool and is easy to use.

CourseBuilder Creates Interactivity

CourseBuilder offers a quick and relatively easy way to keep the learner engaged. In addition to on-line assessments, you can create interactive activities, such as an activity in which the learner explores a simulated toolbar of a software application.

CourseBuilder Makes JavaScript

What is the difference between Coursebuilder and Learning Site?

When you are working with Coursebuilder you are using a tool to design interactions on a single HTML page. Later you may combine them with other pages.

The Learning Site extension to Dreamweaver allows you to take multiple pages and "tie" them together into a course that has a navigational structure. You can include pages you create with Coursebuilder in your Learning Site as well as other HTML-based pages.

If you've done some web page development, you may be familiar with (or at least heard of) JavaScript. JavaScript has become a popular way to create interactivity on web pages because it handles all interactivity through what are called "client-side scripts." Client-side scripts are pieces of code that are actually embedded in the web page or are loaded off the server at the same time the web page is loaded.

The advantage to these types of scripts is that once the learner does something, the web page doesn't have to send any data to the server to make a decision about how to react to the user action. It is all handled on the local machine by the browser. This results in faster processing, making it more likely to keep the learner's attention. Sometimes this type of interactivity is called Dynamic HTML (or DHTML) because the web page can change based on what the user does.

CourseBuilder is nothing more than some very well thought out JavaScript that creates customizable interactivity for the user. Any good JavaScript programmer could create from scratch the types of interactions that CourseBuilder creates, but it would take an enormous amount of time. Also, CourseBuilder creates and edits the JavaScript code without you ever having to know any JavaScript. (You don't even have to see it if you don't want to!).

CourseBuilder Works With Multiple Browsers

CourseBuilder writes JavaScript that is usually compatible with these browsers:

- Internet Explorer 3 (and higher)
- Netscape Navigator 3 (and higher)

 More Information: See *Appendix C: Cross-browser Limitations* for details about how Internet Explorer and Netscape browsers handle different interactions.

If you are developing for multiple browsers, look for our notes on browser-specific issues throughout the book. We'll address them as they pertain to each topic.

Exploring CourseBuilder Possibilities

Now that you know what CourseBuilder is, here are some possible ways you can use this tool:

- In-course interactions to reinforce learning
- In-course topic reviews with remediation
- End-of-lesson quizzes and or skill/knowledge certification
- Test preparation
- Software simulations
- Equipment operation simulations
- Soft-skills training that requires branching based upon responses (for example, call center training)
- End-of-course survey questions that elicit feedback from the learner

Before you get into the details, let's take a look at some finished examples.

CourseBuilder Samples

Perhaps the best way to become acquainted with CourseBuilder is to look at some examples. This is just an overview. You will learn how to create all of the interactions in this section later in this book.

On CD: You can find each sample in this section on the CD-ROM that accompanies this book.

More Information: See *CourseBuilder Basics* later in this chapter for instructions on how to edit any of the examples on the CD-ROM.

Multiple Choice

CourseBuilder allows you to create standard "single correct" Multiple Choice questions as well as "multiple correct" (or "all that apply") questions. CourseBuilder also gives you the option of creating Multiple Choice questions with preset form objects, preset graphics, or custom graphics. CourseBuilder also lets you determine how many choices (often called "distracters") are to be included in the question.

This example is a Multiple Choice question in which the learner must choose "all that apply":

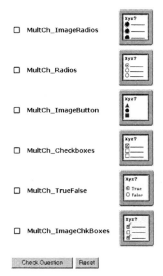

On CD: You can view this example by opening *Sample_3-3_Table.htm* in a browser.

More Information: Learn how to create Multiple Choice questions in Chapter 3: *Multiple Choice and True/False Interaction* .

True/False

True/False is a variation on the Multiple Choice question. Unlike the Multiple Choice example, this example uses preset form objects instead of graphical objects:

On CD: You can view this example by opening *Sample_2-1.htm* in a browser.

More Information: Learn how to create True/False exercises in Chapter 3: *Multiple Choice and True False Interaction* .

Drag-and-Drop

Drag-and-Drop interactions are very popular in e-learning because they are highly interactive and different from traditional quiz question types such as Multiple Choice and True/False.

When Should I Use Drag-and-Drop?

Drag-and-Drop interactions can accommodate several different types of instructional objectives. You can use Drag-and-Drop interactions for:

- Matching
- Identification
- Step-by-step
- Ordering

This Drag-and-Drop exercise is used as a matching exercise:

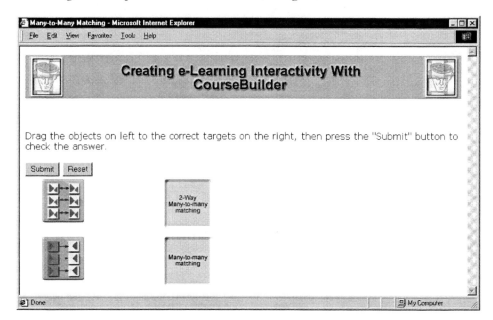

On CD: You can view this example by opening *Sample_4-1.htm* in a browser.

More Information: Learn how to create Drag-and-Drop exercises in Chapter4: *Drag-and-Drop Interaction* .

Text Entry

Text Entry is commonly known as fill-in-the-blank. CourseBuilder offers two different kinds of Text Entry interactions:

- Single-line responses
- Multiple-line responses

Single-line response questions are typical Fill-in-the-Blank interactions. You can use multiple-line responses for essay type questions.

Here is an example of a simple Text Entry interaction:

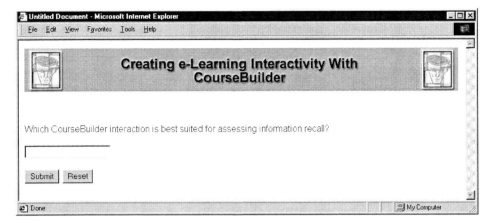

  More Information: Learn how to create Text Entry exercises in Chapter 7: *Text Entry Interactions* .

Slider

In this interesting interaction, the learner slides a "thumb" to different points on the line to give responses to a question. This could be used very easily to pose a question about dates or time of day. It could also be used as a more interactive type of Multiple Choice.

This is an example of a slider used as a learning activity:

On CD: You can view this example by opening *Sample_9-2.htm* in a browser.

More Information: Learn how to create Slider exercises in Chapter 9: *Slider Interactions.*

Button

Button interactions are not really question types. They are simply graphical buttons that are available as interactive objects. Buttons in and of themselves don't do anything useful out-of-the-box. They need to be controlled using the Action Manager (see The Action Manager object below).

Buttons can be used for simple tasks, such as playing a media file, or they can be used within a complex interactive structure where multiple interactions take place on the same page, such as in a simulation of equipment or software.

For example, the following is a sample of a button interaction used in a simple software simulation that simulates adding a new CourseBuilder interaction. The buttons use custom graphics to appear like the buttons in CourseBuilder:

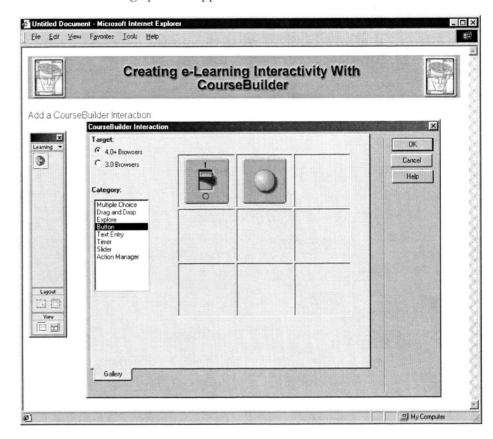

 On CD: You can view this example by opening *Sample_6-3.htm* in a browser.

More Information: Learn how to create button interactions in Chapter 6: *Button Interactions.*

Timers

Use timers to let the learner know how much time they've taken and how much time remains before the allotted time for a question runs out. Only use timers if you are dealing with time-sensitive interactions—otherwise they aren't necessary.

Here is an example of a quiz-style interaction that employs a timer. This timer triggers a brief warning 10 seconds before the time expires:

On CD: You can view this example by opening *Sample_8-3.htm* in a browser.

More Information: Learn how to use timers in the Chapter 8: *Timer Interactions*.

The Action Manager Object

The Action Manager object is unlike any other interaction object in the gallery. This object is a tool you can use to manipulate other interactive objects on the same page. It is invisible and unseen by the user but can control how different interactions work together behind the scenes. You don't have to use this object, but using it expands CourseBuilder's potential uses.

This example uses an unseen Action Manager object as part of a multi-question quiz to display feedback, tally scores, and verify that the learner answered all questions correctly:

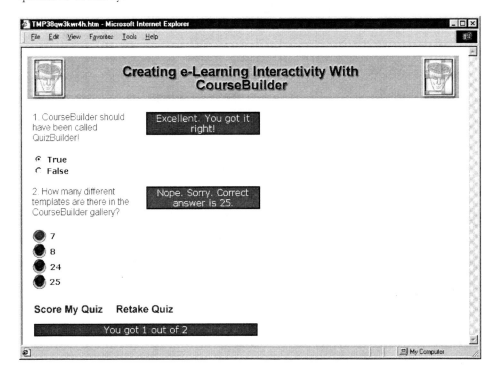

 More Information: Get a more detailed overview of the Action Manger object in Chapter 12: *The Action Manager: An Overview*. Also see other chapters that focus on the Action Manager in Section II: *Extending CourseBuilder*.

Installing CourseBuilder

Macromedia has made installing extensions a snap. Before you can install CourseBuilder you must have these three items:

- Dreamweaver or Dreamweaver UltraDev, version 4 or higher
- The Dreamweaver Extensions Manager. This comes preinstalled with Dreamweaver, version 4 or higher.
- The CourseBuilder install file.

Follow these steps to install the CourseBuilder extension:

1   Access the Dreamweaver or UltraDev Exchange site and find and download the CourseBuilder package file (.MXP).

     Here are the URLs for both Exchange sites:

       ▪   Dreamweaver - *http://www.macromedia.com/exchange/dreamweaver/*
       ▪   UltraDev - *http://www.macromedia.com/exchange/ultradev/*

2   Access the Dreamweaver (or UltraDev Exchange site and find and download the CourseBuilder package file [.MXP]).

     To find the extension, choose Learning from the Browse Extensions drop down box.

Tip: You may want to save this file to the "Downloaded extensions" folder that is within the Dreamweaver folder.

3   Find the package file you downloaded and double-click it or choose Install from the File menu in the Extension Manager (File → Install Extensions). This starts the installation program.

4   Accept the disclaimer and the CourseBuilder extension automatically installs.

     You should be able to view the extension in the Extension Manager.

When you install CourseBuilder, you won't initially notice any significant changes to Dreamweaver.

However, if you look in the Insert menu you will notice a new option: CourseBuilder Interaction:

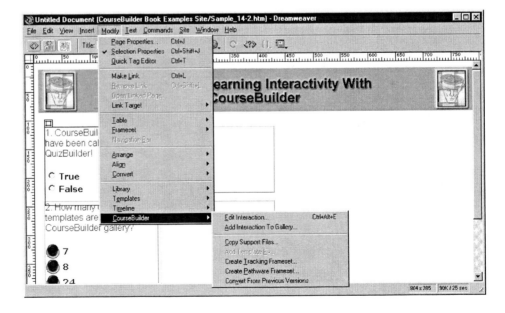

You will also notice that the Modify menu has a new CourseBuilder sub-menu:

CourseBuilder Basics

Before creating your first interaction, you need to know some of the basics.

Inserting a New Interaction

To insert a new interaction do one of the following:

- Choose CourseBuilder Interaction from the Insert menu (Insert →
  Coursebuilder Interaction)

- Click on the Coursebuilder icon [icon] or drag it to your page. You can find this
  icon in the Dreamweaver object panel in the Learning category.

Dreamweaver displays the CourseBuilder Interaction window.

Choosing 4.0 browsers as your target browser offers you the most question types to choose from.

Click the category type to see the interactions in that category.

Click the specific type of interaction to place that interaction template on your web page.

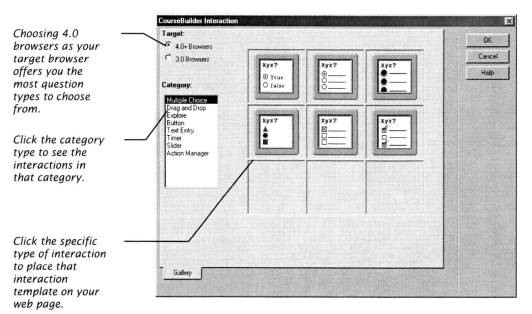

Click the category and interaction you want to put on your page.

CourseBuilder Interaction Window Tabs

After you select the interaction you want to add to your page, CourseBuilder
displays additional tabs that hold the settings for that particular interaction.

The General Tab

We'll discuss the General tab first because it contains elements that are common to nearly all interactions:

```
CourseBuilder Interaction                                                    [x]

  Interaction Name:  MultCh_TrueFalse03                            OK

      Question Text: Put your question text here                   Cancel

                                                                   Help


    Judge Interaction:   ○ when the user clicks a button labeled
                         ● when the user clicks a choice
                         ○ on a specific event (set using the Judge Interaction Behavior)

      Correct When:  Any Correct and None Incorrect  ▼

    Knowledge Track:  ☐ Send results to a management system if present

        Tries Are:  Unlimited  ▼        tries

          Time Is:  Unlimited  ▼        seconds after page text is loaded

           Reset:  ☐ Create a Reset button

           Layer:  ☐ Insert in a layer (4.0+ browsers only)

   Gallery    General    Choices    Action Mgr
```

More Information: See the individual chapters in Section I for detailed explanations of the tab options specific to those question types.

This table describes the options on the General tab that are common to all interactions:

Option	Description
Interaction Name	Each interaction has a name. CourseBuilder supplies a default name. You won't usually change this name unless you are going to refer to it using JavaScript or using the Action Manager. To work through an example where names can be important, see Chapter 14: *The Power of the Action Manager Object.*

Option	Description
Judge Interaction	*When the learner clicks a button labeled….* Choose this option when you want the learner's response evaluated only when he/she clicks a separate button. By default CourseBuilder labels this button Submit. *When the learner clicks a choice* Choose this option when you want the interaction evaluated immediately after the learner chooses a response. This is best suited for Multiple Choice questions. *On a specific event (using the Judge Interaction Behavior)* Choose this option if you want some other action on the web page to evaluate the interaction. You can use this when providing feedback for a quiz that has multiple questions on one page. See Chapter 14: *The Power of the Action Manager Object* for an example.
Correct When	This setting determines when the interaction is considered "correct." This has not only scoring consequences, but also determines what kind of feedback the learner will receive. *Any Correct and None Incorrect* Choose this option when choosing only one right answer means the entire interaction should be considered as correct (i.e. a Multiple Choice question where only one answer is right and all others are wrong). *All Correct and None Incorrect* Choose this option when the learner must choose multiple answers for the entire interaction to be considered correct (i.e. a "choose all that apply" Multiple Choice question).
Knowledge Track	Adds the Tracking tab to the interaction dialog box for student data tracking. See Chapter 21: *Using Learning Site to Track Learner Data.*
Tries Are:	*Unlimited* Allows the learner to try to answer the question correctly as many times as they want. *Limited To* Entering the maximum number of attempts the learner is allowed before the question is "locked, limits the learner to the entered number of tries."

Option	Description
Reset	Creates a button labeled Reset that resets most quiz interactions when clicked. Some form elements (such as radio buttons) may not reset using this method.
Layer	Inserts the whole interaction in a layer. This can be very helpful if you want to hide or move the interaction dynamically or simply for exact positioning in the browser.

Other Tabs

Each interaction has additional tabs that you need to fill out to make sure your interaction works the way you want it to.

This table shows the different tabs that CourseBuilder displays and when, based on the interaction type:

Tab	Interaction
Action Manager	Like the General tab, this tab appears for every interaction. To learn more about the Action Manager tab, see Chapter 11: *The Action Manager – An Overview* and Chapter 12: *Action Manager Basics.*
Choices	Multiple Choice – used to define the different distracters for the Multiple Choice question
Elements	Drag and Drop – used to define what pieces of the interaction are drag objects and which are target objects
Pairs	Drag and Drop – used to define which elements are valid pairs and which pairs are correct and incorrect
Hot Areas	Explore – used to define how many hot areas (or clickable areas) there are and which hot areas are correct and incorrect
Responses	Text Entry – used to define the correct and incorrect responses
Triggers	Timers – defines when triggers fire, or in other words, when CourseBuilder will send a message to the action manager that it needs to be evaluated.

Tab	Interaction
Ranges	Sliders – defines the number and scope of the ranges within which the user can slide the draggable parts of the interaction

Editing and Deleting Existing Interactions

In later chapters you will create CourseBuilder interactions from the ground up. Once you create interactions you'll want to be able to edit them and sometimes delete them altogether.

Selecting an Interaction

To edit or delete an interaction, you have to select it first. To select an existing interaction, do *one* of the following:

- Select the CourseBuilder icon ⊕ from the Dreamweaver page that corresponds with the interaction you are try to edit or delete
- Place your cursor somewhere in the interaction and click the *<interaction>* tag selector `<body> <table> <tr> <td> <interaction>` at the bottom of the screen

Note: When you properly select the interaction, Dreamweaver changes the contents of the Properties panel so it looks like this:

CourseBuilder Interaction	Name MultCh_ImageButton02 ▼	Edit...
	Layer ☐ Insert in layer (4.0+ browsers only)	

Editing an Existing Interaction

Once you have selected your interaction you can edit it by doing one of the following:

- Click Edit on the Properties dialog box.
- Press CTRL+ALT+E

- Choose the Edit Interaction option from the Modify menu (Modify →
  CourseBuilder → Edit Interaction).

Deleting an Existing Interaction

Once you have properly selected your interaction, simply press the DELETE key.
Dreamweaver deletes the interaction and its associated code from the page.

Caution: Make sure to properly select the interaction before deleting it. Deleting just the
layer the interaction is in, or just the visible interactive objects will not really delete the
entire interaction, and will leave some extra code cluttering up your document.

Tip: Deleting the interaction won't delete the source (*src*) references to CourseBuilder's
external JavaScript files. If you don't plan to include a different CourseBuilder interaction
on the page, you may want to delete those references as well. Using Dreamweaver's Code
View you can find them at the top of the page in the HEAD tag. They look like this:

```
<script language="JavaScript" src="scripts/behActions.js"></script>
<script language="JavaScript" src="scripts/behCourseBuilder.js"></script>
<script language="JavaScript" src="scripts/interactionClass.js"></script>
```

Getting Started With CourseBuilder

If you're like us, you want to get into the program right away and try it out.
Chances are you have tried it already, but if you haven't, here's a good starting
point.

Let's start by creating a basic True/False CourseBuilder interaction.

Viewing the Finished Interaction

Before you create this interaction, take a look at what it looks like in its completed
form.

On CD: See this completed exercise by opening *Sample_2-1.htm* in a browser.

Creating this Interaction

Now let's create the interaction you just finished viewing.

Follow these steps to create a basic True/False interaction:

1   Insert a new Coursebuilder interaction into a blank page (or open *BlankPage.htm* on the CD-ROM).

2   Choose the ***Multiple Choice*** category by clicking on ***Multiple Choice*** in the Category box.

3   Click on the first Multiple Choice question type: True/False (when you place your mouse over it, CourseBuilder displays *MultCh_TrueFalse*).

Note: CourseBuilder places the interaction on your web page as you choose options in the dialog box. This makes it easy to see how changes you make in the dialog affect your interaction.

CourseBuilder displays the tabs specific to the question that you chose.

4   Make these changes to the settings on the General tab:

Setting	Value
Question Text	CourseBuilder control navigation and course architecture for you.
Judge Interaction	- Choose when the user clicks a button labeled… - Replace "Submit" with "Am I Right?"
Reset	Select Create a Reset button

5   Make these changes to the setting on the Choices tab:

Choice	Setting	Value
Choice1	Choice Is	Incorrect
Choice2	Choice Is	Correct

6   Click the **OK** button.

Try your True/False interaction in a browser. It should look something like this:

```
┌─────────────────────────────────────────────────────────────────────┐
│ 🖳 Untitled Document - Microsoft Internet Explorer           _ □ ✕    │
├─────────────────────────────────────────────────────────────────────┤
│  File  Edit  View  Favorites  Tools  Help                            │
├─────────────────────────────────────────────────────────────────────┤
│   ┌────┐          Creating e-Learning Interactivity With    ┌────┐   │
│   │    │                   CourseBuilder                     │    │   │
│   └────┘                                                     └────┘   │
│                                                                       │
│   CourseBuilder controls navigation and course architecture for you.  │
│                                                                       │
│   ○ True                                                              │
│   ○ False                                                             │
│                                                                       │
│   [Am I Right?]   [Reset]                                             │
├─────────────────────────────────────────────────────────────────────┤
│ 🖉 Done                                          🖳 My Computer        │
└─────────────────────────────────────────────────────────────────────┘
```

Congratulations! You've created your first CourseBuilder interaction.

Note: You may notice that the **Reset** button doesn t seem to clear the interaction. CourseBuilder 's **Reset** buttons don't clear form–style radio buttons and checkboxes. It does, in fact, clear your answer even though it doesn't look like it (test this by choosing the correct answer, clicking **Am I Right?**, then **Reset**, then **Am I Right?** again). Also, CourseBuilder's **Reset** button *does* clear image-style buttons and checkboxes. For a **Reset** button that will clear form–style buttons and checkboxes, see *Chapter 14: The Power of the Action Manager Object* and look at the Retake Quiz image in the multi-question quiz tutorial.

Using CourseBuilder Help

CourseBuilder comes with some fairly extensive on-line help.

You can access this help from the CourseBuilder Interaction window:

Like other Macromedia products, the help is an HTML-based help system. Most of the CourseBuilder help is content sensitive, so that when you click on the Help button it will take you to a relevant help document.

Summary

With CourseBuilder you can create JavaScript-based learning interactions quickly for both Internet Explorer and Netscape browsers. These interactions include True/False, Multiple Choice, Text Entry, Drag-and-Drop, and Sliders. You learned how to add, edit, and delete interactions from the CourseBuilder Gallery.

CourseBuilder's flexibility and easy-to-use interface require little to no scripting skills, making it an increasingly popular tool. CourseBuilder is also easy to install and comes with context-sensitive help.

If you've never used CourseBuilder as an e-learning development tool, you may find it soon becoming the tool you can't live without.

Multiple Choice and True/False Interactions

3

Multiple Choice and True/False interactions are arguably the most common type of test question presented to learners. In the previous chapter we introduced you to CourseBuilder by having you create a basic True/False interaction. This chapter expands on the True/False interaction and also presents several ways to use the Multiple Choice interaction.

In this chapter you will learn:

- About templates and possibilities for the Multiple Choice, True/False interaction.
- How to create a graphical True/False interaction.
- How to create a Multiple Choice interaction.
- How to create a Multiple-correct interaction (i.e. all that apply).
- Several ways to enhance the Multiple Choice, True/False interaction.

Introducing the Multiple Choice and True/False Interaction

As you learned in Chapter 2, multiple choice is one type of interaction that you can create with CourseBuilder. We used this category in Chapter 2 to create a sample true/false question, just one of the questions types you can create using this category.

In this introductory section you read suggestions for using the Multiple Choice interaction and learn what templates are available from the Gallery as well.

When to Use a Multiple Choice True/False Interaction

Multiple Choice or true/false is generally the first kind of question that people think of when designing a quiz. Keep in mind, though, that since they are the traditional question type used on standardized tests, many think of them as tedious. In addition, many measurement professionals (however, not all) would steer you away from using true/false questions for the reason that they are easier to guess.

Despite these negatives, multiple-choice questions still remain a standard for any quiz. And if you mix in other question types, the quiz becomes much more interactive and interesting.

In addition, you shouldn't limit your reasons for using multiple choice and true/false to just assessment. These question types are also valid for practice, pre-assessment, and on-line surveys.

One variation of the multiple choice question is the multiple-correct question. This is also called an all-that-apply question. This type of question can have more than one correct response. An advantage of this type of question is that it can assess related topics in a single question. From a learner perspective, this type of question is more difficult, and

Writing Quality Multiple Choice Questions

One of the most difficult things in assessment is writing good questions. Although this is true for any question type, multiple choice questions seem to take all the heat.

Here are some online resources to help you write more effective multiple choice questions: *http://www.ed.gov/databases/ ERIC_Digests/ed398236.html*, *http://www2.gasou.edu/psycho logy/courses/dewey/aboutq.htm*, and *http://www.ed.gov/database s/ERIC_Digests/ed398238.html*.

you should consider that when determining scoring.

Here are some questions you can ask yourself to determine whether a multiple-correct question may be appropriate:

- Does the question have more than one correct response?
- Is there more than one way to complete the task?
- Are there several succinct statements that are true about the concept or procedure?

Taking a Look at the Multiple Choice Gallery

The Gallery for the Multiple Choice category consists of 6 different templates. These templates fall under one of three sub-categories:

- True/false questions where there is only one correct answer and only one distracter.
- Traditional multiple choice questions where there is only one correct answer and 2 or more distracters.
- Multiple-correct questions where there can be more than one correct answer and 1 or more distracters.

 Note: It is possible to turn a traditional Multiple Choice interaction into a Multiple-correct or visa versa. However, it saves time if you begin with a template for the type of question you want to create.

Each template also comes with a default appearance. The appearance determines how the choices are presented (for example, radio button, image, and so forth).

This table describes the purpose of each template and displays a thumbnail image showing its appearance. You can change any default setting provided by each template:

Interaction Type	Description
Xyz? ⦿ True ○ False	**True/False.** You have already used this interaction in chapter 2. Although you could turn any multiple choice template into a true/false question by deleting all but one distracter, choosing this template saves you time. This template does not provide a way to change the appearance. Later in this chapter, you will create a graphical true/false question.
Xyz? ⦿___ ○___ ○___	**Multiple Choice Radios.** This template creates a standard multiple choice question using radio buttons. This template does not provide a way to change the appearance.
Xyz? ●___ ●___ ●___	**Multiple Choice Image Radios.** This template creates a standard multiple choice question using graphical image to represent the radio buttons. There are multiple images you can choose from. The representation to the left shows the default image.
Xyz? ▲ ● ■	**Multiple Choice Image.** This template creates a standard multiple choice question using graphic images for the choices instead of text.
Xyz? ☒___ ☐___ ☐___	**Multiple-correct Check Box.** This template creates a multiple-correct question using check boxes. You are provided two correct choices and two incorrect distracters. This template does not provide a way to change the appearance.
Xyz? ☑___ ☐___ ☑___	**Multiple-correct Image Check Box.** This template creates a multiple-correct question using a graphic image instead of a check box. There are multiple images you can choose from. The representation to the left shows the default image. CourseBuilder provides two correct choices and two incorrect distracters to begin with.

Note: Some templates allow you to change the appearance on the Choices tab. There are eleven different appearances to choose from. See *Changing Appearances* later in this chapter.

Multiple Choice True/False Interaction Basics

Creating a Multiple Choice True/False interaction requires these 4 general steps.

1   Insert a new interaction using one of the methods described in chapter 2.

2   Change the question text and feedback settings on the General tab.

3   Configure each choice on the choices tab.

4   Accept or customize the feedback the learner will receive by editing the decision tree in the Action Manager tab.

Steps 2-4, along with other settings and concepts, are described in more detail in the sections that follow.

Changing the Question Text and Feedback Settings on the General Tab

The General tab contains many settings that are included with all interactions. How feedback is handled is important for this interaction:

Question Text field ——

Judge Interaction settings ——

Towards the top of the General tab is a question text field that is unique to the Multiple Choice True/False interaction.

Enter the question text (stem of your question) in this field.

 Tip: You can also change the text directly on the Dreamweaver page without any need to open the CourseBuilder Interaction window.

Common choices for judging a learner response and providing feedback are to choose either **when the user clicks a button** or **when the user clicks a choice**.

 Tip: If you are limiting the learner to a single try at the question, then you probably want to consider judging the interaction when the user clicks a choice to eliminate unnecessary clicking.

 Note: If you limit the learner to a certain number of tries, you probably don't want to include a reset button. The reason for this is that if a learner presses reset after each try, he or she can continue to try the interaction for as long as they want. Open *sample_3-2.htm* from the CD to see an example of this.

Configuring each Choice

Use the Choices tab to establish settings for each choice. This tab is unique to the Multiple Choice True/False interaction:

This tab contains several options. Each option is described in this table:

Option	Description
Choices	This field lists the choices for the question. Select a choice (it becomes highlighted) and change any of its settings in the remaining fields. This is described in more detail in the *Adding, Deleting, and Moving Choices* section later in this chapter.
Name	Enter the name of the choice.
Text	Optional. If you choose to have text for the choice, enter it in this field. You can also change this text directly on the Dreamweaver page.

Option	Description
Image File	Optional. If you wish to use a graphic for the choice, instead of text, click on the **Browse** button and select it. This is not the same as the appearance. The appearance affects the buttons or check boxes while the image file affects the text of the choices.
Place Before Text	Allows you to determine whether the image (if you use one) comes before or after the text. If no text is entered, it doesn't matter what is chosen.
Appearance	Displays the current appearance and allows you to choose a new appearance. This option is described in more detail in the *Changing Appearances* section.
Choice Is	Determines whether the choice is correct, incorrect, or not judged.
Score	Enter a score if you are tracking data with an LMS or Learning Site. See *Chapter 21: Using Learning Site to Track Learner Data* for more information.

Adding, Deleting, and Moving Choices

All multiple choice templates come with four choices. You may need to add or remove choices. You may also want to change the order the choices.

- To add a choice, click the **Add** button. CourseBuilder adds an additional choice and gives it a name of *unamed1*.
- To delete a choice, first select the choice and then click the **Delete** button.
- To change the order of a choice, first select the choice and then click either the **Up** or **Down** button.

Changing Appearances

The appearance is the graphical element that indicates whether the choice has been clicked on or not. It can be as simple as a radio button or as fancy as a switch.

Three of the templates allow you to change the appearance of the button or checkbox. Those templates contain the word *image* in the name (for example, MultCh_ImageRadios and MultCh_ImageChkBoxes).

Note: Don't mix up the appearance up with the image file. An image file is similar to the text of a choice. It presents an option. The graphic image used in the appearance will change the button or check box that is clicked.

There are eleven appearances to choose from. To select another appearance, click the drop down box checkbox_red and choose another option. All eleven appearances are shown in this table with a graphic of how they look before and after being clicked:

Name	Before Being Clicked	After Being Clicked
Checkbox_red	☐	☑
Dial_ridge		
Emboss		
Lighted		
Lighted_mini		
Round_red		
Sphere_blue		
Square_gray		

Name	Before Being Clicked	After Being Clicked
Switch_gray		
Switch_slot		
Switch_zero_one		

To the right of the Appearance field is a **Browse** button. You can define your own appearances and use this button to search for and select the corresponding graphics.

More Information: See the *Creating Your Own Appearances* section later in this chapter for more information.

Customizing Feedback

The default feedback for a Multiple Choice True/False interaction is to pop up a message that says "Correct" or pop up a message that says "Incorrect". You can change this feedback if you wish.

Changing the Correct Feedback

You change the correct feedback by editing the popup message on the Action Manager tab.

Follow these steps to change the correct feedback:

1   Edit an interaction using one of the methods shown in chapter 2.

2   Click the Action Manager tab to access it.

3   Select the Popup Message that is below the *if correct* line:

```
-- if Correct
      Popup Message
```

4   Click the **Edit** button.

5   Change the feedback, and click **OK**.

Changing the Incorrect Feedback

Changing the incorrect feedback uses the same process as changing the correct feedback.

Follow these steps to change the incorrect feedback:

1   Edit an interaction using one of the methods shown in chapter 2.

2   Click the Action Manager tab to access it.

3   Select the Popup Message that is below the *else if incorrect* line:

```
-- else if Incorrect
      Popup Message
```

4   Click the **Edit** button.

5   Change the feedback, and click **OK**.

More Information: When creating a multiple-correct question, you may want to provide partial feedback. This can be done using the Action Manager tab. See *Chapter 13: Customizing the Action Manager Tab.*

Creating a Graphical True/False Interaction

The first step-by-step that we present in this chapter is to create another True/False interaction. We will use graphics in this example as opposed to text that we used in the True/False questions created in chapter 2. This True/False question presents the learner with two screen shots of the object panel in Dreamweaver. By looking at each panel, the learner must choose the one that has CourseBuilder installed and active.

Take time to explore the finished interaction, and then follow the step-by-step instructions to create it.

Viewing the Finished Interaction

Before trying your hand at creating this interaction, first take a look at the finished sample.

 On CD: Take a moment and try out the finished interaction: *sample_3-1*.

As you explore this interaction, you may want to try some of the following tasks.

- Click on both the correct and incorrect choice.
- Notice how the stem of the question is phrased with a graphical True/False.
- Open the interaction inside Dreamweaver and take a look at the settings in CourseBuilder.

Creating the Interaction

Using the step-by-step instructions in this section, you will create a radio button True/False interaction that uses graphics as the options. To follow along with these steps, you must have Dreamweaver or UltraDev opened and have inserted the companion CD in the CD ROM drive.

 More Information: If you need more details about some of the steps, refer to *Chapter 2: Getting to Know CourseBuilder* or section *Multiple Choice True/False Interaction Basics* in this chapter.

Follow these steps to create a graphical True/False interaction:

1   Open a new page and insert a CourseBuilder interaction.

2   Select the *Multiple Choice* category and click on the *MultCh_ImageButton* interaction:

CourseBuilder adds the default interaction to the page. We are using this template instead of a standard True/False template because we are creating a graphical interaction that will allow the learner to click on the graphic instead of a radio button.

3   Click on the General tab.

4   Change the question text so it reads: "Choose the object panel that shows that CourseBuilder is installed and active."

We will use all the default settings for the feedback.

5   Click on the Choices tab.

6   Delete choices 3 and 4 by selecting them and clicking the **Delete** button.

We only need two choices for a True/False question.

7   Select Choice1 and click the **Browse** button next to the ***Appearance*** drop down box. Search for and select *images/sample_images/obj_panel_true.gif.*

Choice Options	
Name:	choice1
Text (optional):	
Image File (optional):	Browse ...
	☑ Place before text
Appearance:	obj_panel_true ▼ Browse...
Choice Is:	Correct ▼ Score: 0

 Note: In this exercise we replace the appearance instead of the image file, because we want the learner to click on the image to indicate a response.

8   Select Choice2 and click the **Browse** button next to the *Appearance* drop
down box. Search for and select *images/sample_images/obj_panel_false.gif.*

We won't make any changes to the popup messages in the action manager tab.

9   Click **OK.**

10   Try the interaction in a browser.

There are two things you will probably notice after trying out this interaction. First,
for this particular question it would be better to display each choice horizontally
across the page instead of vertically. The *Unique Enhancements* section later in the
chapter offers one method for fixing this problem

Second, you cannot click the graphic to indicate your response; you must click the
radio button. This is because the graphic is not used for appearance. The
appearance image is the only image in a Multiple Choice True/False Interaction
that is active.

Tip: You can make the graphic active by using it for the appearance. To do this you will
need to begin with one of the multiple choice image templates and make changes so it *is* a
True/False. You will also need to turn the obj_panel images into the 6 states that
appearance images require. See *Creating Custom Appearances* later in this chapter for
more information.

Creating a Multiple Choice Interaction

This step-by-step tutorial takes you through the process of creating a Multiple Choice interaction. The subject matter for this interaction are the tabs used to create a Multiple Choice interaction.

Take time to explore the finished interaction, and then follow the step-by-step instructions to create it.

Viewing the Finished Interaction

Before trying your hand at creating this interaction, first take a look at the finished sample.

On CD: Take a moment and try out the finished interaction: *sample_3-2.*

As you explore this interaction, you may want to try some of the following tasks:

- Click on both a correct and incorrect choice.
- Try clicking reset after each attempt. In doing so you can try the question multiple times, even though it is limited to 2 attempts.
- Open the interaction inside Dreamweaver and take a look at the settings in CourseBuilder.

Creating the Interaction

Using the step-by-step instructions in this section, you will create a Multiple Choice interaction. To follow along with these steps, you must have Dreamweaver or UltraDev opened and have inserted the companion CD in the CD ROM drive.

More Information: If you need more details about some of the steps, refer to *Chapter 2: Getting to Know CourseBuilder* or section *Multiple Choice True/False Interaction Basics* earlier in this chapter.

Follow these steps to create a Multiple Choice interaction:

1 Open a new page and insert a CourseBuilder interaction.

2   Select the Multiple Choice category and click on the MultCh_ImageRadios
        interaction:

CourseBuilder adds the default interaction to the page.

Note: For this interaction, you could use any of the other multiple choice templates. In fact,
you could choose a multiple-correct or true/false as well. You would just need to make
more changes.

3   Click on the General tab.

4   Make the changes shown in this table to the General tab:

Setting	Information to Enter
Question Text	Enter: *Which tab must you access to change the question text (stem)?*
Judge Interaction	Include a button and label it: "Am I Right?"
Tries are	Limited to 2
Reset	Include a **Reset** button.

The Screen should now look like this:

5 Click on the Choices tab.

6 Change the text of each choice according to this table:

Choice Name	Text
Choice1	The Gallery tab
Choice2	The Choices tab
Choice3	The Action Manager tab
Choice4	The General tab

7 Use the ***Choice is*** drop down box to change Choice1 so it is *incorrect* and Choice4 so that it is *correct*

We won't make any changes to the popup messages in the action manager tab.

8   Click **OK**.

9   Try the interaction in a browser.

Creating a Multiple-correct Interaction

This step-by-step tutorial takes you through the process of creating a multiple-correct interaction. The subject matter for this interaction are the template icons for a Multiple Choice True/False Interaction.

Take time to explore the finished interaction, and then follow the step-by-step instructions to create it.

Viewing the Finished Interaction

Before trying your hand at creating this interaction, first take a look at the finished sample.

On CD: Take a moment and try out the finished interaction: *sample_3-3*.

As you explore this interaction, you may want to try some of these tasks:

- Click on both a correct and incorrect choice.
- Choose some correct and some incorrect.
- Open the interaction inside Dreamweaver and take a look at the settings in CourseBuilder.

Creating the Interaction

Using the step-by-step instructions in this section, you will create a multiple-correct interaction. To follow along with these steps, you must have Dreamweaver or UltraDev opened and have inserted the companion CD in the CD ROM drive.

More Information: If you need more details about some of the steps, refer to *Chapter 2: Getting to Know CourseBuilder* or section *Multiple Choice True/false Interaction Basics* earlier in this chapter.

Follow these steps to create a multiple-correct interaction:

1   Open a new page and insert a CourseBuilder interaction.

2   Select the *Multiple Choice* category and click on the *MultCh_ImageChkBoxes* interaction:

CourseBuilder adds the default interaction to the page.

Note: For this interaction, you could use the other multiple-correct templates. In fact, you could choose a multiple choice or true/false as well—you would just need to make more changes.

3   Click on the General tab.

4   Make these changes to the settings on the General tab:

CourseBuilder Interaction

Interaction Name:	MultCh_ImageChkboxes01
Question Text:	Which multiple choice templates allow you to make changes to the appearance? (Choose all that apply.)

OK
Cancel
Help

Judge Interaction: ⊙ when the user clicks a button labeled |eck Question|
                                ○ when the user clicks a choice
                                ○ on a specific event (set using the Judge Interaction Behavior)

Correct When: | All Correct and None Incorrect ▾ |

Knowledge Track: ☐ Send results to a management system if present

Tries Are: | Unlimited ▾ | [   ] tries

Time Is: | Unlimited ▾ | [   ] seconds after page text is loaded

Reset: ☑ Create a Reset button

Layer: ☐ Insert in a layer (4.0+ browsers only)

| Gallery | General | Choices | Action Mgr |

- Select and change the question text to: *Which multiple choice templates allow you to make changes to the appearance? (Choose all that apply.).*
- Change the label for the judge interaction button to read *Check Question.*

5   Click on the Choices tab.

6   Select Choice4 and use the **Add** button to add two additional choices. Name them choice5 and choice6.

7   Change the text of each choice according to this table:

Choice Name	Text
Choice1	MultCh_TrueFalse
Choice2	MultCh_Radios
Choice3	MultCh_ImageRadios
Choice4	MultCh_ImageButton
Choice5	MultCh_Checkboxes
Choice6	MultCh_ImageChkBoxes

8   Use the *Choice is* drop down box to make Choice3, Choice4, and Choice6 *correct* and Choice1, Choice2 and Choice5 *incorrect.*

9   Include an image file for each choice according to this table:

Choice Name	File Name
Choice1	Images\Sample_Images\MultCh_TrueFalse.gif
Choice2	Images\Sample_Images\MultCh_Radios.gif
Choice3	Images\Sample_Images\MultCh_ImageRadios.gif
Choice4	Images\Sample_Images\MultCh_ImageButton.gif

Choice Name	File Name
Choice5	Images\Sample_Images\MultCh_Checkboxes.gif
Choice6	Images\Sample_Images\MultCh_ChkBoxes.gif

10 Rearrange the choices using the **Up** and **Down** buttons so that they are in the order shown in this graphic:

We won't make any changes to the popup messages in the action manager tab.

11 Click **OK**.

12 Try the interaction in a browser.

Tip: You can spell check all the text you have entered in the CourseBuilder application by spell checking the page. Choose Text → Check Spelling to begin spell checking.

Unique Enhancements to Multiple Choice Interactions

There are a few more advanced ways to enhance the Multiple Choice True/False interaction. We present some of those methods in this section while others are in later chapters. Here we let you know what is possible and either provide instructions or let you know where to look for instructions.

Creating Specific Response Feedback

To improve the learning experience of an on-line course, you may want to provide specific response feedback. The purpose of this type of feedback is to provide instruction when the learner makes an incorrect choice. You can provide different feedback for each distracter and even for the correct response.

Let's say you have a multiple choice question with one correct response and three distracters. Each of the distracters is partially correct but not completely correct. If a learner chooses one of those distracters, you provide feedback pointing out the correct and incorrect portions of the answer.

You can provide specific response feedback using the Action Manager tab.

More Information: You can learn about creating specific response feedback in *Chapter 13: Customizing the Action Manager Tab*.

When creating a multiple-correct question, you may want to provide partial correct feedback. If the learner gets some of the answer right but not all of them, you want to let the learner know. You can provide partial correct feedback using the Action Manager tab.

More Information: See *Chapter 13: Customizing the Action Manager Tab* for information on setting up partial correct feedback.

Branching Based Upon Responses

By choosing the Go to URL action instead of the Popup Message action in the Action Manager tab, you can force CourseBuilder to load a new page into the browser based on a learner's responses.

With branching, you are taking the learner to a new URL for remediation. Therefore the instruction provided by branching should be more in-depth.

More Information: You can learn about branching after a response in *Chapter 13: Customizing the Action Manager Tab.*

Creating Custom Appearances

Each appearance is a button that the learner can click on when making a choice. You can create as many custom buttons as you would like. Here are some reasons why you may want to do this:

- To create an appearance that is unique to your online lesson.
- To create clickable True and False buttons.
- To create graphical multiple choice and true/false questions that allow the learner to click the graphic as if it were a button.

To create you own buttons you will need to work with a graphics editor to create multiple images that represent the different button states.

More Information: See *Chapter 6: Button Interactions* for instructions on creating clickable images (buttons).

Displaying Feedback in a Frame or Layer

The alert box used to display feedback is only one method of providing feedback to a learner. Another alternative is to display feedback in a frame or layer.

More Information: Displaying feedback in a layer is discussed in *Chapter 13: Customizing the Action Manager Tab.*

Displaying Choices Horizontally Across the Page

Occasionally you may want to display the choices to a Multiple Choice or True/False question horizontally across the page instead of vertically. One way to do that is to create a table inside the form added by CourseBuilder.

Follow these steps to move the choices into a table:

1   Click to the right of the last choice in the question to place the cursor at that point.

2   Press RETURN.

3   Insert a table that contains a cell for each choice in the question (e.g. 1 row 4 columns).

4   Click to the right of the last choice again.

5   Click the <span> tag selector:

`<body> <interaction> <div> <form> <p> < span>`

6   Cut the span element.

7 Paste the span element into the last cell of the table:

The span element has been pasted into the cell.

8 Continue this process with the other choices.

9 When you are finished, you may want to customize the table to fit your needs.

That is all there is to it.

Summary

In this chapter you have learned to create True/False, Multiple Choice, and Multiple-Correct interactions, some of the most basic questions used in any assessment. You have also learned what settings are unique to this interaction type.

We also introduced several enhancements. Some of these are covered in more detail in later chapters, but you now know how to create custom appearances and display choices horizontally on the page instead of vertically.

Drag-and-Drop Interactions **4**

Drag-and-Drop interactions are among the most interesting e-learning interactions because they offer a lot of interactivity. In a Drag-and-Drop interaction the learner clicks and drags an object (called a *drag element)* to a target or area (called a *target element)* and drops it.

In this chapter you will learn:

- When to use Drag-and-Drop interactions.

- How to create Drag-and-Drop interactions as matching exercises.

- How to create Drag-and-Drop interactions that teach the order of steps in an activity.

- How to create your own Drag-and-Drop exercise from a template.

- Several ways to enhance Drag-and-Drop interactions.

Introduction to Drag–and–Drop

CourseBuilder gives you several different Drag-and-Drop templates to choose from. In this section you'll learn when to use these types of interactions and the different variations that CourseBuilder makes available to you.

When to Use a Drag–and–Drop interaction

Drag-and-Drop interactions are versatile—they can be used as quiz questions or as learning activities.

As a Quiz Question

Here are a few scenarios in which you might use a Drag-and-Drop interaction as a quiz question:

- **To assess understanding of new terminology.** You can have a column of terms on the left and a column of definitions randomly ordered on the right. The learner has to drag the term to the correct definition.
- **To assess placement of parts of a larger whole, such as parts on a machine.** Place the graphic of the machine on the right. The parts are "cut outs" of the machine and placed on the left. You could use an Explore interaction to explain the machinery parts in the lesson, then use a Drag-and-Drop interaction to assess their knowledge in a quiz.
- **To assess knowledge of procedural steps** (using the Steps in Order type of Drag-and-Drop).

Tip: When used as a quiz question, Drag–and–Drop interactions should generally give feedback after the learner completes all dragging activities using a **Submit** button.

As a Learning Activity

Here are a few scenarios in which you might use a Drag-and-Drop interaction as a learning activity:

- **Teaching step-by-step procedures**
- **Teaching parts of a greater whole.** Have the learner explore where he or she thinks parts might go by dropping parts onto a picture of the whole. Or show

the completed whole and have the learner drop the parts in the appropriate locations for practice.

Tip: When used as a learning activity, you may want to give the learner feedback as soon as an element is dropped. For example, you might want to have the object snap back to its original position if the learner drops it on the wrong target.

Different Kinds of Drag-and-Drop

All Drag-and-Drop exercises are by nature a matching activity where you want the learner to drag an object onto an intended target. However, within the "matching" umbrella there are several different variations.

When you choose the Drag-and-Drop category from the Gallery, CourseBuilder displays several interaction templates to choose from. These interactions fall under two main types:

- Matching
- Ordered steps

This table describes each interaction and points you to the location in this chapter where you can follow step-by-step instructions to create an example:

Interaction Type	Description
	Many-to-many (or one-to-one matching). This is the most common form of matching. Every object on the left can be placed on any target on the right. (*Many* objects on the left match up to *many* objects on the right, hence the term many-to-many). Strangely enough this is also called a one-to-one matching exercise because each object on the left matches only one object on the right.
	2-Way many-to-many (or one-to-one matching either way). This is a variation on the standard many-to-many in which any object becomes a drag object and a target object. In other words, any object can be dropped on any other object, but only one target object is correct for each drag object.

Interaction Type	Description
	One-to-many matching. This interaction creates only one drag object and several target objects. Only one target is correct for the one drag object. You could use this as a more visual type of multiple choice interaction.
	2-Way one-to-many (or one-to-many either way). This interaction has 4 objects that are simultaneously drag and target objects; any object can be dropped on another. This is similar to the one-to-many matching.
	2-Way one-to-one (or "Build Your Own") template. Use this template to build your own Drag-and-Drop exercise. Because it has only two drag/target elements, you don't have to spend needless time deleting unwanted elements.
	Steps in order (or procedures with no distracters). Use this template for most exercises where you want the learner to place steps in a particular order. The learner must drag a single object to targets in the correct sequential order.
	Steps one-to-many (or procedures with a distracter). This is the same template as the Steps in Order type, but contains a distracter step. For example, if there are three steps to a procedure, but the third step is often confused with something else, you can place the erroneous third step as the distracter to see if the learner can choose the correct third step.

Drag-and-Drop Basics

Before you create a Drag-and-Drop interaction, it's important to understand some of the basic skills and concepts relating to this type of interaction.

6 Steps to Drag-and-Drop interactions

Follow these six basic steps to create a Drag-and-Drop interaction:

1 Insert a new interaction using one of the methods described in Chapter 2.

2 Establish the settings on the General tab such as when the learner will receive feedback.

3 Make sure you have the right number of drag elements and the right number of target elements by adding or deleting them on the Elements tab.

4 Define valid pairs of elements on the Elements tab. A pair is simply one drag element and one target element. Define each pair as correct or incorrect. A defined pair does not mean it is the correct pair, it simply means the target is a location where the learner can drop the drag element and it will get evaluated as correct or incorrect. CourseBuilder determines other areas on the screen that are not defined as pairs as "undefined" and they will not affect the score. You'll usually want to define all possible pairs.

5 Accept or customize the feedback the learner will receive by editing the decision tree in the Action Manager tab.

6 Move the drag and target layers on the Dreamweaver page to an appropriate locations.

More Information: See *Chapter 13: Customizing the Action Manager Tab* for different ways to customize feedback.

When to Give the Learner Feedback

Determining when to give the learner feedback is an important decision for the Drag-and-Drop interaction. Choosing "when the learner clicks a button labeled…" for the Judge Interaction setting is usually the best option because it allows the learner to finish dragging and dropping every drag object in the interaction before finding out how they are doing.

By default CourseBuilder selects this setting for you:

```
⊙  when the user clicks a button labeled │Submit                │
```

If you are using this interaction to teach or introduce a concept, you may want to give them feedback every time the learner drops an object:

○ when the user drops a drag element

How Should the Element React When Dropped?

CourseBuilder gives you three ways to handle what happens when the learner drops a drag element:

- Snap back if incorrect
- Snap back if not dropped on target
- Allow the learner to drop the drag element anywhere on the screen

CourseBuilder provides these settings on the General tab:

Reaction: ☐ Snap back if incorrect
          ☑ Snap back if not dropped on target

You can select both of these setting at the same time or none at all if desired. Each setting is described in the sections that follow.

Snap Back if Incorrect

When you choose this setting, CourseBuilder resets the location of the drag element if the learner drops it on an incorrect target. Obviously you wouldn't want to use this in a testing environment, but it can be very useful for reinforcing what is correct and incorrect in a learning activity.

When used with the **Snap To** settings on the Pairs tab, you may even want to forego any other kind of feedback.

Note: Don't confuse the "incorrect" in **Snap Back if Incorrect** with the "correctness" of the whole interaction. Choosing this setting simply means to snap the element back when a single element is dropped on an incorrect target. It does not replace feedback for the whole interaction when the learner clicks the **Submit** button at the end of the interaction (that is if you choose to have them click a Submit button).

On CD: To see an example of the *Snap Back If Incorrect* setting in action, view *Sample_4-1.htm* on the CD ROM.

Snap Back if Not Dropped on a Target

In every Drag-and-Drop interaction, you have to define what elements are "target" elements. These elements are the pre-defined objects onto which you can drop drag elements.

If the learner drops a drag element someplace else on the screen, how do you want CourseBuilder to react? If you turn on this setting, a drop onto an unknown target returns the drag element to its original location. If you leave this setting unselected, the drag element simply drops onto the unknown area without any kind of response.

 Note: A drop onto an unknown area is neither correct or incorrect.

Allow the Learner to Drop Anywhere on the Screen

If you want the learner to be able to drop the drag element anywhere on the screen, deselect both settings:

Reaction: ☐ Snap back if incorrect

☐ Snap back if not dropped on target

You might want the interaction to behave this way if your interaction takes up the entire web page. By not providing them any kind of feedback when they drop the drag element, anything on the page except the correct targets acts as a distracter.

Defining Drag–and–Drop Elements

An "element" is an object on the page that can be dragged (called a "drag element") or an defined area on the page where an object can be dropped (called a "target element"). Defining both drag and target elements is an important part of this interaction. You may need to add or delete elements depending on how many drag and target elements you need to complete your interaction.

Adding and Deleting Elements

If you need to add or delete drag and target elements, click the **Add** and **Delete** buttons on the Element tab.

Defining Element Options

Each element has three properties that you can define:

- Name
- Image File (optional)
- Element Is (either a drag element, target element, or both)

This table explains these options:

Property	Explanation	Special Considerations
Name	A valid name is any combination of letters and numbers, but may not contain any spaces.	Naming your elements can be very helpful if you are referencing them in the Action Manager or using JavaScript. Otherwise, there is no need to name them.
Image File	Use this option to use custom graphics for your drag or target elements.	This setting is optional, meaning that you could clear this setting and the drag or target element would simply be a Dreamweaver layer instead of an image in a layer.
Element Is	This setting defines whether the element is a drag element, target element, or both.	Most of the time an element is only going to be one or the other. Choose both only if you really want the learner to be able to drag-and-drop both sides of the match.

Defining Drag-and-Drop Pairs

Any two elements in a drag-and-drop exercise can be a "pair." A pair defines what is a recognized and acceptable target element for a drag element:

You define pairs on the Pairs tab.

We describe the options on this tab in the following sections.

Adding and Deleting Pairs

To help you avoid confusion, the drop down box at the top of the Pairs tab lists all possible pairs between the drag and target elements listed on the Elements tab:

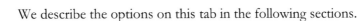

For example, in an interaction that has four drag elements and four target elements there are a sixteen possible pairs!

Note: By default CourseBuilder already creates all possible pairs for each preset drag and target element in any template. You only need to define pairs for drag and target elements that you add to a template. However, you may need to set the *Choice Is* setting for existing pairs to make sure they are designated appropriately as correct or incorrect.

To add one of the possible pairs, select the pair in the drop down list, then click the **Add** button.

To delete one of the pairs, select the pair in the Pairs box below the drop down box and click the **Delete** button:

Pairs:
| Drag1:Target1 (correct) |
| Drag1:Target2 (incorrect) |
| Drag1:Target3 (incorrect) |
| Drag2:Target1 (incorrect) |
| Drag2:Target2 (correct) |
| Drag2:Target3 (incorrect) |
| Drag3:Target1 (incorrect) |
| Drag3:Target2 (incorrect) |

Tip: If you want to add all possible pairs, keep clicking the Add button until you see the text *<all pairs created>* in the drop down box:

| <all pairs created> |

Defining Pair Options

Each pair has a set of unique options that determine how that pair acts.

This table explains those unique options. (Other options such as the Choice Is and Score are similar across all interaction types).

Property	Explanation	Special Considerations
Snap If Within	When learners drop the drag element, they will most likely not drop it *exactly* on top of the target element. The issue here is, "How close is close enough?" Enter the number of pixels that defines the range that is acceptable for the drag element to be dropped.	Usually the higher the number the better. However, be careful. If you are creating rectangular elements, remember the *Snap If Within* range is a number of pixels in any direction from the center of the object. Don't accidentally overlap these Snap If Within areas. See *Defining a Target's "Hot" Area* later in this chapter.

Property	Explanation	Special Considerations
Snap To	**Center** – snaps the center of the drag element to the center of the target element **Left** – snaps the drag element to the left side of the target element. **Right** – snaps the drag element to the right side of the target element. **Top** – snaps the drag element to the top of the target element **Bottom** – snaps the drag element to the bottom of the target element **Custom** – Snaps the drag element to the location you define. You enter the number of pixels down and to the right of the target element's upper left corner.	By default CourseBuilder selects Center as the Snap To setting. You may want to change this if it is important to see the drag and target elements side by side. This can be important for learning reinforcement. See *Defining the Snap To Area* later in this chapter.

Defining the Target's "Snap To" Area

Understanding how to properly define the target's "Snap To" area is critical when creating Drag-and-Drop interactions.

Note: The main thing to remember about the *Snap To* area is that it is circular, even if your target element is square or rectangular.

Suppose you have a rectangular target element that is 150 pixels wide and 50 pixels high with a *Snap If Within* setting of 60 pixels. The "Snap to" area is shown here: (60 pixels in each direction from the center of the target element.)

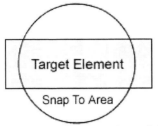

A *Snap If Within* setting of 60 pixels obviously wouldn't be enough because someone could drop the object *on* the target but outside the Snap To area:

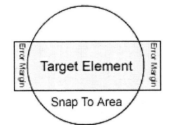

So, will increasing the *Snap If Within* setting to 75 give us better results?

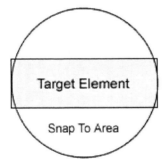

The answer is *perhaps*. Now there is very little room for error when dropping the drag element. However, we now run into a different problem.

Most Drag-and-Drop interactions have more than one target element. If the target elements are placed too closely together, you can quickly see the problem: the *Snap To* areas overlap:

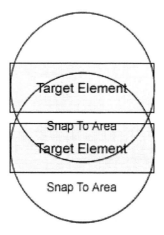

To solve this problem, place the objects far enough apart vertically or horizontally to avoid the overlap:

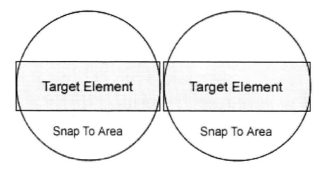

Note: We've used a rectangular target element to illustrate how the ***Snap To*** area works. If your target elements are circular or square, setting the Snap To area is much easier. Because of this we recommend using circular or square target elements where possible.

Caution: Remember that the "Snap if Within" setting measures from the center of the target layer, **not** from the center of any graphics you might have in the layer. If you change the graphic of a target layer, you may need to resize the layer to make the *Snap To* functionality work the way you are expecting.

Matching Exercises

In this section you'll learn more about and be able to create the different kinds of matching interactions.

Many-to-Many

To create the most common type of matching interaction, choose the first CourseBuilder template from the gallery—many-to-many:

View the Finished Interaction

Before creating this interaction, take a moment to explore the finished product.

On CD: Open *Sample_4-1.htm* on the CD ROM to see an example of the many-to-many interaction.

When viewing this interaction, here are some things to look for:

- Drop the drag elements onto an invalid area and see what happens.
- Drop the drag elements near, but not right on, the target elements. How close do you have to be before the drag element snaps to the target?
- Click the **Submit** button to view feedback.
- Click the **Reset** button to start the interaction over.

Create this Interaction

Now that you've seen how this interaction works, try creating it yourself.

Follow these steps to create the matching exercise:

1 Open a blank Dreamweaver page, insert a new interaction on the page, and choose the many-to-many, Drag-and-Drop interaction type.

CourseBuilder inserts the interaction on the page.

2   Leave all settings on the General tab unchanged.

3   Click on the Elements tab.

4   Delete elements named Drag3 and Target3.

5   Define the remaining four elements with these settings. The image files are located on the CD.

Element	Settings
First Drag Element	**Name:** Drag1 **Image File:** *images/sample_images/ dragDrop2WayM2M.gif* **Element Is:** Drag element
Second Drag Element	**Name:** Drag2 **Image File:** *images/sample_images/ dragDropM2M.gif* **Element Is:** Drag element
First Target Element	**Name:** Target1 **Image File:** *images/sample_images/ dragDrop2WayM2MTarget.gif* **Element Is:** Target element
Second Target Element	**Name:** Target2 **Image File:** *images/sample_images/ dragDropM2MTarget.gif* **Element Is:** Target element

Your elements tab should look like this:

*Click the Browse
button to search
for custom
images.*

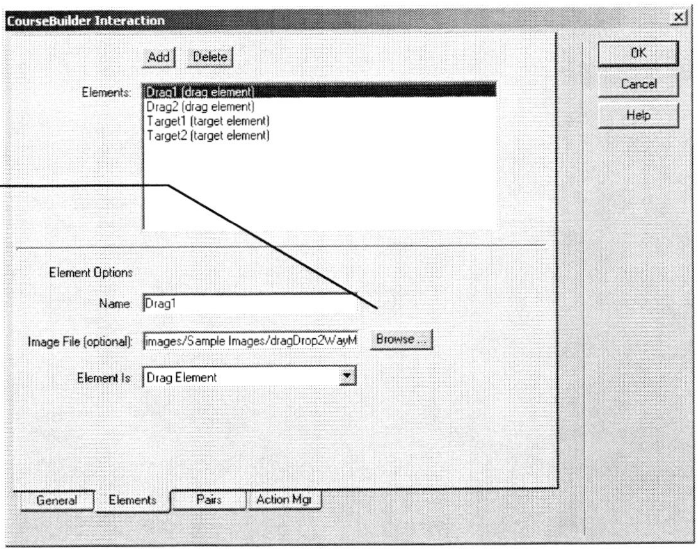

6   Click the Pairs tab.

Since all you did was delete some of the default elements on the Elements tab,
all remaining pairs are already defined for you.

7   The graphics we are using for our elements are 76 pixels wide, so change the
Snap If Within setting to *76* pixels.

Your Pairs tab should look something like this:

Click on each pair to define settings for that pair.

Make sure to do this for every pair. Leave all other settings unchanged.

Tip: Sometimes when defining many pairs, pairs will disappear from the list of pairs on the Pairs tab. This can be very confusing. But don't worry, your pairs are still there; you just can't see them until you select them. But since you can't see them it is hard to know which one to select. One way around this is to start with a pair you can see and use the up and down arrow keys to move through the list (instead of your mouse).

Note: By default CourseBuilder selects each corresponding pair (i.e. Drag1:Target1, Drag2:Target2, etc.) as correct responses. If you were adding additional elements and pairs, you would need to set the *Choice Is* setting for each additional pair.

8   Click **OK**.

Your interaction should look something like this:

Even though we've completed all of the CourseBuilder settings, we still have some cleanup to do on the page itself.

9   Move the drag and target layers beneath the question text:

10   Switch the positions of the drag layers so that the correct answer isn't straight across from each drag layer.

11   View the page in a browser and try it out.

You've created a basic matching interaction. Of course in most interactions you would have more than two pairs. Simply add more pairs and you're on your way.

2-Way Many-to-Many

Though similar to the standard many-to-many interaction, the 2-Way many-to-many differs in one major way: you can drag any object in the interaction, not just the ones on the left. In other words, all objects in the interaction are both drag elements *and* target elements:

One-to-Many Matching

Use this Drag-and-Drop type when you feel distracters would be helpful. The default template supplies you with one drag element and three target elements. Only one of the target elements is correct. You can think of it as a more interactive type of multiple choice:

Viewing the Finished Interaction

Before creating this interaction, take a moment to explore a sample of the completed interaction.

On CD: Open *Sample_4-2.htm* on the CD ROM to see an example of the one-to-many matching interaction.

When viewing this interaction, here are a few things to look for:

- Drop the drag element on a target. Where does it "snap to"?
- How many drag elements are there?
- How many target elements?
- How do you know that you have dropped the drag element on a valid target element?

- What is distracting about the way the cursor behaves when the mouse is placed over the drag elements?

Create this Interaction

Now try creating this interaction yourself.

Follow these steps to create a one-to-many matching exercise:

1   Open a new Dreamweaver page, insert a new interaction on the page, and choose the one-to-many, Drag-and-Drop interaction type.

   CourseBuilder inserts the interaction on the page.

2   Do not change any settings on the General tab.

Note: The default selection for the Judge Interaction setting is *when the learner drops a drag element*. This is because there is only one drag element in the interaction, so there is no reason to delay the feedback.

3   On the Pairs tab, change each pair to *Snap To the Left* of the target element. Leave all other settings on the Elements tab unchanged.

4   Click **OK**.

   Dreamweaver displays the interaction on the page:

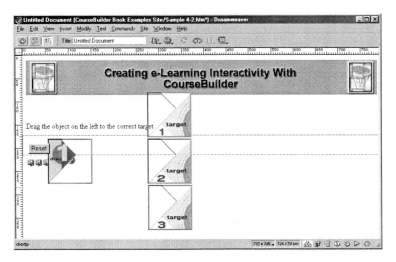

5   Replace the image in the drag layer with this text: *CourseBuilder is....*

6   Replace the images in the target layers, starting with the first, with this text:

- *…a Dreamweaver extension.*
- *…a Dreamweaver behavior.*
- *…a Dreamweaver object.*

7   Position the drag and target layers beneath the **Reset** button.

8   Resize the drag and target layers so the text displays on a single line.

9   Change the question text to: *Complete the sentence by dragging the text on the left to the correct target on the right.*

Your Dreamweaver page should now look something like this:

That's it! You've completed a one-to-many Drag-and-Drop interaction.

10   Try out your interaction in a browser.

More Information: Most users would not assume that the text in this sample is draggable without instructions. See *Drag-and-Drop 3-D Magic* and *Changing the Cursor to a Hand When the Mouse is Placed Over a Drag Element* later in this chapter for some solutions to this usability issue.

2-Way One-to-Many Matching

Though similar to the one-to-many interaction, the 2-Way many-to-many differs in one way: you can drag any object in the interaction, not just the ones on the left. In other words, all objects in the interaction are both drag elements *and* target elements.

Steps in Order

The other type of interaction that CourseBuilder offers you in the drag-and-drop category is Steps in Order (also called procedures).

Ordered Steps interactions require the learner to drop one drag element on multiple target elements in sequential order. If the learner drops the drag element out of sequence, the interaction pops-up some feedback.

More Information: For different ways to display feedback, see Chapter 13: *Customizing the Action Manager Tab.*

Steps in Order With No Distracters

As with most interactions in CourseBuilder, you can find an application for both teaching and assessing for the Steps in Order template. In this section you will create a simple interaction that requires the learner to place the steps in the correct order:

View the Finished Interaction

Before creating this interaction, take a moment to explore the finished product.

On CD: Explore a Steps in Order sample by opening *Sample_4-3.htm* on the CD ROM. Try it out in the browser to see how it works (this exercise was designed for Internet Explorer—you may experience some differences if using another browser).

When viewing this interaction, here are some things to look for:

- What happens if you drop the arrow on Step 2 first?
- What happens when you drop the arrow on Step 1?

More Information: This sample was created from a basic Steps in Order interaction template, but it has some special things added in the Action Manager tab to replace the step graphics with text. See *Changing the Look and Feel of Drag-and-Drop interactions* later in this chapter for more details.

Create this Interaction

In this example we'll create a Steps in Order interaction that teaches the learner certain steps.

Follow these steps to create a Steps in Order interaction:

1   Begin by opening *Sample_4-3_Start.htm* on the CD (this exercise was designed for Internet Explorer—you may experience some differences if using another browser).

This page already has the interaction inserted for you.

2   Edit the CourseBuilder interaction on this page.

Note: The interaction on this page has had some advanced Action Manager logic added to make the exercise more meaningful.

3   On the Elements tab, select the settings of each element according to the values in this table (don't change any other settings):

Element	Settings
Drag Element	**Image File:** *images/sample_images/greenArrow.gif*

Element	Settings
Target Element 1	**Image File:** *images/sample_images/Step1.gif*
Target Element 2	**Image File:** *images/sample_images/Step2.gif*

4   Click the Pairs tab and set the ***Snap To*** setting to *Left*.

5   Click **OK**.

6   Arrange the drag and target layers so they look like this:

7   Replace the question text with: *To learn the basic steps to setting up a CourseBuilder interaction, drag the arrow on the left to the steps on the right in sequential order.*

8 Try the interaction in a browser:

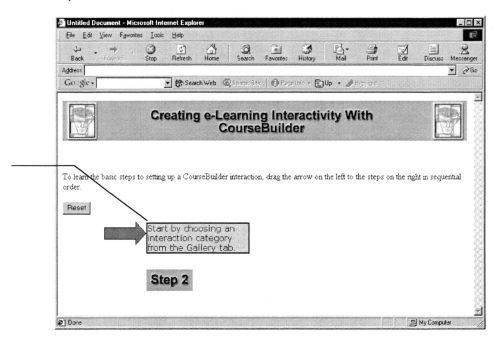

When viewed in a browser, the behavior in which the purple "step" graphic changes to text is controlled in the Action Manager tab. This is not inherent behavior to the Steps in Order question type, but is shown in this example as one way this type of question could be implemented.

Steps in Order With Distracters

This interaction type works the same way as the basic Steps in Order without distracters, except that it has one or more target elements that act as distracting alternatives. This type works best as a quiz question:

Creating a Custom Drag–and–Drop Interaction

To build your own Drag-and-Drop interaction, you can start with one of the other templates and delete unnecessary elements and/or add others. However, it may be easier to start with the one-to-one, or build-your-own, template:

Follow these steps to use this template:

1   Click on the one-to-one interaction from the Drag-and-Drop category of the Gallery tab.

CourseBuilder displays the new interaction on the page and displays the Elements, Pairs, and Action Manager tabs.

 Note: CourseBuilder creates two elements for you, but notice that they are defined as both Drag *and* Target elements (meaning each can act as a Drag or Target element). You still need to define what types of elements you want these to be, as well as add and define other drag and target elements.

2   Click the Elements tab and add and define additional drag and target elements.

3   Click the Pairs tab and define needed pairs.

4   Click **OK.**

You have created a custom Drag-and-Drop interaction.

 More Information: To learn how to add this interaction to your gallery so you can reuse it at a later time, see Chapter 15: *Creating Custom CourseBuilder Interactions.*

Unique Enhancements to the Drag–and–Drop Interaction

Now that you know how to create basic Drag-and-Drop interactions, learn how to improve them. In this section you'll find several ways to get the most out of these fun interactions.

Changing the Look and Feel of a Drag-and-Drop interaction

Here are some ways you can customize the look and feel of a Drag-and-Drop interaction:

- Change the placeholder graphics
- Use text instead of graphics
- Add a style from a cascading style sheet to text-only drag and/or target elements

Changing the Placeholder Graphics

To change the placeholder graphics use one of these methods:

- Choose a different image for the Image File setting on the Elements tab
- Delete the graphics from the Dreamweaver page and insert them using standard Dreamweaver tools and techniques.

Use Text Instead of Graphics

Using text for your drag-and-drop exercises (instead of graphics) saves on bandwidth. To use text, replace the placeholder graphics in the drag and target layers with text of your choice.

Tip: If you choose to use text elements instead of graphical elements, spruce up your interaction by assigning style sheet classes to the drag and target layers.

More Information: To learn how to use styles with CourseBuilder interactions, see *Chapter 11: Using CSS to Enhance CourseBuilder.*

Drag-and-Drop 3-D Magic

If you choose to use text-based Drag and Target elements (instead of graphics), you can use styles to create the appearance of a 3-D drag object that looks raised off the page and a 3-D target object that looks inset. This works well for drag-and-drop exercises such as matching terms with definitions.

On CD: To see an example of a 3-D Drag-and-Drop interaction using text and a stylesheet, open *Sample_11-2.htm* on the CD ROM.

More Information: To follow a step-by-step tutorial on how to create this type of enhancement, see *Chapter 11: Using CSS to Enhance Coursebuilder.*

Changing the Cursor to a Hand When the Mouse Is Placed Over a Drag Element

To indicate to the learner that a Drag element is an *interactive* element on the page (i.e. the learner can and should do something with it), you may want the cursor to change to a hand when the mouse is placed over the drag element.

To do this, create a style that changes the cursor to a hand (or whatever other cursor style you choose) and apply that style to the drag layer in Dreamweaver.

More Information: To follow a step-by-step tutorial on how to create this type of enhancement, see *Chapter 11: Using CSS to Enhance Coursebuilder.*

Enhancing What Happens When the Learner Drops the Drag Element

By default, the only thing that happens when the learner drops a drag element on a target element is that it snaps into place. Working with the Action Manager tab, you can use the dropping action as a trigger to make other things happen.

Because of the variety of actions provided in the Action Manager, there are dozens of things you could do. Here are a few examples to get you thinking.

After the learner drops the drag element you could:

- Change the contents of the target layer to show different text, replace the graphic, or show some other layer altogether.
- Play a Macromedia Flash movie somewhere else on the page.
- Reset other drag elements to their original positions so the learner can only have one object on any one of the targets at a time.
- Display another page in a different frame.

On CD: To see an example of an interaction that uses the Action Manager to do more than just display a popup message after the learner drops the interaction, open *Sample_4-3.htm* and explore the contents of the Action Manager tab.

More Information: To learn more about the Action Manager, see the chapters on the Action Manager in Section II of this book, *Extending CourseBuilder.*

Summary

In this chapter you've learned how to create Drag-and-Drop interactions. Drag and Target elements make up the interactive parts of these types of interactions. Drag-and-Drop interactions can be used for matching exercises or for procedural step assessment or instruction. You can also create your own custom Drag-and-Drop interactions.

As a reminder, when creating Drag-and-Drop interactions, ask yourself if you've completed these steps:

- Have all of the necessary elements and pairs been created?
- Are the *Snap If Within* and *Snap To* **settings** for each pair defined correctly? (Remember, these settings are not global across pairs and must be set for every pair.)

Drag-and-Drop interactions are more complicated than some of the interactions in the CourseBuilder gallery, but by using the templates and with a little practice, customizing them to fit your particular needs should not be difficult for you.

Explore Interactions 5

The Explore interaction is a bit different from many other CourseBuilder interactions. Most of the other CourseBuilder interactions lend themselves to quiz type questions. The Explore interaction is best suited for an instructional activity that involves the learner learning about the parts of an object or a series of concepts. However, you can use it for quiz questions as well.

In this chapter you will learn:

- About templates and possibilities for the Explore interaction.
- The different settings available for the Explore interaction.
- How to create a random exploration.
- How to create a structured exploration.
- How to create explore quiz questions.
- Several ways to enhance the Explore interaction.

Introducing the Explore Interaction

The Explore interaction is best suited for an instructional exercise that allows the learner to click on hot areas to receive additional information. The hot areas consist of HTML layers. The layers can contain images, text, or remain empty and invisible.

The Explore interaction can be set up to let the learner explore parts of an object or concepts in any order (random explore), or you can structure it to suggest an order that the learner needs to explore (structured explore).

When Should You Use an Explore Interaction?

The most common reason to use an Explore interaction is to teach the parts of something. A random Explore interaction and a structured Explore interaction may have different applications.

When to Use A Random Explore Interaction

Here are a few situations where you may find it useful to use a random Explore interaction to:

- Teach about the different elements of a new software product's user interface.
- Describe the purpose of a series of menu options.
- Teach the names and descriptions of parts on a piece of equipment.
- Provide more detailed information about a flowchart.
- Provide more information about a series of related objects.
- Provide a more detailed explanation of related concepts.
- Describe different locations on a map.

These are just a few ways to use a random Explore interaction. Undoubtedly, you can think of many more.

 On CD: Try out *sample_5-1.htm* to see how a random Explore interaction works.

When to Use a Structured Explore Interaction

A structured Explore interaction is not as versatile, but there are situations where it is very useful. Remember, a structured explore, by default, does not require the learner to explore the information in a prescribed order, it simply suggests an order by the way the hot areas are organized.

Tip: You can use the Action Manager to force an order if you would like. This is covered in *Chapter 13: Customizing the Action Manager Tab.*

Here are a couple of situations where you may want to use this type of interaction:

- To provide more information about a series of steps.
- To teach a series of concepts that build upon each other.

On CD: Try out *sample_5-2.htm* to see how a structured Explore interaction works.

How Does the Explore Interaction Work?

When a learner interacts with an explore interaction, they click on different areas of the page and are provided with information. Normally there is a representation of some object displayed on the page. The learner explores the object by clicking on different parts. The object may consist of several text descriptions instead of a graphic image.

The Explore interaction lets you to place a graphic or text in the background. You then place hot areas (layers) over the top of certain parts of the graphic or text. As the learner clicks on that hot area, a text description displays.

Note: In traditional web design, this type of interaction is called an *image map*. While this concept has been used for navigation for many years, this interaction uses it to enhance learning.

Choosing a Template

The Explore interaction Gallery consists of three templates as shown here:

Visible Random Explore

Transparent Random Explore

Structured Explore

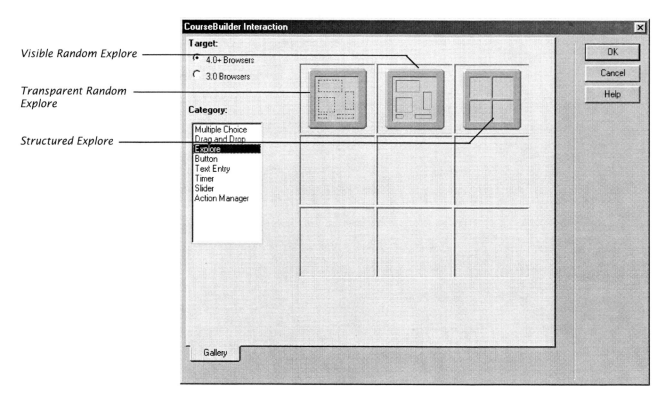

This table describes the purpose of each template and displays a thumbnail image showing its appearance. You can change any of the default setting provided by each template:

Interaction Type	Description
	Transparent Random. The template creates a random exploration activity using transparent layers (the layers do not contain a visible graphic image). The layers are not placed in any particular order. You are initially provided with five hot areas.

Interaction Type	Description
	Visible Random. The template creates a random exploration activity using visible layers. A default graphic image is provided for each layer. The layers are not placed in any particular order. You are initially provided with five hot areas.
	Structured. This template creates a structured exploration by providing layers in a prescribed order. Because the hot areas are organized in a particular order it sends a message to the learners to explore the information in that order.

How Dreamweaver Implements the Explore Interaction

The Explore interaction works only in version 4 or later browsers, due to how the interaction is implemented. (You can also use them in Netscape 3 if you don't use any transparent images.) The main reason for this is that the hot areas are actually layers (div tag for those of you that know HTML). Layers are only supported in later browsers.

Each hot area (layer) may contain a graphic, text, or remain transparent. Basically, anything you can put in a layer can go in the hot area. Moreover, because they are layers you can position and resize them.

As with all interactions, a fair amount of JavaScript code makes the interaction work.

Explore Interaction Basics

Creating an Explore interaction requires these 6 basic steps which we elaborate in the section that follow:

1 Insert an interaction using a method discussed in chapter 2. Choose a template from the Gallery.

2   Add and delete hot areas as necessary.

3   Replace the placeholder graphics with your own graphics.

4   Make changes to the popup description text on the Action Manager tab.

5   Align the hot area layers.

6   Modify the default instructions.

 Tip: You may find it helpful to first create an Explore interaction before tackling the next several sections. Step-by-step instructions are presented later in this chapter. Look for the hands-on icon.

Adding or Deleting Hot Areas

Each explore template provides you with some hot areas to get started. Occasionally you may create an Explore interaction that requires the same number of hot areas that are provided by default. However, most of the time you need to add or delete hot areas to get the right number for what you are teaching.

You add and delete hot areas on the Hot Areas tab.

Follow these steps to add hot areas:

1   Click the Hot Areas tab to access it.

The Hot Areas tab appears:

The Add and Delete buttons.

```
CourseBuilder Interaction                                    [x]
                          Add    Delete                     OK
         Hot Areas:  HotArea1 (not judged)                  Cancel
                     HotArea2 (not judged)                  Help
                     HotArea3 (not judged)
                     HotArea4 (not judged)
                     HotArea5 (not judged)



         Hot Area Options

             Name:  HotArea1

         Text (optional):  [                        ]

         Image (optional):  images/transparentSquare.gif   Browse...

         Hot Area Is:  Not Judged  ▼   Score: 0

       Gallery | General | Hot Areas | Action Mgr
```

Hot Areas tab

2 Select a hot area.

3 Click the **Add** button.

Note: Hot areas are added immediately following the hot area that is selected.

Follow these steps to delete hot areas:

4 Click the Hot Areas tab to access it.

5 Select the hot area that you want to delete.

6 Click the **Delete** button.

Replacing the Placeholder Graphics

An Explore interaction comes with a default background graphic and default hot area graphics. If you are creating a transparent Explore interaction, you will want to use the default transparent graphics CourseBuilder supplies you with for each hot area that you will want to use. Otherwise you will need to replace both the background graphic and all of the hot area graphics.

Replacing the Background Graphic

The background graphic is usually a complete graphic that shows all of the parts you are trying to teach. However, in some Explore interactions you may choose to eliminate the background graphic altogether.

The background graphic information is kept on the General tab.

What is the Purpose of the Background Graphic?

How you use the background image depends on the type of Explore interaction you are creating. For example, if you are teaching about the buttons on a toolbar, then you will want to use a graphic of the toolbar as your background image. However, if you want to teach concepts or steps, then the background image may simply be something that provides some visual appeal and ties everything together.

Background Image

Follow these steps to replace or remove the background graphic:

1   Click the General tab.

2   To remove the background image, select the filename in the ***Backdrop Image*** field and press DELETE.

To change the background image, click the **Browse** button that is to the right of the ***Backdrop Image*** field and search for a new graphic.

Replacing the Hot Area Graphics

If you are not using the transparent graphics for an Explore interaction, then you will want to replace the hot area placeholder images with graphics that fit your topic. For example, instead of a placeholder image, the graphic may represent the concept or step being taught.

If you want to use transparent images, you don't need to replace the hot area graphics—simply use the ones that are supplied by default.

More Information: To see some examples of how graphics can be used, see the tutorials on Random and Structured interactions later in this chapter.

Follow these steps to replace the hot area graphics:

1   Click the Hot Areas tab to access it.

2   Click a hot area in the ***Hot Areas*** field.

3   Click the **Browse** button that is to the right of the optional ***Image*** field. Search for and select the graphic you want to use for that hot area.

To delete the graphic, select the file name and press the DELETE key.

Tip: It is helpful to name the hot areas before replacing the graphics. When the hot area has a name, it is easier to know which image you need to select.

4   Repeat steps 2-3 for the remaining hot areas.

Tip: You can replace and delete images using standard Dreamweaver techniques as well.

Changing the Description Text

In an Explore interaction, the learner clicks on a hot area in the interaction and the web page displays a description of that element in a popup box. The learner reads the text and then clicks **OK**. You need to change this text so that the correct information is presented to the learner.

Tip: You can also change this interaction so that the text that displays will show up in a layer. See *Chapter 13: Customizing the Action Manager Tab* for more information.

Follow these steps to make changes to the text:

1   Click the Action Manager tab.

2   Select the popup message for the first hot area.

The popup Message is preceded by an *if* statement that contains the name of the first hot area:

CourseBuilder Interaction   ☒

Add	Segment ▼	Cut	Copy	Paste	OK
Edit..	Cancel
	+ Segment: Check Time Help
Rename..	-- Segment: HotArea1 Feedback
	-- if HotArea1 Selected
	Popup Message

Popup message for first hot area ——

```
+ Segment: Check Time
-- Segment: HotArea1 Feedback
   -- if HotArea1 Selected
        Popup Message
-- Segment: HotArea2 Feedback
   -- if HotArea2 Selected
        Popup Message
-- Segment: HotArea3 Feedback
   -- if HotArea3 Selected
        Popup Message
-- Segment: HotArea4 Feedback
   -- if HotArea4 Selected
        Popup Message
-- Segment: HotArea5 Feedback
   -- if HotArea5 Selected
        Popup Message
-- Segment: Correctness
   -- if Correct
        Popup Message
   -- else if Incorrect
        Popup Message
   -- else if Unknown Response
        Popup Message
+ Segment: Check Tries
```

Expand
Collapse

| Gallery | General | Hot Areas | Action Mgr |

Tip: Name the hot areas before working with the Action Manager tab so you are clear which popup message you are working on.

3   Click the **Edit** button.

4   Change the text and click **OK**.

Aligning the Hot Area Layers

Once you have made all of the changes in the CourseBuilder Interaction window and clicked **OK**, you need to resize and reposition the hot area layers.

Each hot area is implemented as a layer with an image. The image is transparent for transparent interactions. To make sure that the hot areas are in the correct location, you need to position those layers. You may also need to resize them.

Positioning Hot Area Layers

You can position hot area layers by either dragging the layer with the mouse or by selecting the layer and using the arrow keys to move the layer.

Follow these steps to position a layer:

1   Select the layer by clicking its border or tab.

When a layer is selected, you will see select boxes all around the layer as shown here:

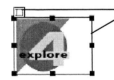
Click the either the border or the tab to select the layer.

If you click in the middle of the layer you will only select the image and it will display as shown here:

The layer tab.

Notice that select boxes do not surround the layer. If you have selected the image, just click the layer tab to reselect the layer.

2   Move the layer to its correct position. You can do this by clicking the layer tab and dragging with the mouse or by selecting the layer and using the arrow keys to move it in small increments.

Resizing Hot Area Layers

You won't normally need to resize the hot areas unless you are using transparent layers. When using transparent layers you are usually trying to position the layer over some portion of the background object.

When you resize a transparent layer, it is important to resize the graphic image as well. You can resize a graphic or layer by selecting it and dragging the select handles.

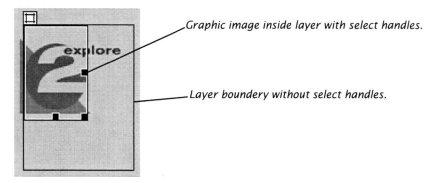

Graphic image inside layer with select handles.

Layer boundery without select handles.

You can also enter new values in the Width and Height fields of the Property Inspector:

Width and Height fields.

To avoid frustration, remember these simple rules when you are resizing layers.

▪   If you need to make the layer larger, resize the layer first and then the graphic (or just resize the graphic and the layer resizes with it).

> ■ If you need to make the layer smaller, resize the graphic first and then resize the layer. You cannot make the layer smaller than the graphic.

 More Information: Refer to your Dreamweaver manual for more information about working with layers.

 Note: For some browsers (Internet Explorer, for example) it is not necessary to have a transparent image in the layer. CourseBuilder implements the interaction just using the layer.

Replacing the Default Instructions

When you add the Explore interaction to the page, these default instructions are added: "Click on a hot area." Before you finalize the Explore interaction, you will want to modify these instructions to fit your own personal preferences.

 # Creating a Random Exploration

The first step-by-step tutorial that we present in this chapter is an Explore interaction that teaches the purpose of the different fields on the Hot Areas tab. As we mentioned in the beginning of the chapter, one of the ways you can use random exploration is to teach about the different parts of software.

Once you have viewed the finished interaction, you can follow the step-by-step instructions to recreate it.

Viewing the Finished Interaction

Before trying your hand at creating this interaction, take a look at the finished sample.

 On CD: Take a moment and try out the finished interaction: *sample_5-1*.

As you work with this interaction, you may want to try some of the following tasks.

■ Click on each field to view the description.
■ Click outside of the fields to view the unknown response.

- Open the interaction from inside Dreamweaver so you can see the layers. Try selecting the layers and the images.

Creating the Interaction

Using the steps in this section, you will create a random Explore interaction that uses transparent layers. To follow along with these steps, you must have Dreamweaver or UltraDev opened and access to the sample files on the CD.

More Information: If you need more details about some of the steps in this section, refer to *Chapter 2: Getting to Know CourseBuilder* and the *Explore interaction Basics* section in this chapter.

Follow these steps to create a random Explore interaction:

1 Open a new page, and insert a CourseBuilder interaction.

2 Select the *Explore* category and click the *Explore_Transparent* interaction:

CourseBuilder adds the default interaction to the page and additional tabs appear.

3 Click the General tab:

The only thing you need to change on this tab is the background image. Right now it is set to the default which is Explore_Random.gif.

4   Click the **Browse** button next to the ***Backdrop Image*** field. Select file *images/sample_images/hotareas_tab.gif.*

If CourseBuilder prompts you to copy the image to your site folder, you may want to choose "yes" so that the image is in your root folder.

The background image on the page should change to a graphic of the Explore interaction Hot Areas tab.

5   Click the Hot Areas tab.

The Hot Areas tab appears:

For this sample interaction you do not need to add or delete hot areas.

6   Name each of the hot areas by selecting the hot area and entering a new name in the *Name* field. Use these names:

Hot Area	New Name
HotArea1	HotAreas
HotArea2	Name
HotArea3	Text
HotArea4	Image
HotArea5	Judging

You do not need to make any additional changes. Since it is a transparent interaction, you won't change the hot area images. You also won't use any text for this interaction.

7   Click the Action Mgr tab.

The Action Mgr tab appears:

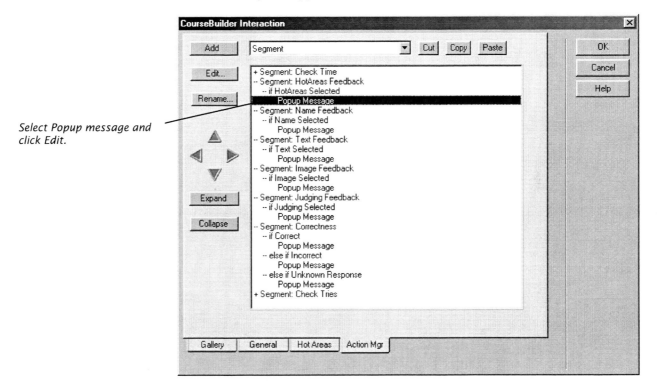

Select Popup message and click Edit.

As you can see, the names of the hot areas show up on this tab. This makes it easier to edit the Popup Message.

8   Change the Popup Message for the 5 hot areas by selecting the *Popup Message* below each hot area name (e.g. if Text Selected) and clicking the **Edit** button. Use these messages:

Hot Area Name	Popup Message
HotAreas	Use this field to display a list of all the hot areas in the interaction. Use the **Add** and **Delete** buttons to add and delete hot areas.

Hot Area Name	Popup Message
Name	Use this field to name a hot area. This makes the interaction easier to work with.
Text	Use this field to enter text that will display as part of the hot area.
Image	Use this field to enter the name of a graphic image that will display in the hot area.
Judging	Use the drop down box to determine whether the interaction is judged or not. If you decide to have it judged, you can enter a score.

9   Click the **OK** button.

The window is closed. Now you need to position and resize the hot areas. The background image is a screen shot of the Hot Areas tab with all of the fields. Each layer needs to be positioned over its corresponding field in the graphic image.

10 Find the name of each layer by selecting it or using the Dreamweaver layers panel. Once you know the name of the layer, move it so it covers the field that it describes.

11 Resize each layer so it is just a little larger than the field it covers.

Tip: Remember to size the image first if you are trying to make the layer smaller.

This screen shot shows the layers positioned of each field of the background graphic:

The five layers positioned over the five fields on the graphic image.

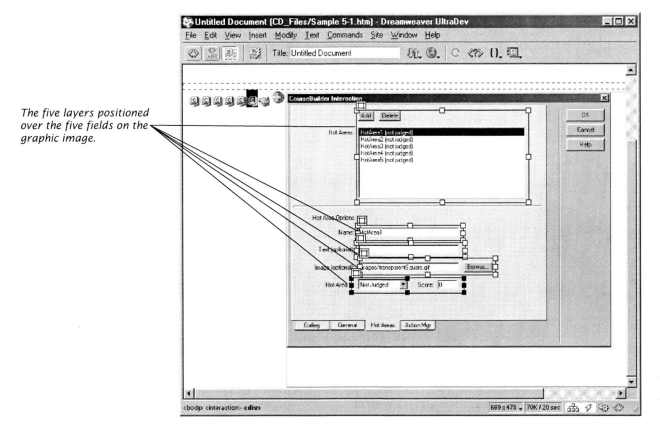

12 Change the instructions to read: *Click on each of the fields to learn more about the Hot Areas tab.*

13 Try the interaction in a browser and make adjustments as necessary.

More Information: You may want to use some of the suggestions in *Unique Enhancements to Explore interactions* to improve this interaction.

Creating a Structured Exploration

This step-by-step tutorial takes you through the process of creating a structured Explore interaction. The purpose of the interaction is to teach the steps required to install the CourseBuilder extension. We use a structured interaction in this case, because we want to present the steps in a logical order.

Viewing the Finished Interaction

Before trying your hand at creating this interaction, take a look at the finished product.

On CD: Take a moment and try out the finished interaction: *sample_5-2.*

As you explore this interaction, you may want to try some of the following tasks:

- Click on each step to view the description and see how we have used this interaction to provide more information about each step.
- Click outside of one of the fields to see the unknown response.
- Open the interaction from inside Dreamweaver so you can see the layers. Try selecting the layers and the images.

Creating the Interaction

Using the step-by-step instructions in this section, you will create a structured Explore interaction that uses visible layers. To follow along with these steps, you must have Dreamweaver or UltraDev opened and have inserted the companion CD in the CD ROM drive.

More Information: If you need more details about some of the steps, refer to *Chapter 2: Getting to Know CourseBuilder* and the *Explore Interaction Basics* section earlier in this chapter.

Follow these steps to create a structured Explore interaction:

1   Create a new page and insert a CourseBuilder interaction.

2   Select the *Explore* category and click the *Explore_Areas* interaction:

CourseBuilder adds the default interaction to the page and additional tabs appear.

Note: The structured explore template comes without a background image.

3 Click on the Hot Areas tab:

Delete this hot are. ——————

For this sample interaction we need only three hot areas. So, let's delete one.

4 Select *HotArea4* and delete it.

5 Choose a new image for the three remaining hot areas. Use these image files:

Hot Area	New Name
HotArea1	Image/Sample_Images/install_step1.gif
HotArea2	Image/Sample_Images/install_step2.gif
HotArea3	Image/Sample_Images/install_step3.gif

6 Click the Action Mgr tab:

Change these popup messages.

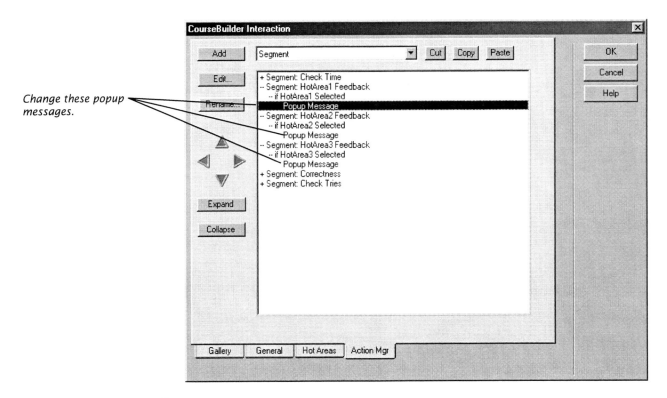

7   Change the *Popup Message* for the 3 hot areas. Use these messages:

Hot Area	Popup Message Text
HotArea1	You can download the package file (.MXP) from http://www.macromedia.com/ exchange/dreamweaver/) or (http://www.macromedia.com/exchange /ultradev/).
HotArea2	You can start the installation by double-clicking the package file or by choosing Install from the File menu in the Extension Manager.
HotArea3	Click OK to accept the disclaimer.

8   Click the **OK** button.

The window is closes. Now you need to position the hot areas.

9 Position each layer so that each subsequent step is below the previous step as shown here:

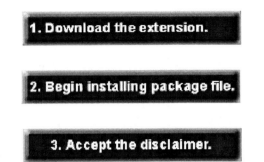

10 Change the instructions for the interaction to say: *Click on each step to learn more.*

The finished interaction should look like this:

The instructions after they have been changed.

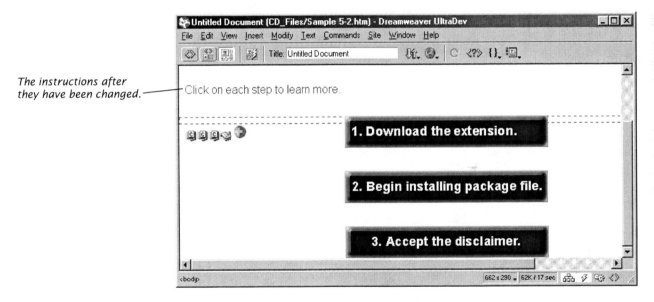

11 Test the interaction by previewing the page in a browser.

 More Information: You may want to use some of the suggestions in the *Unique Enhancements for the Explore interactions* section to improve this interaction.

Using the Explore Interaction as a Quiz Question

You can use the Explore interaction as a quiz question. It functions pretty much like a Multiple Choice question. For example, you may want to test learners on their knowledge of the location of certain parts.

In this step-by-step tutorial you create a quiz question that tests the learner on the names of the three Explore interaction templates.

Once you have viewed the finished product, you can follow the step-by-step instructions to recreate it.

Viewing the Finished Quiz Question

Before trying your hand at creating this interaction, take a look at the finished product.

On CD: Take a moment and try out the finished interaction: *sample_5-3*.

As you explore this interaction, you may want to try some of these tasks:

- Click on an incorrect hot area as well as a correct hot area.
- Click outside one of the fields to view the unknown response.
- Open the interaction from inside Dreamweaver so you can see the layers. Try selecting the layers and the images.

Creating the Interaction

Using the step-by-step in this section, you will create a quiz question using visible layers. In order to follow along with these steps, you must have Dreamweaver or UltraDev opened and have inserted the companion CD in the CD ROM drive.

More Information: If you need more details about some of the steps, refer to *Chapter 2: Getting to know CourseBuilder* or the *Explore Interaction Basics* sections earlier in this chapter.

Follow these steps to create an explore quiz question:

1 Create a new page, name it, and insert a CourseBuilder interaction.

2 Select the *Explore* category and click on the *Explore_Random* interaction:

CourseBuilder adds the default interaction to the page and additional tabs appear. Since we need to turn this Explore interaction into a quiz question, we need to make several entries on the General tab.

3 Click on the General tab and establish these settings:

Setting	Value
Correct When:	All Correct and None Incorrect
Tries Are:	Limited to 1 try
Background Image (Optional):	Select the background image and press the delete key to delete it.

4 Click on the Hot Areas tab.

For this interaction you only need three hot areas, so you will delete two of them:

HotArea4 and HotArea5

5   Select and delete *HotArea4* and *HotArea5*.

6   One by one, select and name the three remaining hot areas according to this table:

Hot Area	New Name
HotArea1	ExploreTransparent
HotArea2	ExploreRandom
HotArea3	ExploreAreas

7 Choose a new image for the three remaining hot areas using these image files:

Hot Area	New Name
HotArea1	Image/Sample_Images/explore_transparent_icon.gif
HotArea2	Image/Sample_Images/explore_random_icon.gif
HotArea3	Image/Sample_Images/explore_areas_icon.gif

8 Set the *exploreAreas* hot area to be correct with a score of 1. The other two should be incorrect with a score of 0:

The first two hot areas are incorrect. The last one is correct.

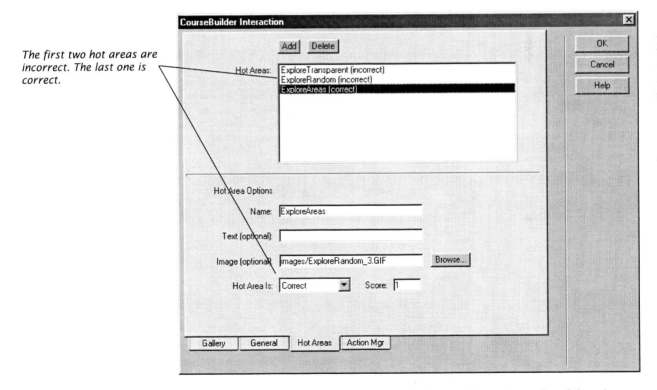

Because you are using this interaction as a quiz question, you need to delete the popup message for each hot area on the Action Mgr tab.

9 Click the Action Mgr tab:

Delete these three Popup messages.

Don't delete these ~~Popup~~ messages.

CourseBuilder Interaction

Add | Segment | ▼ | Cut | Copy | Paste | OK

Edit... | Cancel

Rename... | Help

+ Segment: Check Time
-- Segment: ExploreTransparent Feedback
   -- if ExploreTransparent Selected
      Popup Message
-- Segment: ExploreRandom Feedback
   -- if ExploreRandom Selected
      Popup Message
-- Segment: ExploreAreas Feedback
   -- if ExploreAreas Selected
      Popup Message
-- Segment: Correctness
   -- if Correct
      Popup Message
   -- else if Incorrect
      Popup Message
   -- else if Unknown Response
      Popup Message
+ Segment: Check Tries

Expand

Collapse

Gallery | General | Hot Areas | Action Mgr

10 Select the popup message for each hot area (ExploreTransparent, ExploreRandom, ExploreAreas) and delete it by clicking the **Cut** button.

Make sure you do not delete the popup message for getting the question correct.

Note: If you do not delete the popup messages for these hot areas, a default message appears when the learner clicks the hot area.

More Information: Refer to the action manager chapters in *Section II: Extending CourseBuilder* for more information on the Action Manager.

11 Click the **OK** button on the CourseBuilder Interaction window.

The window closes.

12 Position the layers so they are next to each other as shown here:

13 Change the instructions at the top to read: *Click on the Explore_Areas template.*

14 Try the interaction in a browser and make adjustments as necessary.

More Information: You may want to use some of the suggestions in the *Unique Enhancements for the Explore interaction* section to improve this interaction.

Unique Enhancements for the Explore Interaction

There are a few more advanced ways to enhance the Explore interaction. In this section we let you know what is possible and provide you with instructions or refer you to a more advanced chapter for instructions.

Removing or Changing the Unknown Response

You may have noticed that in an Explore interaction, if a learner clicks somewhere outside a hot area, CourseBuilder displays an alert box with Unknown Response:

Microsoft Internet Explorer ☒

⚠ Unkown Response.

[OK]

This alert box only occurs if you include a background graphic and the learner clicks on the background graphic.

On CD: Try *sample_5-1* to see this happen. Click somewhere on the CoruseBuilder Interaction Window but not on the fields.

In many situations this may be more of a distraction than help. For that reason, you may want to delete the Unknown Response or change the message. (For example, you could change the message to: *You clicked on an undefined area. Please try again.*).

You change or delete the Unknown Response on the Action Mgr tab. The popup message is located towards the bottom and immediately follows the line: *else if Unknown Response.* Once you have selected that *popup message*, you can either change it or delete it.

- To change the response, select it and click the **Edit** button, enter the new response and click **OK**.

- To delete the response, select it and click the **Cut** button.

Displaying Feedback in a Frame or Layer

The alert box used to display the description when a hot area is clicked can be quite annoying. You can avoid the beep and the alert box by displaying the description in a layer.

More Information: Displaying feedback in a layer is discussed in *Chapter 13: Customizing the Action Manager Tab.*

Adding Text to Hot Areas

With some interactions you may find it helpful to include text that labels the hot area. This may also make the instruction more effective. You can label an object so that when the learner clicks it, CourseBuilder displays a description.

On CD: Open *sample_5-4.htm* to see an example of this type of interaction.

To add text to a hot area, enter a label in the Text field on the Hot Areas tab.

Creating a Mouse-Over Highlight

When you are creating an Explore interaction that uses transparent hot areas such as *sample 5-1.htm*, you may also want the object you are teaching highlighted as the mouse passes over it. This technique lets learners know that when they cursor over an object they can click on it.

On CD: Open sample_5-5.htm to see an example of a mouse-over highlight.

There is really no secret to creating a mouse-over highlight. First, create a highlight graphic for each layer, and second, use the swap image and swap image restore behaviors in Dreamweaver to implement it.

Follow these steps to create a mouse-over highlight:

1 Create a transparent Explore interaction.

2 Select the image in each layer and write down its pixel size. (View pixel size in the Property Inspector.)

   By getting the pixel size of the transparent image, you can create a highlight image of the same size so it displays without distortion.

3 Create a red rectangle as a highlight graphic for each layer. Use no fill color and make sure you export the GIF image with transparency.

4 Add a swap image behavior to each layer in the interaction. Dreamweaver automatically adds a swap image restore behavior.

5 Test your interaction.

That is all there is to it. You now have a more effective interaction.

Changing the Cursor

Changing the cursor to a hand when the mouse is placed over it is a way of indicating an Explore interaction is active.

To do this, create a style that changes the cursor to a hand (or whatever other cursor style you choose) and apply that style to the explore layer in Dreamweaver.

More Information: For more information on creating this type of enhancement, see *Chapter 11: Using CSS to Enhance Coursebuilder.*

Tracking Responses

If you choose to use the Explore interaction as a quiz question, you may also want to track learners' responses. See *Chapter 20: Using Learning Site to Track Learner Data.*

Forcing an Order in a Structural Explore

The structural Explore interaction used in this chapter does not force the learner to click hot areas in any particular order. You may come across an instructional situation where it might be advantageous to force learners to explore in a defined order. This is possible using the Action Manager.

 More Information: You can find an example of a structural explore that forces the learner to follow a defined order in *Chapter 13: Customizing the Action Manager Tab.*

Summary

Explore interactions let you provide the learner with an engaging exercise. An Explore interaction provides several hot areas that the learner clicks to learn more information. The hot areas are implemented as HTML layers.

The main difference between an Explore interaction and other CourseBuilder interactions is the Hot Areas tab. On this tab you define the different hot areas in the interaction.

We provided step-by-step instructions to create both a random interaction with visible images and a random interaction with transparent images. Although this interaction is not best suited for creating quiz questions, it is still possible to create them as shown in the last step-by-step tutorial.

Finally, there are several ways you can enhance the Explore interaction to make it more useful.

Button Interactions   **6**

By themselves, buttons are not really interactions. However, they are an important building block for interactions. To make full use of buttons, you also need to understand the Action Manager well. See the Action Manager chapters in *Section II: Extending CourseBuilder.*

In this chapter you will learn:

- About templates and ways to use buttons.
- How to create custom buttons.
- How to create navigational buttons.
- How to create general purpose buttons.
- How to create simulation buttons.
- A few ways to enhance buttons.

Introducing the Button Interaction

Think of buttons as building blocks that help you build interactions. To make full use of buttons as building blocks, you need to be very familiar with the Action Manager.

Note: As we talk about buttons in this chapter, we are not referring to standard buttons that are used inside of forms. We are referring to clickable images.

In this section we take a look at some of the situations where you may want to use buttons. We also discuss how CourseBuilder buttons differs from regular buttons you create in Dreamweaver.

When to Use a Button

Since CourseBuilder buttons act like other clickable images you have used in the past, you can probably think of many situations to use a button. Here are some situations where we have used buttons in the past:

- To provide navigation in a course
- To provide interaction (The learner clicks a button to show more information on a topic.)
- To start a Macromedia Flash® movie or some other form of media
- To simulate software
- To pop-up a picture of a concept

As you can see from these examples, CourseBuilder buttons are used in the same situations as normal buttons. In fact, they are normal buttons controlled by CourseBuilder. So this brings up the question: *Why use CourseBuilder buttons?* We address this question in the next section.

How are CourseBuilder Buttons Different from Regular Buttons?

Since CourseBuilder buttons are used in the same situation as clickable images in Dreamweaver or Macromedia Flash buttons, what makes them different and why use them over these others?

Here are some of the advantages to using a CourseBuilder buttons.

- They generally have more states (six total), making the button more interesting and more interactive.
- They use the power of the Action Manager, letting you do a lot without knowing much JavaScript.
- They come with a couple of settings that let you easily establish the initial state and the mouse-over state of the button.

Basics of the Button Interaction

CourseBuilder buttons are not difficult to use. There are only two templates to choose from and a couple of settings. If you want to create custom buttons, then you need to spend a little more time in a graphics editor. In this section we discuss each of these topics.

Taking a Look at the Button Gallery

The Button interaction consists of two templates: Button_toggle and Button_push.

Each template comes with a default button image, but you can change that image to any that are available in the ***Appearance*** drop down box on the General tab. The main difference between the two templates is how the buttons work.

This table describes both templates and provides a thumbnail of each:

Interaction Type	Description
	Toggle Button. This template comes with a default appearance of a switch. When the toggle button is clicked, it keeps the up or down state until it is clicked again.
	Push Button. This template comes with a default appearance of a round push button. When the push button is clicked, it immediately returns to its normal state.

The toggle button stays in its clicked state until it is clicked again. The push button immediately returns to its normal state after it is pushed. If you want a button that acts like a switch, choose the button_toggle template. If you want a standard push button, choose the button_push template.

Button Settings

The Button interaction doesn't have any unique tabs. However, there are several new settings on the General tab:

These settings at the top are unique to the Button interaction.

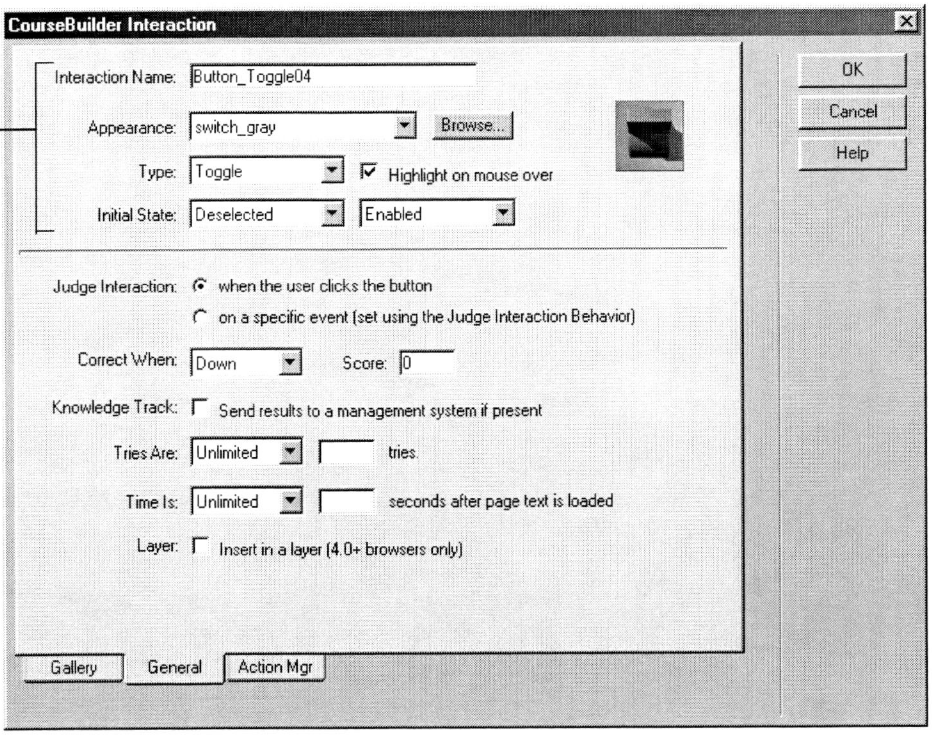

Each setting is described in this table:

Setting	Description
Interaction Name	This field contains the name of the interaction.
Appearance	This drop down box contains a list of the different buttons you can choose. A thumbnail of the current button is shown to the right. You can click on the browse button to choose a button you have created and stored in another folder.
Type	In the Type drop down box, you choose either toggle or push.
Highlight on mouse over	This check box lets you determine whether or not a button highlights (changes) when the cursor passes over it.

Setting	Description
Initial State	Initial state consists of two drop down boxes that allow you to determine the initial state of a button. In the first drop down box, you choose whether the button is selected (already clicked) or not. In the second drop down box, you choose whether the button is enabled or disabled.

These settings are an advantage of a CourseBuilder button. With them you can easily control the state and response of each button.

The *Judge Interaction* settings on the General tab don't normally apply to a Button interaction because they aren't being used for quiz questions. However, you may want to use the information these settings provide for other purposes. For example, maybe you want something to happen after the learner clicks a button twice. You do that by having the action manager react when the number of tries equals two.

The Action Manager Tab

We mentioned that to make full use of CourseBuilder buttons, you must use the action manager tab. Lets look a little closer at the Action Manager tab:

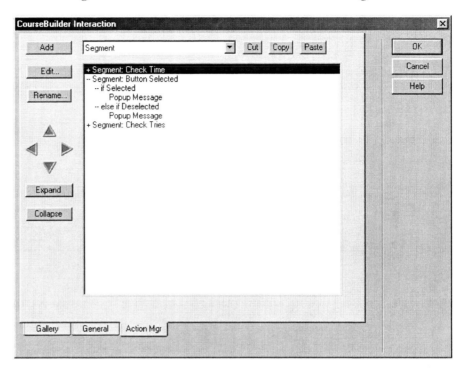

The action manager tab can be very powerful if you know how to use it. Every button interaction comes with a default action on the Action Manager tab. That default action is to display a popup message when the learner either pushes or selects the button. You can change these popup messages to a myriad of other actions.

The Action Manager tab displays the brains behind the interaction. In one sense the Action Manager tab uses programming logic to make decisions about how to handle the learner's response. While you don't need to know a programming language to use the Action Manager tab, you need to follow a specific order and format (also called "syntax") to tell Coursebuilder how to make the right decisions and do the right things.

In this chapter, we simply show and tell you what is possible. You will learn more about the Action Manager tab in later chapters.

More Information: For more information on the Action Manager, see *Section II: Extending CourseBuilder.*

Creating Custom Buttons

CourseBuilder comes with 11 buttons to choose from. You can create additional buttons if you would like.

Before you can create your own custom buttons, you need to understand these concepts:

- The different states of a button
- The file naming convention
- The storage location
- The basic steps to creating a button

The Six States of a Button

Each button used in CourseBuilder consists of 6 states. This means that they can appear 6 different ways depending upon what the learner is doing. This may surprise someone that has used Coursebuilder extensively because the 6 states aren't always apparent. In most cases there are only slight differences.

Each state consists of a single graphic image. That means you need to create 6 images for each button.

The 6 states are described in this table:

Name	Description	Example
Normal	This state is the one most commonly seen by the learner. This is what the image looks like before the learner begins interacting with it.	☐
Mouse Over	This state appears when the learner moves the cursor over the top of the image.	☐
Mouse Over Selected	This state occurs when the learner clicks on the image and passes the cursor over the image after they have already selected the choice.	☑

Name	Description	Example
Normal Selected	This state is how the image appears after it has been clicked on and the cursor is not over it.	☑
Normal Disabled	This state occurs when the question is disabled. For example, the learner has run out of time or has been limited to a certain number of tries.	☐
Selected Disabled	This state occurs when the question is disabled and the choice has been selected.	☑

 On CD: To help you see the different states in action, we have created a simple True/False question (*sample_6-1.htm*) using a circle for a button. The circle changes color for each state: normal = red, mouse over = yellow, mouse over selected = black, normal selected = green, normal disabled = blue, selected disabled = purple. Try the question 3 times and it will disable.

File Naming Conventions

To get a button to work correctly, you must create a different image for each of the six states and name the images correctly. CourseBuilder finds the image by the name that is used.

 Caution: Create all six states or the button will not work correctly.

To name the files correctly, create the image for the normal state first. You can name this image anything you want, but the name of the other 5 images must begin with the same name used for the normal image.

This table identifies the naming convention you need to use:

State	Naming Convention	Example
Normal	You can name this file anything you want.	Sample.gif
Mouse Over	Combine the name of the normal file and "_hlt" to name this file.	Sample_hlt.gif

State	Naming Convention	Example
Mouse Over Selected	Combine the name of the normal file and "_sel_hlt" to name this file.	Sample_sel_hlt.gif
Normal Selected	Combine the name of the normal file and "_sel" to name this file.	Sample_sel.gif
Normal Disabled	Combine the name of the normal file and "_dis" to name this file.	Sample_dis.gif
Selected Disabled	Combine the name of the normal file and "_sel_dis" to name this file.	Sample_sel_dis.gif

File Storage Location

You can save your image files in any location. However, if you would like the new button that you created to show up in the **Appearance** drop down box on the General tab, then you need to save these files in the *images\buttons* folder.

Note: If you save the images in the *images\buttons* folder, they will also appear in the Appearance drop down box on the Choices tab for a Multiple Choice interaction. You can use it as a part of a Multiple Choice interaction.

This graphic shows the Appearance drop down box with a new button selected. The name of the image is test.gif. Notice that it shows up as test:

```
test                    ▼
lighted                 ▲
lighted_mini
round_red
sphere_blue
square_gray
switch_gray
switch_slot
switch_zero_one
test                    ▼
```

A thumbnail of the button you choose is shown to the right of the Appearance drop down box. When you create a new button, you may notice that the image looks distorted. That is because it enlarges the image to display it in an area of 100 pixels by 100 pixels.

Tip: To make the thumbnail graphic appear like all other thumbnail graphics, create a transparent GIF that is 100x100 pixels and place a small composite image of the button in the center. Name it the same as the normal graphic with "_tnail" attached to the end.

Creating a Custom Button

We can summarize the process of creating a custom button using these three steps:

1 Use a graphics program to create 6 states for the new button. Name them using the correct naming convention.

2 If you want the button to show up in the *Appearance* drop down box, store the files in the *images\buttons* folder.

3 From the choices tab select the new button. If you stored the files in the buttons folder, select it from the drop down box. If you stored them in another folder, click the **Browse** button, search for and select the normal state graphic. (We recommend storing the buttons in the buttons folder.)

That is all there is to it.

Creating Navigation Buttons

The purpose of a navigation button is to let the learner move through the course. You can create navigational buttons using the Button interaction.

The best way to create a navigational framework for your course is to use Learning Site. Learning Site also lets you to create your own navigational buttons; however, those buttons only have two states.

More Information: You can learn more about Learning Site in *Section III: Using Learning Site Command for Course Architecture.*

If you choose not to use Learning Site, we suggest you create customs buttons and place them in a frameset. You can then program the buttons using JavaScript functions.

You could place the navigational buttons on each page and use the Go To URL behavior in Dreamweaver, but this makes a course difficult to maintain.

More Information: For more information on framesets, see a Dreamweaver reference manual.

Creating General Purpose Buttons

Buttons have several uses in the instructional portion of any course. One of those uses is to display some additional information. To illustrate this type of button, we use an example that shows a Macromedia Flash movie when clicked.

Once again, you could create this same interaction without using CourseBuilder buttons. If you like the advantages that CourseBuilder buttons offer then you can use them to create this interaction.

Viewing the Finished Interaction

When you are presenting information and some of that information is in a Macromedia Flash movie, you may not want the movie to start as soon as they enter the page. For example, you may want them to read some text first. In a scenario like this, you can use a button to show a Macromedia Flash movie. This example shows that type of scenario.

Why Use Macromedia Flash in e-Learning?

Macromedia Flash is a tool that allows you to create low bandwidth animations or movies.

Sometimes the best way to explain a concept is through an animation or a movie. When you are trying to explain a concept that is difficult, try creating a Macromedia Flash movie. This interaction shows you how to incorporate flash, not the best method of applying it.

On CD: Open *sample_6-2.htm* to see a Button interaction that shows a Macromedia Flash movie. This interaction was designed for Internet Explorer.

While viewing this interaction, make sure you try the following:

- Click the button to show the movie.
- Open the interaction in Dreamweaver to see how it was implemented.

Creating the Interaction

To complete this interaction, you will need to use the Action Manager tab.

Follow these steps to create an interaction that starts a Macromedia Flash movie:

1 Create a new page, name it, and insert a push button interaction.

2 Click **OK**.

The CourseBuilder Interaction window closes and leaves a button and text on the page:

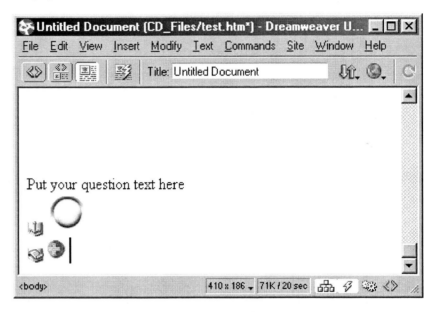

3 Add a layer to the page, name it, and insert this Macromedia Flash movie *siteintro3.swf* into the layer. (Use Insert → Media → Flash or click the **Flash** button on the Objects panel.)

The Macromedia Flash movie shows as a gray image with a flash icon:

4   Uncheck autoplay in the Property Inspector (Window → Properties) and enter *flashobj* as the **ID** and the name for the movie:

5   Choose Window → Layers to access the Layers panel and hide the layer:

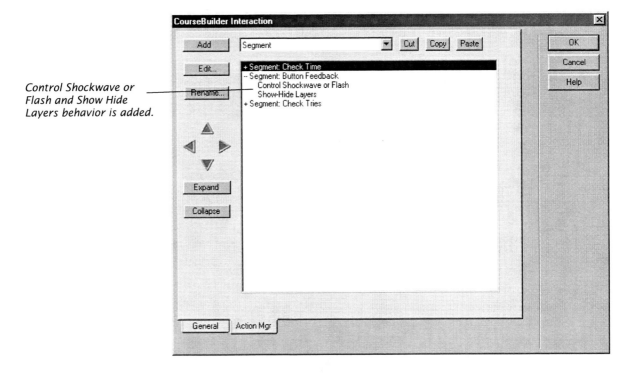

Layer is hidden.

6 Edit the Button interaction and click on the Action Manager tab.

7 Change the *Button Feedback* segment by deleting the Popup message and adding a Control Shockwave or Flash behavior and a Show-Hide Layers behavior. You need to show the layer and start the Macromedia Flash movie playing.

Note: We have found that the *Control Shockwave or Flash* behavior does not always work well with Netscape Navigator.

Here is what the completed Action Manager tab looks like:

Control Shockwave or Flash and Show Hide Layers behavior is added.

The Action Manager includes the same behaviors that you have access to in Dreamweaver. Showing a layer and playing the Macromedia Flash movie are both behaviors.

 More Information: See the chapters in *Section II: Extending CourseBuilder* to learn how to make these changes.

8   Click **OK** and test the interaction in a browser.

You can use this same technique to hide and show a graphic or any other type of information.

 Tip*:* You can create an interaction that will show and hide the Macromedia Flash movie when the button is clicked. See *Unique Enhancements to the Button Interaction* later in this chapter for more information.

Creating Simulation Buttons

Simulations are one of the most challenging things to do in e-learning. Simulating software involves, to some extent, recreating the software. This includes buttons. If those buttons contain multiple states and may be disabled at times, you can use CourseBuilder to help simulate those buttons.

In this example, we illustrate the very simple simulation of clicking the CourseBuilder icon on the objects panel. When the learner clicks the icon, the CourseBuilder Interaction window opens. For simplicity sake, the only button we simulate on that window is the Cancel button. When the learner clicks Cancel, the window closes.

Viewing the Finished Interaction

Before creating this simple simulation, take a moment to view what it looks like.

On CD: Open *sample_6-3.htm* to see this simple simulation.

While you are looking at this interaction, try the following:

- Click the CourseBuilder icon to open the CourseBuilder Interaction window.
- While the CourseBuilder interaction window is still opened, try to click the icon.

- Click the Cancel button on the CourseBuilder Interaction window.

- Open the page in Dreamweaver and see how it was created. Notice how the simulation button is offset from the graphic image, yet in the browser it lines up correctly. This is one of the quirks of layers.

Creating the Interaction

Before you can create a simulation that uses buttons, you must first create all of the graphics for the buttons using the steps outlined in *Creating Custom Buttons*. A screen capture utility such as SnagIt® (see *www.snagit.com*) works well for this type of task. For this exercise the button graphics are already created for you on the CD ROM.

To follow along with these steps, you must have Dreamweaver or UltraDev opened and have access to the files from the CD.

Follow these steps to create a simple simulation:

1   Open a new page and name it.

2   Add a layer and insert *images\sample_images\obj_panel.gif* in the layer.

3   Add another layer and insert *images\sample_images\course_inter_win.gif* in the layer.

4   Position the layers side by side with the layer that contains the *course_inter_win.gif* image on the right side.

   The page should now look like this:

5   Insert a push Button interaction.

6   On the General tab check the *Layer* check box.

By placing the button in a layer, you can move the entire interaction around the screen.

7   To place an image in the *Appearance* field, click the **Browse** button and select *images\sample_images\obj_icon.gif.*

Change the appearance and place the button in a layer.

8 Click **OK** and close this interaction for now.

9 Insert another Button interaction.

10 Select *Layer* to place this interaction in a layer

11 To place an image in the *Appearance* field, click the **Browse** button, search for and choose file *images\sample_images\cancel_butt.gif* for the *Appearance*.

12 Click **OK** and close this interaction for now.

13 Delete the question text for each Button interaction.

14 Use the Property Inspector (Window → Properties) to change the *Z-index* for the two interaction layers (probably named G01layer and G02layer) to a 3:

Change Z-index to a 3.

	Layer ID	L	18px	W	54px	Z-Index	3	Bg Image	
	G01Layer	T	186px	H	49px	Vis	visible	Bg Color	

Tag DIV   Overflow   Clip L   R

T   B

This places these two layers on top of the first two layers you created.

15 Position the button layers so that the buttons appear in the correct place. You may need to view the results in a browser several times before you get it right. You probably can't place the button layer directly over the image of the button on the graphic and get them to line up correctly.

This screen shows an example of the offset button layers:

The two button layers are offset a bit so they will line up correctly.

16 Use the Layers panel (Window g Layers) to hide the CourseBuilder Interaction window layer and the layer with the Cancel button:

The layers with the CourseBuilder window and the cancel button are hidden (eye shut).

Name	Z
G01Layer	3
G02Layer	2
Layer2	2
Layer1	2

Now the layers should be set up and ready to add the actions from the Action Manager.

17 Edit the interaction that contains the CourseBuilder icon button and complete these tasks:

- On the General tab limit the tries to 1. This disables the button once it is clicked. While the CourseBuilder Interaction window is opened, the learner shouldn't be able to click this button.

- On the Action Manager tab delete the popup message for check tries segment. (You don't want a message popping up when the learner clicks on the button.)

- On the Action Manager tab add a show/hide layer behavior to show the CourseBuilder Interaction window layer and the Cancel button layer:

Show-Hide Layer behavior showing the two layers that contain the CourseBuilder window and the Cancel button.

18 Edit the interaction that contains the **Cancel** button and complete these tasks.

- On the Action Manger tab, add a show/hide layer behavior and hide the **Cancel** button layer and the Course Builder Interaction widow layer.

- Add a reset interaction behavior and reset CourseBuilder icon Button interaction (probably button_push01) so that the learner can click on it again once the window is closed:

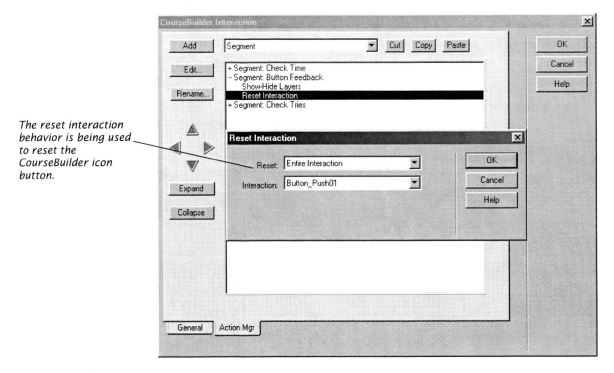

The reset interaction behavior is being used to reset the CourseBuilder icon button.

More Information: To learn how to edit the Action Manager tab see the chapters in *Section II: Extending CourseBuilder*.

19 Test the interaction in a browser.

Let's Review

This interaction was a bit complex, so let's review what we covered.

To begin with we had you add two layers to a blank Dreamweaver page and inserted a graphic image into each layer. The purpose of the graphic image is to give the look of the software that is a part of the simulation.

We then had you create two CourseBuilder Button interactions. The purpose of the first button was to simulate the **CourseBuilder** button on the Objects panel. The second button simulates the **Cancel** button on the CourseBuilder window. Once these were created it was necessary to positioned the layers so that everything lined up correctly. Before editing the Action Manager tab we had you hide the two layers for the cancel button.

Next we had you edit the Action Manager tab for the **CourseBuilder** button interaction so that when it was clicked, it would display the correct layers. You also limited the tries on this interaction to 1. This causes the interaction to disable after it is clicked once.

Finally, we had you edit the Action Manager tab for the **Cancel** button. In this tab you hid the layers again and reset the CourseBuilder button interaction. This way learners could try the simulation again if they wanted to.

There are a lot of steps to making a simple simulation, because simulations do take some time to create. These steps give you the basic idea of how to construct a simulation. However, we don't intend to communicate the idea that this is all there is to it. Simulations can be very complex. The more closely they simulate actual functionality, the more complex they become.

Unique Enhancements to Button Interactions

Since Button interactions are really building blocks to other interactions, there are not a lot of enhancements we can add. However, we do want to mention a couple of things.

Showing and Hiding a Flash Movie

When you create a button that shows information such as a Macromedia Flash movie, you may also want the button to hide that movie if it is clicked again.

A simple way to do this is to use a toggle button instead of a push button. With a toggle button, you are given a place in the action manager tab to enter actions for the selected and deselected state of the button.

When the button is selected, you can show the layer and start the Macromedia Flash movie. When it is deselected, you can stop the movie and hide the layer.

Scoring Multiple Interactions

A nice use of the Button interaction is to score multiple interactions on a single page. This is much easier to do with the action manager than trying to get all the JavaScript code right.

More Information: See *Chapter 14: The Power of the Action Manager Object* for more information.

Removing the Focus from a Simulation Button

Whenever you click on an image or a button, it retains the focus. As you probably know, when an image or button has the focus, it is surrounded by a dotted line. This changes the look of the simulation button and may be something that you want to avoid.

You can remove the focus with a simple line of JavaScript: *OnFocus="this.blur()"*

The ***onFocus*** event causes the script to execute. *This* refers to the object being clicked: the button. The *blur()* method removes the focus from the object.

Note: The blur() method does not work in early browsers (Netscape 2 or Internet Explorer 3).

The easiest way to add this line of JavaScript is by editing the HTML code. If you try to use the Call JavaScript behavior, use the actual name instead of the term *this*.

Follow these steps to remove the focus from a simulation button:

1 Display the HTML code (View → Code or click the **Show Code View** button).

2 Find the <a> tag that defines the button. The name should be something like: G01elemInp.

3 Place the line of code inside the <a> element. Here is an example of how the code may look.

This line was added. ──────────

```
<a name="G01elemInp" href="#"
onClick="G01.e['elem'].update('onclick');return false"
onFocus="this.blur()"
onMouseOver="G01.e['elem'].update('onmouseover');"
onMouseOut="G01.e['elem'].update('onmouseout');"
onMouseDown="G01.e['elem'].update('onmousedown');">
```

4   Test the interaction.

Summary

The Button interaction is really a building block for other interactions. There are two types of buttons available: toggle and push button. You also have access to 11 different appearances. If you choose to you can create as many appearances as you would like. These become custom buttons.

Even though there are multiple ways to create buttons in Dreamweaver, CourseBuilder buttons offer some advantages. They consist of multiple states, and you can use CourseBuilder to set those states.

CourseBuilder buttons have multiple purposes. In addition to using them as part of an interaction, you can use them for navigation. However, we recommend Learning Site for this purpose.

Finally, simulations can be difficult to create even with CourseBuilder. However, if the simulation consists of buttons, use the Button interaction and the Action Manager tab to simulate them.

Text Entry Interactions 7

Text Entry interactions are commonly known as fill-in-the-blank. The Text Entry interaction allows you to gather brief text responses from the learner. These can be single words or complete phrases.

In this chapter you will learn:

- About fill-in-the-blank templates and basic settings.
- The basic steps to creating a Text Entry interaction.
- How to create single response interactions.
- A few ways to modify Submit and Reset buttons.
- How to modify the text field.
- Different methods of displaying feedback.
- How to set the focus to the text field.
- How to submit the answer when pressing RETURN.

Introducing the Text Entry Interaction

The Text Entry interaction is an effective interaction for assessing recall. As opposed to the other types of interactions, it is very difficult for the learner to guess the answer. For that reason there are certain situations when you will want to use this type of question (see *When to Use a Text Entry interaction* later in this chapter).

In a Text Entry interaction you set up a single-line or multi-line input field. The learner must type the answer in that field. The answer is then compared against a series of possible answers. As you are setting up the possible responses, you can determine how strict the judging is.

You can display feedback with this interaction as you can with other interactions discussed in this book.

When to Use a Text Entry Interaction

Since Text Entry interactions require the learner to enter text, you should probably consider using this interaction in these situations:

- To assess exact recall of information
- To assess correct capitalization
- To assess correct spelling
- To conduct a survey or evaluation

You may also want to use this type of interaction for short answer essay questions. This type of interaction may be a little more difficult to set up but it is a very valid way of assessing certain types of content.

Taking a Look at the Text Entry Gallery

The Text Entry Gallery consists of 2 templates as shown here:

The only difference between the text_singleline template and the text_multiline template is that the single-line template provides only one line to enter an answer while the multi-line template allows you to enter several lines of text.

This table describes both templates and provides a thumbnail of each:

Interaction Type	Description
	Single-Line Text Entry. This template comes with a text field that accepts one line of text. Use this template for short one- or two-word responses.
	Multi-Line Text Entry. This template comes with a text field that accepts multiple lines of text. Use this template for responses that consists of more than a few words or for survey questions.

Text Entry Basics

The Text Entry interaction comes with a Responses tab in addition to the General tab and the Action Manager tab. Determining the possible responses is a large part of setting up a Text Entry interaction.

Creating a Text Entry interaction requires these five basic steps:

1   Insert an interaction using one of the methods discussed in chapter 2 and choose a Text Entry template from the Gallery.

2   Determine what type of judging should occur and if you want to include initial text in the text field. Make these changes on the General tab.

3   Add or delete responses and establish settings for each response.

4   Make changes to feedback on the Action Manager tab (optional).

5   Change the question text.

Steps 2-5 are covered in more detail in the sections that follow.

Establishing Settings on the General Tab

In addition to the settings on the General tab that are common to all interactions, the Text Entry interaction supplies you with one new setting: the initial text value. You may also want to change the name of the **Submit** button.

Entering Initial Text

The *initial text* setting on the General tab exists for this interaction only:

Initial Text: [   ]

If you would like the question to appear with text already entered in the field (such as "Type your answer in this field"), then make an entry in this field. If you are requiring the learner to enter a phrase, you may want to enter text that helps him recall that phrase. Whether or not you use this option depends on the purpose of the question.

Changing the Name of the Submit Button

The Text Entry interaction comes with a **Submit** and **Reset** button by default. Having learners click the **Submit** button to indicate they are done entering the answer is probably the most logical way. However, you may not want this button called *Submit*.

You can change the name of this button by editing the name in the Judge Interaction field:

Judge Interaction: ⊙   when the user clicks a button labeled │Submit

Perhaps you may want to label the button "Check Question", "Finished", "Am I Right", or "Go".

 More Information: If you would like to change the label on the Reset button see the *Unique Enhancements to the Text Entry Interaction* section.

Determining Responses

To make the most effective use of the Text Entry interaction, you need to understand how to set up responses on the Responses tab:

CourseBuilder Interaction	
Add Delete	OK
Possible Responses: Response1 (correct) / Response2 (incorrect) / Response3 (incorrect)	Cancel
	Help

Response Options

Name: │Response1

Must Contain: │word1

☐ case sensitive   ☐ exact match required

Match Is: │Correct ▼   Score: │0

Any Other Response Is: │Not Judged ▼

Gallery │ General │ Responses │ Action Mgr

Each setting on the response tab is described in more detail in this table:

Setting	Description
Possible Responses	A list of all possible responses. To make changes to individual responses, first select the response in this field. Use the **Add** and **Delete** buttons to add or remove responses.
Name	A name for the response. In some situations naming the response can make it easier to work with. The name cannot contain any spaces. Changing this setting is optional as CourseBuilder already supplies a default name for the response.
Must Contain	A word or phrase that the answer must contain. See sections *Checking for an Exact Match* and *Checking for Key Words* later in this chapter for more information about how to make entries.
Case Sensitive	Check this box if the answer must match the capitalization used in the responses.
Exact Match Required	Check this box if the answer must be an exact match to be correct. See sections *Checking for an Exact Match* and *Checking for Key Words* for more information about this setting.
Match Is:	Whether the response is considered a correct match or an incorrect match. You can also assign a score to the response. See *Section IV: Tracking Learner Data* for more information on scoring and tracking results.
Any Other Response Is:	Determines how entries that don't match the responses are handled. Are they considered correct, incorrect, or not judged? For most interactions you will want to consider all other responses incorrect.

Both templates come with three default responses. One is correct and two are incorrect. If you use this default setup, you will enter a word or phrase for the correct response and then incorrect words or phrases for the others. All other responses are not judged, meaning they are neither correct nor incorrect. This is set using the *Any Other Response is* setting at the bottom of the response tab.

If you use this default setup, it means the learner receives an incorrect response if they enter the word or phrase that exists in one of the incorrect responses.

Generally, with fill-in-the-blank exercises, you want any response other than the correct one to be considered incorrect.

The preferred method for setting up the responses is to establish several correct responses then judge all other responses as incorrect. In these correct responses account for any word or misspelling that could be considered correct. For example, if the correct answer to a question is "hypotenuse triangle," you may need to enter both "hypotenuse" and "hypotnuse" as correct responses. You would consider other responses incorrect. (Of course, if you are assessing their ability to spell then you will not want to include misspellings as correct responses.)

Adding and Deleting Responses

You may need to add additional responses or delete some that are already there. For example, if the answer can match only one word to be correct, then you may want to set only one correct response and all others as incorrect. However, if there are multiple misspellings and other ways to enter a phrase that could be correct, then you may want to add additional responses.

Follow these steps to delete a response:

1   Click on the response that you want to remove. This selects it.

2   Click the **Delete** button.

Follow these steps to add a response:

1   Click the response that contains settings that are most like the one you want to add.

2   Click the **Add** button.

CourseBuilder adds the new response immediately below the response you have selected.

Checking for an Exact Match

Checking for an exact match is simply a matter of checking the ***exact match check*** box:

☐ exact match required

This means that the answer must match exactly the text entered in the ***Must contain*** field (same spelling, same spacing, and same punctuation).

 Note: Remember that when you check this box, it is set for only one of the responses. If you want to use this setting for other responses, you must select them one-by-one and check the box.

Checking for Key Words

If you just want to make sure the learner enters the correct key words or phrases, then *do not* check the exact match check box. Instead, enter a key word in the ***Must Contain*** field and uncheck this box. You may need to enter key words in several responses to get the results you are after.

When you are trying to match a key word, CourseBuilder does not require you to enter the answer in exactly the same way. For example, if we asked "What is the name of the Dreamweaver extension that adds navigation to a course?" The learner may respond with "learning site" or "learning site command". If we enter "learning site" in the must contain field without an exact match, then both answers would be correct. In fact the learner could enter a complete phrase such as "Learning site is an extension that provides navigation" and still get it correct.

What if the learner were to enter "site command" as the response in this scenario? In this case CourseBuilder would consider that incorrect because the learner did not include the keyword "learning". We would need to add another response with the text "site command" as part of the response. If we were to add a response with just the word "site", then the learner could type anything as long as the word "site" appeared somewhere in the answer.

Making Changes to Feedback

As is the case with most CourseBuilder interactions, Text Entry comes with default feedback that displays the words "correct", "incorrect," or "unknown response". If this type of feedback works for the interaction you are creating, then you don't need to make any changes. If not, you will need to edit the popup messages on the Action Manger tab.

Three popup messages are available. One for "correct", one for "incorrect", and one for "unknown response."

Three Popup messages are available.

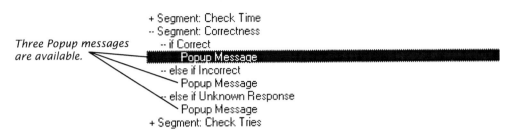

The correct popup message is selected in this sample graphic.

Follow these steps to change a popup message:

1   Click the popup message to select it.

2   Click the **Edit** button.

CourseBuilder displays the Popup Message window:

3   Make changes to the text and click **OK**.

More Information: Changing feedback on the Action Manager tab is discussed in more detail in *Chapter 13: Customizing the Action Manager Tab.*

Changing the Question Text

Once you have finished defining the Text Entry interaction and you click OK, the interaction is added to the page with a default question as shown here:

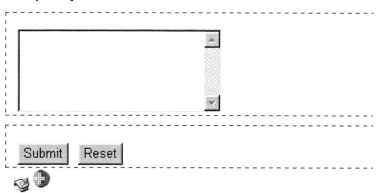

Put your question text here

"Put your question text here" is the default question text. Select that text and enter you own question to make the interaction ready to use.

 Note: In some interactions you can replace the question text in the CourseBuilder Interaction window. The Text Entry interaction is an example of one type that requires you to make this change on the Dreamweaver page.

Creating a Single-Line Interaction

The first step-by-step tutorial that we present in this chapter is for a single-line response.

After viewing the finished interaction, you can use the step-by-step instructions to recreate the question.

Viewing the Finished Interaction

Before trying to create this interaction, take a moment to examine the finished sample.

On CD: Open *Sample_7-1.htm* to see a single-line, Text Entry interaction.

While viewing this interaction, make sure you try the following:

- Enter "fill in the blank" as a response (no hyphens).
- Enter "text entry" as a response.
- Enter "fill-in-the-blank" as a response (with hyphens).
- Enter "fill-in-the-blank question" as a response.
- Enter an incorrect response.
- Open the interaction in Dreamweaver and see how it is set up.

Creating the Interaction

Using the step-by-step instructions in this section, you will create a Text Entry interaction that asks the learner this question: *Which CourseBuilder interaction is best suited for assessing information recall?*

To follow along with these steps, you must have Dreamweaver or UltraDev opened and access to the files on the CD.

More Information: If you need more details about some of the steps, refer to *Chapter 2: Getting to Know CourseBuilder* and the *Basics of the Text Entry interaction* section earlier in this chapter.

Follow these steps to create a single-line interaction:

1 Open a new page and insert a CourseBuilder interaction.

2 Select the *Text Entry* category and click on the *text_singleline* template:

Don't make any changes to any settings on the General tab.

3 Click on the Responses tab.

4 Add one more response by clicking on *Response1* and clicking the **Add** button. Name this response *Response4*.

5 Establish these settings for each of the responses.

Response	Settings
Response1	Make sure the match to this response is correct. Enter *fill in the blank* in the **Must Contain** field. Uncheck the **Exact Match** check box.
Response2	Make sure the match to this response is correct. Enter *fill-in-the-blank* in the **Must Contain** field. Uncheck the **Exact Match** check box.
Response3	Make sure the match to this response is correct. Enter *text entry* in the **Must Contain** field. Uncheck the **Exact Match** check box.
Response4	Make sure the match to this response is correct. Enter *text entry* in the **Must Contain** field. Uncheck the **Exact Match** check box.

6 Set the ***Any Other Response Is*** setting to *Incorrect*.

Don't make any changes to the popup messages on the Action Manager tab.

7 Click **OK**.

8 Replace the default question text on the Dreamweaver page with *Which CourseBuilder interaction is best suited for assessing information recall?*

Caution: When you select the default question text, make sure the entire interaction isn't selected or you could delete it.

9 Test the interaction in a browser.

That is all it takes to create a single-line interaction.

Unique Enhancements to Text Entry Interactions

There are a few, more advanced ways to enhance the Text Entry interaction. We cover those methods in this section. Some advanced techniques contain references to other chapters.

Displaying Feedback in a Frame or Layer

The alert box that is used to display feedback is only one way that you can provide feedback to a learner. Another alternative is to display feedback in a frame or layer, which requires you to use the Action Manager.

More Information: Displaying feedback in a frame or layer is discussed in *Chapter 13: Customizing the Action Manager Tab*.

Creating Specific Response Feedback

To improve the learning experience of an on-line course, you may want to provide specific response feedback. The purpose of this type of feedback is to provide instruction when the learner makes an incorrect choice or even a correct choice. You can provide different feedback for each possible response.

Let's say you have a fill-in-the-blank question with a couple of responses that you have judged to be correct. However, those responses may be spelled incorrectly or might be missing a word from a phrase. If a learner enters one of these responses, you can provide correct feedback but also point out how the answer could be more accurate. This same scenario would work for incorrect responses.

You can provide specific response feedback using the Action Manager tab.

More Information: You can learn about creating specific response feedback in *Chapter 13: Customizing the Action Manager tab*.

Modifying the Reset and Submit Buttons

Since the **Reset** and **Submit** buttons are a default for the Text Entry question, you may want to change their labels or the way they look.

Changing the Label on the Reset Button

Earlier we showed you how to change the label for the **Submit** button. You can use Dreamweaver to do the same to the **Reset** button.

Follow this step to change the label on the reset button:

1   On the Dreamweaver page, select the **Reset** button. In the Label field on the Property inspector enter a new term such as *Try Again.*

Replacing the Standard Submit and Reset Buttons

You can replace the **Submit** and **Reset** buttons with a button of your own making if you would like. Since the **Submit** and **Reset** buttons are almost standard for Text Entry interactions, you will probably want to make this change.

You can make this change to any CourseBuilder interaction. Therefore, we have included the steps on how to do this in *Chapter 10: Global Interaction Enhancements.*

Creating Essay Questions

Essay questions can be effective at assessing a learner's comprehension of steps to a process, how interconnected pieces of a model relate to one another, or any other more complex subject that may be difficult to assess using Multiple Choice, True/False, or other common types of interactions. The problem with essay questions is that they generally require a human to check them. You can use a multi-line template to allow the learner to enter an essay question, but then you need to either send that answer to an LMS or communicate with a server to send it out as an email message.

More Information: You need a CGI script to send email. For more information here are a couple of web sites: *http://web.mit.edu/wwwdev/cgiemail/* and *http://www.worldwidemart.com/scripts/formmail.shtml.*

Modifying the Text Field

When CourseBuilder creates a Text Entry interaction, it creates a standard HTML form with a text field and buttons. The text field is where the learner enters responses. You may find a need to make changes to this text field.

For example, you may want to set the *Char Width* of the field to make it larger. Or you may want to specify a maximum number of characters the learner can type.

You can make these and other changes on the Property Inspector for the field:

TextField	Char Width	Type ⦿ Single line	○ Multi line	○ Password
G01eleminp	Max Chars	Init Val		
	Wrap			

More Information: You can also make changes to the text field using Cascading Style Sheet styles. See *Chapter 11: Using CSS to Enhance CourseBuilder*.

Setting the Focus to the Text Field When the Page Loads

To make this interaction a little easier for the learner, you can automatically set the focus to the text field when the page loads. This way the learner doesn't need to click in the text box before typing the answer.

You can do this by using the Call JavaScript behavior on the body tag. We will provide the JavaScript for you.

Follow these steps to set the focus to the text field when the page loads:

1   Open sample_7-2.htm from the CD.

Before you can enter the JavaScript that sets the focus, you must find out the name of the text field and the form it is in.

2   Click on the text field so it is selected.

Dotted lines appear around the field when it is selected:

3   Open the Property Inspector and write down the name shown:

Name

The name will normally be *G01elemInp*, but it is a good idea to always check.

4   While the text field is selected, click on the <form> tag selector at the bottom of the Dreamweaver window:

`<body> <interaction> <div> <form> <input>`

This selects the form that contains the text field.

Caution: Be careful to select the correct form. A Text Entry interaction consists of two forms.

5   Open the Property Inspector and write down the name shown for the form:

The name will normally be *G01elem*. But once again it is always good to check.

We will now attach the JavaScript code to the body tag.

6 Click on the body tag selector at the bottom of the Dreamweaver window:

<body> <interaction> <div> <form> <input>

7 In the Behaviors panel select the ***Call JavaScript*** action. Don't worry that other actions are already included.

The Call JavaScript window displays:

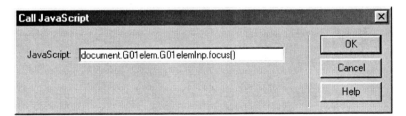

8 Enter *document.G01elem.G01elemInp.focus()*.

In place of G01elem enter the form name if it is different. In place of G01elemInp enter the field name if it is different:

Call JavaScript	✕
JavaScript: document.G01elem.G01elemInp.focus()	OK Cancel Help

The focus() method is what places the focus in that field.

9 Click **OK**.

10   The default event should be *onLoad*. If it is not, choose *onLoad* as the event
for the behavior:

OnLoad event ————————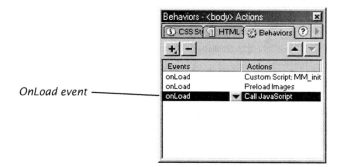

11   Try the interaction in a browser.

The cursor should blink in the field when it is opened.

Submitting the Answer with the Enter Key

A natural inclination of most computer users is to press the ENTER key after typing
information in a field. Learners that use your course may have the same tendency.
For this reason you may want to modify your interaction so that pressing the
ENTER key submits the answer.

This enhancement requires that you create and call a JavaScript function. We
provide the function for you.

Taking a Look at the Function

We have included the function in sample_7-2.htm. You may open that file and view
the function as we talk about it.

You must place JavaScript between JavaScript tags: *<script language="JavaScript">*
and *</script>*. Although there are several tags of this type in sample_7-2.htm, if you
look close, you will be able to find the function *function
processOnEnter(interactionName, evt)*.

Here is the code:

```
function processOnEnter(interactionName, evt) {
    var keycode = document.layers ? evt.which : document.all ?
    evt.keyCode : evt.keyCode;
    if (keycode == "13")
            {
            G01.e['elem'].update()
            MM_judgeInt(interactionName);
            }
    else
            return false;
    }
```

When this function is called, it determines if the key pressed is the ENTER key (13). It then calls the appropriate CourseBuilder functions: update() and MM_judgeInt(interactionName).

To include this enhancement in any interaction, you must enter this function inside the head tags. Make sure you surround it with the JavaScript tags. If you want, you can copy and paste the function from sample_7-2.htm.

To call this function, you need to add an ***onKeyPress*** event to the text field. See the steps in the next section.

Calling the Function

For this function to work, you must call it.

Follow these steps to call the function:

1   Open file *sample_7-2.htm*.

2   Select the text field.

3   Open the behaviors panel and choose the Call JavaScript behavior.

The JavaScript Window displays.

4   Enter *processOnEnter['G01',event]* into the Call JavaScript window.

This will call the function and pass it the name of the interaction and the event (key). The first interaction added to a page is always G01. The second is G02 and so forth. Make sure you use the correct name.

5   Click **OK**.

6   Change the event for the behavior to ***onKeyPress***.

7   Test the interaction in a browser by typing a response and pressing ENTER.

   Note: You can also place the code onKeyPress=processOnEnter('G01', event) directly inside the input tag for the text field and not use the Call JavaScript behavior. Both methods work, but this is cleaner for you JavaScript purists.

Summary

The Text Entry interaction is very good at assessing the ability of a learner to recall information instead of just recognizing the correct response. Whether using a single-line response or a multi-line response, it is very important to fill out the responses correctly. You need to have a clear understanding of what is correct and what the learner may enter before establishing the settings.

Text Entry interactions come with the same default popup messages for feedback as other interactions. You can make changes to these if you wish. You may also want to display the feedback in a frame or layer or respond to feedback differently depending on the response.

Essay questions are possible with a Text Entry interaction, but to judge them you'll have to have someone review the response which may require you to send the response to a database.

You can set the focus to the text field when the page opens. You may also want to process the answer when the learner presses the ENTER key. Both are possible.

Timer Interactions 8

Timers are unlike the other interactions in CourseBuilder. Timers don't require a response from the learner. Instead, they simply define when certain events happen (or are *triggered*).

In this chapter you will learn:

- To use a timer to display the maximum amount of time a learner has to complete an interaction.
- To use a timer to disable an interaction when the maximum amount of time expires.
- To use a timer to display a warning before the maximum amount of time expires.
- To choose the appearance of a timer.
- To use custom graphics for a timer.

Introduction to Timers

Timers are made up of a sequence of graphics that are cycled through to give the learner the appearance of animation. You can use them to start any action at specific moments (also called *triggering*).

Note: Don't confuse timer interactions with the ***Time is Limited To*** setting on the General tab of most interactions. The ***Time is Limited To*** setting does not display anything visually like Timer interactions. To learn more about the ***Time is Limited To*** setting, see *Chapter10: Global Interaction Enhancements*.

When to Use Timers

Use timers whenever you are assessing time-sensitive knowledge or skills. Here are some scenarios in which using a timer might be effective:

- Assessing first aid skills
- Testing memory recall for customer service questions
- Designing an interactive activity in which the learner determines a certain grade of material (such as determining the grade of stone from a quarry or wood from a saw mill)

Be careful when using timers. You may find that timers are not effective when used in many other types of assessment situations. Timers tend to make learners feel uneasy and thereby may compromise their ability to answer the question correctly.

Different Timer Templates

When you choose the Timer category on the Gallery tab, CourseBuilder displays these interaction templates to choose from:

Interaction Type	Description
	One-trigger timer – comes preset with one trigger setting. Use this timer when you want to cause the time to expire for an interaction without an explicit warning.
	Two-trigger timer – comes preset with two triggers. Use this timer when you want to provide an explicit warning before the time expires.

Tip: Even though the intention of single and multiple triggers is to disable the interaction when the time expires and to give a warning to the learner, triggers on any template can be used for any action available in the Action Manager (see the Action Manager chapters in Section II: *Extending CourseBuilder*).

Timer Basics

Before you create a Timer interaction, it's important to understand some basic concepts about it:

5 Steps to Creating a Timer Interaction

To create a Timer interaction, follow these general steps:

1　Insert a timer interaction onto the page.

2　Choose the appearance and set the duration of the timer.

3   Insert the timer interaction into a layer so you can easily position it on the page (optional).

4   Set up triggers that tell CourseBuilder to execute certain actions when the timer reaches that trigger.

5   Establish what happens when the timer reaches each trigger (usually displaying a warning or disabling an interaction).

Each of these steps is described in more detail later in this chapter.

Choosing the Timer Appearance

CourseBuilder supplies several timer styles to choose from.

This table displays CourseBuilder's pre-designed timer styles:

Name	Appearance
Clapboard	
Gradient	
Hourglass	
Rising_Bars	
Small_Gradient	
Small_Rising_Bars	

Follow these steps to choose a timer style:

1   Edit a timer interaction.

2   Click the General tab.

More Information: The settings below the horizontal line on the General tab are common to all interactions (see Chapter 2: *Getting to Know CourseBuilder* for more details).

3 Choose a timer style from the drop down list at the top of the tab:

This style is called "Gradient".

To cause timer images to display in reverse order (i.e. to have a gradient fill start completely filled and gradually change to empty), select the *Reverse Image Order* setting on the General tab:

☐ Reverse image order

4 Click **OK.**

CourseBuilder displays the timer with the new style you selected.

More Information: To learn how to use custom images with timers, see *Using Custom Timer Graphics* later in this chapter.

Setting the Duration of the Timer

One of the first settings you need to establish for a timer is the overall duration. To set the overall duration, enter the number of seconds in the ***Duration*** field on the General tab:

Duration: 30   seconds

Tip: To set the duration for a number of minutes you still need to enter the duration in seconds. For example, to set the duration for three and a half minutes, you would enter 210 in the Duration field (60 seconds x 3 + 30 seconds).

Inserting the Timer into a Layer

Placing interactions in layers allows you to position them where you want on the Dreamweaver page. This can be especially useful for Timer interactions because you almost always use Timer interactions in conjunction with other interactions. You may want to position the timer near another interaction to make it obvious to the learner that the time remaining applies to that interaction.

To insert the timer into a layer, follow these steps:

1   Edit the timer interaction.

2   Click the General tab.

3   Select the ***Layer*** setting:

Layer: ☑ Insert in a layer (4.0+ browsers only)

CourseBuilder places the timer in a layer.

4   Click **OK**.

5   Reposition the timer layer on the Dreamweaver page to the desirable location.

To reposition a layer, select the layer by clicking its border or tab, then drag it to another location on the page.

When you select a layer, you see select boxes all around the layer as shown here:

If you click in the middle of the layer, you select the image only, and it displays as shown here:

   *The layer tab.*

Notice that select boxes do not surround the layer. If you have selected the image, just click the layer tab to select the layer.

To move the layer, drag it with the mouse or use the arrow keys to move it in small increments.

More Information: You may want to check a Dreamweaver reference for more information on how to move layers.

Defining Timer Triggers

A timer is only a visual display if it doesn't have any triggers. To make the timer do something at a certain number of seconds into its duration, add a trigger. Then use the Action Manager tab to define what happens when the trigger fires.

Adding and Deleting Triggers

You add and delete triggers on the Triggers tab:

Triggers tab

To add a new trigger, click the **Add** button. CourseBuilder adds the new trigger directly beneath the selected trigger.

To delete an existing trigger, select the trigger you want to delete and click the **Delete** button.

Defining Trigger Options

You can specify these settings for each trigger on the Triggers tab:

- *Name*
- *Trigger Once After* (a certain number of seconds)
- *Trigger Is* (correct, incorrect, or not judged)
- *Score*

This table defines trigger settings:

Property	Explanation	Special Considerations
Name	A valid name is any combination of letters and numbers, but may not contain any spaces.	Naming your triggers can be very helpful if you are referencing them in the Action Manager or using JavaScript. By default CourseBuilder names them *unnamed1*, *unnamed2*, etc. You may want to rename them *Trigger1*, *Trigger2*, etc. or use a name that refers to when they fire such as *5Seconds*, *10Seconds*, etc.
Trigger Once After	The number of seconds after the timer starts that this trigger fires. A trigger usually causes some kind of action to happen in the Action Manager.	See the Caution statement below this table.
Trigger Is	The options for this setting are Not Judged, Correct, and Incorrect.	Usually leave this Not Judged.
Score	Enter the numeric value the learner receives when this trigger is met.	Usually "0" unless you want the learner to receive a score for reaching a trigger (such as in some type of endurance exercise).

Caution: CourseBuilder doesn't prevent you from entering a trigger that is larger than the duration of the timer. If you do, the trigger will never get fired because the timer will run out before the trigger is met.

Also on the Triggers tab is a setting that determines whether the entire interaction is correct, incorrect, or not judged before the timer reaches the first trigger:

Interaction Is: | Not Judged ▼ | before timer reaches first trigger

By default the ***Interaction Is*** setting is set to *Not Judged* because you usually don't want to rule the interaction correct or incorrect before the timer reaches the first trigger.

Defining What Happens When the Timer Reaches a Trigger

When the timer reaches a trigger it can cause something to happen. You define what happens on the Action Manager tab.

More Information: For more details on working with the Action Manager, see the Action Manager chapters in Section II: *Extending CourseBuilder.*

Every time you add a new trigger, CourseBuilder creates a condition in the Action Manager tab that checks to see if the trigger has already been met. You simply need to define what happens when that trigger is met.

Follow these steps to define what happens when the timer reaches a trigger:

1   Edit the timer interaction.

2   Click the Action Manager tab.

3   Select the condition that corresponds with the trigger action you want to define. For example, to define trigger actions for a trigger named Trigger2, select the condition *if Trigger2 Selected:*

```
-- Segment: Trigger2 Feedback (state transition)
   -- if Trigger2 Selected
```

4   Choose the action from the action drop down list:

```
Set Text of Layer                    ▼
Show-Hide Layers                     ▲
Swap Image
Swap Image Restore
Validate Form
------------------------ Set Text
Set Text of Frame
Set Text of Layer
Set Text of Status Bar
Set Text of Text Field               ▼
```

5   Click the **Add** button to add the action.

CourseBuilder displays a dialog window for whichever action you added:

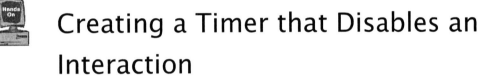

6   Define the action options and click **OK**.

7   Repeat steps 4 through 6 to define multiple actions for a single trigger.

8   Click **OK** to close the CourseBuilder Interaction window.

Creating a Timer that Disables an Interaction

CourseBuilder's default response when a timer reaches a trigger is to display a popup message. Beyond letting the learner know that the time has expired, you may want to disable the interaction so he or she can't continue to try to respond to the interaction.

In this section, you will create a timer that disables the interaction after displaying this message in a layer: *The allotted time for this question has expired" in a layer and disables the interaction.*

Viewing the Finished Interaction

Before creating the interaction, take a look at the completed interaction.

On CD: Take a moment and try out the finished sample by opening Sample_8-1.htm (this exercise was designed for Internet Explorer—you may experience some differences if using another browser).

As you try out this interaction, here are some things to think about:

- What happens to the Multiple Choice interaction when the timer runs out?
- What type of message is displayed when the time runs out? (What action in the action manager can make this happen?)

Creating this Interaction

In this section, you will create the interaction you just viewed.

To follow along with these steps, you must have Dreamweaver or UltraDev opened.

Follow these steps to create a timer that disables an interaction:

1   In Dreamweaver, open *Sample_8-1_Start.htm* on the CD ROM (this exercise was designed for Internet Explorer—you may experience some differences if using another browser).

The file should look like this:

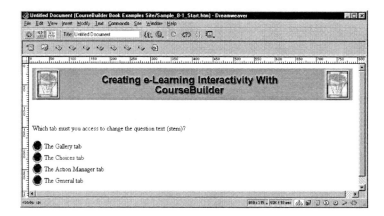

2   Insert a new layer (Insert→Layer) using the Property Inspector to name it *TimerFeedback*

3   With the *TimerFeeedback* layer still selected, apply the *incorrectFeedbackText* style from the attached stylesheet.

This style displays white text on a red background.

More Information: For more details on attaching styles to layers, see a Dreamweaver reference. Also see Chapter 11: *Using CSS to Enhance CourseBuilder.*

4   Place your cursor inside the layer and enter this text: *The allotted time for this question has expired.* (You may want to resize the layer to fit the text)

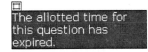

5   Insert a one-trigger Timer interaction using one of the techniques we described in Chapter 2:

 Caution: Make sure the cursor is at the beginning of the document so that you don't insert the timer interaction inside the multiple choice *<interaction>* tag.

6   Establish these settings on the General tab:

Setting	Value
Appearance	Small_Gradient
Duration	10 seconds
Reset	Deselect this option so there is no **Reset** button
Layer	Select this option to place the timer in a layer for easy positioning.

7   Click the Triggers tab and set the ***Trigger Once After*** setting to *10*.

Setting the ***Duration*** and the ***Trigger Once After*** settings to the same value causes the Action Manager to execute the actions as soon as the entire duration has lapsed.

8   Click the Action Manager tab.

The first thing you'll do with the Action Manager is put the message text in a layer. To do this, you need to replace the popup message action with a *Set Text of Layer* action.

9   To delete the popup message default action, select *Popup Message* and click Cut.

Now you are ready to tell the Action Manager to display the timer feedback layer.

10   Select the condition *if Trigger1 Selected*.

11   Choose *Show-Hide Layers* from the action drop down list:

12   Click **Add**.

CourseBuilder displays the Show-Hide Layers window:

Show-Hide Layers

Named Layers:
layer "G02Layer"
layer "TimerFeedback"

Show   Hide   Default

OK
Cancel
Help

13   Select *layer "TimerFeedback"* and click **Show**.

CourseBuilder displays *(show)* next to the selected line:

layer "G02Layer"
layer "TimerFeedback" (show)

14   Click **OK** to accept these settings.

Now you're ready to make the Action Manager disable the Multiple Choice interaction on the page.

15   Choose *Set Interaction Properties* from the action drop down list.

16 Click **Add**.

CourseBuilder displays the Set Interaction Properties window:

*By default,
CourseBuilder chooses
the Disabled property
of the interaction and
sets the value to TRUE.
Simply choose the
correct interaction
from the Interaction
drop down list.*

17 Choose *MultCh_ImageRadios01* from the Interaction drop down list:

Note: If you had more than one interaction on a page and you wanted to disable them all, you would need to add the ***Set Interaction Property*** action several times and make sure you have the correct interaction selected in the ***Interaction*** drop down list of the Set Interaction Properties window.

More Information: There are many other things you can do with the Set Interaction Properties action beyond disabling the interaction. For more details, see the Action Manager chapters in *Section II: Extending CourseBuilder*.

18 Click **OK** to accept these settings.

You Action Manager tab should look like this:

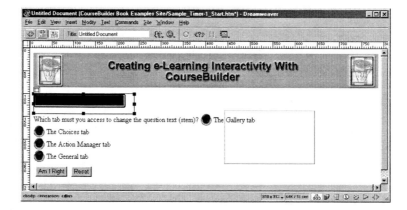

19 Click **OK** to close the CourseBuilder Interaction window.

Now you need to reposition the timer and reposition the timer feedback layer.

20 Select the timer layer and place it above the Multiple Choice interaction:

Tip: You may find it useful to turn off invisible elements when positioning layers (View→Visual Aids→Invisible Elements). You may also want to resize the layer so that it fits a little more closely around the Timer interaction.

21 Select the *TimerFeedback* layer and place it to the right of the Multiple Choice interaction.

22 Hide the *TimerFeedback* layer so the learner doesn't see the message you placed in the layer when the page loads. To do this, choose *hidden* for the **Visible** property on the Property panel.

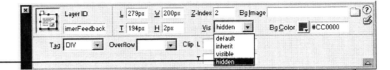

Choosing "hidden" hides the entire layer.

23 Preview the page in a browser.

 Tip: Even though you disable the interaction, the learner can refresh the browser and reload the page to re-enable the interaction. This is currently a limitation of CourseBuilder. If you're serious about limiting time, one way to avoid this would be to navigate to another page when the time expires using the *Go to URL* action in the Action Manager. To prevent the learner from clicking the **Back** button, you would need to display the course in a browser window that does not display the browser toolbar (using the *Open Browser Window* behavior).

Creating a Timer that Displays a Warning

In the previous section you created a timer that disabled a quiz interaction. You may want to display a warning to the learner when a certain amount of time is remaining. For example, if the timer disables the interaction after 30 seconds, you may want to display a warning when the timer reaches 20 seconds.

In this section you create a timer that warns the learner before disabling the interaction.

Viewing the Finished Interaction

Before creating this interaction, take a moment to view the completed sample.

 On CD: Take a moment and try out the finished sample *Sample_8-2.htm* (this exercise was designed for Internet Explorer—you may experience some differences if using another browser).

As you try out this interaction, here are some things to look for:

- How many times can you answer the question before the question disables?
- How does the warning message appear after the timer reaches 20 seconds?
- What happens to the text entry field when the timer expires?

Creating this Interaction

Now, let's create the Timer interaction you just finished viewing.

Follow these steps to create a timer that displays a warning before disabling the interaction:

1   In Dreamweaver, open Sample_8-2_Start.htm (this exercise was designed for Internet Explorer—you may experience some differences if using another browser).

This sample file already contains a Text Entry interaction that displays feedback in a layer called *Feedback*. We've also created a layer called *TimerFeedback* in which we will display the messages triggered by the timer. Both of these layers are already hidden.

More Information: To learn how to display feedback in a layer, see Chapter 13: *Customizing the Action Manager Tab.*

2   Place your cursor at the top of the document (after the banner graphic) and insert a two-trigger Timer interaction using one of the techniques we described in Chapter 2:

3   On the general tab, choose *small_rising_bars* as the appearance:

Appearance: [Small_Rising_Bars ▼] [Browse...]   [|||||||]

4   Deselect the **Reset** setting to remove the Reset button:

Reset: ☐ Create a Reset button

Because you've placed the Timer interaction above the Text Entry interaction, there is no need to place the timer in a layer. Leave all other setting on the General tab as the default settings.

5   Click the Triggers tab.

This template comes preset with two triggers, one at 15 seconds and one at 30 seconds. The intended use of these triggers is to warn the learner at 15 seconds and disable the interaction at 30 seconds.

You want to warn the learner at 20 seconds, not 15 seconds, so you need to change the ***Trigger Once After*** setting for the first trigger.

6   Click the first trigger in the *Triggers* field.

7   Enter *20* in the ***Trigger Once After*** field.

The other trigger is already set up to trigger at 30 seconds, so you'll leave that one set up as is.

8   Click the Action Manager tab.

CourseBuilder displays a separate condition in the Action Manager for each trigger created on the Triggers tab:

The two conditions are: "if Trigger1 Selected", and "if Trigger2 Selected".

Display the warning and the final message in layers instead of popup messages. To do so, delete the **Popup Message** actions and replace them with *Set Text of Layer* actions.

9 Select the first *Popup Message* action and click **Cut**.

10 Select the second *Popup Message* action and click **Cut**.

The Action Manager tab should look like this:

```
CourseBuilder Interaction                                                    [x]
┌────────┐  ┌────────────────────┐ ┌───┐ ┌────┐ ┌─────┐     ┌──────────┐
│  Add   │  │ Segment          ▼ │ │Cut│ │Copy│ │Paste│     │    OK    │
└────────┘  └────────────────────┘ └───┘ └────┘ └─────┘     └──────────┘
┌────────┐  ┌──────────────────────────────────────────┐    ┌──────────┐
│  Edit..│  │ -- Segment: Trigger1 Feedback (state transition) │    │  Cancel  │
└────────┘  │    -- if Trigger1 Selected                 │    └──────────┘
┌────────┐  │ -- Segment: Trigger2 Feedback (state transition) │    ┌──────────┐
│ Rename.│  │    -- if Trigger2 Selected                 │    │   Help   │
└────────┘  │                                            │    └──────────┘
            │                                            │
     ▲      │                                            │
   ◄   ►    │                                            │
     ▼      │                                            │
┌────────┐  │                                            │
│ Expand │  │                                            │
└────────┘  │                                            │
┌────────┐  │                                            │
│Collapse│  │                                            │
└────────┘  └──────────────────────────────────────────┘
      ┌─────────┬─────────┬───────────┐
      │ General │ Triggers │ Action Mgr │
      └─────────┴─────────┴───────────┘
```

11 Select the *if Trigger1 Selected* condition by clicking on it.

12 Choose **Set Text of Layer** from the Action drop down list.

13 Click **Add**.

14 Select *layer "Timer Feedback"* from the drop down list:

15 In the New HTML field enter this text: *You have 10 seconds remaining to complete the question.*

16 Click **OK**.

17 Choose **Show-Hide Layers** from the Action drop down list.

18 Click **Add**.

19 Select *layer "TimerFeedback"* and click Show.

Show-Hide Layers	×

Named Layers: layer "feedback"
                layer "TimerFeedback" (show)

          Show Hide Default

OK   Cancel   Help

20 Click **OK**.

21 Select the *if Trigger2 Selected* condition by clicking on it.

22 Choose *Set Text of Layer* from the Action drop down list.

Note: CourseBuilder always displays the last action you chose in the drop down list, so you may not need to choose the **Set Text of Layer** action.

23 Click **Add**.

24 Select *layer "Timer Feedback"* from the drop down list.

25 In the **New HTML** field enter: *Sorry, the time allotted to complete this question has expired.*

26 Click **OK**.

27 Add and define a **Set Interaction Properties** action to disable the Text Entry interaction when the timer reaches the second trigger.

More Information: For more information about disabling an interaction using the Set Interaction Properties action, see *Creating a Timer that Disables an Interaction* earlier in this chapter.

The Action Manager tab should look like this:

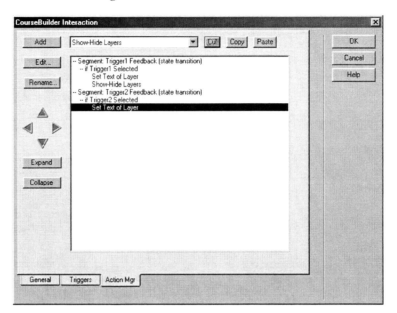

28 Click **OK** to close the CourseBuilder Interaction window.

29 Test the interaction in a browser.

Unique Enhancements to Timer Interactions

There are many ways you can enhance a timer. Here are a few things that can make using timers even more effective:

- Create your own timer graphics to fit the look and feel of your learner interface.
- When using warnings, make the warning appear in a layer for just a few seconds, then disappear.
- Showing Timer messages as text in a layer rather than as popup messages.

Using Custom Timer Graphics

Timers look animated because CourseBuilder displays a series of graphics one after another at certain intervals based on the timer's duration setting (a lot like animated GIFs).

Each timer has a certain number of graphics associated with it. These images are located in the images/timers/ directory. For example, the *small_gradient* timer style uses these graphics (there are actually more than these, but this is a representative sample so you can see the concept):

To create your own custom timer, you need to create a series of images in this fashion.

Where to Place Custom Graphics

To use custom graphics, place your own timer graphics in the images/timers/ directory. This causes them to appear in the ***Appearance*** drop down list on the General tab.

File Naming Convention

Timer images need to be named with the same root name and increasing numeric extensions. For example, if you have five graphics called *dots* you want CourseBuilder to cycle through, the files need to be named *dots_01.gif, dots_02.gif...dots_05.gif*.

Making a Warning Appear and Disappear

Displaying a warning can be a nice touch to a Timer interaction. However, if the warning appears and stays on the page until the timer expires, the learner may not be alerted to the change of the message when the timer expires.

To resolve this usability problem, cause the timer message to appear for a second or two, then disappear.

On CD: To see an example of this usability problem, open *Sample_8-2.htm* on the CD ROM in a browser.

Viewing the Finished Interaction

Before creating this interaction, take a moment to view the completed sample interaction.

On CD: To view the completed interaction, open Sample_8-3.htm on the CD ROM (this exercise was designed for Internet Explorer—you may experience some differences if using another browser).

As you view this interaction, here are some things to look for:

- What Action Manager action do you think we are using to display the warning and final notification?
- How many seconds does the warning stay visible?
- What is the timer doing while the warning is visible?

Creating this Interaction

Follow these steps to cause a timer message to appear and disappear:

1 In Dreamweaver, open Sample_8-3_Start.htm on the CD ROM (this exercise was designed for Internet Explorer—you may experience some differences if using another browser).

This interaction already displays a warning and expiration message in a layer. You are simply going to make that layer show for a few seconds then hide.

2 Click the Triggers tab.

3 Select trigger *Trigger2*.

4 Click the **Add** button.

CourseBuilder displays a new trigger named *unnamed1:*

Triggers:	Trigger1 (not judged)
	Trigger2 (not judged)
	unnamed1 (not judged)

5 Name the trigger *Trigger3* and set the ***Trigger Once After*** setting to *23*.

Trigger1 is set to fire at 20 seconds. Set Trigger3 to fire at 23 seconds. Trigger1 shows the timer message layer that displays the warning, and Trigger3 hides it three seconds later.

Note: Timer triggers do not have to be ordered sequentially in the ***Triggers*** field on the Triggers tab. In this example, Trigger1 fires at 20 seconds, Trigger2 fires at 30 seconds, and Trigger3 fires at 23 seconds.

6   Click the Action Manager tab:

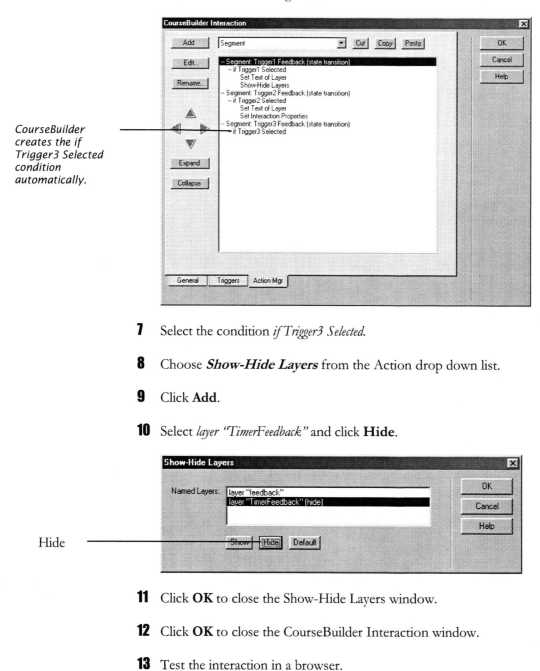

CourseBuilder creates the if Trigger3 Selected condition automatically.

7   Select the condition *if Trigger3 Selected*.

8   Choose ***Show-Hide Layers*** from the Action drop down list.

9   Click **Add**.

10 Select *layer "TimerFeedback"* and click **Hide**.

Hide

11 Click **OK** to close the Show-Hide Layers window.

12 Click **OK** to close the CourseBuilder Interaction window.

13 Test the interaction in a browser.

Showing Timer Messages as Text in a Layer

Though we've already covered this enhancement in some of our previous exercises, here are a few things to consider when designing how your timer displays messages.

While popup messages can be somewhat effective (they get the learner's attention), they create some usability problems for Timer interactions. The main problem is that as soon as a popup message appears, the browser stops displaying any changes to the timer's appearance. In other words, while the popup message is still open, the timer keeps ticking but visually it doesn't show any progress. This is a problem especially for timers that display warnings.

This can cause the learners to think they have more time than they do, especially if they continue to think about how to answer the question while the popup message is open. If the learner waits long enough, this can result in the timer disabling the interaction as soon as the learner closes the popup warning message.

To avoid this usability problem, use the **Set Text of Layer** action instead of the popup message action to display timer messages.

More Information: For more information on using the *Set Text of Layer* action, see *Chapter 13: Customizing the Action Manager Tab*. Also see these step-by-step examples earlier in this chapter: *Creating a Timer that Disables an Interaction* , and *Creating a Timer that Displays a Warning*.

Letting the Learner Start the Timer

By default, all CourseBuilder timers start as soon as the page loads. You may want the Learner to be able to start the timer. In this section you'll create an interaction in which the learner will click an image labeled "Start Interaction". By clicking the button the learner will display the interaction and start the timer.

Viewing the Finished Interaction

Before creating this interaction, take a moment to view a completed example.

On CD: Open *Sample_8-4.htm* in a browser (this exercise was designed for Internet Explorer—you may experience some differences if using another browser).

Here are some things to consider as you view the sample interaction:

- What happens when you click the "Start Interaction" image?
- What behavior actions do you think make this happen?
- What interaction settings do you think you have to choose to be able to hide and show the entire interaction?

Creating this Interaction

In this section you'll modify an existing interaction to create the sample you just viewed.

Follow these steps to let the learner start the timer:

1   In Dreamweaver open *Sample_8-4_Start.htm* (this exercise was designed for Internet Explorer—you may experience some differences if using another browser).

You created this sample in the previous hands-on tutorial:

Now you'll add functionality to show the timer when the leaner clicks an image.

2   Edit the Timer interaction.

3   Select the *Layer* setting to insert the timer into its own layer:

4   Click **OK** to close the CourseBuilder Interaction window.

5 Edit the Text Entry interaction.

6 Select the *Layer* to insert the Text Entry interaction into its own layer.

7 Click **OK** to close the CourseBuilder Interaction window.

The Dreamweaver page should look something like this:

The layer that contains the timer and the layer containing the Text Entry interaction are stacked on top of each other.

8 Resize and reposition the Timer and Text Entry layers so they look like this:

Placing the interactions in layers allows you to show and hide them using Dreamweaver behaviors.

9 Just under the banner image at the top of the page, insert this graphic: *images\sample_images\start_interaction.gif*.

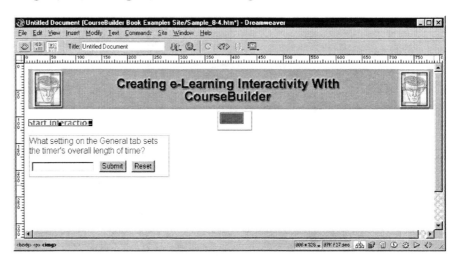

10 Go to Dreamweaver's Code View and locate the **<body>** tag:

The <body>
tag.

The onLoad
event.

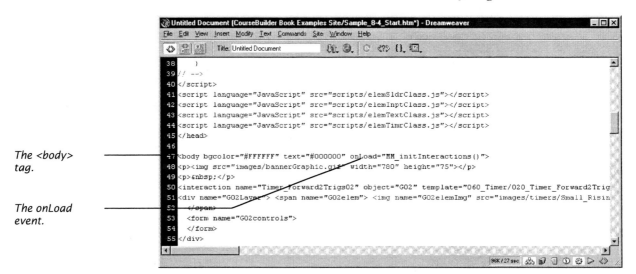

11 Select and Copy the code after the *onLoad* between the quotation marks.

The entire code you should copy is:

```
MM_initInteractions()
```

This code initializes (or creates) the interaction objects so the browser recognizes them as objects.

12 Select the *Start Interaction* image and add a ***Call JavaScript*** behavior action.

Dreamweaver displays the Call JavaScript window.

13 Paste the code you copied into the ***JavaScript*** field:

14 Click **OK** to close the ***Call JavaScript*** window.

15 Make sure the event in the Behaviors panel is *onClick*:

16 With the *Start Interaction* image still selected, click the Action drop down list and choose ***Show-Hide Layers*** to add a ***Show-Hide Layers*** action.

17 Select layer *G01Layer* and click **Show**. Do the same for *G02Layer*.

Both the G01Layer and G02Layer are set to show.

These are the interaction layers. By adding this action you are not only initializing the interactions (with the code you pasted in the Call JavaScript action) but also showing them to the learner.

You should see these two events in the Behaviors panel:

onClick		Call JavaScript
onClick	▼	Show-Hide Layers

18 Choose Dreamweaver Code View again.

19 Delete the entire *onLoad* event and its accompanying code. The code you should delete is:

```
onLoad="MM_initInteractions()
```

The *<body>* tag should now look like this:

```
<body bgcolor="#FFFFFF" text="#000000">
```

20 Choose Dreamweaver Design View.

21 Display the Layers panel (Window→Layers):

Layers	☒
🗀 Layers ⊞ Frames > History	⑦ ▶

☐ Prevent Overlaps

👁	Name	Z
👁	TimerFeedback	2
👁	⊟ G01Layer	1
👁	└ feedback	1
👁	G02Layer	1

22 Hide the *G01Layer* and *G02Layer* layers by clicking the eye symbol next to hide the layers so the interaction page loads with the layers hidden.

Dreamweaver hides the layers and changes the symbol to a shut-eye symbol.

23 Test the interaction in a browser.

More Information: This tutorial is based on a tutorial from the Macromedia website. To see that tutorial, see *www.macromedia.com/coursebuilder* and look in the Support and Training section for CourseBuilder. Click on CourseBuilder Extension for DW and UD Concepts and choose Customizing.

Stopping the Timer Early

CourseBuilder can stop the timer when the learner clicks the Submit button, when the learner's response is correct, or based on any other desired event. To do this, use the ***Set Interaction Properties*** action and set the timer interaction's *Disabled* property to True.

On CD: To see an example of an interaction that disables (stopping) the timer when the correct answer is chosen but not when the incorrect answer is chosen, try *Sample_8-5.htm* in a browser (this exercise was designed for Internet Explorer—you may experience some differences if using another browser).

Summary

In this chapter you've learned to create timers that display messages when triggers fire, timers that disable other interactions, and timers that display warnings.

You also learned some enhancements to the Timer interaction that can make using it more learner friendly.

Remember that timers are not restricted to disabling interactions and displaying messages. Any action in the Action Manager can be executed when a timer reaches a trigger.

Slider Interactions 9

In a Slider interaction the learner slides a *thumb* to different points on a line to give responses to a question. This interaction can be used very easily to pose a question about dates or time of day. It can also be used as a more interactive type of multiple choice.

In this chapter you will learn how to:

- Use basic slider skills.
- Create sliders used as learning activities (range sliders).
- Create sliders used as a quiz question (point sliders).
- Change the look and feel of the slider.
- Use custom graphics with a slider.
- Create a slider that "snaps" into place when released.

Introduction

When you choose the Slider category CourseBuilder displays two templates to choose from. In this section you'll learn about the different templates and when to use them.

Different Slider Types

This table describes the two different Slider templates that come with CourseBuilder. The page number refers you to a page in this chapter where that template is discussed.

Template	Description
	Range – meant for learning activities, this interaction is preset to execute actions that are specific to a certain range. The default action is to popup a message. The ranges in this template are preset as "Not Judged".
	Point – meant for assessments, this interaction comes preset to execute actions corresponding to the ranges on which the thumb is dropped and also judges the interaction as correct or incorrect. There are three ranges in this template. The first range is considered too low and incorrect; the middle range is considered correct; and the third is considered too high and incorrect.

When to Use Sliders

Sliders can be used for quizzes and for learning activities. In this section we describe a slider's potential uses for both applications.

Using a Slider as a Quiz Question

Here are a few learning scenarios in which you might use a Slider interaction as a quiz question:

- **To assess comprehension of points on a scale,** such as a thermometer.
- **To assess comprehension of a timeline**, such as with important dates.
- **To assess step-by-step procedures**. Make a graphic that lists the procedures in equally sized graphics running from left to right. Line up the slider under it and have the learner choose which step accomplishes a certain task.

Using a Slider as a Learning Activity

Here are just a few ways a slider could be used as a learning activity:

- **To describe elements of a graphic**, such as a toolbar for a software simulation. Place the graphic horizontally on the page and the slider underneath. As the learner drags the thumb to each element of the graphic, display the description in a layer.
- **To describe points on a scale,** such as the boiling and freezing temperature on a thermometer.
- **To describe dates on a timeline**. Display the important dates graphically horizontally or vertically. As the learner drags the thumb near a date, have the thumb snap to that date, display a picture and text in a layer that describe the importance of that date.

Slider Basics

Before you create a Slider interaction, it's important to understand the basic skills necessary to work with this type of interaction.

The 5 Steps to Slider Interactions

To create a Slider interaction you need to complete five basic steps:

1 Insert a new interaction using one of the methods described in Chapter 2.

2 Choose the appearance of the slider, the range of the slider (for example 0 to 100), the initial value, and other options on the General tab.

3   Define the specific sub-ranges of the slider.

4   Modify the Action Manager tab contents to define what happens when the
        learner drags the thumb to each range.

5   Position the slider on the Dreamweaver page.

 More Information: See also *Chapter 13: Customizing the Action Manager Tab.*

Choosing the Appearance of the Slider

Sliders come in both horizontal and vertical formats. CourseBuilder provides
several styles to choose from in each format.

To choose a slider style, follow these steps:

1   Edit the Slider interaction using one of the techniques described in Chapter 2.

2   Click on the General tab.

3   Choose a slider style from the drop down list at the top of the tab:

Learn how to add your own styles to this list later in this chapter!

CourseBuilder Interaction

Interaction Name: Slider_CorrectRange01

Appearance: green_horiz ▼   Browse...
  gray_horiz
  gray_vert
  green_horiz
  green_vert
Range:
  red_horiz
Initial Value: red_vert
  umber_vert
  violet_horiz
Judge Interaction: violet_vert ▼ labeled [   ]
    ⦿ when the slider thumb has been released
    ○ on a specific event (set using the Judge Interaction Behavior)

Correct When: Any Correct and None Incorrect ▼

Knowledge Track: ☐ Send results to a management system if present

Tries Are: Unlimited ▼ [   ] tries

Time Is: Unlimited ▼ [   ] seconds after page text is loaded

Reset: ☑ Create a Reset button

Layer: ☐ Insert in a layer (4.0+ browsers only)

General | Ranges | Action Mgr

OK   Cancel   Help

4   Click **OK**.

CourseBuilder displays the slider with the new style you selected.

This table displays CourseBuilder's pre-designed styles:

Name	Appearance
black_h_penta	
black_v_penta	
blue_ball	
blue_h_dmnd_arrow	
blue_h_dmnd	
blue_h_dmnd_notch	
blue_v_dmnd_arrow	
blue_v_dmnd_notch	
blue_v_dmnd	

Name	Appearance
blue_vert	
grey_horiz	
grey_vert	
green_horiz	
green_vert	
red_horiz	
red_vert	
umber_vert	
violet_horiz	
violet_vert	

More Information: To learn how to use custom graphics with sliders, see *Using Custom Graphics* later in this chapter.

Setting the Overall Range

Once you've chosen the style, you need to set the overall range of the slider. The overall range sets the minimum and maximum values of the slider.

Follow these steps to set the overall range of a slider:

1 Edit the Slider interaction.

2 Click the General tab.

3 Enter the minimum value of the range in the first *Range* field and the maximum value in the second field.

For example, if you want to set the slider's range from 1900 to 2000, the Range values would look like this:

Range: 1900   to 2000

4 Click **OK**.

Setting the Initial Value

By default, when the page loads in the browser, CourseBuilder places the thumb of the slider at the minimum value of the overall range. (See *Setting the Overall Range* earlier in this chapter.)

Follow these steps to change the beginning value of the slider, and consequently the location of the thumb, when the page loads:

1 Edit the Slider interaction.

2 Click on the General tab.

3 Change the value in the *Initial Value* field.

For example, if the slider's range is from 0 to 100 and you want the thumb of the slider to appear in the middle of the range when the page loads, enter 50 in the *Initial Value* field:

4   Click **OK**.

5   Test the interaction in a browser.

When the page loads, CourseBuilder displays the thumb in the position that corresponds to the *Initial Value* setting:

Defining the Slider's Ranges

When creating a Slider interaction, you define the overall range on the General tab. The overall range defines the minimum and maximum values the learner can choose. You can divide the overall range into *sub-ranges*. Sub-ranges (also called *ranges*) define the areas on the slider that correspond to specific feedback.

For example, if the overall range were for a Fahrenheit thermometer ranging from 0 to 300 degrees, you might define the ranges from 0 to 32 degrees, 33 degrees to 212 degrees, and 213 to 300 degrees. Defining three different ranges allows you to provide three different feedback responses. If the learner drags the slider to the first range, your feedback might say something about the degrees below water's freezing temperature. If the learner drags the slider to the second range, you might say something about the degrees above water's freezing temperature and the 212 degree boiling point. If the learner drags the slider to the third range you might display feedback about the degrees above water's boiling point.

Adding and Deleting Ranges

You define a slider's ranges on the Ranges tab:

Ranges tab

To add slider ranges, click the **Add** button on the Ranges tab. To delete slider ranges, select the range by clicking it, then click the **Delete** button.

Defining Range Options

Each range has these settings:

- Name
- Range value in units
- Range is correct, incorrect, or not judged
- Score

This table explains these options:

Property	Explanation	Special Considerations
Name	Any combination of letters and numbers, but no spaces.	Naming a range can be very helpful if you are referencing the range in the Action Manager or with JavaScript; otherwise there is no need to name a range.
Range value in units	This setting has two fields: • Minimum number in the range • Maximum number in the range	Make sure the sub-range is within the overall range of the slider on the General tab. Setting a sub-range that is outside the overall range in effect nullifies that sub-range, preventing the learner from ever selecting that range.
Range Is	This setting determines the correctness of the range. Choose from Not Judged, Correct, and Incorrect.	For learning activities, choose Not Judged. For quizzes, choose Correct or Incorrect.
Score	This field contains the score the learner receives if the thumb is dropped on this range.	Only add a score here if you are using a slider as a quiz, or if your learning activity is totaling points. Otherwise, leave it 0.

Modifying the Default Feedback Responses

CourseBuilder's default response to dropping the thumb on a particular sub-range is: "Range n hit" (where n refers to the range number).

Follow these steps to change CourseBuilder's default feedback response:

1 Edit the Slider interaction.

2 Click the Action Manager tab.

3 Select *Popup Message* under the line that reads *if Range1 Selected:*

Select this
line.

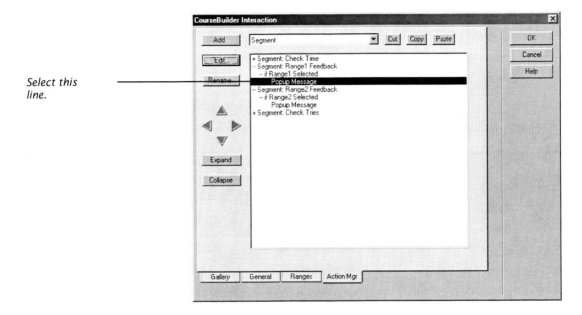

4 Click the **Edit** button.

CourseBuilder displays the Popup Message window:

5 Replace the text in the ***Message*** field with the new message text and click **OK**.

6 Repeat these steps for each range.

More Information: To display the feedback in a more elegant way than a popup message, see Chapter 13: *Customizing the Action Manager Tab.*

Positioning the Slider on the Page

When you are finished choosing the slider's settings, you will usually want to move the Slider interaction from its original location on the Dreamweaver page. CourseBuilder places slider graphics in layers. By viewing the Layers panel (Windows→Layers) in Dreamweaver, you can see the names of the layers:

The first layer contains the track graphic on which the thumb slides. CourseBuilder also puts the current value field in this layer. The value of the current value field changes as the learner drags the thumb up and down the track.

The second layer is nested under the first and contains the thumb image.

To reposition the Slider interaction, select the first layer and drag it to a new location on the Dreamweaver page.

Note: Being nested, the second layer always moves its position relative to the position of the first layer. This makes positioning the slider easier—if you reposition the first layer, the second repositions with it.

By default CourseBuilder does not place other elements of the interaction (such as the question text and any buttons you may choose to display with the interaction) in layers. To reposition these other elements, choose the *Layer* setting on the General tab:

Layer: ☑ Insert in a layer (4.0+ browsers only)

Choosing this option places the other elements of the interaction in another layer so you can easily reposition them.

More Information: To learn more about the "Insert in a layer" setting on the General tab, see *Chapter 10: Global Interaction Enhancements.*

Caution: If you choose not to insert the interaction in a layer, you can reposition other elements of the Slider interaction. Do this by cutting and pasting them onto another area of the Dreamweaver page, such as onto another table cell. Be careful though! Remember that each interaction has a lot of underlying code that goes along with it. Even though in design view it looks as if you have selected all of the interaction, you may have unintentionally selected only part of the code that needs to go with it. To be safe, use the *Layer* option on the General tab.

Creating a Range Slider

A range slider is the first template in the Slider category:

A range slider allows you to define sub-ranges to which the slider thumb can be dragged. Once the learner releases the mouse button CourseBuilder determines which range the thumb was dragged to and executes a response (such as popping up a message or displaying the message in a layer). Range sliders are best suited for learning activities.

In this section, you will create a range slider that displays information about the five steps it takes to successfully set up a Slider interaction.

Viewing the Completed Interaction

Before creating this interaction, take a moment to explore the finished product.

On CD: Open *Sample_9-1.htm* to see an example of a completed range slider.

When viewing this interaction, here are a few things to look for:

- What happens when you drag the slider under each number in the image?
- How many ranges do you think this slider has?

- What is the overall range of the slider?
- What numbers appear in the text box beneath the slider track?

Creating this Interaction

To create a range slider, follow these steps:

1   Open a new page.

2   Insert a new layer on the page (Insert → Layer).

3   Position your cursor inside the layer and insert this image (Insert→Image): */images/sample_images/5_steps_to_slider.gif*

4   Position the layer near the top of the page:

5   Insert another new layer and name it *Explanation* in the Property Inspector:

Layer name

This layer holds the explanation of each step when the learner drops the thumb on the range to which the step corresponds.

6 Insert a new range Slider interaction on the page using one of the techniques described in Chapter 2.

7 On the General tab change only these settings:

Setting	Value
Appearance	**violet_horiz**
Reset	**Deselected**. By deselecting this option, CourseBuilder removes the **Reset** button.
Layer	**Selected**. By choosing to insert this interaction in a layer, you'll be able to reposition easily later.

8 Click the Ranges tab.

9 On the Ranges tab, click on the second range in the *Ranges* field.

10 Add three ranges by clicking the **Add** button three times:

Newly created ranges.

11 Click on each unnamed range and name it in sequential order so that you have five ranges named Range1, Range2, …Range5.

12 Define each range with these settings:

Range	Settings
Range1	**Range:** 0 to 20 **Range is:** Not Judged **Score:** 0
Range2	**Range:** 21 to 40 **Range is:** Not Judged **Score:** 0
Range3	**Range:** 41 to 60 **Range is:** Not Judged **Score:** 0
Range4	**Range:** 61 to 80 **Range is:** Not Judged **Score:** 0
Range5	**Range:** 81 to 100 **Range is:** Not Judged **Score:** 0

13 Click on the Action Manager tab.

14 Select *Popup Message* under *if Range1 selected:*

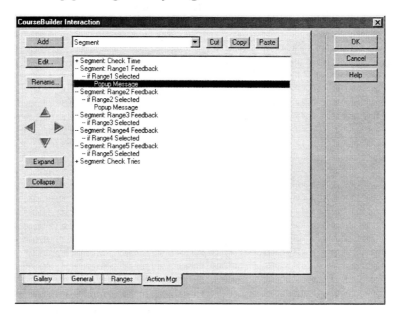

15 Click **Cut** to delete the *Popup Message* action.

16 Click on *if Range1 Selected*.

17 Choose ***Set Text of Layer*** from the action drop down list.

18 Click **Add**.

CourseBuilder displays the Set Text of Layer window:

Set Text of Layer	✕
Layer: layer "Explanation" ▾	OK
New HTML:	Cancel
	Help

Note: CourseBuilder always adds new actions below the currently selected line.

19 Choose *layer "Explanation"* from the drop down list. (This layer may already be selected.)

20 In the ***New HTML*** field, enter: *Step 1 – Enter a new interaction.*

21 Click **OK**.

22 Repeat steps 14 through 21 for each range, setting the following text for each Explanation layer.

Range	Message Text
Range2	Step 2 - Establish the overall range.
Range3	Step 3 - Establish individual sub-ranges.
Range4	Step 4 - Accept or customize feedback.
Range5	Step 5 - If necessary, arrange the interaction layer to match a corresponding graphic or other text.

23 Click **OK** to accept your changes and close the CourseBuilder Interaction window.

24 Reposition the question text layer so the question text appears above the 1 through 5 graphic:

Place question text here.

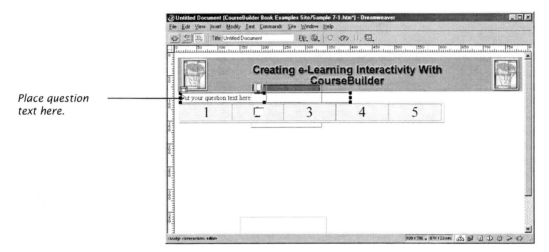

25 Reposition the layer containing the track graphic underneath the 1 through 5 graphic. (The layer containing the thumb layer will reposition at the same time.)

Place the track graphic layer here.

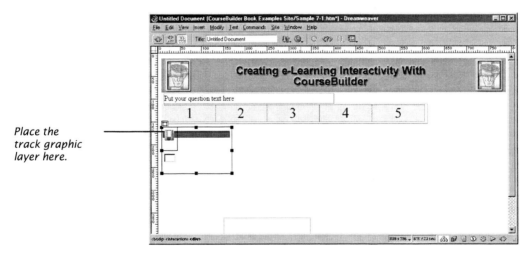

26 Select the track graphic:

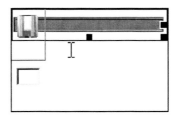

27 Use the Properties panel (Windows→Properties) to set the width of the image to 608 pixels:

*Set the width
here*

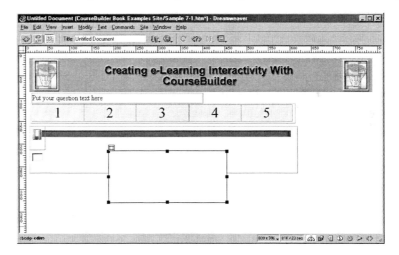

Changing the width stretches the track graphic to the length of the image above it.

28 Resize and reposition the Explanation layer so that it looks something like this:

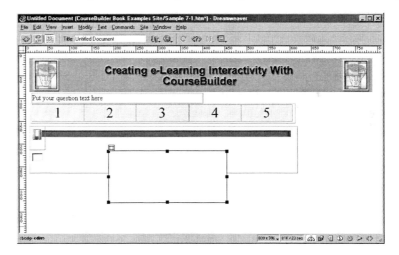

29 Change the interaction text to: *To learn the 5 main steps to creating a Slider interaction, click and drag the slider to each step.* (You may have to resize the layer to accommodate this text.)

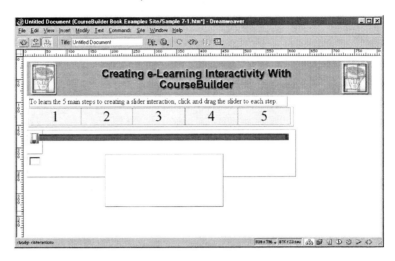

30 Test the interaction in a browser.

In this exercise you learned not only how to create a range slider but also how to make the explanation text appear in a layer instead of a popup message.

 More Information: For more information on the *Set Text of Layer* action in the Action Manager, see *Chapter 13: Customizing the Action Manager Tab.*

Creating a Point Slider

A point slider differs from a range slider in that it determines which range is correct. It is better suited for quiz questions while the range slider is better suited for learning activities.

Follow these steps to create a point slider:

1 Insert a point slider by using one of the techniques to insert new interactions discussed in chapter 2.

2 On the General tab, set the overall range and choose any other options common to the General tab:

3 Click on the Ranges tab.

By default, CourseBuilder makes the first range *Incorrect*, the second range *Correct*, and the third range *Incorrect*.

4 Add or delete ranges as necessary to your interaction.

5 Establish the range settings for each range (see *Defining the Slider's Ranges* earlier in this chapter).

6 Click on the Action Manager tab and make any desired changes to the feedback (see *Modifying the Default Feedback Responses* earlier in this chapter).

7 Click **OK** to close the CourseBuilder Interaction window.

8 Reposition the slider on the Dreamweaver page as necessary (see *Positioning the Slider on the Page* earlier in this chapter).

Unique Enhancements to the Slider Interaction

There are a few ways you can enhance the Slider interaction. In this section you will learn what is possible and how you can do it.

Creating Custom Appearances

As we discussed in *Choosing the Appearance* earlier in this chapter, you can choose from a list of preset slider styles that come with CourseBuilder. You can also create your own custom graphics to use with sliders.

Sliders are made up of three graphics:

- The *thumb* image—the graphic the learner drags along the slider track
- The *track* image—the graphic on which the thumb *slides.*
- The *thumbnail* image—the graphic that shows the style of the slider in the CourseBuilder Interaction window

To create custom slider graphics, simply create three graphics, one each for the thumb, track, and thumbnail. These graphics must follow a specific naming convention and be placed in a specific location.

Image	File Naming Convention	Location
Thumb	*graphicname*_**thm.gif** (i.e. redball_thm.gif)	…/images/sliders/
Track	*graphicname* _**trk.gif** (i.e. redball_trk.gif)	…/images/sliders/
Thumbnail	*graphicname* _**tnail.gif** (i.e. redball_tnail.gif)	…/images/sliders/

Note: Though the graphics all have different endings (the _thm, _trk, and _tnail suffixes), the name of the graphic before the ending must be the same for all three graphics.

Tip: To make the thumbnail graphic appear like all other thumbnail graphics, create a transparent GIF that is 100x100 pixels and place a small composite image of the slider in the center.

Creating a Slider that Snaps To the Center of a Range

By default you can drag the thumb of a slider to any point in any range on the slider. You may occasionally want to cause the thumb to snap to the center of a range when the mouse button is released. To do this you need to use the Action Manager to set the value of the *selected* property of the interaction. In this section we will show you how to create this type of interaction.

More Information: To learn more about using the Action Manager, see the Action Manager chapters in Section II: *Extending CourseBuilder.*

Viewing the Finished Interaction

Before creating this interaction, first take a look at the completed interaction.

On CD: Take a moment and try out the finished sample by opening *Sample_9-2.htm* (this exercise was designed for Internet Explorer—you may experience some differences if using another browser).

As you explore this interaction, you may want to try some of the following tasks.

- Drag the thumb to the middle of each range.
- Drag the thumb to the beginning of each range.
- Drag the thumb to the ends of each range.

Creating the Interaction

In this section you'll create the interaction you just finished viewing.

Follow these steps to create a slider that snaps the thumb to the center of the range on which it is dropped:

1   Open *Sample_9-2_Start.htm* (this exercise was designed for Internet Explorer—you may experience some differences if using another browser).

To let you focus on certain tasks in this exercise, we've already created and set up the Slider interaction, a layer called *Explanation* (and we applied a CSS style to it), and a layer containing a graphic.

We've also positioned the Slider interaction under the graphic and stretched the slider's track graphic to be approximately the same width as the graphic above it:

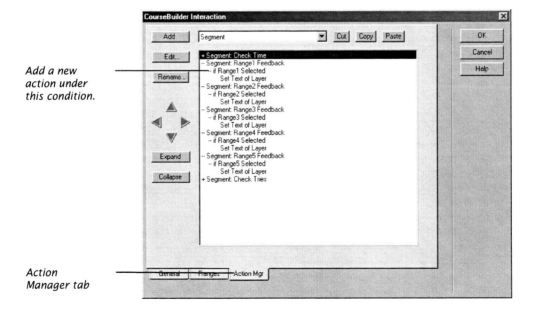

2 Edit the interaction using one of the methods described in Chapter 2.

3 Click on the Action Manager tab if it isn't already selected:

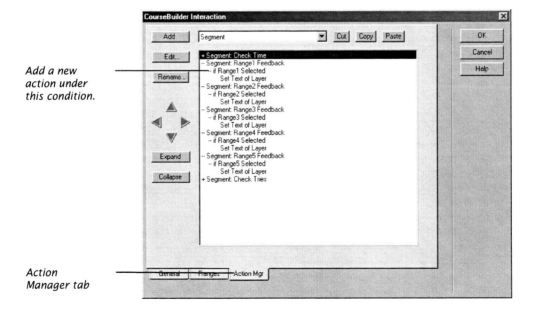

Add a new action under this condition.

Action Manager tab

4 Click on *if Range1 Selected.*

5 Choose ***Set Interaction Properties*** from the drop down list:

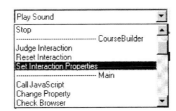

6 Click **Add**.

CourseBuilder displays the Set Interaction Properties window.

More Information: For more information on the ***Set Interaction Property*** action, see *Chapter 13: Customizing the Action Manager Tab.*

7 Choose these settings for this window:

Property	Value
Set	Interaction
Interaction	**First drop down list:** Slider_2Ranges01 **Second drop down list:** Slider "elem" (This tells CourseBuilder you are setting properties for the thumb image layer.)
Property	Value
Type	Number
Number	10

This first range spans from 0 to 20, so setting the value of the slider thumb layer to 10 will cause the thumb to *snap to* the center of the range:

Set Interaction Properties	
Add Delete	OK
	Cancel
Assignments: Slider "elem" Value = 10	Help
Set: Interaction	
Interaction: Slider_2Ranges01 Slider "elem"	
Property: Value	
Equal To	
Type: Number	
Number: 10	

8 Click **OK**.

9 Add a Set Interaction Properties action for each range setting the value of the slider's thumb layer (named "elem") to these values:

Range	Thumb Layer Value
Range2	30
Range3	50
Range4	70
Range5	90

Tip: To save time, select the Set Interaction Properties action for the first range and click **Copy**. Select *if Range2 Selected* and click **Paste**. CourseBuilder pastes the *Set Interaction Properties* action. Click Edit and change the necessary settings. Repeat for each range.

Your Action Manager tab should look like this:

10 Click **OK** to close the CourseBuilder interaction window.

11 Test the interaction in a browser.

Summary

In this chapter you've learned how to create and enhance Slider interactions. The two different kinds of sliders are range and point sliders. The main difference between the two is that range sliders are not judged correct or incorrect while point sliders are.

You also learned how to create custom graphics to enhance the appearance of a slider as well as how to create a slider that snaps the thumb to the center of the range.

Global Interaction Enhancements 10

In previous chapters you learned how to create CourseBuilder interactions and make some enhancements. Most of the enhancements you learned in previous chapters are unique to the respective interactions. This chapter covers some additional ways of enhancing Coursebuilder interactions that apply to all interactions.

In this chapter you will learn:

- How to show and hide interactions based on a specific event by placing the interactions in a layer.
- How to evaluate the learner's responses based on a specific event (using the Judge Interaction behavior).
- How to place a limit on the number of attempts a learner has to complete an interaction.
- How to place a limit on the amount of time a learner has to complete an interaction.
- How to make customize the standard **Submit** and **Reset** buttons.

Introduction

There are potentially countless ways to enhance a CourseBuilder interaction. It's up to your imagination or what your e-learning course requires. CourseBuilder supplies some out-of-the-box enhancements that can be confusing to a new CourseBuilder user, but can also be very useful. We chose to separate these enhancements out from the other interaction-specific chapters because they apply to all interactions.

More Information: To look at advanced enhancements to CourseBuilder interactions, see Section II: *Extending CourseBuilder.*

Placing Interactions in Layers

A setting on the General tab of each interaction allows you to place the interaction in a *layer.*

A layer is an HTML object that retains its position on the web page regardless of what is happening to the browser or other objects on the page. Any JavaScript *event* can hide or show layers, move layers along a Dreamweaver timeline, replace the layer contents, or any other behavior in Dreamweaver.

JavaScript events include button clicks on the web page, a mouse being placed over a picture, or any number of other events that browsers recognize.

More Information: See a JavaScript and/or Dreamweaver reference for more information about events and behaviors.

At the bottom of the General tab in the CourseBuilder Interaction window, CourseBuilder displays this setting:

> Layer: ☐ Insert in a layer (4.0+ browsers only)

The *Layer* setting is available for every type of interaction. To choose this setting, click the checkbox.

When you choose this setting, CourseBuilder places the entire interaction within a Dreamweaver layer (in HTML known as a *<div>* tag).

Creating an Interaction that Shows and Hides

In this section you will create a page that presents some information and provides a clickable **Quiz Me** image. Clicking the **Quiz Me** image displays a multiple-correct question about the information just presented.

Viewing the Finished Interaction

Before working through the step-by-step tutorial, take a look at a completed sample.

On CD: Open *Sample_10-1.htm* in a browser and try it out.

While viewing this sample, here are a few things to look for and think about:

- What event causes the interaction to appear?
- Where does the interaction appear?
- What happens to the topic content?
- Why is placing the interaction in a layer any better than placing it at the bottom of the screen after the topic content?

More Information: To see a more extensive example of showing and hiding interactions, see *Chapter 14: The Power of the Action Manager Object.*

Creating this Interaction

As you create this interaction you will:

- Insert the interaction into a layer.
- Add a rollover image to the layer.
- Attach behaviors to rollover images to hide and show the appropriate layers.
- Position the layer on the page.

All of the content and the interaction has been created for you so you can focus on the use of layers.

1   Use Dreamweaver to open *Sample_10-1_Start.htm* on the CD ROM.

2   Edit the interaction by using one of the methods described in Chapter 2.

3   Click the General tab.

4   Check *Insert in a layer*:

Layer: ☑ Insert in a layer (4.0+ browsers only)

When you choose to place the interaction in a layer, CourseBuilder creates a new layer and gives it a name. The name is always the title of the object followed by the word "Layer". For example, if the interaction you are working on is the first interaction on the web page, it's title is *G01*. The second would be *G02* etc. So the name of the layer for the first interaction would be *G01Layer* and the name for the second, *G02Layer*.

More Information: For more information about the interaction object, see Chapter 16: *Behind the Scenes: Deciphering CourseBuilder's JavaScript.*

5   Click **OK.**

Your screen should look something like this:

This layer contains the topic content.

You'll use these other elements later in the exercise.

When you select the Layer setting, CourseBuilder places the entire interaction inside a new layer.

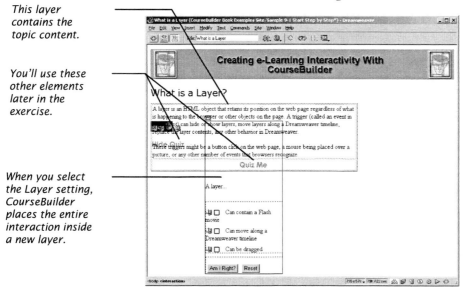

6 Resize the layer so the multiple choice question text fits on one line:

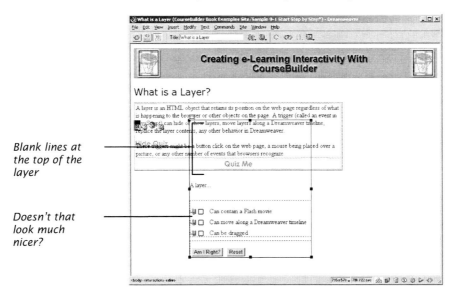

Blank lines at the top of the layer

Doesn't that look much nicer?

7 To make the interaction layer easier to work with, hide the topic content layer (*Layer1*) by clicking the *eye* symbol next to *Layer1* on the Dreamweaver Layers panel (Window→Layers). The eye symbol changes to a shuteye symbol:

8 Delete the blank lines at the top of the interaction layer.

The interaction layer (*G01Layer*) should now look like this:

```
┌──┐
│  │
A layer...
- - - - - - - - - - - - - - - - - - - - - -
 ☐  Can contain a Flash movie
 ☐  Can move along a Dreamweaver timeline
 ☐  Can be dragged
- - - - - - - - - - - - - - - - - - - - - -
[Am I Right?]  [Reset]
```

9 Move the Hide Quiz rollover image into the interaction layer by copying an pasting it into this location (you may need to hide or move the topic content layer aside to get to it):

```
┌──┐
│  │
A layer...
- - - - - - - - - - - - - - - - - - - - - -
 ☐  Can contain a Flash movie
 ☐  Can move along a Dreamweaver timeline
 ☐  Can be dragged
- - - - - - - - - - - - - - - - - - - - - -
[Am I Right?]  [Reset]

Hide Quiz
```

New location for the Hide Quiz image inside the interaction layer

10 Show the topic content layer (*Layer1*) by clicking on the shut-eye icon in the Layers panel.

11 Position the interaction layer (*G0Layer1*) so that its top left corner sits over the top left corner of the topic content layer (*Layer 1*):

Layers match
on top-left
corner

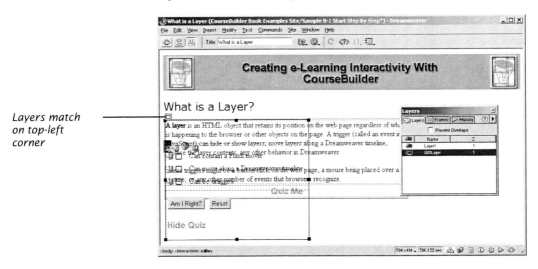

Now you're ready to attach a behavior to the Hide Quiz rollover image that will hide the interaction layer and show the topic content layer.

12 Select the Hide Quiz rollover image and attach a ***Show/Hide Layers*** behavior using the Behaviors panel (Window→Behaviors→+→Show-Hide Layers).

More Information: Refer to a Dreamweaver reference guide or Dreamweaver's online help to learn more about adding behaviors to Dreamweaver objects.

13 Set the interaction layer (*G0Layer1*) to hide and the topic content layer (*Layer1*) to show:

14 Click **OK**.

Now you need to attach a similar behavior to the Quiz Me image. Except this behavior will hide the topic content layer and show the interaction layer.

15 Use the layer panel to hide the interaction layer (*G0Layer1*).

16 Select the Quiz Me rollover image and attach a ***Show-Hide Layers*** behavior using the Behaviors panel (Window→Behaviors).

17 Set the interaction layer (*G0Layer1*) to show and the topic content layer (*Layer1*) to show:

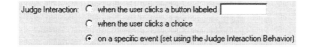

18 Click **OK**.

19 Test the interaction in a browser.

Judging an Interaction Based on a Specific Event

As we discussed in Chapter 2, the General tab displays three options for determining when the interaction gets judged. In previous chapters you've learned how to use the first two options. In this section you'll learn how to use the third option: *on a specific event (set using the Judge Interaction Behavior)*.

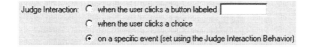

What Does the Specific Event Option Mean?

Every interaction has default settings in the Action Manager tab. The Action Manger makes decisions about what CourseBuilder should do when the learner responds to the question.

 More Information: To learn about the Action Manager in depth, see the Action Manager chapters in Section II: *Extending CourseBuilder*.

By default, the Action Manager is already set up to handle three main decisions Those three decisions are identified on this sample Action Manager tab:

Segment Check Time decides what to do if the user didn't complete the interaction within the allotted time.

Segment Correctness decides what to do if the user completed the question correctly or incorrectly.

Segment Check Tries decides what to do if the user didn't complete the interaction within the allotted number of tries.

CourseBuilder Interaction

| Add | Segment ▼ | Cut | Copy | Paste | | OK |

Edit..

Rename...

+ Segment: Check Time
  Segment: Correctness
  -- if Correct
       Popup Message
  -- else if Incorrect
       Popup Message
  -- else if Unknown Response
       Popup Message
+ Segment: Check Tries

Cancel

Help

Expand

Collapse

Gallery | General | Choices | Action Mgr

The Judge Interaction options allow you to determine when to process the decision tree on the Action Manager tab.

By choosing the third option, on a "specific event", you are telling CourseBuilder to process the contents of the Action Manager tab based on some JavaScript event determined somewhere else on the Dreamweaver page. Most of the time you won't use this option, but it is available so you can customize your interaction.

For example, you could wait to process the Action Manager tab until the learner had completed all five questions in a multi-question quiz.

Other uses for this option could include processing the Action Manager tab when the learner leaves the page (*onUnload* event), when the learner places the mouse over some object on the page (*onMouseOver event*), or when the learner double-clicks a button (*onDblClick*). These are just a few examples—you can use the any JavaScript event available to you from the Behaviors panel (Windows→Behaviors).

More Information: For a step-by-step tutorial on how to setup and score a multi-question quiz, see *Chapter 14: The Power of the Action Manager Object.*

How Do I Use It?

You can judge the interaction based on any specific JavaScript event by assigning the Judge Interaction behavior to an HTML object like a button, an image, or a layer.

For example, suppose you want to process the Action Manager tab when the learner places the mouse over an object, such as a rollover image. To do this, simply add the Judge Interaction behavior to that rollover image.

Follow these steps to judge an interaction based on a specific event:

1   Edit the interaction.

2   On the General tab, choose to judge the interaction on a specific event:

Choose this option to judge the interaction based on a JavaScript event.

CourseBuilder Interaction	☒

Interaction Name: MultCh_ImageRadios01

Question Text: Put your question text here:

OK
Cancel
Help

Judge Interaction: ○ when the user clicks a button labeled
  ○ when the user clicks a choice
  ● on a specific event (set using the Judge Interaction Behavior)

Correct When: Any Correct and None Incorrect ▾

Knowledge Track: ☐ Send results to a management system if present

Tries Are: Unlimited ▾ [   ] tries

Time Is: Unlimited ▾ [   ] seconds after page text is loaded

Reset: ☐ Create a Reset button

Layer: ☐ Insert in a layer (4.0+ browsers only)

General | Choices | Action Mgr

3   Click **OK**.

4   Select the HTML object that you want to use to trigger the Judge Interaction setting. This can be a button, an image, a layer, the *<body>* tag, or any valid HTML object.

5 Open the Behaviors window (Windows→Behaviors) and choose Judge Interaction from the CourseBuilder category:

Choose Judge Interaction from the CourseBuilder sub-menu.

CourseBuilder displays the Judge Interaction window:

6 Choose the CourseBuilder interaction you want to judge from the drop-down list.

7 Click **OK**.

CourseBuilder displays the behavior in the Behaviors window with the default *onClick* event.

8   Choose the event that you want to trigger this behavior:

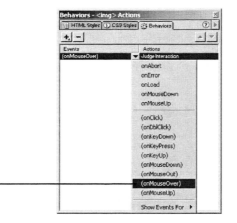

This example uses the onMouseOver event

The interaction will now be judged when that event occurs.

 More Information: To go through a tutorial with a sample that uses this Judge Interaction setting, see *Chapter 14: The Power of the Action Manager Object.*

 # Placing a Limit On the Number of Tries

CourseBuilder allows you to limit the number of attempts the learner has to complete an interaction. When the learner completes the number of tries, CourseBuilder disables the interaction.

In this section you will open an existing CourseBuilder interaction and place a limit on the number of tries using the ***Tries Are*** setting.

Viewing the Finished Interaction

Before using the ***Tries Are*** setting you may want to see a completed example of an interaction that limits the number of tries.

 On CD: Open and try *Sample_10-2.htm* in a browser.

Here are a few things to look for and think about while viewing this sample:

▪   How many tries do you get?

- What message do you get when your tries are used up?
- What happens visually to the interaction when your tries are used up?

 More Information: To learn how to change the message the learner gets when the tries are used up, see *Changing the Default Message* later in this section.

Creating this Interaction

In this section you'll create an interaction that you just finished viewing.

Follow these steps to practice using the *Tries Are* setting in an interaction:

1 In Dreamweaver open *Sample_10-2_Start.htm* on the CD ROM.

2 Edit the interaction.

3 Click the General tab.

4 Choose *Limited To* from the ***Tries Are*** drop down box.

CourseBuilder automatically places 3 in the *Tries* field.

Tries Are: [Limited To ▼] [3] tries

5 In the *Tries* field enter *1*.

Your General tab should look like this:

6   Click **OK**.

7   Test the interaction in a browser.

Changing How the Feedback Message is Displayed

When the learner has met the allotted number of tries, Coursebuilder displays a default popup message:

To display the message in a more elegant manner, display the feedback message in a layer instead of popping up a dialog box. In this section you'll learn how to display feedback in a layer rather than a with the popup message box.

Viewing the Finished Interaction

Before creating the interaction, take a look at the finished example:

 On CD: To see this completed example, open *Sample_10-3.htm* on the CD ROM.

This example shows the feedback in a layer beneath the interaction.

Feedback displaying in a layer

Creating this Interaction

Follow these steps to change the default message when a learner has completed the maximum number of tries:

1   Add a layer to your web page and name it *Feedback*. You may also want to assign it a style from a stylesheet.

2   Edit the interaction.

3   Click the Action Manager tab.

4   Click the line that reads: *Segment: Check Tries*.

5   Click **Expand** to show the segment's nested content beneath it.

CourseBuilder displays the contents of the Check Tries segment:

*Choose
actions from
this drop
down list.*

*You'll replace
this Popup
Message
action with a
Set Text of
Layer action.*

6   Under *if Tries At Limit* click *Popup Message*.

7   Click **Cut** at the top of the window to remove the *Popup Message* action.

8   Choose *Set Text of Layer* from the drop down box at the top of the window:

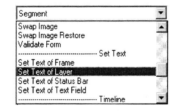

9   Click **Add** at the top of the window.

CourseBuilder displays the Set Text of Layer window:

10 If it doesn't appear by default, choose the layer named *Feedback* from the drop down box.

11 In the New HTML field enter: *<b>You have reached the maximum number of tries allowed for this interaction.</b>*

The <b> tag makes the text bold.

> **Tip:** When you are using the Set Text of Layer action you are really replacing all of the HTML in the layer so you can use HTML tags and/or JavaScript variables.

12 Click **OK** to close the Set Text of Layer window.

13 Click **OK** to close the CourseBuilder Interaction window.

14 Test the interaction in a browser.

> **More Information:** For more alternatives for showing feedback, see *Chapter 13: Customizing the Action Manager Tab*. Also, we have provided numerous examples throughout the book that use the ***Set Text of Layer*** action to display feedback. Check the index for more tutorials that use this action.

Placing a Limit on the Amount of Time

In some assessments you may want to limit the amount of time the learner has to complete the interaction. This can be a critical component, depending on the material. Examples of such topics might be first-aid training or customer support training (such as how to help a customer with a down system that is critical to their business).

There are two ways to limit the allotted time a learner has to complete an interaction. First, you can give the ***Time Is*** setting on the general tab a specific value. Second, you can use a CourseBuilder Timer interaction from the Gallery.

Using the *Time is Limited* Setting

On the General tab for each interaction there is a ***Time Is*** field.

Time Is: Unlimited ▾ [ ] seconds after page text is loaded

By default it is set to *Unlimited.* To limit the amount of time, enter the maximum number of seconds the learner has to complete the interaction in the *seconds after page text is loaded* field.

Time Is: Limited To ▾ [30] seconds after page text is loaded

CourseBuilder automatically changes the drop down box to *Limited To.* As the setting describes, the time starts counting down once the text of the web page is loaded into the browser window.

When the time expires, CourseBuilder displays a default popup message (*You are out of time*) and disables the interaction.

Note: Unlike Timer interactions, this timer is invisible—it starts and finishes without any visible cue to the learner. See *Chapter 8: Timer Interactions* for information about visible timers.

Tip: You can change what happens when the time expires by editing the Check Time segment on the Action Manager tab. To learn more about the Action Manager and how to edit it, see the Action Manager chapters in Section II: *Extending CourseBuilder.*

Using Timer Interactions

A Timer interaction can also limit the time a learner has to complete an interaction, but unlike the *Time is* setting on the General tab, a Timer interaction is visible. There are also more ways to customize a Timer interaction.

More Information: See *Chapter 8: Timer Interactions* for more details about using visible timers.

Customizing the Submit and Reset Buttons

CourseBuilder gives you the option to add two default buttons to your interaction: **Submit** and **Reset.** You can add these buttons by selecting settings on the General tab for any interaction:

*Choose this setting to add a **Submit** button.*

*Choose this setting to add a **Reset** button.*

```
CourseBuilder Interaction                                                        [x]

    Interaction Name:  MultCh_Radios03                                   ┌──────────┐
                                                                         │    OK    │
      Question Text:   Put your question text here                  ▲    ├──────────┤
                                                                         │  Cancel  │
                                                                         ├──────────┤
                                                                    ▼    │   Help   │
                                                                         └──────────┘

   Judge Interaction  ⦿ when the user clicks a button labeled │Submit │
                       ○ when the user clicks a choice
                       ○ on a specific event (set using the Judge Interaction Behavior)
      Correct When:  │Any Correct and None Incorrect ▼│
   Knowledge Track:  ☐ Send results to a management system if present
         Tries Are:  │Unlimited  ▼│ │      │ tries
          Time Is:  │Limited To ▼│ │30    │ seconds after page text is loaded

            Reset:  ☑ Create a Reset button
            Layer:  ☐ Insert in a layer (4.0+ browsers only)

     │ Gallery │   General │ Choices │ Action Mgr │
```

Learners click the **Submit** button to submit their response to the interaction and receive feedback. Uses click the **Reset** button to reset the interaction to try it again.

Changing the Button Label

You can change the name of the submit button by entering a new name on the General tab:

⊙ when the user clicks a button labeled [Go]

You cannot change the name of the **Reset** button in the CourseBuilder Interaction window. However, you can do this in Properties panel (Windows→Properties) in Dreamweaver.

To change the name of the Reset button, follow these steps:

1 Add a **Reset** button to your interaction by selecting the *Reset* setting on the General tab:

Reset: ☑ Create a Reset button

CourseBuilder creates a form-style button labeled **Reset** and displays it on the page.

2 After completing all other settings in the CourseBuilder Interaction window, click **OK** to close the CourseBuilder interaction window.

3 Select the **Reset** button on the Dreamweaver page.

4 Open the Properties panel (Windows→Properties):

This is where you change the label of standard CourseBuilder buttons.

Button Name	Label Reset	Action ○ Submit form ⊙ None
G0lreset		○ Reset form

5 Replace the text in the Label field with your new label:

Button Name	Label Try Again	Action ○ Submit form ⊙ None
G0lreset		○ Reset form

Dreamweaver changes the button label:

[Try Again]

Making the Submit and Reset Buttons Graphical

If you enhance your interaction using colors and styles (see *Chapter 11: Using CSS to Enhance CourseBuilder*) the standard form-style **Submit** and **Reset** buttons start to look out of place. In this section you'll learn how to make the **Submit** button a graphical rollover button. You can apply the same technique to the **Reset** button.

To make the Submit button a rollover image style button follow these steps:

Note: To complete these steps you need two graphic images, one that is for the *normal* state of the rollover image and another that is for the *rollover* state (when the learner places the mouse over the image).

1   If you've already added a **Submit** button to your interaction, delete it (or choose to judge the behavior *on a specific user event* set on the General tab).

2   Insert a rollover image onto the Dreamweaver page (Insert→Interactive Image→Rollover Image).

Dreamweaver displays the Insert Rollover Image window:

Insert Rollover Image			
Image Name: Image2			OK
Original Image:		Browse...	Cancel
Rollover Image:		Browse...	Help
☑ Preload Rollover Image			
When Clicked, Go To URL:		Browse...	

3   Click the **Browse** button next to the *Original Image* field and select the graphic that represents the normal state of the button.

4 Click the **Browse** button next to the ***Rollover Image*** field and select the
     graphic that represents the highlighted state of the button:

Normal state

*Highlighted
state*

5 Click **OK**.

6 Select the rollover image and open the Dreamweaver Behaviors panel
     (Windows→Behaviors):

7 Click on the plus icon ⊞ to display a list of behaviors.

8 Select the ***Judge Interaction*** action (Coursebuilder→Judge Interaction) from
     the popup behavior list.

     CourseBuilder displays the Judge Interaction window. This behavior submits
     the learner's response to be judged:

9 Select the CourseBuilder interaction you want the **Submit** button to judge from the drop down list. (If you have only one interaction on the page, only one interaction displays in this list.)

10 Click **OK.**

11 Make sure the Event that triggers the behavior is *onClick.*

12 Test the page in a browser.

 On CD: View *Sample_10-4.htm* on the CD-ROM to see a simple completed example of a rollover image style Submit button.

Summary

There are many ways to enhance CourseBuilder interactions. In this chapter you learned some of the ways that apply to all interactions. You learned how to:

- Place interactions in a layer. allowing you to hide and show the entire interaction.
- Evaluate the learner's response based on a specific event.
- Limit the number of attempts and time allowed to complete the interaction.
- Display feedback in a layer.

Section II:
Extending CourseBuilder

You've learned the basics. Now it's time to turn it up a notch. Using Cascading Style Sheets (CSS), the Action Manager, and JavaScript, you'll learn to add functionality that doesn't come "out-of-the-box."

Using CSS to Enhance CourseBuilder

11

By now you should know how to create basic CourseBuilder interactions. And you've learned some pretty nice ways to enhance them in each chapter.

In this chapter we're going to discuss how to enhance CourseBuilder interactions using styles from a Cascading Style Sheet (CSS). You can implement any of the examples in this chapter without using a style sheet by creating individual styles in each document. But since using a style sheet is more efficient when you are applying styles across several pages, that's the approach we'll take.

The beautiful thing about styles is that they add so much visual appeal to an interaction without adding the bandwidth that is required for images.

In this chapter you will learn:

- To use styles to ensure consistent visual design.
- To use styles to enhance user input areas.
- To use style borders to create 3-D appearances.
- To use styles to manipulate the cursor appearance to enhance usability.
- To use styles to enhance feedback.

Introduction

Cascading Style Sheets have long been used for web pages to ensure consistent design throughout a website. You can use the same principles to ensure consistent design throughout an e-learning course. Styles can control the font type, size, font color, background color, border styles, and other text settings. Moreover, you can use styles to create a number of effects that can enhance the learner experience.

For example, in one project we worked on, we used CSS to enhance various text input areas so that we could use them to appear and act like a mainframe computer software application we needed to simulate. We made the borders of the text input objects black and their backgrounds black, then made the text green. By placing these in layers on top of the black background of the screenshot of the application, we were able to produce the desired effect. With the use of styles combined with some JavaScript functions we were able to simulate the software without any plugin required (much to our client's delight!).

Caution: Be careful when using styles if you need to develop for multiple browsers. Not all browsers support all style attributes. For example, most hands-on exercises in this chapter work well in Internet Explorer but won't work well in Netscape. You may also want to see *Appendix C: Cross-browser Limitations.*

Complete coverage of styles and style sheets is beyond the scope of this chapter (and this book). However, let's review some Dreamweaver stylesheet basics.

Creating a Stylesheet Using Dreamweaver

A style sheet is simply a text file that defines different styles. Each style can have multiple attributes (font size, font style, font typeface, etc.). You can, of course, define these all by hand. But why not let the stylesheet do the work for you?

More on Style Sheets

For more information about style sheets see these websites for tutorials and examples:

- *http://www.fourlevel.com/ dreamweaver/CSS/*

- *http://hotwired.lycos.com/ webmonkey/reference/ stylesheet_guide/*

- *http://www.faqts.com/ knowledge_base/index.phtm fid/337*

- *http://wsabstract.com/ dhtmltutors/css1.shtml*

- *http://www.htmlhelp.com/*

Tip: You may want to ask your IT department if there is an existing style sheet you should use. See *Attaching an Existing Style Sheet* later in this chapter.

Follow these steps to create a style sheet in Dreamweaver:

Note: There are several ways to create a style sheet in Dreamweaver. These steps show you a way to create a style sheet while you are creating your first style.

1   Open the CSS Styles panel in Dreamweaver (Windows→CSS Styles).

Dreamweaver displays the CSS Styles window:

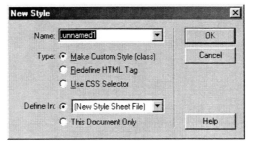

New Style button

2   Click the **New Style** button at the bottom right of the panel.

Dreamweaver displays the New Style window:

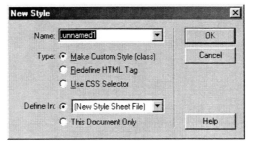

In the New Style window, you are creating both a style sheet and a new style at the same time.

The *Name* drop down box refers to the name of the specific style, not the style sheet. The style sheet file is referenced in the *Define In* option at the bottom.

3   Choose *New Style Sheet File* from the **Define In** drop down list. (It may already be selected.)

Choosing this option means that when you click **OK** Dreamweaver will create a new style sheet for you.

4   Enter the name of the new style in the **Name** drop down box. Preface it with a period (i.e. ".questionText").

5   Click **OK**.

Dreamweaver prompts you to give the new style sheet a name and file location.

6   Type a name in the name field, navigate to the folder in your Dreamweaver site where you want to save it, and click **Save**.

Dreamweaver saves your new style sheet with a *.css* extension and opens the Style Definition window:

7   Choose the style attributes in this window and click **OK** (see Dreamweaver's online help for details about what all of the options mean).

You've created a new stylesheet and one new style.

Attaching an Existing Style Sheet

In many cases you may already have a style sheet created that you want to attach to the Dreamweaver web page. One reason you may want to do this is to help the look and feel of your interactions fit in with the look and feel of a larger internet or intranet site.

Follow these steps to attach an existing style sheet to a Dreamweaver page:

1   Open the CSS Styles panel in Dreamweaver (Windows→CSS Styles).

Dreamweaver displays the CSS Styles window:

Attach Style Sheet button.

2   Click the **Attach Style Sheet** button at the bottom right of the CSS Styles panel.

Dreamweaver displays the Select Style Sheet File window.

3   Select the style sheet you want to attach to this document and click Select.

Dreamweaver populates the CSS Styles panel with the styles defined in the stylesheet you selected:

That's it! Now you can use any of the styles defined in that stylesheet.

Creating a Custom Style Class

Style sheets typically define what are called *classes*. These are custom styles that you can apply to almost any HTML object to assign the attributes of the style class to that object. For example, as part of the sample site on the companion CD ROM there is a style sheet that contains a class called *feedbackText*. We created this class to be able to assign the same attributes to most of our feedback layers throughout the samples. One change to the class changes all objects that use that class throughout the site.

Follow these steps to create a style class in a style sheet that is already attached to a Dreamweaver page:

1   Open the CSS Styles panel.

2   Click the **New Style** button at the bottom right of the panel.

3   Type a period (.) and the new style class name in the Name drop down box (the period prefix defines this style as a class):

The period (.)
prefix

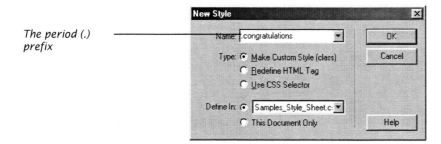

4   Click **OK**.

Dreamweaver displays the Style Definition window.

5   Choose the attribute definitions you want to apply to this style and click OK.

Dreamweaver lists your new style in the CSS Styles panel:

Dreamweaver
displays your
new style

You now have a new style class!

Using Styles to Ensure Consistent Visual Design

The most common reason to use styles with CourseBuilder is to ensure consistent design. After all, ensuring consistent design is what styles are for.

To ensure consistent design, you may want to apply style classes to the interaction question text as well as any text that may be part of the different elements of the interaction (such as distracters in a Multiple Choice question).

By default, CourseBuilder does not apply any formatting to the text that appears with an interaction. The text appears in the default type face the browser is set to.

Applying Styles to Interaction Question Text

In most cases, you can't apply a style to text in the CourseBuilder Interaction window—you have to do it on the Dreamweaver page.

Follow these steps to apply a style to the question text of an interaction:

1   On the Dreamweaver page, select the question text:

Selected question text

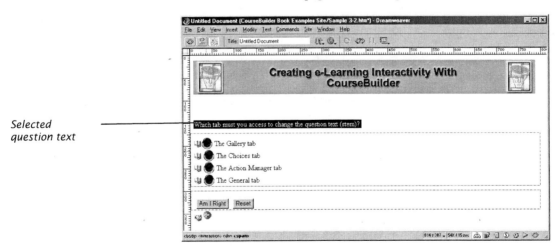

2   Open the CSS Styles panel (Windows→CSS Styles).

3   On the CSS Styles panel click the style you want to apply:

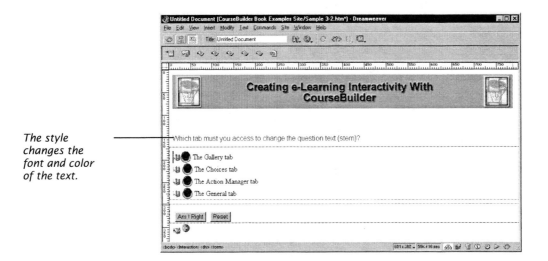

Dreamweaver immediately applies the style to the selected text:

The style changes the font and color of the text.

Applying Styles to Other Text or Objects

You may want to apply styles to other elements of an interaction. For example, in a Multiple Choice question, you may want the choice text to acquire the attributes of a particular style.

Tip: You also may want to apply a style to the **Submit** and **Reset** buttons to format the text color, background color, etc. You apply styles to **Submit** and **Reset** buttons the same way you apply styles to text. Select the button and click on the style you want to apply. Remember, to see some changes you'll need to preview the interaction in a browser.

To apply a style to other text in an interaction, select the text and follow the same steps you would for applying a style to the question text. Repeat the steps for each element to which you want the style applied.

Using Styles to Enhance User Input/Interaction Areas

Some interactions use default form objects to receive learner input. For example, by default, Text Entry interactions use a generic form text field to receive the learner's answer. The non-graphical Multiple Choice interactions use form radio buttons and check boxes.

Note: You can apply styles to radio buttons and check boxes, but the style only applies to the area surrounding the button and check box. Unlike text input fields, the look of the radio button and checkbox does not change.

You can make an interaction appear cleaner and more inviting by applying styles to some of these areas.

In this section we'll apply styles to the question text, the text input field, and the **Submit** and **Reset** buttons in a Text Entry interaction.

More Information: To learn more about Text Entry and Multiple Choice interactions, see *Chapter 7: Text Entry Interactions* and *Chapter 3: Multiple Choice and True/False Interactions.*

As an example, by default a form text field is white and appears inset:

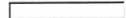

By applying a style, you can change the background color, the font color, and the borders. In this section you'll apply styles to the elements of an existing Text Entry interaction:

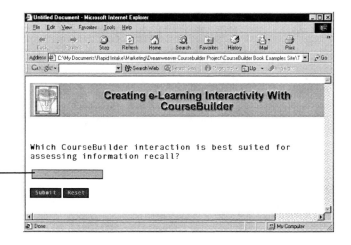

With the style applied the form has a different background color and border.

Viewing the Finished Interaction

Before creating this interaction, take a moment to view the completed example.

On CD: In Internet Explorer open *Sample_11-1.htm*. When finished viewing it in the browser, open it in Dreamweaver (this exercise was designed for Internet Explorer—you may experience some differences if using another browser).

Note: Please note that not all styles are supported by all browsers. Internet Explorer has traditionally supported more style attributes than Netscape.

Here are some things to look for when viewing this example:

- What color is the border of the text field?
- What color is the background of the text field?
- Type an answer in the text field. How far does the text indent from the left side of the text field?
- What other elements on the page have styles applied to them?
- In Dreamweaver, what color are the borders and background?

Creating this Interaction

In this section you'll create the interaction you just finished viewing.

Follow these steps to attach styles to existing elements of CourseBuilder interactions:

Note: All but one of the styles need for this exercise has already been created for you.

1 In Dreamweaver, open *Sample_11-1_Start.htm* (this exercise was designed for Internet Explorer—you may experience some differences if using another browser).

2 Apply the *textEntryInstructions* style class to the question text (we've already created this style for you).

3 Apply the *submitButton* style class to the Submit and Reset buttons (we already created this style for you too).

4 Create a new style class called *textField*:

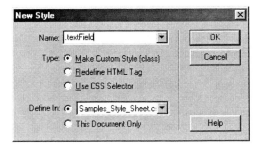

5 Click **OK**.

6 In the *Type* category, set the Font to *Andale Mono, Ariel.*

7 In the *Background* category, set the Background Color to *#00FF99.*

8 In the *Block* category, set the Text Indent to *3.*

9   In the Border category, select these settings:

Attribute	Value
Top	**Width** – thin **Color** – #006633
Right	**Width** – thin **Color** – #006633
Bottom	**Width** – thin **Color** – #006633
Left	**Width** – thin **Color** – #006633
Style	Solid

10   Click **OK**.

Dreamweaver displays the new style, *textField*, in the CSS Styles panel:

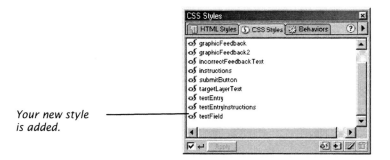

Your new style
is added.

11   Click the *Text Entry* field to select it.

12   Click the *textField* style in the CSS Styles panel.

Dreamweaver applies the style to the text field:

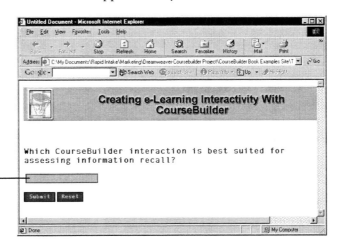

With the style applied the form has a different background color and border.

 Note: Even though Dreamweaver applies the style to the text field, it only displays some of the attributes of the style in Dreamweaver design view. To see all of the style attributes, you have to view the page in a browser.

Using Styles to Create 3-D Appearances and Manipulate the Cursor

One of the effects you can produce by using styles is a three-dimensional appearance. By creating a style with certain border colors, a layer can appear raised or inset. This can be especially useful for Drag-and-Drop interactions.

 More Information: To learn more about Drag-and-Drop interactions, see *Chapter 4: Drag-and-Drop Interactions.*

If you choose to use text-based drag and target elements (instead of graphics), you can use styles to create the appearance of a 3-D drag object that looks raised off the page and a 3-D target object that looks inset. This works well for Drag-and-Drop exercises such as matching terms with definitions.

Viewing the Finished Interaction

Before creating this interaction, take a moment to view the completed example.

On CD: In a browser, open *Sample_11-2.htm* and try this interaction (this exercise was designed for Internet Explorer—you may experience some differences if using another browser).

When viewing this interaction, here are some things to look for:

- What is it about the drag layers that make them look raised?
- What is it about the target layers that make them look inset?
- When do you receive feedback in this interaction?

Creating this Interaction

In this section you will apply styles that will create a three-dimensional appearance to an existing Drag-and-Drop interaction.

Follow these steps to create a 3-D appearance using styles:

1 In Dreamweaver, open *Sample_11-2_Start.htm* (this exercise was designed for Internet Explorer—you may experience some differences if using another browser).

We've already created the interaction for you, as well as a table of definitions. You will edit the interaction and create styles to apply to the drag and target layers:

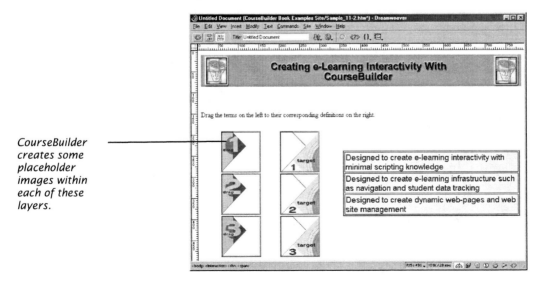

CourseBuilder creates some placeholder images within each of these layers.

2   Delete the placeholder images in the drag and target layers by clicking each image and pressing the DELETE key.

After you delete a placeholder image, the layer is still there, but its size shrinks to a small square.

Resized layer without the placeholder h image.

3   In the first drag layer enter *Dreamweaver.*

4   In the second drag layer enter *CourseBuilder.*

5   In the third drag layer enter *Learning Site.* You may need to resize this layer so the text fits horizontally without wrapping:

First drag layer

Second drag layer

Third drag layer

6   In the Properties panel (Windows→Properties), set the width of all drag and target layers to *130*.

Making the drag and target layers the same size makes it easier for the learner to know where to drop the drag elements.

7   Create a new style class called *.dragLayer*.

New Style	
Name: .dragLayer	OK
Type: ⦿ Make Custom Style (class) ○ Redefine HTML Tag ○ Use CSS Selector	Cancel
Define In: ⦿ Samples_Style_Sheet.c ○ This Document Only	Help

8   Click **OK**.

Dreamweaver displays the Style Definition window.

9   In the *Type* category, specify these attributes:

Attribute	Value
Font	Verdana
Size	14
Color	#FFFCC

10   In the Background category, set the *Color* to *#6600CC*.

11   In the Block category, set the *Text Align* attribute to *Center*.

The next step is to create the 3-D effect. Take a moment to look at these buttons, found at the bottom of the Style Definition window:

Cancel	Apply	Help

The illusion of lighting makes the buttons look raised. The top and left borders are lighter and the bottom and right borders are darker. So all we need to do to create the 3-D *raised* effect is to do the same thing to our drag layers.

12 In the Border category, specify these settings:

Attribute	Value
Top	**Width** – thin **Color** – #CCCCCC
Right	**Width** – thin **Color** – #000000
Bottom	**Width** – thin **Color** – #000000
Left	**Width** – thin **Color** – #CCCCCC
Style	Solid

Since we are defining the styles that we will apply to the drag layers, we need to take something else into consideration. When learners places their mouse over the drag layer, we want them to know they can click and drag it. The default cursor for a draggable layer is a vertical cursor indicating they can select text. It makes more sense to the learner if the cursor turns into the hand pointer when the mouse is placed over the layer.

You can change the cursor by choosing an Extensions style attribute.

13 In the Extension category, choose *Hand* from the **Cursor** drop down list:

```
Style Definition for .dragLayer in Samples_Style_Sheet.css          [×]

 Category:              Extensions
 Type
 Background                               Page Break
 Block
 Box                               *Before: [          ▼]
 Border
 List                              *After:  [          ▼]
 Positioning
 Extensions
                                          Visual Effect

                                  *Cursor: [hand      ▼]

                                  *Filter: [            ▼]



                          * Indicates styles not currently displayed in Dreamweaver.


                          [  OK  ]  [ Cancel ]  [ Apply ]  [ Help ]
```

Choosing "hand" causes the cursor to change to a hand when the mouse is placed over the object to which the style is applied.

14 Click **OK** to accept the style definition settings.

15 Apply the *dragLayer* style class to each drag layer by selecting the layer and clicking *dragLayer* in the CSS Styles panel (Windows→CSS Styles).

Again, you may need to resize the layers so the text fits horizontally.

Note: Dreamweaver cannot display border styles. To view them you need to preview the page in a browser.

16 Preview the page in a browser to see the 3-D effect applied to the drag layers.

Your drag layer buttons should now look like this when viewed in a browser:

The color of the borders makes these Drag layers look like raised buttons.

> Dreamweaver

> CourseBuilder

> Learning Site

Now you need to create the style for the target layers.

17 Right-click on the *dragLayer* style and choose Duplicate.

Dreamweaver displays the Duplicate Style window with *.dragLayerCopy* displayed as the name.

18 Name the new style *.targetLayer*.

Rename the style to ".targetLayer".

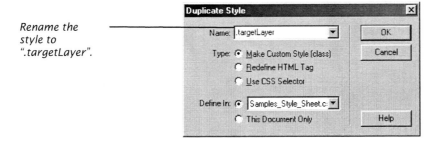

19 Click **OK** to close the Duplicate Style window.

Dreamweaver displays the new style in the CSS Styles panel (Windows→CSS Styles):

Your new style

20 Right click on the *targetLayer* style and choose Edit.

Dreamweaver displays the Style Definition window.

21 Change the ***Background Color*** to #FFFFCC.

Now all you need to do is change the borders so the style creates an "inset" or "sunken" appearance.

22 Set the attributes of the Border category according to this table:

Attribute	Value
Top	**Width** – thin **Color** – #000000
Right	**Width** – thin **Color** – #CCCCCC
Bottom	**Width** – thin **Color** – #CCCCCC
Left	**Width** – thin **Color** – #000000
Style	Solid

23 In the Extensions category, delete *Hand* from the Cursor drop down box by selecting the text within the drop down box with your mouse and pressing the DELETE key.

24 Apply the *targetLayer* style to the target layers.

All that remains to do is reposition the drag and target layers near the definitions.

25 Reposition the layers so they look like this:

26 Preview the interaction in the browser.

Follow-up

Now that you've completed the step-by-step instructions, here are a couple of other things to be aware of regarding this specific interaction.

The reason this interaction displays correct or incorrect feedback when you drop the drag layers is for these two reasons:

- We set the *Judge Interaction* setting to *when the user drops a drag element*.
- We set the *Correct When* setting to a*ny correct and None incorrect*.

By choosing both of these options the interactions displays correct feedback when you drop a single drag layer on the correct target layer—it considers the whole interaction correct.

Using Styles to Enhance Feedback

In several Section I chapters we discussed using the Set Text of Layer action in the Action Manager to display feedback (see also *Chapter 13: Customizing the Action Manager Tab*). You can make the Set Text of Layer action even more useful by applying a style to the layer.

In this tutorial we edit an existing Multiple Choice interaction and enhance the feedback by applying one style to correct feedback and a different style to incorrect feedback.

Viewing the Finished Interaction

Before creating the interaction, take a moment to view the completed example.

On CD: In a browser, open *Sample_11-3.htm* and try the interaction (this exercise was designed for Internet Explorer—you may experience some differences if using another browser).

Here are some things to look for while viewing the interaction:

- What color is the feedback when you get the correct answer?
- What happens to the feedback when you get the incorrect answer?

- What action do you think we're using in the Action Manager to show the feedback?

Creating this Interaction

In this section we'll dynamically add styles to the feedback text, using the **Set Text of Layer** action, so that the correct feedback displays differently than the incorrect feedback.

Follow these steps to use styles with the *Set Text of Layer* action:

1 In Dreamweaver, open *Sample_11-3_Start.htm* (this exercise was designed for Internet Explorer—you may experience some differences if using another browser).

The interaction on this page is a Multiple Choice interaction using graphics. We've already created the interaction as well as added a layer called *Feedback*. We've also created two styles: *feedbackText* and *incorrectFeedbackText*.

2 Edit the interaction.

3 Click the Action Manager tab:

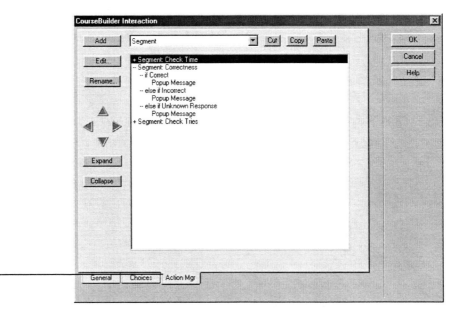

Action Manager tab

4 Click *Popup Message* under *if Correct* to select it.

5 Click the **Cut** button.

6 Choose *Set Text of Layer* from the action drop down list.

7 Click the **Add** button.

CourseBuilder displays the Set Text of Layer window:

Choose the correct layer from this drop down list.

8 Make sure *layer "Feedback"* is selected in the *Layer* drop down list.

You're not only going to set the text of the layer, but assign the correct style to the layer as well.

Tip: Even though the name of this action is *Set Text of Layer,* you are really replacing the entire HTML of the layer. This means you can enter HTML and JavaScript in the New HTML field.

9 Enter this text in the *New HTML* field:
*<p class = "feedbackText">Good job! That's right.
Always make sure that you're going to insert the interaction into the body of the document. If you're not careful, it's easy to insert it into another layer on the page or into an existing interaction.</p>*

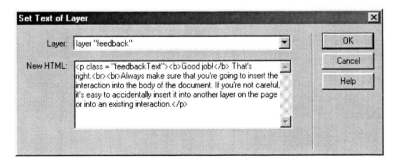

The *class = "correctFeedback"* portion of the HTML assigns the style to the text that follows. The *<b>* tag bolds the text it surrounds. The *
* tag inserts a line break.

More Information: You may want to reference one of the hundreds of books and excellent online sources on HTML for more details about tags and styles.

10 Click **OK** to close the Set Text of Layer window.

11 Click *Popup Message* under *if Incorrect* to select it.

12 Click the **Cut** button.

13 Choose *Set Text of Layer* from the action drop down list.

14 Click **Add**.

15 Make sure *layer "Feedback"* is selected in the **Layer** drop down list.

16 Enter this text in the **New HTML** field:
<p class = "incorrectFeedbackText"><b>Sorry!</b> That's incorrect.</p>

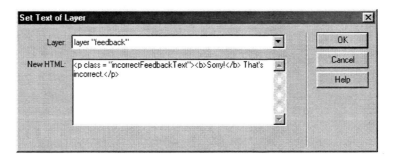

17 Click **OK** to close the Set Text of Layer window.

18 Click **OK** to close the CourseBuilder interaction window.

19 Try the interaction in a browser.

As you can see, applying a style to feedback requires some knowledge of HTML. But as you also experienced, you can drastically change the way the feedback text appears.

Summary

In this chapter you learned how to add styles to the question text and other elements of the interaction. We also discussed how to use styles to add certain effects (such as 3-D) and how to use styles to enhance learner feedback.

As you work with styles, remember that some styles are only supported by certain browsers. Internet Explorer appears to support more styles than Netscape browsers.

There are certainly many more ways you can use styles with CourseBuilder, but this chapter hopefully started your creative wheels turning.

The Action Manager: An Overview **12**

Even if this is the first chapter you're reading in this book, you've probably come across the Action Manager as you've worked with CourseBuilder. If you've read all of our preceding chapters then you've already used the Action Manager in some of our earlier tutorials that were specific to certain interactions.

In the settings for each CourseBuilder interaction there is an Action Manager tab. There is also an Action Manager interaction object in the CourseBuilder Gallery.

In this chapter you will learn:

- The difference between the Action Manager tab and the Action Manager object.
- How to use the building blocks of the Action Manager: segments, conditions, and actions.
- About the different Action Manager actions that are available.
- Action Manager basics by editing an existing Action Manager decision tree.

The Action Manager Tab vs. the Action Manager Object

The first thing to know about the Action Manager is that it offers you tremendous power and flexibility when creating interactive e-learning. Once you understand all of the elements of the Action Manager and how to use them, there is virtually no limit to the kinds of interactions you can create with CourseBuilder.

The second thing to know about the Action Manager is that the Action Manager *object* and the Action Manager *tab* are not the same thing! Even though they are named the same, they serve two very different purposes. In this chapter you'll learn what the purposes of each are and how they differ.

The Action Manager Tab

Before tackling the Action Manager interaction object, you should become familiar with the Action Manager tab:

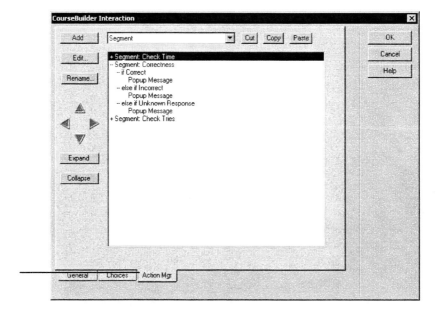

Action Manager tab

Every interaction has an Action Manager Tab. Once you understand the Action Manager tab, you will have an easier time mastering the Action Manager object.

What is it for?

When a learner interacts with a CourseBuilder question (i.e. they choose a response, they press the **Submit** button, they drag and drop an object, etc.), CourseBuilder must decide what to do next. In a nutshell, the Action Manager tab contains all of the instructions that tell CourseBuilder what to do in response to a learner's interaction.

For example, when the learner chooses a response, CourseBuilder has to determine if it is the correct response. It also has to decide what to do if the learner selected the correct response or the incorrect response. The Action Manager tab for each interaction takes care of all this. Of course, it can also be customized, which is why it can be so powerful.

Why does it look so complicated?

What you're seeing when you look at the contents of the Action Manager tab are the brains behind the interaction. Even though you don't have to know how to program JavaScript or another language to use CourseBuilder, the Action Manager tab uses programming logic to make decisions about how to handle what the learner is doing.

We'll call the contents of the Action Manager tab a "decision tree." To tell CourseBuilder how to make the right decisions and do the right things, you need to follow a specific order and format (also called "syntax").

Macromedia has made the interface fairly easy to use and you won't have to type any real code if you don't want to (and for those that do, lookup the ***Call JavaScript*** action in the index). With a little practice you'll be customizing interactions in no time.

So what can I do with it?

Use the Action Manager tab to customize the interactivity of a CourseBuilder interaction for your particular needs. For example, most CourseBuilder interactions show feedback by popping-up a JavaScript alert window. Using the Action Manager tab you could change any interaction to show the feedback in a layer, or a frame, or in a text field instead. Other possibilities include showing response-specific feedback or showing progressive feedback (sometimes called "layered feedback").

 More Information: For more information on customizing feedback, see *Chapter 13: Customizing the Action Manager Tab.*

Beyond feedback, other uses include:

- Controlling the number of tries allowed per interaction.
- Controlling the amount of time allowed per interaction.
- Branching to other parts of the course for remediation based on learner responses.
- Forcing the learner to follow a sequential order in an Explore interaction.
- Many other uses you'll discover as you work through the rest of this book.

These are all applications of the concepts you'll learn in this and the following chapters on the Action Manager. Who knows, you might even come up with ways to use the Action Manager that no one has thought of before!

The Action Manager Object

In the CourseBuilder Gallery, you'll find a category called Action Manager. This category contains only one interaction: the Action Manager:

Action Manager category

Think of the Action Manager object as an external tool you can use to manipulate other interactions.

The Action Manager object carries the same name as the Action Manager tab, and that causes a little confusion. Remember, the Action Manager *tab* controls the interactivity within any given interaction. Every CourseBuilder interaction has an Action Manager tab (in fact, even the Action Manager object has its own Action Manager tab). On the other hand, the Action Manager *object* can affect many different interactions.

For example, suppose you want the learner to answer a series of questions all on the same page, but you don't want to score them or show any feedback until the learner has completed all of the questions on the page. The specific feedback for each question would be handled in the Action Manager tab of each question, but checking to make sure the learner has answered all of the questions and calculating the total score would be handled using an Action Manager object.

 More Information: You can find more information on setting up and scoring a multi-question quiz in *Chapter 14: The Power of the Action Manager Object.*

Another way to think of the Action Manager object is to think of it as an entire *page tool* whereas the Action Manager tab is a single *interaction tool*. The decision-making logic in the Action Manager object can reach any interaction on the page, whereas the Action Manager tab is used mainly to change the interactivity for only that specific interaction.

Action Manager Building Blocks: Segments, Conditions, Actions

To effectively use the Action Manager, it's important to understand its basic building blocks:

- **Segments** define an area of the Action Manager devoted to one particular decision.
- **Conditions** decide what actions should take place based on learner responses to the interaction.
- **Actions** do things, such as popping up a message, displaying text in a layer, playing a Macromedia Flash movie, and so forth.

This image identifies the Action Manager building blocks:

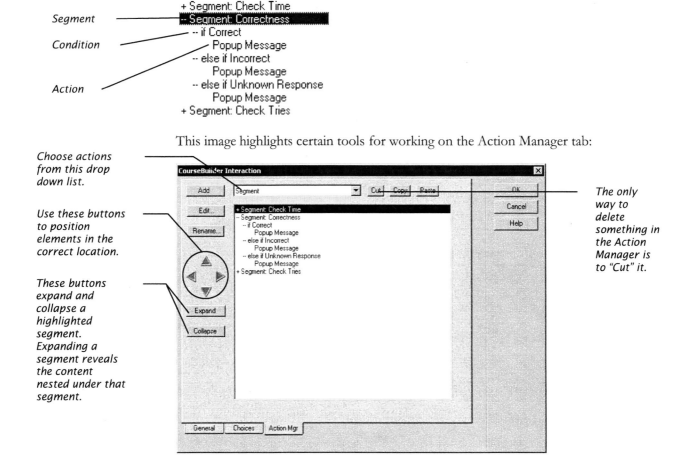

This image highlights certain tools for working on the Action Manager tab:

Segments

Segments define, or "rope off," an area of the action manager devoted to one particular decision. For example, you might name a segment "Correctness," "Limit Tries," "Limit Time," or "Verify Learner Answered All Questions." These examples are simply names that remind you what the intended purpose of that section of the Action Manager decision tree is for. Most CourseBuilder interactions come with some preset segments. Within a segment, conditions make the decisions and actions define what will happen based on the decisions.

In the example screen shot above, the segment we identify is called "Correctness".

Adding a Segment

Adding a segment is easy. Defining what is in the segment can be more challenging.

Follow theses steps to add a segment:

1 Choose *Segment* from the drop down list at the top of the Action Manager tab.

2 Click **Add**.

CourseBuilder displays the Segment Editor window:

This table defines the option in this window:

Attribute	Value
Segment Name	This name appears in the Action Manager tab. Name the segment something relevant so it is easy to understand the purpose later

Attribute	Value
Segment Evaluation	***Always evaluate from the beginning –*** whenever the interaction is judged, the action manager gets processed. This setting tells CourseBuilder to process this segment from the beginning of the segment to the end of the segment every time the interaction gets judged. In other words, if the learner interacts more than once (answers twice for example), this setting will ensure that the segment reacts the same way each time. You will almost always use the *Always evaluate from the beginning* option. ***State Transition*** - this setting tells CourseBuilder to process the segment from the beginning until it finds a condition that is true. It processes that condition, then stops. The next time the interaction is judged, CourseBuilder *remembers* that the condition had already been met and skips it and goes on to the next.

3   Enter the name of the segment in the Segment Name field.

4   Choose the ***Segment Evaluation*** setting.

5   Click **OK**.

More Information: See *Chapter 13: Customizing the Action Manager Tab* and *Chapter 14: The Power of the Action Manager Object* to work through tutorials that use segments.

Conditions

Conditions make decisions. They decide which actions take place based on learner interactions. A condition always asks the question "If the learner does such and such…?"

For example, if the learner clicks the "Am I Right?" button, what should happen? If the learner clicks "Am I Right?" but didn't answer the question, what should happen? If the learner drops an element of a drag and drop exercise onto a wrong answer, what should happen? If the learner clicks the "Reset Question" button, what should happen? If the learner clicks the "Show Correct Answer" button, what should happen?

Obviously the list could go on and on. Conditions are the "artificial intelligence" behind how the interaction will respond to the learner. In a large part, they are what make the interaction intriguing.

In this example screen, the condition we've identified is called "Correct":

The name of this condition is "Correct". The "if" is inserted by CourseBuilder.

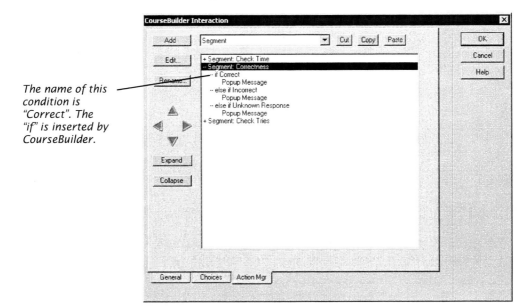

Adding Conditions

Adding your own conditions exploits the real potential of the Action Manager. By customizing the action manager with your own criteria you can create interactions that meet your specific needs.

Follow these steps to add an Action Manager condition:

1   Choose ***Condition*** from the drop down list at the top of the Action Manager tab.

2   Click **Add**.

CourseBuilder displays the Condition Editor window:

If you are trying to test a specific interaction element, choose the specific choice here.

Choose the comparison operator (equals/not equals)

This table explains the options of the Condition Editor window:

Setting	Description
Condition Name	This name appears in the Action Manager tab. Name the condition something relevant so it is easy to understand the purpose later
Expression	This field displays the condition that must be met for the Action Manager to continue. CourseBuilder automatically populates this field as you choose specify other settings in this window.

Setting	Description
Type	Choose the type of condition. **Interaction** – Choose this type when you are testing a property of the interaction (such as a specific choice selected). **Action Manager** – Choose this type when you want to test a segment of an Action Manager tab. **Document Tag** – Choose this type to test properties of an HTML object on the page (such as the visibility of a layer, or a value in a text field). If you choose this type you also have to select the object on the page you are testing. **JavaScript** – Choose this type to enter your own JavaScript condition (such as *myVariable == "TRUE"*).
Interaction	Choose the interaction that must meet the condition. The first drop down list displays the interactions on the page. The second drop down list displays the elements of that interaction (i.e. for a multiple choice, the individual buttons). You can create a condition that tests the property of the entire interaction or a property of a single element of the interaction.
Property	Choose the property you are testing from the drop down list. This list changes based on what you choose for the *Interaction* setting.
Type (2nd)	The Type setting at the bottom of the window is the type of value you are comparing to. You have several options here, but CourseBuilder usually displays the appropriate one based on the Interaction and properties you choose above. The second drop down list under Type contains the actual value you are comparing to.

3   Choose the appropriate settings on the Condition Editor window.

4   Click **OK**.

More Information: See *Chapter 13: Customizing the Action Manager Tab* and Chapter 14: *The Power of the Action Manager Object* to learn more about conditions.

Actions

Actions cannot make decisions—they act! An action almost always follows a condition. If the condition were *if the learner clicks the Reset Question button* then the action might be *reset the CourseBuilder interaction.*

This action is called Popup Message

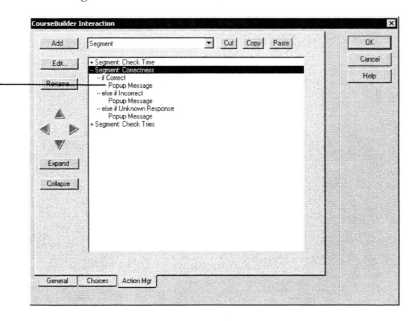

One of CourseBuilder's nicest features is that all Dreamweaver behaviors are available to you as actions. This includes behaviors you may have added as extensions to Dreamweaver, often created by third parties.

Triggering Actions

Being able to trigger actions based on what happens elsewhere on the page is what makes a web page interactive and dynamic.

Actions can be triggered by something on the Action Manager tab or outside of CourseBuilder interaction altogether using Dreamweaver Behaviors. Actions can be triggered in several different ways:

- When the learner responds to the interaction by clicking a choice, dragging an object, etc.
- When the learner clicks a button.
- By meeting a condition in the Action Manager.

- By an event on a Dreamweaver timeline (such as reaching a certain frame).
- By any JavaScript event listed in the Dreamweaver Behavior's panel:

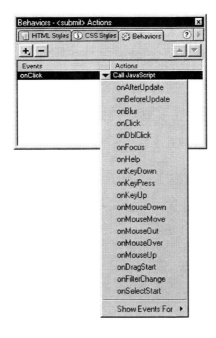

 More Information: In this book we primarily focus on using actions from within CourseBuilder interactions. You may want to look at a good Dreamweaver guide for information on how to use actions outside of CourseBuilder.

Choosing Actions

You choose an action from the drop-down list at the top of the dialog box:

Actions drop down list

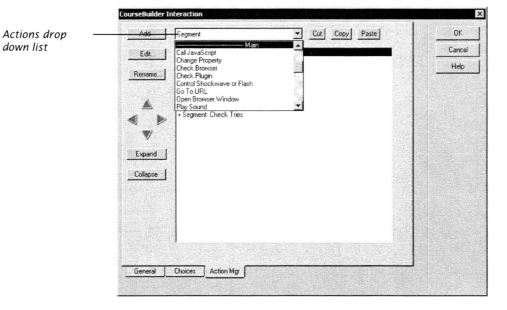

This list of actions determines what you can customize with CourseBuilder. Generally speaking, if it isn't in this list, you can't do it with CourseBuilder. (The exception to this rule is if you use the ***Call JavaScript*** action, which opens up a lot of extra customization beyond what CourseBuilder provides "out of the box".

More Information: See *Chapter 13: Customizing the Action Manager Tab* for some good examples using the Call JavaScript action with CourseBuilder. Also see Call JavaScript in the Index.

The items in the action drop down list are divided into seven categories, separated by dashed text and a category name. The first four items (Segment, Condition, Else, Stop) are used to create Action Manager segments and conditions. The remaining items are actions.

The following table describes each action in the order that they appear in the drop-down box. The first column lists the action in the drop-down list, the second column provides a brief description, and the third column gives you the page number later in this book where you can find an example of this action in use:

Action	Description
CourseBuilder	
Judge Interaction	Executes everything in the Action Manager tab for a specific interaction.
Reset Interaction	Clears settings and learner input for a specific interaction, elements within an interaction, or Action Manager segments that are tracking state transitions
Set Interaction Properties	Sets properties of a specific interaction or an action manager segment. You set properties by selecting specific properties and setting values, or you can use JavaScript.
Main (these are general Dreamweaver behaviors)	
Call JavaScript	Type in a specific JavaScript command or call a JavaScript function.
Change property	Set the property of any object on the HTML page.
Check Browser	Route a navigation path to different locations based on the browser type.
Check Plugin	Checks for a specific plug-in, such as the Macromedia Flash player, and routes navigation based on whether or not it exists.
Control Shockwave or Flash	Plays, stops, rewinds, or goes to a frame in a Shockwave or Flash movie.
Go to URL	Opens a new page in the current window or frame.
Open Browser Window	"Pops-up" a new browser window according to the dimensions and attributes specified.

Action	Description
Play Sound	Plays a designated sound file. Also, see the Caution statement following this table.
Popup Message	Displays JavaScript alert with your text. You can embed JavaScript in your text.
Show-Hide Layers	Shows/Hides layers in the current window or in other frames—excellent for visual interaction.
Swap Image	Swaps one image for another by changing the *src* attribute of the *<img>* tag. Another good choice for visual interaction. May want to use with Swap Image Restore.
Swap Image Restore	Restores an image that was replaced with the Swap Image action.
Validate Form	Checks contents of text fields to make sure the learner has entered the correct type of data.
Set Text (these are general Dreamweaver behaviors)	
Set Text of Frame	Replaces not only the text, but also the entire HTML of a frame—an alternative way to display feedback.
Set Text of Layer	Replaces not only the text, but also the entire HTML of a layer. This is our preferred way to show feedback.
Set Text of Status Bar	Shows a message in the status bar at the bottom left of the browser window (where you normally see URL information when you place your mouse over a link).
Set Text of Text Field	Replaces the text of an input text field with the text you specify.
Timeline (these are general Dreamweaver behaviors)	
Go to Timeline Frame	Moves a Dreamweaver timeline playback head to a specific frame.

Action	Description
Play Timeline	Starts a Dreamweaver timeline.
Stop Timeline	Stops a Dreamweaver timeline.
Tracking *	
Send Interaction Info	Send specific information to a server running a Learning Management System (LMS). Tracking was specifically designed to communicate with LearningSpace® but should work with any AICC-compliant LMS.
Send Lesson Status	Sends status of a lesson or group of interactions to an LMS.
Send Lesson Time	Sends how long it took a learner to complete a lesson or group of interactions to an LMS.
Send Objective Info	Sends information about the object or lesson objective, as specified on the Tracking tab of the CourseBuilder Interaction dialog box, to an LMS.
Send Score	Sends the score for an individual interaction or for a lesson (group of interactions) to an LMS.

Note: These actions refer to settings on the Tracking tab. To see the tracking tab you must choose the Knowledge Track option on the General tab.

Tip: The items in this table and the order they appear are based on the html document *ActionMenu.htm* (usually found at c:\program files\macromedia\Dreamweaver 4\CourseBuilder\Config). You can move the items you use most to the top of the list by editing this document.

Caution: When using the Play Sound action, be careful as different browsers and different end-user machines may be set up to play sounds differently than yours. See Appendix D: *Using Media With CourseBuilder.*

Adding an Action

To add an action to the Action Manager, choose the action from the drop down list at the top of the Action Manager tab and click the **Add** button. Each action displays a different window with different settings.

More Information: See *Chapter 13: Customizing the Action Manager Tab* and Chapter 14: *The Power of the Action Manager Object* to work through tutorials that use actions.

Getting Started

The easiest way to get your feet wet in the Action Manager is to simply change an existing action. Almost every CourseBuilder interaction comes preset with some Segments, Conditions, and Actions. Probably the most common use of the Action Manager is to provide feedback. CourseBuilder's preset feedback is to pop-up some text.

To practice using the action manager, follow these steps to change the text in a sample interaction:

1 Create a Multiple Choice interaction on a blank Dreamweaver page.

2 Click on the Action Manager tab.

3 Under the condition *if Correct* click on the *Popup Message* line and click the Edit button.

4 Change the text to: *Way to go! You got it right* (or whatever text you like).

5 Click **OK** to go back to the Dreamweaver page and try out the interaction in the browser. Of course you'll have to answer the question correctly to see your change.

CourseBuilder displays your feedback:

Microsoft Internet Explorer
⚠ Way to go! You got it right!
OK

This is a very simple use of the Action Manager. To become more proficient, make sure to complete the tutorials in Chapter 13 and Chapter 14.

 More Information: See *Chapter 13: Customizing the Action Manager Tab* for many other hands-on exercises as well as more elegant ways of displaying feedback.

Summary

The Action Manager tab and Action Manager object are different, even though they use the same elements: segments, conditions, and actions. The difference is really their scope—the Action Manager tab affects only that particular interaction, whereas the Action Manager object is generally used to manipulate other CourseBuilder interactions on the same page.

To learn more about the Action Manager and how to apply what you've learned in this chapter, take a look at these chapters:

- Chapter 13: *Customizing the Action Manager Tab*
- Chapter 14: *The Power of the Action Manager Object*
- Chapter 16: *Behind the Scenes: Deciphering CourseBuilder's JavaScript*

Also see the Unique Enhancements section of each chapter in Section I for enhancements that might use the Action Manager

Customizing the Action Manager Tab **13**

If you've worked through the tutorials in the preceding chapters, you've already been introduced to the Action Manager. As we discussed in Chapter 12, the Action Manager tab is mainly used to control what happens within a single interaction. To control what happens *between* interactions or to control all of the interactions on a page, use the Action Manager object (see Chapter 14).

To learn the Action Manager tab or object, it is best to work with it in some kind of relevant context. In this chapter you will learn how to deliver feedback to the learner using different methods by manipulating the contents of the Action Manager tab. You will also enhance an Explore interaction (see Chapter 5) using the Action Manager to create a mandatory exploring order.

In this chapter you will learn how to:

- Show feedback in a layer by using the ***Set Text of Layer*** action.
- Provide specific feedback for different question distracters.
- Provide feedback for a partially correct response.
- Provide multiple layers of feedback (i.e. a hint the first time the learner responds incorrectly, a less subtle hint the second time, and a link to the correct answer the third time).
- Branch to a specific part of the course for remediation when the learner responds incorrectly.
- Create an ordered Explore interaction (see Chapter 5).

Showing Feedback in a Layer

Once you've experienced feedback delivered via the JavaScript popup message box several times, you may start looking for more elegant ways to display feedback. The popup message box serves its purpose, but the beeping and the caution sign may be less "friendly" than you want.

There isn't much you can do to change the popup message box—its functionality is built into the browser functionality. However, you can choose to display your feedback in alternative ways. We suggest the cleanest way is to show the feedback in a layer.

Displaying feedback in a layer offers you these advantages:

- You don't annoy the learner with the JavaScript popup message box (our favorite benefit!).
- You can hide and show feedback at will using the Action Manager.
- You can swap graphics, text, and styles in and out of the layer to make the feedback more dynamic.
- You can display links to other areas of the course in a layer (for remediation).

To display feedback in a layer, use the ***Set Text of Layer*** action. When using the ***Set Text of Layer*** action:

- You must target 4.0 browsers or higher.
- Your page must contain at least one layer.
- You can show feedback that includes text, HTML, and JavaScript variables (for showing the score or other interaction information).

Viewing the Finished Interaction

Before creating this interaction, take a look at what you'll end up with by viewing the completed example.

On CD: Open *Sample_13-1.htm* in a browser.

Here are a few things to look for as you view this interaction:

- Where does the feedback appear?
- What color is the feedback?

- What other formatting do you notice about the feedback?

Creating this Interaction

In this hands-on exercise you'll set up feedback for correct and incorrect responses using the ***Set Text of Layer*** action.

Follow these steps to show feedback in a layer:

1   Open *Sample_13-1_Start.htm* in Dreamweaver and edit the interaction.

2   Click on the action *Popup Message* just beneath the *if Correct* condition:

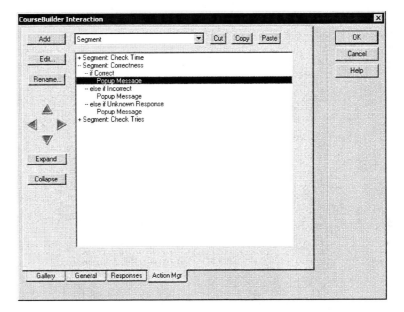

3   Click the **Cut** button.

Note: There is no **Delete** button in the Action Manager, so the only way to "delete" a line is to use the **Cut** button.

4   Click the *if Correct* condition to select it.

Note: Coursebuilder always adds segments, conditions, and actions beneath the current line. By clicking this condition, anything you add will appear directly beneath it.

5   Choose *Set Text of Layer* from the drop down list:

```
Segment                                  ▼
Swap Image Restore                       ▲
Validate Form
-------------------------- Set Text
Set Text of Frame
Set Text of Layer
Set Text of Status Bar
Set Text of Text Field
-------------------------- Timeline
Go To Timeline Frame                     ▼
```

6   Click the **Add** button.

Coursebuilder displays the Set Text of Layer dialog box.

7   Choose the correct layer from the drop down box. For this example, choose the layer called *Feedback*.

8   In the *New HTML* field, enter this text:

<font color=green>That's right!</font><p>You tell CourseBuilder which answers are correct and incorrect on the Choices tab.

The Set Text of Layer window should look like this:

```
┌─────────────────────────────────────────────────────────────────────┐
│ Set Text of Layer                                                  ⊠  │
│                                                                       │
│     Layer:  [layer "Feedback"                              ▼]  [ OK ] │
│                                                                       │
│  New HTML:  [<font color=green><b>That's right!</b></font><p> You tell│  [Cancel]
│             Coursebuilder which answers are correct and incorrect on  │
│             the <b>Choices</b> tab.                                   │  [ Help ]
│             [                                            ]            │
│                                                                       │
└─────────────────────────────────────────────────────────────────────┘
```

Notice that this sample feedback has HTML embedded within it. What you're doing is replacing the contents of the layer, not just replacing the text. So you can use HTML tags, JavaScript, and CSS styles along with whatever text you're entering.

Tip: Because the *Set Text of Layer* action allows you to embed HTML tags with the text, you could add images to your feedback by adding an *<img>* tag in the *New HTML* field and setting its *src* property to a graphic on your site or somewhere else on the web. See your favorite HTML reference for more information on the *<img>* tag.

9   Click the **OK** button to close the Set Text of Layer dialog box.

Now you'll set up the feedback for the *else if Incorrect* condition.

10 Delete (i.e. "cut") the *Popup Message* action beneath the *else if Incorrect* line and add the ***Set Text of Layer*** action (see Step 6 if you need help adding this action).

11 Enter this text in the ***New HTML*** field: *Sorry, that's incorrect.*

12 Click **OK** to close the Set Text of Layer window.

More Information: We use the Set Text of Layer action in several examples throughout this book. See *Set Text of Layer* in the index for references to more tutorials using this valuable action.

13 Click **OK** to close the Coursebuilder Interaction window.

14 When you try out your interaction in a browser you should see your new feedback appear in the *Feedback* layer:

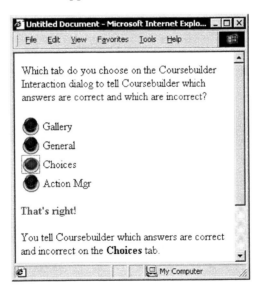

Providing Response–Specific Feedback

We all know you can't learn from your mistakes unless you know what you did wrong. That's as true for e-learning as it is for life. If a learner chooses an incorrect answer, it's often very useful to explain why it is incorrect. Unless you are designing a certification exam you may even want to give them a hint that would guide them to the right answer.

In this section you will learn to create conditions in the Action Manager that detect when the learner chooses a certain answer. You can then supply feedback specific to that response.

Viewing the Completed Interaction

Before creating this interaction, take a look at the completed example.

 On CD: Open *Sample_13-4.htm* in a browser.

Here are some things to look for as you view the interaction:

- What feedback do you get when you answer correctly?
- What feedback do you get when you answer incorrectly?
- How does the feedback differ from response to response?

Creating this Interaction

In this section you'll create the interaction you just viewed.

Follow these steps to create response-specific feedback:

1 Open *Sample_13-4_Start.htm* in Dreamweaver.

We've already created the interaction as well as a layer in which to display feedback.

2   Edit the interaction and click the Action Manager tab:

Replace these popup messages.

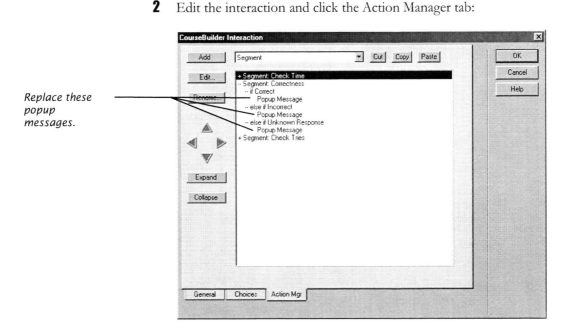

3   Replace the Popup Message action under *if Correct* with a ***Set Text of Layer*** action for the Feedback layer that says: *That's right. You set the question text on the General tab.*

   More Information: See *Showing Feedback in a Layer* earlier in this chapter for detailed instructions.

4   Remove the Popup Message under *else if Incorrect* by selecting it and clicking **Cut**.

To provide response-specific feedback, if the learner chooses an incorrect answer, you want to know which incorrect answer they chose. To find out you need to add a condition under *else If Incorrect* for each possible incorrect choice.

5   Choose *Condition* from the drop down list at the top of the window:

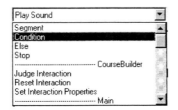

6   Click **Add**.

CourseBuilder displays the Condition Editor window:

7   Enter *Learner Chose Choice One* in the **Condition Name** field.

8   Choose *Interaction* for the **Type**.

9   Choose *MultCh_ImageRadios01* in the first **Interaction** drop down list.

10   Choose *Button "choice1"* from the second **Interaction** drop down list:

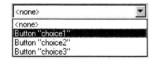

11   Choose *Selected* in the **Property** drop down list and *equals* in the drop down list just under it.

12   Choose *True/False* in the second **Type** drop down list and *True* in the drop down list just under it.

The expression in the **Expressions** field should now read: *Button "choice1" Selected equals True.*

CourseBuilder
displays the
entire
expression in
this field.

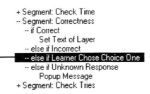

Condition Editor

Condition Name:	Learner Chose Choice One

Add   Delete

Expressions: Button "choice1" Selected equals True

Type: Interaction

Interaction: MultCh_ImageRadios01   Button "choice1"

Property: Selected

equals

Type: True/False

True

and

OK
Cancel
Help

This means that the *Selected* property of the interaction's first choice has to be true for this condition to be met. In other words, the learner has to select the first choice to meet this condition.

13 Click **OK** to close the Condition Editor window.

CourseBuilder displays the new condition:

```
+ Segment: Check Time
-- Segment: Correctness
   -- if Correct
       Set Text of Layer
   -- else if Incorrect
      -- else if Learner Chose Choice One
   -- else if Unknown Response
       Popup Message
+ Segment: Check Tries
```

Before the
condition is
indented.

14 With the condition still selected, click the **Indent** button ▷.

This indents the condition so that it is only evaluated when the *if Incorrect* condition is met:

```
+ Segment: Check Time
-- Segment: Correctness
   -- if Correct
       Set Text of Layer
   -- else if Incorrect
       -- if Learner Chose Choice One
   -- else if Unknown Response
       Popup Message
+ Segment: Check Tries
```

After the
condition is
indented.

Note: CourseBuilder changes the condition from *else if* to *if*. This indicates it is a new condition nested within the *if Incorrect* condition structure.

15 With *if Learner Chose Choice One* still selected, add a Set Text of Layer feedback message that reads:

The segment offsets all of the conditions and actions under it from other action manager segments, but it does not decide what action gets taken. Try again!

Now you're ready to create a condition that tests to see if the learner chose the third option. There's no need to recreate the next condition from scratch. Save yourself some time by copying and pasting.

Tip: CourseBuilder not only copies the current selection, but copies any actions or conditions nested under it. This really saves time because in many cases, as in this example, you may want to duplicate the same actions but with different settings.

16 Select *if Learner Chose Choice One* and click the **Copy** button.

17 With *if Learner Chose Choice One* still selected, click the **Paste** button.

CourseBuilder pastes the new condition and the action beneath it in the new location:

```
+ Segment: Check Time
-- Segment: Correctness
        Show-Hide Layers
    -- if Correct
            Set Text of Layer
    -- else if Incorrect
        -- if Learner Chose Choice One
                Set Text of Layer
        -- else if Learner Chose Choice One
                Set Text of Layer
    -- else if Unknown Response
            Popup Message
+ Segment: Check Tries
```

When you paste the condition, actions nested under it get pasted also.

Now we just need to edit the condition and action so that they are set up correctly for the third option.

18 With the second *else if Learner Chose Choice One* still selected, click **Edit**.

19 Change the **Condition Name** to *Learner Chose Choice Three* and change the interaction element selection to *Button "choice3"*:

Changing just the name won't change the functionality of the condition.

Make sure to change the interaction element selection.

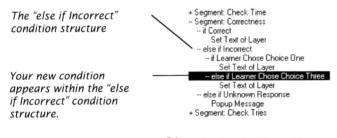

20 Click **OK** to close the Conditions Editor.

Your Action Manager tab should now look like this:

The "else if Incorrect" condition structure

Your new condition appears within the "else if Incorrect" condition structure.

```
+ Segment: Check Time
-- Segment: Correctness
    -- if Correct
        Set Text of Layer
    -- else if Incorrect
        -- if Learner Chose Choice One
            Set Text of Layer
        -- else if Learner Chose Choice Three
            Set Text of Layer
    -- else if Unknown Response
        Popup Message
+ Segment: Check Tries
```

21 Edit the *Set Text of Layer* action under *else if Learner Chose Choice Three* and change the message text to:

An Action is what takes place when the Action Manager makes a decision, but an action in and of itself cannot decide what to do. Try again!

The Set Text of Layer window should look like this:

> **Set Text of Layer**
>
> Layer: layer "Feedback"
>
> New HTML: An Action is what takes place when the Action Manager makes a decision, but an action in and of itself cannot decide what to do. Try again!
>
> OK
> Cancel
> Help

22 Click **OK** to close the Set Text of Layer window.

Finally, you need to make the Feedback layer appear when the interaction is judged, regardless of the response. You can do this by adding a ***Show-Hide Layers*** action in the Correctness segment before any of the if statements.

Note: You can tell the Feedback layer is initially hidden on the page because of the closed–eye symbol next to its name in the Layers panel (Windows→Layers):

> **Layers**
>
> Layers | Frames | History
>
> ☐ Prevent Overlaps
>
> | 👁 | Name | Z |
> |----|----------|---|
> | 👁 | Feedback | 3 |

Indicates the layer is hidden.

23 Click *Segment: Correctness* and add a ***Show-Hide Layers*** action.

CourseBuilder displays the Show-Hide Layers window:

> **Show-Hide Layers**
>
> Named Layers: layer "Feedback"
>
> Show | Hide | Default
>
> OK
> Cancel
> Help

24 With the *Feedback* layer selected, click the **Show** button:

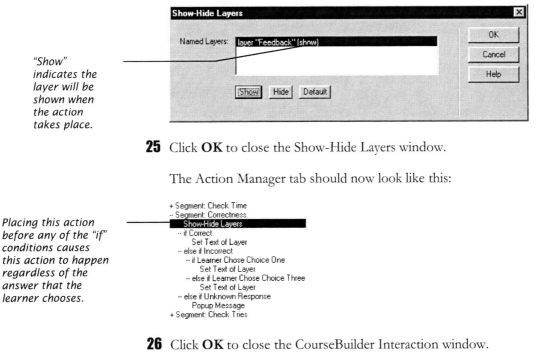

"Show" indicates the layer will be shown when the action takes place.

25 Click **OK** to close the Show-Hide Layers window.

The Action Manager tab should now look like this:

Placing this action before any of the "if" conditions causes this action to happen regardless of the answer that the learner chooses.

```
+ Segment: Check Time
-- Segment: Correctness
      Show-Hide Layers
   -- if Correct
        Set Text of Layer
   -- else if Incorrect
      -- if Learner Chose Choice One
           Set Text of Layer
      -- else if Learner Chose Choice Three
           Set Text of Layer
   -- else if Unknown Response
        Popup Message
+ Segment: Check Tries
```

26 Click **OK** to close the CourseBuilder Interaction window.

27 Test the interaction in a browser. Clicking each option should trigger a separate response.

In Review

Here are a few things to remember about this example. Our main goal was to deliver feedback that varied based on the learner's response. To accomplish this we made the Action Manager check first if the interaction was answered correctly. If it was, we responded with feedback for the correct answer. If the answer was not correct, we had it check to see which response they chose and display feedback for those specific responses.

Providing Feedback for a Partially Correct Response

Sometimes you may want to provide feedback for a partially correct responses. Giving this kind of feedback can help the learner make final distinctions between similar distracters. This type of feedback usually arises during interactions where there are multiple responses necessary by the learner, such as a "select all that apply" Multiple Choice interaction.

In this section you'll modify an existing interaction and add a condition in the Action manager to see if any correct responses are among the selected responses. If the correct response is among the learner's response but the entire interaction isn't correct, then you'll provide partial feedback.

Viewing the Finished Interaction

Before creating this interaction, take a look at the finished sample.

On CD: In a browser open *Sample_13-8.htm* (this exercise was designed for Internet Explorer—you may experience some differences if using another browser).

When you are viewing this interaction:

- Select all correct answers. What is the feedback?
- Select two correct answers. What is the feedback?
- Select two correct answers and the incorrect answer. What is the feedback?
- Select just the one incorrect answer. What is the feedback?

Creating this Interaction

Now let's create the interaction you just finished looking at.

Follow these steps to modify an existing interaction to provide feedback for partially correct responses:

1   In Dreamweaver, open *Sample_13-8_Start.htm* (this exercise was designed for Internet Explorer—you may experience some differences if using another browser).

Note: We've left the method of feedback as Popup Message simply to focus this exercise on how the action manager determines whether the learner gave a partially correct response or not. You can obviously change the method of feedback to use Set Text of Layer or whatever method you prefer. The conditions would remain the same.

2   Edit the interaction and click the Action Manager tab.

Start adding a condition after the *if Unknown Response* line:

```
+ Segment: Check Time
-- Segment: Correctness
   -- if Correct
         Popup Message
   -- else if Incorrect
         Popup Message
   -- else if Unknown Response
         Popup Message
+ Segment: Check Tries
```

Unknown
Response line

3   Click *if Unknown Response.*

4   Add a condition with settings from this table:

Property	Value
Condition Name	Partially Correct Response
Type	Interaction
Interaction	MultCh_ImageChkboxes
Interaction 2nd Dropdown	Button "choice1"
Property	Selected equals
Type	True/False
Type Value	True

Your condition should look like this:

Condition Editor	☒
Condition Name: Partially Correct Response	OK Cancel Help
Add Delete	
Expressions: Button "choice1" Selected equals True	
Type: Interaction	
Interaction: MultCh_ImageChkboxes▼ Button "choice1" ▼	
Property: Selected	
equals ▼	
Type: True/False ▼	
True ▼	
and ▼	

5   Now, choose "or" from the drop down list in the bottom right-hand corner:

or ▼
and
or

6   Click the **Add** button to add another test to this condition using the *or* operator.

The *Expressions* field should look like this:

This phrase of —————— Button "choice1" Selected equals True or
the expression   Correct State equals "Not Judged"
is added by
default.

7   Complete this test of the condition according to the values this table:

Property	Value
Type	Interaction
Interaction	MultCh_ImageChkboxes

Property	Value
Interaction 2nd Dropdown	Button "choice2"
Property	Selected equals
Type	True/False
Type Value	True

8   Click **Add** to add another *or* test with the values from this table:

Property	Value
Type	Interaction
Interaction	MultCh_ImageChkboxes
Interaction 2nd Dropdown	Button "choice4"
Property	Selected equals
Type	True/False
Type Value	True

Your *Expressions* field should now look like this:

```
Button "choice1" Selected equals True or
Button "choice2" Selected equals True or
Button "choice4" Selected equals True
```

By using *or,* you are checking to see if any of the responses are correct. If the learner chooses even one correct response, this expression will be True and you can supply partially correct response feedback.

9   Click **OK** to close the Condition Editor.

The Action Manager tab should look like this:

```
+ Segment: Check Time
-- Segment: Correctness
    -- if Correct
        Popup Message
    -- else if Incorrect
        Popup Message
    -- else if Unknown Response
        Popup Message
    -- else if Partially Correct Response
+ Segment: Check Tries
```

10 With *else if Partially Correct Response* still selected, add a Popup Message action with the message text: *That's partially correct. You have selected at least once correct answer. Please try again.*

The Action Manager tab should now look like this:

```
+ Segment: Check Time
-- Segment: Correctness
    -- if Correct
        Popup Message
    -- else if Incorrect
        Popup Message
    -- else if Unknown Response
        Popup Message
    -- else if Partially Correct Response
        Popup Message
+ Segment: Check Tries
```

If we stop here and try this interaction in a browser, the popup message you just entered would never be shown (go ahead and try it if you like). Do you know why? The reason lies in the order of the conditions in this tab.

Because of the *Correct When* setting on the General tab, this interaction only gets evaluated as correct if *all are correct and none incorrect*:

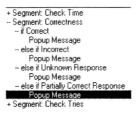

This means that if learners choose even one incorrect, then they will receive feedback under the *else if Incorrect* condition.

We could just delete that condition, but then if learners were to choose the one incorrect answer in this interaction they wouldn't receive any feedback at all. So the solution lies in editing the *else if Incorrect* condition.

11 Edit the *else if Incorrect* condition line.

Edit this condition.

```
+ Segment: Check Time
-- Segment: Correctness
  -- if Correct
       Popup Message
  -- else if Incorrect
       Popup Message
  -- else if Unknown Response
       Popup Message
  -- else if Partially Correct Reponse
       Popup Message
+ Segment: Check Tries
```

12 Change the condition so the ***Expression*** field reads (using similar techniques to those you used in steps 4-9):

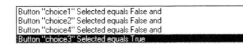

```
Button "choice1" Selected equals False and
Button "choice2" Selected equals False and
Button "choice4" Selected equals False and
Button "choice3" Selected equals True
```

By verifying that all correct responses are not selected (i.e. their *Selected* property is *False*), and at the same time verifying that the learner did select the third choice, we are sure that the only choice selected is the third choice. If we had created the condition so it simply read *Button 'choice3' Selected equals True,* then learners would receive the feedback for being incorrect even if they had selected other choices as well. In this case we want the learners to receive a different kind of feedback for those responses that include an incorrect response, but are not entirely incorrect.

13 Click **OK** to close the Condition Editor.

14 Click **OK** to close the CourseBuilder Interaction window.

15 Test the interaction in a browser.

Providing Progressive Feedback

In many cases you may want to provide multiple layers (progressive) feedback. In other words, the first time the learners respond incorrectly, the feedback displays that it is incorrect then gives them the opportunity to try again. If they respond incorrectly a second time, the feedback displays a hint. If they respond incorrectly the third time, the feedback displays the correct answer and directs them to another part of the course for remediation.

More Information: See also *Branching Based on a Learner Response* later in this chapter.

Progressive feedback is very helpful when you are using CourseBuilder interactions to teach rather than test. In our experience, online learners tend to want to figure it out on their own the first time, but after a few tries they can easily get frustrated.

If learners cannot get to needed help to complete the interaction correctly, they can become discouraged and are then less likely to approach the rest of the course with a positive approach.

In this section you'll modify a Multiple Choice interaction to provide progressive feedback.

To modify an interaction to provide progressive feedback, you'll need to use these elements of the Action Manager:

- ***Set Text of Layer*** action
- ***Call JavaScript*** action
- ***JavaScript*** condition type

 Note: If you are unfamiliar with JavaScript, you may want to review *setting global variables* and how to create *if* statements in your favorite JavaScript reference.

Viewing the Finished Interaction

Before creating this interaction, take a look at the completed sample.

 On CD: Open *Sample_13-5.htm* in a browser (this exercise was designed for Internet Explorer—you may experience some differences if using another browser).

Here are some things to look for while viewing this sample:

- What happens when you respond correctly?
- What happens when you respond incorrectly?
- What happens when you respond incorrectly for a second and third time?

Creating this Interaction

Now let's create the interaction you just looked at.

To create this interaction you'll follow these general procedures:

- **Part I (steps 1-6):** Create a variable that will store a value that indicates how many times the learner has responded incorrectly.

- **Part II (steps 7-11):** You'll modify the feedback the learner receives if they respond correctly to the interaction.
- **Part III (steps 12-18):** You'll add a condition that will check to see if the learner has responded to the interaction incorrectly just once. You'll also define what actions take place if that is the case.
- **Part IV (steps 19-21):** You'll add a condition that will check to see if the learner has responded incorrectly twice and corresponding actions if so.
- **Part V (steps 22-25):** You'll define what happens if the learner responds incorrectly to the interaction three times.

Part I (steps 1-6)

Follow these steps to modify an existing interaction to provide progressive feedback:

1 Open *Sample_13-5_Start.htm* in Dreamweaver (this exercise was designed for Internet Explorer—you may experience some differences if using another browser).

So you can focus on the techniques in this section, we've already created the interaction, modified the choices, and created a feedback layer for you.

The first thing you need to do is create a global JavaScript variable that will keep track of the number of incorrect tries the learner makes.

2 Display the contents of the *<head>* tag in Design view (View→Head Content):

Dreamweaver displays the Head Content pane.

These scroll icons represent script tags.

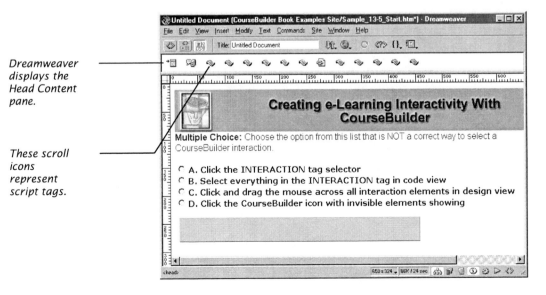

Note: If you know JavaScript you can, of course, enter the code using the Dreamweaver's Code view.

3   Click in the Head Content area and insert a *<script>* tag (Insert→Invisible Tags→Script).

Dreamweaver displays the Insert Script window:

```
┌─────────────────────────────────────────────────────────┐
│ Insert Script                                        [x]  │
│                                                           │
│  Language:  [JavaScript ▼]            ┌──────────┐        │
│                                       │    OK    │        │
│  Content:   ┌──────────────────┐ ▲   ├──────────┤        │
│             │                  │     │  Cancel  │        │
│             │                  │     ├──────────┤        │
│             │                  │     │   Help   │        │
│             │                  │     └──────────┘        │
│             │                  │ ▼                       │
│             │ ◄               ►│                         │
│             └──────────────────┘                         │
└─────────────────────────────────────────────────────────┘
```

4   Make sure JavaScript is selected for the *Language* setting.

5   In the *Content* field type this text: *var answered*

6   Click **OK** to close the Insert Script window.

Now that you've created the variable to track the number of times the learner has responded incorrectly, you're ready to edit the interaction.

Part II (steps 7–11)

In this part of the tutorial you modify the feedback the learner receives if they respond correctly to the interaction.

7   Edit the Multiple Choice interaction and go to the Action Manager tab:

```
+ Segment: Check Time
-- Segment: Correctness
   -- if Correct
         Popup Message
   -- else if Incorrect
         Popup Message
   -- else if Unknown Response
         Popup Message
+ Segment: Check Tries
```

8 Select the segment named *Correctness* and click **Edit** to change the name of the segment to *Progressive Feedback*:

9 Click **OK** to close the Segment Editor.

10 Remove all Popup Message actions within the *Progressive Feedback* segment by selecting each one and clicking the Cut button.

The Action Manager tab should look like this:

11 Select *if Correct* and insert a ***Set Text of Layer*** action with this message in the Feedback layer: *That's Right!*

```
+ Segment: Check Time
-- Segment: Progressive Feedback
    -- if Correct
            Set Text of Layer
    -- else if Incorrect
    -- else if Unknown Response
+ Segment: Check Tries
```

Now you're ready to move on to Part III.

Part III (steps 12–18)

In this part of the tutorial you'll add a condition that will check to see if the learner has responded to the interaction incorrectly just once. You'll also define what actions take place if that is the case.

12 Select *else if Incorrect* and add a condition.

CourseBuilder displays the Condition Editor.

13 Use the values in this table to complete the Condition Editor:

Property	Value
Condition Name	Answered Once
Type	JavaScript
JavaScript	answered == null

The Condition Editor should look like this:

As a word of explanation, every time the learner responds you will increment the value of the *answered* variable. If the *answered* variable is *null* (meaning empty), then this is the first time the learner responded to the question. This technique lets you know how many times the learner has answered the question.

14 Click the **OK** button to close the Condition Editor.

CourseBuilder displays the new condition in the Action Manager tab:

New condition

You want this condition evaluated only if the response is incorrect, so you need to indent it so it is nested under the *else if Incorrect* condition.

15 With *else if Answered Once* selected, click the **Indent** button ▷.

CourseBuilder indents the condition and removes *else* so that it reads *if Answered Once*:

```
+ Segment: Check Time
-- Segment: Progressive Feedback
   -- if Correct
        Set Text of Layer
   -- else if Incorrect
        -- if Answered Once
   -- else if Unknown Response
+ Segment: Check Tries
```

Now add the actions that the Action Manager performs the first time the learner answers incorrectly.

16 With *if Answered Once* still selected, add a *Call JavaScript* action.

CourseBuilder displays the Call JavaScript window.

17 In the JavaScript field enter *answered = 1*:

This sets the value of *answered* to *1*. You'll check this value later to determine how many times the learner has answered the question.

18 Add a *Set Text of Layer* action that sets the text of the Feedback layer to: *Oops! That's incorrect*:

Now you're ready to add the next condition.

Part IV (steps 19–22)

In this part of the tutorial you add a condition that will check to see if the learner has responded incorrectly twice. You also define what actions take place if that is the case.

19 Select *if Answered Once* and add a new condition (choose Condition from the drop down list and click **Add**). Complete the Condition Editor with the values shown in this table:

Property	Value
Condition Name	Answered Twice
Type	JavaScript
JavaScript	answered == 1

The Condition Editor should look like this:

The only way the *answered* variable could equal "1" is if the learner had already responded once, meaning this would be their second response.

Now let's add the actions the Action Manager performs if the learner answers incorrectly for the second time.

20 Click the **OK** button to close the Condition Editor.

The Action Manager tab should look like this:

```
+ Segment: Check Time
-- Segment: Progressive Feedback
    -- if Correct
          Set Text of Layer
    -- else if Incorrect
       -- if Answered Once
             Call JavaScript
             Set Text of Layer
       -- else if Answered Twice
    -- else if Unknown Response
+ Segment: Check Tries
```

21 Increment the *answered* variable by adding a *Call JavaScript* action and entering this text in the JavaScript field: *answered +=1*

The "+=" adds whatever comes after it (in this case "1") to the existing value of *answered*. Since *answered* already has a value of 1, incrementing it by one gives it a value of 2.

22 Add a ***Set Text of Layer*** action that updates the ***Feedback*** field with this text: *Are you sure you're clicking the one that does NOT apply?*

The Action Manager tab should look like this:

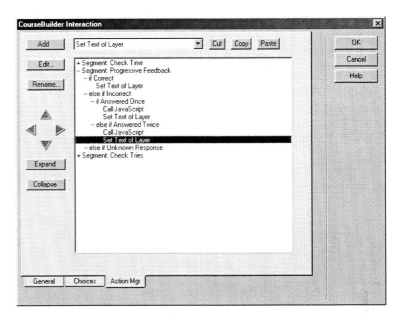

Now you're ready to add the final condition and actions.

Part V (steps 23-26)

In this part of the tutorial you'll define what happens if the learner responds incorrectly to the interaction three times.

23 Select *else if Answered Twice* and add another condition, completing the Condition Editor according to the values in this table:

Property	Value
Condition Name	Answered Three Times
Type	JavaScript
JavaScript	answered == 2

The Condition Editor should look like this:

This condition is checking to see if the "answered" variable has a value of "2". If the variable contains a "2" it means the learner has answered twice already.

The Action Manager tab should look like this:

```
+ Segment: Check Time
-- Segment: Progressive Feedback
    -- if Correct
        Set Text of Layer
    -- else if Incorrect
        -- if Answered Once
            Call JavaScript
            Set Text of Layer
        -- else if Answered Twice
            Call JavaScript
            Set Text of Layer
        -- else if Answered Three Times
        -- else if Unknown Response
+ Segment: Check Tries
```

If the learner answers this question incorrectly three times you're going to suggest they review the information by navigating to another area of the course for remediation.

24 With *if Answered Three Times* still selected, add a ***Set Text of Layer*** action with this text in the ***New HTML*** field:

Sorry, that's still not right. Would you like to review the material? Click <a href= "selecting_an_interaction.htm">here</a>.

Note: Remember, one of the most powerful things about the *Set Text of Layer* action is that you can change the entire HTML contents of the layer, not just the text. In other hands-on exercises in this book we have used styles and HTML formatting within the *Set Text of Layer* action. Here we use the *<a>* tag to display a link for the learner. To change the link, simply change the contents of the *href* property to a different URL.

Tip: An alternative to having the learner navigate to another page is a pop-up window (see *Sample_13-6.htm*). To do this, enter this HTML text in the *Set Text of Layer* action under the *if Answered Three Times* condition:

Sorry, that's still not right. Would you like to review the material? Click <a href="#" onClick=window.open("selecting_an_interaction.htm","","width=400,height=500, scrollbars=yes")>here</a>.

25 Click **OK** to close the CourseBuilder Interaction window.

26 Test the interaction in a browser.

Note: If you are unfamiliar with JavaScript, it is easy to make a mistake when writing the code. Remember, JavaScript doesn't know what you intend, so if you don't enter the code correctly, it probably won't work the way you were expecting. If your interaction doesn't work as intended, go back and check the conditions and make sure the JavaScript is entered correctly. Check the Call JavaScript actions for typos as well. If you still can't find the problem, compare your work with the completed example by viewing *Sample_13-5.htm*.

On CD: We've included a screen movie on the CD ROM for this tutorial so you can watch us perform the steps to this tutorial if needed. Open *Movie1.wmv*.

Branching Based on a Learner Response

Short concise feedback usually works best. In other scenarios, you may want to direct the learner to more content for remediation. This is especially the case when a firm grounding in the current topic may be required to progress to the next topic.

If you are serious about requiring a base of knowledge, you may want to require the student to take a complete skill certification exam (see the next chapter, *The Power of the Action Manager Object*) or you may simply want to ask them a single question in the form of a progress check. In either case you can automatically branch to a different area of the course if the learner responds incorrectly or give the learner the choice of either branching or moving on.

Generally it's better to give the learner the choice (the hands-on exercise in the *Displaying Progressive Feedback* earlier in this chapter uses this approach) rather than forcing them to go through remediation. But there may be occasions when you want to prevent learners from moving forward until they answer the question correctly.

To branch the navigation based on a learner response, use the ***Go to URL*** action.

In this section you'll modify the interaction you created in *Displaying Progressive Feedback* earlier in the chapter so that if the learner gets the answer wrong, the interaction gives the learner the choice to receive remediation or continue with the training.

Branching and Business Simulations

Another useful application of branching is for business scenario simulations. For example, suppose you're developing a course on sales skills. Once the learner has gone through the course you could simulate a sales scenario with the question text being the comments of the customer and the responses being the comments back from the salesperson in training. If the learner applies the skills well, the courses branches to interactions that eventually lead to a sale. If the learner don't answer well, the course navigates to interactions that eventually lead to an upset customer and losing money on the deal.

Viewing the Finished Interaction

Before doing the hands-on, take a minute to view the finished interaction.

 On CD: Open *Sample_13-7.htm* in a browser (this exercise was designed for Internet Explorer—you may experience some differences if using another browser).

As you're viewing it, here are a few things to look for:

- How is this interaction similar to *Sample_13-5.htm?*
- How does it differ?

- What purpose does the popup message serve and why do you think we used that method rather than displaying the message in a layer?

Creating this Interaction

Now let's create the interaction you just finished looking at.

Follow these steps to modify an interaction so it branches based on the learner's response:

1 In Dreamweaver, open *Sample_13-7_Start.htm* (this exercise was designed for Internet Explorer—you may experience some differences if using another browser).

2 Edit the Multiple Choice interaction and select the Action Manager tab:

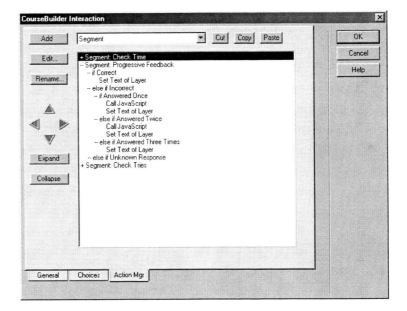

In this example, you are going to automatically branch learners if they answer incorrectly three times.

3 Select *Set Text of Layer* beneath *else if Answered Three Times* and click **Cut** to delete it.

4 Add a *Popup Message* action beneath *else if Answered Three Times* with this text as the message:

You have unsuccessfully answered this question three times. You will now be taken to another area of the course to review the material. When finished, click the Back button and try this question again.

5   Add a ***Go to URL*** action beneath the *Popup Message* action by choosing ***Go to URL*** from the drop down list and clicking **Add**.

CourseBuilder displays the Go to URL window:

Go To URL	☒
Open In: Main Window	OK
	Cancel
	Help
URL:	Browse...

6   In the URL field enter *selecting_an_interaction.htm*.

 Note: The *Open In* field displays the Main Window as the only option unless the page with the CourseBuilder interaction you are working on is part of a frameset. If it is, you can choose to display the URL in a different frame.

7   Click **OK** to close the Go to URL window.

The action manager tab should look like this:

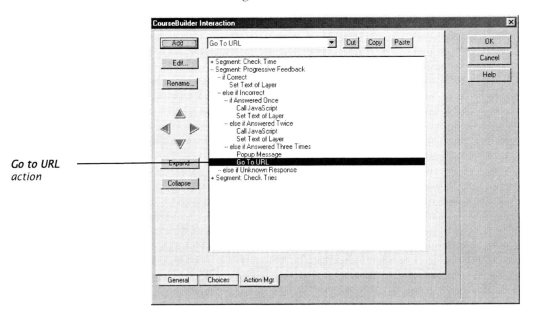

Go to URL action

8 Click **OK** to close the CourseBuilder interaction window.

9 Test the interaction in a browser.

That's it! Remember that you can use the *Go to URL* action for any navigational purpose. Here you have used it to make sure the learner gets the information they need to complete the interaction successfully.

Note: Throughout the book we've guided you away from using the *Popup Message* action for feedback because there are often more effective ways to provide feedback (such as using the *Set Text of Layer* action). However, in this example the Popup Message action works very effectively, because it prohibits the browser from performing the navigation until the learner acknowledges that they are being taken to a new location.

Creating an Ordered Explore Interaction

In Chapter 5 you learned how to create Explore interactions that allow the learner to click on certain areas of an image to receive information. You learned how to create a *structured* Explore interaction that guided the learner through the interaction in a certain order.

On CD: To see that example again, view *Sample_5-2.htm* on the CD ROM.

In this section we'll enhance the structured Explore interaction you made in Chapter 5 to force the learner to click on the images in a certain order. We'll also make the response to the learner appear in a layer and dynamically move that layer to a position near the image the learner clicked.

To force the clicking order, you'll follow these general procedures:

- **Part I (steps 1-5):** You'll create two JavaScript variables that keep track of what was clicked (see *Providing Progressive Feedback* earlier in this chapter for more on JavaScript variables).

- **Part II (steps 6-12):** You'll define the actions that take place when the learner clicks the first hot area. One of these actions will be setting a corresponding variable to *True*. When the learner clicks the second image, if that variable is not *True* (meaning they haven't clicked the first image yet), we'll pop up a message telling the learner to click the first image. If it is *True* then we'll display the image's corresponding explanation in the layer.

- **Part III (steps 13-20):** You'll define the actions that take place when the learner clicks the second hot area. You'll set a corresponding variable to "true" to record that the learner has clicked the second hot area. You'll also add a condition to only do these actions if the variable you set in Part II has a value of *True*.

- **Part IV (steps 21-34):** You'll define what actions that take place when the learner clicks the third hot area. You'll also add a condition to check the variable you set to *True* in part III.

To position the explanation layer, we'll use the Change Property action to change the *Top* position property of the layer.

Viewing the Finished Interaction

Before creating this interaction, take a look at the finished sample.

 On CD: In a browser, open *Sample_13-9.htm* (this exercise was designed for Internet Explorer—you may experience some differences if using another browser).

Here are some things to consider while viewing this interaction:

- What happens when you click the steps out of order?
- Once you click the first step, then the second, can you click the first step again?

Creating this Interaction

Now let's create the interaction you just finished viewing.

Part I (steps 1–5)

In this part of the tutorial you will create two JavaScript variables. One for each of the first two hot areas. These variables will keep track of what was clicked and in what order.

Follow these steps to create an ordered Explore interaction:

1 In Dreamweaver, open *Sample_13-9_Start.htm* (this exercise was designed for Internet Explorer—you may experience some differences if using another browser).

You may notice a couple of alterations to the original interaction from Chapter 5. We added a layer called *explanation* in which the explanation that corresponds with each image will be displayed. We also moved the hot area layers to the left to make room for the explanation layer.

The first thing you need to do is set up the JavaScript variable that is going to track which images the learner clicked.

2 If it's not already showing, display the page's head content in Dreamweaver's design view (View→Head Content) and select it by clicking in the Head Contents area.

3 Insert a script (Insert→Invisible Tags→Script).

Dreamweaver displays the Insert Script window.

4 Make sure the *Language* is *JavaScript* and the *Contents* contain this script:

var img1Clicked
var img2Clicked

The Insert Script window should look like this:

This script declares these variables as global variables (see your favorite JavaScript reference for more details on global variables if needed).

5   Click **OK** to close the Insert Script window.

Now you're ready to modify the interaction.

Part II (steps 6–12)

In this section you define the actions and conditions for the first hot area.

6   Edit the Explore interaction and on the Action Manager tab, delete the Popup Message under *if HotArea1 Selected* (remember, the only way to delete an action in the action manager is to select it and click the **Cut** button).

7   Add a Set Text of Layer action and paste in the text you just copied, but make these changes so that the text lines become links:

*<p class='explanation'>You can download the package file (.MXP) by clicking the link that corresponds with your authoring tool:
 <a href='http://www.macromedia.com/exchange/dreamweaver/' target='_blank'>Dreamweaver</a> <a href='http://www.macromedia.com/exchange/ultradev/' target='_blank'>UltraDev</a></p>*

Note: This example is a good illustration of including other elements beyond text, such as HTML, JavaScript, and CSS styles with the **Set Text of Layer** action.

8   Add a **Change Property** action beneath the *Set Text of Layer* action you just added.

CourseBuilder displays the Change Property window:

9 Fill out this window using the settings in this table:

Property	Value
Type of Object	Layer
Named Object	Layer "explanation"
Property	Select: style.top
New Value	160

The Change Property window should look like this:

Setting the "top" property of the layer moves the layer to the correct vertical position on the screen so that its position corresponds with the images the learner clicks. *160* means it will be positioned 160 pixels down from the top of the page.

Note: Moving layers is only supported in version 4 and later browsers, so make sure you have selected either NS4 or IE4 in the browser version drop down list. This technique should work with either Internet Explorer® or Netscape® browsers.

10 Click **OK** to close the Change Property window.

The next thing we need to do if the learner clicks *HotArea1* is set the JavaScript variable.

11 Add a Call JavaScript action and enter this text in the JavaScript field: *img1Clicked = true*

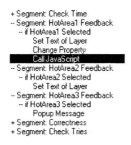

12 Click **OK** to close the Call JavaScript window.

The action manager tab should look like this:

```
+ Segment: Check Time
-- Segment: HotArea1 Feedback
    -- if HotArea1 Selected
        Set Text of Layer
        Change Property
        Call JavaScript
-- Segment: HotArea2 Feedback
    -- if HotArea2 Selected
        Set Text of Layer
-- Segment: HotArea3 Feedback
    -- if HotArea3 Selected
        Popup Message
+ Segment: Correctness
+ Segment: Check Tries
```

Now you're ready to add the conditions and actions for *HotArea2*.

Part III (steps 13-20)

In this section you'll define the actions for the second hot area. You'll define the actions first then add a condition that will require that the learner click the first hot area before those actions can take place.

13 Edit the Popup Message under *if HotArea2 Selected* and Copy (CTRL+C) its text message.

14 Cut the Popup Message action from *if HotArea2* Selected and add a ***Set Text of Layer*** action. Use the text you just copied for the layer text. Remember to apply the *explanation* style class:

<p class="explanation">You can start the installation by double-clicking the package file or by choosing Install from the File menu in the Extension Manager.</p>

15 Add a ***Call JavaScript*** action with this script: *img2Clicked = true*

16 Add a ***Change Property*** action to change the *Top* position of the Explanation layer. Set the text of the ***New Value*** field to *240*:

The Action Manager tab should look like this:

```
+ Segment: Check Time
-- Segment: HotArea1 Feedback
   -- if HotArea1 Selected
      Set Text of Layer
      Change Property
      Call JavaScript
-- Segment: HotArea2 Feedback
   -- if HotArea2 Selected
      Set Text of Layer
      Call JavaScript
      Change Property
-- Segment: HotArea3 Feedback
   -- if HotArea3 Selected
      Popup Message
+ Segment: Correctness
+ Segment: Check Tries
```

17 Click *Set Text of Layer* under *if HotArea2 Selected* and add a condition with the values shown in this table:

Property	Value
Name	Already clicked img 1
Type	JavaScript
JavaScript	Img1Clicked = true

The Condition Editor should look like this:

```
Condition Editor                                                    [x]

Condition Name:  already clicked img 1                        [  OK   ]
                                                             [ Cancel ]
                 [ Add ] [ Delete ]                          [  Help  ]

Expressions:   (img1Clicked == true)




Type:  [ JavaScript        ▼]
JavaScript:  [img1Clicked == true                      ]







                                          [ and        ▼]
```

 Note: Remember, you don't need to put parentheses around the expression like you would if you were entering an *if* statement in a JavaScript function.

The *Hot Area 2* section of the Action Manager tab should look like this:

```
-- if HotArea2 Selected
     Set Text of Layer
     Call JavaScript
     Change Property
   -- if already clicked img 1
```

18 Select *Set Text of Layer* and move it down three levels by clicking the down arrow three times. This will place it below the *if already clicked img 1*. Do the same for *Call JavaScript* and *Change Property*.

Your Action Manager tab should look like this:

By moving these actions beneath the *if already clicked img 1* condition, they will happen only if the variable *img1Clicked* has a value of "true". The only way it gets a value of "true" is because the learner selected the first hot area.

19 With *Set Text of Layer* selected, choose *Else* from the action drop down list and click **Add**:

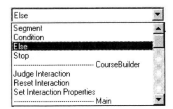

This adds an *else* line to the action manager. *Else* means "otherwise". So, if the learner has already clicked the first image, you'll display the text in the layer. Otherwise, you'll popup a message telling them to click the first image before they can click the second.

20 With *–else* selected, add a ***Popup Message*** with this text: *Please click the first step before clicking the second.*

Now we need to do the same thing for the third hot area. The easiest way to do this is to copy and paste the segment for HotArea2 and make a few changes. First let's delete the segment for HotArea3 so we can replace it with a copy of the one we just finished.

Part IV (step 21–34)

In this part of the tutorial you will define the actions for the third hot area. You'll also add a condition to check to see if the leaner has clicked the previous two hot areas in order.

21 Select *Segment: HotArea3 Feedback* and click **Cut**.

22 Select *Segment: HotArea2 Feedback*, click **Copy**, then click **Paste**.

CourseBuilder duplicates the *HotArea2 Feedback* segment. The Action Manager tab should look like this:

This segment
should appear
identical to the one
above it since you
just copied and
pasted it.

```
+ Segment: Check Time
-- Segment: HotArea1 Feedback
   -- if HotArea1 Selected
      Set Text of Layer
      Change Property
      Call JavaScript
-- Segment: HotArea2 Feedback
   -- if HotArea2 Selected
      -- if already clicked img 1
         Set Text of Layer
         Call JavaScript
         Change Property
      -- else
         Popup Message
-- Segment: HotArea2 Feedback
   -- if HotArea2 Selected
      -- if already clicked img 1
         Set Text of Layer
         Call JavaScript
         Change Property
      -- else
         Popup Message
+ Segment: Correctness
+ Segment: Check Tries
```

23 Edit the Segment name and rename it to: *Segment: HotArea3 Feedback*.

24 Edit the *if HotArea2 Selected* condition and change the interaction element value to *HotArea3*. Also change the name of it to *HotArea3 Selected:*

Change the name here.

Choose "HotArea3" here.

25 Click **OK** to close the Condition Editor.

26 Edit *if already clicked img 1* condition and change the name to *already clicked img 2* and the JavaScript to: *img2Clicked == true*

27 Click **OK**.

28 Replace the text in the Set Text of Layer action with:

<p class="explanation">Click OK to accept the disclaimer.</p>

29 Since this is the last image the learner should click, select the *Call JavaScript* action under the condition *if already clicked img 2* and click the **Cut** button to delete it.

The Action Manager should now look like this:

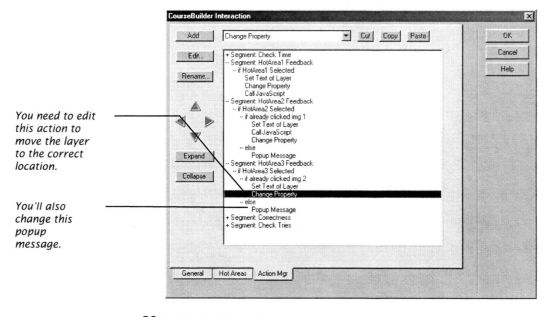

You need to edit this action to move the layer to the correct location.

You'll also change this popup message.

30 Edit the *Change Property* action and set the *style.top* value to *320:*

31 Click **OK** to close the Change Property window.

32 Edit and change the Popup Message in this segment to read: *Please click steps one and two before clicking the third step.*

33 Click **OK** to close the CourseBuilder Interaction window.

34 Test the interaction in a browser.

 On CD: We've included a screen movie on the CD ROM for this tutorial so you can watch us perform the steps if needed. Open *Movie2.wmv.*

Let's Review

This was a fairly lengthy exercise, so let's review how you did a few things.

First of all, your main task was to force the learner to click the images in a certain order. You accomplished this by declaring two JavaScript variables (img1Clicked and img2Clicked) and setting their values (using the Call JavaScript action) to true when their corresponding images were clicked. Before displaying the explanation text you checked to see if the variable corresponding to the preceding image was set to true (meaning it had been clicked). If it was, you displayed the explanation text. Otherwise (remember *else*), you displayed a popup message.

You can apply this same techniques to any interaction you want to order.

You also used the Change Property action to set the *top* property of the layer to different pixel positions. This made the explanation layer appear in a more relevant position and made the page more dynamic.

Summary

In this chapter you've learned some additional ways to customize interactions using the Action Manager tab. Specifically you learned how to:

- Use the ***Set Text of Layer*** action to display feedback in a layer.

- Add conditions that displayed different feedback for each possible response.

- Add conditions that tested a JavaScript variable to determine how many times the learner had answered the question.

- Use the ***Call JavaScript*** action to increment a global variable to keep track of how many times the learner had answered the question.

- Use the ***Go to URL*** action to redirect the learner to other areas of the course.

- Use global variables to help force the learner to follow an order in an Explore interaction.

- Use the ***Change Property*** action to dynamically move a layer to a different position on the page.

Now that you've learned how to customize the Action Manager tab, you're ready for to move on to the Action Manager object.

The Power of the Action Manager Object

14

The Action Manager object is your key to truly extending CourseBuilder beyond its normal capabilities. We use the word "power" in the chapter title because once you learn how to use it, you get all sorts of new ideas about what you can do with CourseBuilder.

Like the Action Manager tab, learning to use the Action Manager object is best learned in some kind of meaningful context. In this chapter you'll learn to use the Action Manager object as you create and score a multi-question quiz.

In this chapter you will learn how to:

- Use a scoring variable to calculate and display scores.

- Create a "Show Answer" button.

- Create a multi-question quiz on one page that waits to deliver feedback to the learner until after the learner responds to each question.

- Tally and display the score from a multi-question quiz.

- Add decision-tree logic that prevents the learner from receiving feedback and a score until all questions have been answered.

Introduction

The Action Manager object (or interaction template) is one of the most underutilized and misunderstood CourseBuilder features. Many CourseBuilder users that we've encountered feel intimidated by it. If you're like them, you might have asked yourself these questions. What does it do? How is it different from the Action Manager tab (see Chapter 12)? Should I be doing something with it, or should I be ignoring it? Is it already doing something behind the scenes that I'm not aware of?

These are all questions we had as we first began learning CourseBuilder ourselves. In this chapter, you'll not only learn what it is, but you'll be guided through some tutorials that we hope will open your mind to its possibilities. Using this object in conjunction with other interactions has great potential for creating complex and engaging interactions. This chapter should get you jump started. After that, let your imagination be your guide!

Along with the Action Manager object, we'll cover some of the Dreamweaver behaviors that you are installed by CourseBuilder. You can use these behaviors outside of an interaction.

Three CourseBuilder Behavior Actions

When you install CourseBuilder, the extension installs three new "learning" actions:

- *Judge Interaction*
- *Reset Interaction*
- *Set Interaction Properties*

In earlier chapters you've seen some examples of the ***Set Interaction Properties*** action used in the Action Manager tab. Many CourseBuilder users fail to realize that you can use these actions outside of the Action Manager tab. In fact, you don't have to be within an interaction at all to use them if you don't want to. You can trigger these actions based on any JavaScript event (i.e. *onClick*, *onMouseOver*, etc.).

Let's take a look at what these actions do.

Judge Interaction

The *Judge Interaction* action executes everything in the Action Manager tab for a specific interaction. It does this whether or not the Action Manager tab actually judges the interaction. In other words, when you choose this action you are saying, "Do what's in the Action Manager tab of such-and-such interaction."

Of course, usually your Action Manager tab *does* indeed judge the interaction and provide feedback—hence the name.

Follow these steps to use the Judge Interaction action:

1 Open the Behaviors panel (Windows→Behaviors) and click the **Plus** (+) button (or click the action drop down list on the Action Manager tab).

2 Choose *Judge Interaction* (CourseBuilder→Judge Interaction) from the popup list (or if using this action in the Action Manager just choose Judge Interaction from the drop down list).

When you choose this action CourseBuilder displays the Judge Interaction window:

3 If you have multiple interactions on one page, choose the desired interaction from the drop down list.

4 Click **OK**.

As you can see, it's pretty simple. Moreover, any event could trigger it. Remember, all it's doing is executing whatever is in the action manager tab of the interaction you choose from the list. Can you begin to see some of the potential?

Reset Interaction

The *Reset Interaction* action does what it says—it resets the interaction to its initial state.

Tip: If your interaction uses common form elements such as form-style radio buttons or check boxes, these elements do not appear to be reset even though you use this interaction. You may need to use the Change Property action to set the values of the actual form elements themselves. Or, in some cases you can perform what is called a "hard" reload or refresh of the entire web page by using the Call JavaScript action and entering "*window.location.reload(true)*". We'll use this exact code string later in this chapter.

Follow these steps to use the *Reset Interaction* action:

1   Open the Behaviors panel and click the **Plus** (+) button (or if using this action in the Action Manager, click the action drop down list).

2   Choose ***Reset Interaction*** (CourseBuilder →Reset Interaction) from the popup list (or just Reset Interaction from the drop down list in the Action Manager).

When you choose this action, CourseBuilder displays the Reset Interaction window:

The Reset drop down list.

Reset Interaction	✕
Reset: Entire Interaction ▼	OK
Interaction: ActionMgr03 ▼	Cancel
	Help

The Reset drop down list has three options that are explained in this table:

Option	Description
Entire Interaction	Resets all properties of the interaction including all of the interaction's elements, scores, etc.
Elements Only	Displays an "Elements" drop down list. From this drop down list choose the elements of the interaction, such as drag and target elements of a Drag-and-Drop interaction.

Option	Description
Action Manager Only	When you first create a segment in the action manager you have to designate it as an "always evaluate from the beginning" or as a "state transition" type of segment. You can reset the segment of the action manager that tracks the state transition. (See Chapter 12 for more information about state transition segments.)

3 Choose an option from the **Reset** drop down list.

4 Choose any other applicable options in the window.

5 Click **OK**.

Set Interaction Properties

The Set Interaction Properties action can be very powerful. Using this action you can set properties of an interaction "on the fly" based on any browser event.

For example, later in this chapter, you'll create a "Show Answer" button. This button will use the Set Interaction Properties action to set the "Selected" property of certain elements of an interaction to True. By setting the Selected property of the correct element to True, the learner will can view the correct response.

More Information: You can get a complete list of CourseBuilder interaction properties by looking for *Properties* in the index of CourseBuilder's online help:

Select properties under the CourseBuilder Interaction sub-heading.

Follow these steps to use the Set Interaction Properties action:

1 Open the Behaviors panel and click the **Plus** (+) button (or if using the Action Manager, click the action drop down list on the Action Manager tab).

2 Choose ***Set Interaction Properties*** (CourseBuilder → Set Interaction Properties) from the popup list (or just Set Interaction Properties from the drop down list in the Action Manager).

When you choose this action CourseBuilder displays the Set Interaction Properties window:

If needed, select specific elements of the interaction from this drop down list.

Note: In some ways this window looks a lot like the Condition Editor. Don't let that confuse you. When you are creating a condition in the Action Manager you are testing a value. The Set Interaction Properties doesn't do any testing, but rather sets the value of the property.

This table describes the different fields in this window:

Option	Description
Set	This is where you choose what type of property you are setting. **Interaction** – choose this option when you want to set a property of the interaction without using JavaScript. **Action Manager** – choose this option to enable, disable, and reset specific nodes of a "state transition" segment (see Chapter 12 for more information about state transition segments). **JavaScript** – choose this option to set a property of an interaction using JavaScript. For example, you might have a custom function to which you send the value of an interaction property. Based on the value you send the function could determine to set an interaction property one way or another.

Option	Description
Interaction	A drop down list of interactions whose properties you want to set. Select the specific element from the drop down list to the right (if you are setting a property of a specific element such as the Selected property of a choice in a Multiple Choice interaction).
Property	Dependent on what you choose in the Interaction drop down list. If you choose an entire interaction it shows the properties for the interaction. If you also choose an element it shows the properties that pertain to that element. These properties are specific to the type of interaction you are working with. (For example, the Drag-and-Drop interaction has some different properties than a Multiple Choice interaction.)
Type	The value of this drop down list changes based on what you choose in the Property drop down list. For example, if the Property is set to Selected, the Type list has True/False and JavaScript in it. If the Property is set to Score, the Type list changes to Number and JavaScript. The field beneath the Type drop down list changes as you choose different options in the Type list.

3   Choose the interaction that contains the properties you want to set.

4   Choose the correct properties and set it to the new value.

5   Click **OK** to close the Set Interaction Properties window and save your changes.

Creating a "Show Answer" Button

In this section you'll explore one way to use the *Set Interaction Properties* action by creating a clickable image that shows the learner the correct response.

In some scenarios you may want to supply the learner with a button that displays the correct answer to a question. Unless it is a skill certification situation, it may be helpful to supply learners with the correct answer and then have them try it again for reinforcement.

Viewing the Finished Interaction

Before creating this interaction, take a moment to view the finished example.

On CD: In a browser, open *Sample_14-1.htm* (this exercise was designed for Internet Explorer—you may experience some differences if using another browser).

As you view this interaction, here are some things to look for:

- What happens when you click the *Show Answer* image? What property of the interaction do you think we might be setting?
- What happens when you click the *Try Again* image?

Creating this Interaction

Let's create the interaction you just finished looking at.

Follow these steps to create a "Show Answer" button:

1 In Dreamweaver, open *Sample_14-1_Start.htm* (this exercise was designed for Internet Explorer—you may experience some differences if using another browser).

You may recognize this sample from the Drag-and-Drop chapter (chapter 4) in Section I. It contains a very simple Drag-and-Drop activity.

Note: We've made some enhancements to this interaction since you saw it last. We attached a Change Property behavior to the drag layer to make it highlight when the mouse is placed over it. We also added styles to the Drag and Target layers. We also provide feedback in a layer using different styles for correct and incorrect responses. Finally, using the Change Property action in the Action Manager we changed the background color of the target layer when it is dropped on the correct target element. You might want to take a moment to explore the enhancements to this interaction before proceeding.

The principle behind showing the correct answer is to create an image and attach a behavior using a Set Interaction Properties action that triggers on the *onClick* event. This is an example of using Dreamweaver in conjunction with CourseBuilder. This behavior sits outside any interaction, but uses the CourseBuilder actions to dynamically change the interaction.

2 Insert a rollover image (Insert → Interactive Image → Rollover Image) directly after the interaction instructions. Use these images: */images/Sample Images/ShowAnswer.gif* and */images/Sample Images/ShowAnswer_mo.gif.*

This graphic shows you where to place the images for this tutorial:

Complete the sentence by dragging the text on the left to the correct target on the right. **Show Answer**

3 Click the Show Answer image.

4 Open the Behaviors panel (Windows→Behaviors) and attach a Set Interaction Properties action (CourseBuilder→Set Interaction Properties).

Dreamweaver displays the Set Interaction Properties window:

5 Complete this window according to the values in this table:

Option	Value
Set	Interaction
Interaction	Drag_1ToMany01
Interaction Element	Pair: "Drag1:Target1"

Option	Value
Property	Selected
Type	True/False
Type Value	True

Note: When creating "Show Answer" buttons, make sure to choose the correct element of the interaction. For Drag-and-Drop interactions it's "pairs" but for other types of interactions you would choose a different element, such as "choices" for a Multiple Choice interaction.

6   Click **OK**.

7   Make sure the event for the behavior is *onClick*:

Choose the onClick event

(onMouseOut)	Swap Image Restore
(onMouseOver)	Swap Image
onClick	Set Interaction Properties

Now you need to create a clickable image that resets the interaction so the learner can try again once he or she has seen the correct answer.

8   Insert a rollover image (Insert → Interactive Image → Rollover Image) directly after the Show Answer image. Use these images: */images/Sample Images/tryAgain.gif* and */images/Sample Images/tryAgain.gif*.

> Complete the sentence by dragging the text on the left to the correct target on the right. **Show Answer   Try Again**

9   Click the *Try Again* image to select it.

10   Open the Behaviors panel and attach a ***Reset Interaction*** action (CourseBuilder→Reset Interaction).

Dreamweaver displays the Reset Interaction window:

Reset Interaction

Reset:	Entire Interaction
Interaction:	Drag_1ToMany01

OK   Cancel   Help

11 Complete the Reset Interaction window with the values from this table:

Option	Value
Reset	Entire Interaction
Interaction	Drag_1ToMany01

12 Click **OK**.

13 Test the interaction in a browser.

In review, we completed the following procedures in this exercise:

- We attached a ***Set Interaction Properties*** action to the Show Answer image triggered by the *onClick* event. This action selects the correct elements of the interaction.

- We attached a ***Reset Interaction*** action to the Try Again image triggered by the *onClick* event.

Remember, so far, we haven't used the Action Manager object. These actions were all added outside the Action Manager. To reiterate, you can use them as part of the Action Manager or completely independent of the Action Manager.

Tip: Other ways of creating a "Show Answer" button could include using the Show–Hide Layers action to show a layer containing an image (such as an arrow) that points to the correct answer or using the Change Property behavior to change the background color of a layer or the color of the text of the correct answer.

Note: You might be asking yourself, "Why do I need to use the Action Manager then?" Here's a rule of thumb. If what you're trying to do requires a logical decision tree, use the Action Manager (unless you want custom JavaScript functions to handle logical decision making). If you don't need a logical decision tree (such as with the Show Answer and Reset images we just created), use standard Dreamweaver techniques to attach behaviors.

Creating a Multi-question Quiz

The Action Manager object in the gallery is nothing more than an invisible interaction that has an Action Manager tab that you can customize. You primarily use the Action Manager object to manipulate other interactions on the same web page.

In this section you'll learn how to use the Action Manager object by creating a quiz that has multiple questions, all on one web-page. The Action Manager *tab* in each interaction determines *what* feedback the learner receives, but the Action Manager *object* determines *when* the learner receives the feedback. In the example you will create, learners receive feedback after completing all of the interactions in the quiz.

In addition to judging the interactions on the page, the Action Manager object determines whether or not the learner has completed all interactions on the page before showing the feedback. It displays a reminder message if they haven't.

Viewing the Finished Quiz

Before creating the mult-question quiz, take a moment to view the finished interaction to see how it works. Try the quiz first in the browser. Then you might want to take a look at how it is constructed in Dreamweaver.

 On CD: In a browser, open *Sample_14-2.htm* (this exercise was designed for Internet Explorer—you may experience some differences if using another browser).

Here are a few things to try while viewing this interaction:

- Answer both questions correctly and click the Score My Quiz image.
- What happens to the feedback when you answer the questions incorrectly?
- Reset the quiz, answer only one question, and click the Score My Quiz image.
- Reset the quiz, don't answer any of the questions, and click the Score My Quiz image.

Creating the Quiz

Let's create the quiz that you've just looked at. During this tutorial, we'll guide you step by step. Before we begin let's identify the three main things you'll be doing and the order you'll do them:

- **Part I (steps 1-15):** Make sure each interaction is set up to display the feedback you want it to display once it eventually gets judged.
- **Part II (steps 16-21):** Add an Action Manager object to the page that judges all other interactions on the page once the learner has completed all questions.

- **Part III (steps 22-40):** Add segments, conditions, and actions to the Action Manager object's Action Manager tab (that's a mouthful!). This detail will make sure all questions were answered before judging the interactions.

- **Part IV (steps 41-46):** Attach behaviors to the Score My Quiz rollover image to trigger the Action Manager object so that when the learner clicks the Score My Quiz image the Action Manager judges all interactions on the page.

- **Part V (steps 47-50):** Add a behavior to the Reset Quiz image to make it reset the quiz.

- **Part VI (steps 51-58):** Modify the Action Manager object to tally and show the score of the entire quiz when it judges the interactions.

Part I (steps 1–15)

In this part of the exercise you will modify the existing interactions to make sure that each one is set up to display the appropriate feedback once it eventually gets judged by the Action Manager object.

Follow these steps to create a multi-question quiz scored by the Action Manager object:

1   In Dreamweaver, open *Sample_14-2_Start.htm* (this exercise was designed for Internet Explorer—you may experience some differences if using another browser).

We've done a lot of the groundwork for you so we can focus on using the Action Manager object and not on creating the individual interactions (even so this is a very long tutorial). We have created the quiz interactions, added Score My Quiz and Retake Quiz rollover images, created two layers for interaction-specific feedback, and a layer that eventually displays the score.

Here is an explanation of each of the different layers on this quiz page:

Question 1 feedback layer

Question 2 feedback layer

Score My Quiz and Retake Quiz rollover images. Like everything else on this page, these objects are in layers to ensure exact positioning.

The score will be displayed in this layer.

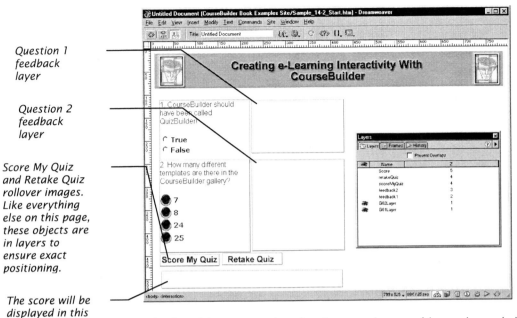

The first thing you need to do when creating a multi-question quiz is make sure that every interaction is set up to work independently the way it should. We've created the interactions for this quiz, but you need to use the Action Manager tab on each interaction to determine the feedback for each interaction.

2 Edit the True/False interaction and go to the Action Manager tab.

We've already deleted the default feedback actions:

Default feedback actions normally follow each of these conditions.

```
-- Segment: Correctness
  if Correct
  else if Incorrect
  else if Unknown Response
```

3 Select the *if Correct* line and add a Set Text of Layer action for the *Feedback1* layer. Place this text in the New HTML field: *<p style class = "feedbackText">Excellent. You got it right!</p>*

Set Text of Layer

Layer: layer "feedback1"

New HTML: <p style class = "feedbackText">Excellent. You got it right!</p>

OK
Cancel
Help

4 Click **OK** to close the Set Text of Layer window.

5 Select the *if Incorrect* line in the Action Manager tab and add a Set Text of Layer action for the *feedback1* layer. Place this text in the New HTML field: *<p style class = "incorrectFeedbackText">Whoops! That's not right.</p>*

Set Text of Layer

Layer: layer "feedback1"

New HTML: <p style class = "incorrectFeedbackText">Whoops! That's not right.</p>

OK
Cancel
Help

Note: We assign a different stylesheet class for correct and incorrect because we want to use color to draw the learner's attention to those questions they answered incorrectly. The *incorrectFeedbackText* style has a red background as opposed to the blue background of *feedbackText*. We've already created these style classes for you.

6 Click **OK** to close the Set Text of Layer window.

7 Click the General tab.

Look at the ***Judge Interaction*** setting:

Judge Interaction: ○ when the user clicks a button labeled [   ]
                    ● when the user clicks a choice
                    ○ on a specific event (set using the Judge Interaction Behavior)

The quiz should display feedback for all of the questions when the learner clicks the Score My Quiz image. It shouldn't display the feedback immediately after the learner responds to the question, so you need to choose the *on a specific event (set using the Judge Interaction Behavior)* option.

8 Choose the *on a specific event* option for the Judge Interaction setting:

> Judge Interaction: ⃝ when the user clicks a button labeled [   ]
> ⃝ when the user clicks a choice
> ⦿ on a specific event (set using the Judge Interaction Behavior)

By choosing this option you are telling CourseBuilder to wait until some other browser event happens before judging this interaction.

Later in the tutorial you'll use the ***Judge Interaction*** action and choose this interaction to activate this setting. Remember, judging the interaction simply means processing whatever is on the Action Manager tab.

9 Click **OK** to close the CourseBuilder Interaction window and save your changes.

Now you need to do the same things to the next quiz question.

10 Edit the Multiple Choice interaction and on the General tab, choose the *on a specific event* option for the ***Judge Interaction*** setting.

11 On the Action Manager tab, select the *if Correct* line and add a ***Set Text of Layer*** action for the *feedback2* layer. Place this text in the ***New HTML*** field:
<p style class = "feedbackText">Yep, if you count all templates there are 25.</p>

The Set Text of Layer window should look like this:

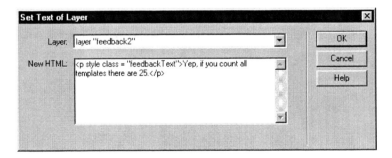

12 Click **OK** to close the Set Text of Layer window.

13 Select the *if Incorrect* line of the Action Manager tab and add a ***Set Text of Layer*** action for the *feedback2* layer. Place this text in the ***New HTML*** field:
<p style class = "incorrectFeedbackText">Nope. Sorry. Correct answer is 25.</p>

Set Text of Layer	☒
Layer: `layer "feedback2"` ▼	OK
New HTML: `<p style class = "incorrectFeedbackText">Nope. Sorry. Correct answer is 25.</p>`	Cancel
	Help

14 Click **OK** to close the Set Text of Layer window.

15 Click **OK** to close the CourseBuilder Interaction window.

Now you are ready to add the Action Manager object to the page.

Part II (steps 16–21)

In this part of the tutorial you will add an Action Manager object to the page.

16 Place your cursor at the top of the Dreamweaver page in design view. Make sure the insertion point is not within another interaction.

If you can still see the *<interaction>* tag selector at the bottom left of your screen, your insertion point is within an existing interaction:

`<body> <interaction> <div> <span>`

Place the cursor higher in the page until you see the tag selector look like this:

`<body>`

17 Insert a new interaction and choose the Action Manager object from the Action Manager category in the template Gallery:

These are the only tabs an Action Manager object has.

CourseBuilder displays the General and Action Manager tabs.

18 Click the General tab:

Notice how the Judge Interaction setting is set to *on a specific event* by default. Leave this setting selected because you want to process the logic and actions you'll put on the action manager tab when the learner clicks the Score My Quiz image.

19 Select the *Insert in a Layer* setting.

Tip: We recommend choosing this setting because the Action Manager is not an object you can see on your CourseBuilder page. It is invisible. All it really does is add some JavaScript code behind the scenes. So finding it to edit can be somewhat difficult. By placing it in a layer you can resize the layer to be very small, and place it in an inconspicuous place, such as on top of the banner at the top of the page. That way, whenever you want to edit it, you can simply select the layer and edit the interaction just as you would any other interaction.

20 Click **OK** to close the CourseBuilder Interaction window.

Dreamweaver displays the new layer containing the Action Manager object:

*Action
Manager
object layer*

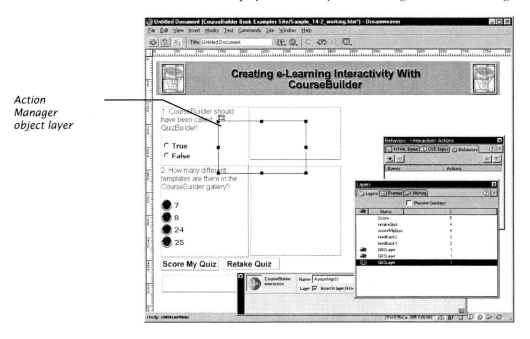

21 Resize the layer and move it on top of the banner image at the top of the page:

Action Manager layer resized

The layers panel indicates the name of the Action Manager layer.

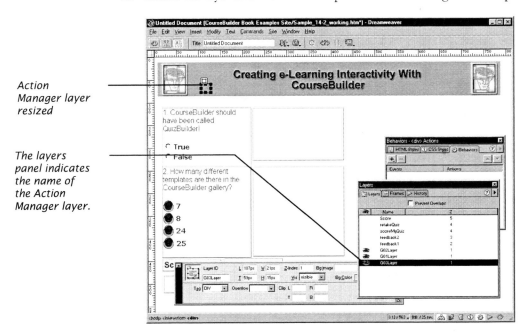

Since the Action Manager object is invisible, this layer can be as small as you want.

Part III (steps 22-40)

In this section of the tutorial you will add segments, conditions, and actions to the Action Manager tab of the Action Manager object. Doing will ensure that the learner answers all questions before the Action Manager object judges the interactions (and thereby provides feedback).

22 Edit the Action Manager object.

23 Click the Action Manager tab.

As you can see, by default this tab is empty. You'll add a new segment for each quiz question on the page.

24 Add a segment called *Judge Question 1* (choose Segment from the drop down list and click **Add**):

Now you're ready to add a condition that verifies all questions have been answered before judging the interactions.

25 Add a condition and complete the Condition Editor using the values in this table:

Setting	Value
Name	Answered All Questions
Type	Interaction
Interaction	MultCh_TrueFalse01
Interaction Element	<none>
Property	Known Response
Condition Operator	Equals
Type (lower)	True/False
Type Value	True

26 With *and* selected in the at the bottom-right corner of the Condition Editor, click the **Add** button to add another phrase to the expression:

*Click **Add** to add another phrase (or requirement) to the expression. This is important when you need the condition to meet multiple requirements.*

Choose "and" here so that all requirements of the condition must be met. If you were to choose "or", any of the requirements could be met.

27 Complete the next part of the expression according to the values in this table:

Setting	Value
Type	Interaction
Interaction	MultCh_ImageRadios02
Interaction Element	<none>
Property	Known Response
Condition Operator	Equals
Type (lower)	True/False
Type Value	True

The expression in the condition editor should look like this:

The Known Response property indicates whether or not the learner responded at all to the interaction. By default it is set to False. When the learner responds by clicking a choice, the Known Response property is set to True. So this condition is basically asking the question: "Has the learner chosen an answer for question 1 and has the learner chosen an answer for question 2?" The *and* between the two phrases requires that both conditions be met before the entire expression is True.

Note: For most multi-question quizzes, you will have more than two questions. Therefore, you would have to add a new phrase to the expression for each question in the quiz. Make sure the Boolean operator (*and/or*) is set to *and*.

28 Click **OK** to close the Condition Editor.

The Action Manager tab should look like this:

-- Judge Question 1
   -- if Answered All Questions

If all questions were answered, then you want the Action Manager object to judge the interaction.

29 Add a ***Judge Interaction*** action and choose *MultCh_TrueFalse01* from the drop down list:

30 Click **OK** to close the Judge Interaction window:

-- Judge Question 1
   -- if Answered All Questions
      Judge Interaction

31 Select *if Answered All Questions* and add a condition.

32 Complete the Condition Editor with the values in this table:

Setting	Value
Name	Question 1 unanswered

Setting	Value
Type	Interaction
Interaction	MultCh_TrueFalse01
Interaction Element	<none>
Property	Known Response
Condition Operator	Equals
Type (lower)	True/False
Type Value	False

You want to know if the Known Response property of question 1 is False because if it is, you'll want to take some action in response. In this case it should pop up a message reminding the learner to answer question number one.

33 Click **OK** to close the Condition Editor.

Your Action Manager tab should look like this:

```
-- Judge Question 1
    -- if Answered All Questions
        Judge Interaction
    -- else if question 1 unanswered
```

34 With *else if question 1 answered* selected, add a Popup Message action with this message: *Please answer question #1.*

```
-- Judge Question 1
    -- if Answered All Questions
        Judge Interaction
    -- else if question 1 unanswered
        Popup Message
```

That's all you need to do for this segment. Now you're ready to tackle the segment for question two. Instead of creating it from scratch, just duplicate segment one and make a few changes.

35 Select *Judge Question 1* and click **Copy** then **Paste**.

You should now have two identical segments:

Original

Duplicate

```
- Judge Question 1
    -- if Answered All Questions
        Judge Interaction
    -- else if question 1 unanswered
        Popup Message
- Judge Question 1
    -- if Answered All Questions
        Judge Interaction
    -- else if question 1 unanswered
        Popup Message
```

36 Edit the second segment and name it *Judge Question 2.*

You don't need to do anything to the *if Answered All Questions* condition because it is testing all questions on the page, not just one specific question.

37 Edit the *Judge Interaction* action in the second segment and choose *MultCh_ImageRadios02* as the interaction to judge.

38 Edit the *else if question 1 unanswered* condition in the second segment and change these settings:

Setting	Value
Name	Question 2 unanswered
Interaction	MultCh_ImageRadios02

39 Edit the Popup Message action in the second segment and change the text to: *Please answer question #2.*

Your Action Manager tab should look like this:

With changes added

```
-- Judge Question 1
    -- if Answered All Questions
        Judge Interaction
    -- else if question 1 unanswered
        Popup Message
-- Judge Question 2
    -- if Answered All Questions
        Judge Interaction
    -- else if question 2 unanswered
        Popup Message
```

Note: For multi-question quizzes with more than two questions, repeat steps 35 through 39 making changes so they correspond with for the correct question.

40 Click **OK** to close the CourseBuilder Interaction window.

Now you need to make the Score My Quiz image process the Action Manager object when the learner clicks the image.

Part IV (steps 41–46)

In this part of the tutorial you will attach behaviors to the Score My Quiz image to trigger the Action Manager object so that when the learner clicks the Score My Quiz image, the Action Manager judges all interactions on the page.

41 Select the Score My Quiz image:

> Score My Quiz

42 Open the Behaviors panel (Windows→Behaviors) and add a ***Judge Interaction Behavior*** (CourseBuilder→Judge Interaction Behavior).

43 In the Judge Interaction window, choose interaction ActionMgr03 (this is name of the Action Manager object):

44 Click **OK** to close the Judge Interaction window.

45 Make sure the event for the Judge Interaction action is *onClick*.

The behaviors for the Score My Quiz image should look like this:

46 Take a moment to test the quiz in a browser.

You should be able to take the quiz, click the Score My Quiz, and see the feedback layers populate with the right text and styles:

Feedback for correct answers should be blue.

Feedback for incorrect answers should be red.

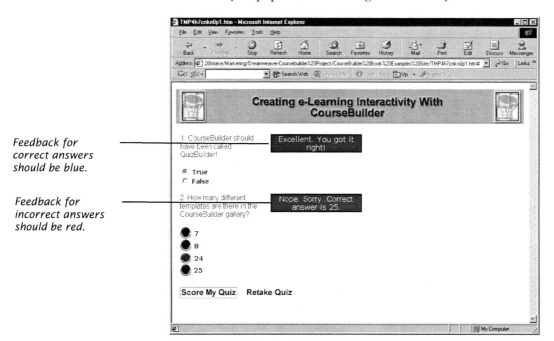

Also, you might want to refresh the browser and try it again, not answering any questions. The reminder popup messages should appear:

Now you're ready to activate the *Retake Quiz* image. Instead of resetting each question individually, just attach a script to the image that refreshes the browser with what's called a "hard reload." This action resets all elements on the page.

Part V (steps 47–50)

In this part of the tutorial you will add a behavior to the Retake Quiz image to cause it to reset the quiz when clicked by the learner.

47 Select the Retake Quiz image.

48 Add a Call JavaScript behavior action with this code: *window.location.reload()*

Call JavaScript

JavaScript: window.location.reload()

OK
Cancel
Help

49 Click **OK** to close the Call JavaScript window.

50 Test the quiz in a browser.

When the Retake Quiz button is clicked, the page should refresh and clear all quiz interactions (including the form-style True/False interaction that doesn't normally clear on a normal Refresh).

Your quiz is now very close to being finished (and you would hope so after 50 steps!). All you have left to do is tally and display the score. To do this, you need to update the Action Manager object.

Part VI (steps 51–58)

In this final part of the tutorial you will modify the Action Manager object to tally and show the score of the entire quiz when it judges the interactions.

51 Edit the Action Manager object and click the Action Manager tab.

```
-- Judge Question 1
    -- if Answered All Questions
        Judge Interaction
    -- else if question 1 unanswered
        Popup Message
-- Judge Question 2
    -- if Answered All Questions
        Judge Interaction
    -- else if question 2 unanswered
        Popup Message
```

The first thing you need to do is add a new segment to the Action Manager tab.

52 Select *Judge Question 2* and add a new segment called *Show Scores*:

Segment Editor

Segment Name: Show Scores

Segment Evaluation: ⊙ Always evaluate from the beginning
○ State transition

OK
Cancel
Help

Leave this setting selected by default.

53 Select *if All Questions Answered* from either of the earlier segments and click **Copy**.

54 Select the *Show Scores* segment and click **Paste**.

Your action manager should look like this:

```
-- Judge Question 1
    -- if Answered All Questions
        Judge Interaction
    -- else if question 1 unanswered
        Popup Message
-- Judge Question 2
    -- if Answered All Questions
        Judge Interaction
    -- else if question 2 unanswered
        Popup Message
-- Show Scores
    -- if Answered All Questions
        Judge Interaction
```

Instead of judging an interaction if all of the questions have been answered correctly, in this segment you need to tally and show the score. Therefore, delete the ***Judge Interaction*** action.

55 Select the *Judge Interaction* action in the *Show Scores* segment and click **Cut**.

Now you're ready to add the action that calculates and display the score.

56 Add a Set Text of Layer action for the "Score" layer and add this text in the New HTML field:

<p style class = feedbackText>You got {G01.score + G02.score} out of {G01.possCorrect + G02.possCorrect}</p>

Each CourseBuilder interaction is an HTML *object*. These objects are titled with the prefix of "G" followed by a number (i.e. if it is the first interaction added to the page it's *G01*). The score is stored as a property of that object. Because of this you can use "dot syntax" to reference it. Hence, "G01.score" is the score for the interaction titled G01. Adding the score for each interaction gives us the total score.

More Information: See *Using Scoring Variables* in *Chapter 16: Behind the Scenes: Deciphering CourseBuilder's JavaScript* for more details on working with interaction scores.

Your Action Manager tab should now look like this:

```
-- Judge Question 1
     -- if Answered All Questions
          Judge Interaction
     -- else if question 1 unanswered
          Popup Message
-- Judge Question 2
     -- if Answered All Questions
          Judge Interaction
     -- else if question 2 unanswered
          Popup Message
-- Show Scores
     -- if Answered All Questions
          Set Text of Layer
```

57 Click **OK** to close the CourseBuilder Interaction window.

58 Preview the quiz in a browser.

That's it! You did it! That was a long exercise, but we hope it was well worth it. It could have been much longer had we included more questions in the quiz. We hope you can see how to extend the same functionality to a multi-question quiz with more questions.

Let's Review

Since this tutorial was so long, it might be helpful to take a moment to review a few things. The first question you might ask is, "So what exactly did the Action Manager object do for us?"

In this example, the Action Manager acted as the overseer for the whole quiz. It determined if all questions were answered by the learner. Determining that all questions were answered it then told each interaction to process its Action Manager tab (through the ***Judge Interaction*** action). It also computed and displayed the score in a separate layer.

Another question you might ask is, "So why did I need the Action Manager to do all of this? Isn't there another way I could have done it?" First of all, you needed some way to take an action based on decisions. If the learner hadn't responded to all of the questions, you didn't want to process the feedback and scoring.

Certainly there are other ways you could accomplish this. You could have written your own JavaScript function to check to see if all questions were answered and called these functions manually. However, why do that when you use the Action Manager object to save you time and the headache of debugging all of your code?

Finally, some people may not like having all of the quiz questions on one page. If there are too many questions, learners have to scroll through the page which can be annoying. Of course you could place all questions on separate pages, but then you'd have to find some way to track the scoring results across multiple pages (which can be tricky, but see the More Information reference below for solutions).

The short answer to these issues is that you would need to create a frameset in which to store the scores from each interaction in some kind of variable (preferrably an array) that you could then add up later and display. We decided not to cover the details of doing this in our book because the Learning Site extension to Dreamweaver does all of this for you! See Section III and IV on using Learning Site.

More Information: A quiz with multiple questions on one page will not work with Learning Site. If you want to transfer scores and student data using Learning Site you need to create a multi-question quiz in which the interactions are placed on separate web-pages. See *Chapter 18: Defining a Learning Site* for a solution. Also see the following URL for a solution for multi-page, multi-question quizzes created from scratch:

```
http://www.macromedia.com/support/coursebuilder/scoring/
multi_page_track/
```

More Information: For another (even more complicated but very intriguing) tutorial using the Action Manager object, see this URL:

```
http://www.macromedia.com/support/coursebuilder/interactions/
bikelane/
```

Summary

The Action Manager object is meant to sit, in a sense, "above" the rest of the interactions on the page and oversee the how the overall page works. In this chapter you learned how to use Scoring variables, create a "Show Answer" button, and manage a multi-question quiz.

Remember that even though the Judge Interaction, Reset Interaction, and Set Interaction properties are often used in the Action Manager, they can also be used as Dreamweaver behaviors by attaching them to any object.

Creating Custom CourseBuilder Interactions

15

By now you've probably thought of a lot of ways you would like to apply what you've learned to your own organization's needs. Perhaps you have already tried using your own style sheet with interactions. Perhaps you've started creating some custom graphics that fit your e-learning initiative's look and feel.

In this chapter you'll learn how to:

- Build custom reusable libraries of interactions that you can share with your e-learning development team members.

- Add a customized interaction to the CourseBuilder Gallery so it can be reused again and again.

- Delete unwanted interaction templates from the Gallery.

- Share a customized Gallery with other team members.

Adding a Customized Interaction to the CourseBuilder Gallery

As you know, Coursebuilder comes with a preset gallery of interactive quiz objects. If you find yourself constantly changing them to fit the style of your particular website or course, you can create a custom interaction and add it into the gallery to re-use later.

This functionality can be particularly useful if you have already applied styles from an external style sheet, selected custom graphics, or designed complex feedback responses in the Action Manager and you want to reuse the same objects without having to choose all of those settings every time.

For example, it is fairly common to use the ***Set Text of Layer*** behavior to display feedback rather than use the pop-up JavaScript error message boxes. By creating a reusable object you won't have to recreate the **Set Text of Layer** behavior every time.

Follow these steps to add a customized interaction to the CourseBuilder gallery, follow these steps:

1 Apply your styles or other changes to an interaction you want to re-use.

2 Once you have it looking and working the way you want, select the entire interaction using one of the methods explained in Chapter 2.

3 Open the Add Interaction to Gallery window (Choose Modify →
Coursebuilder → Add Interaction).

The Add Interaction to Gallery dialog box appears:

Select this option to add your custom interaction to an existing category.

Select this option to create new categories within the gallery.

4 Choose the category you want to add it to or create your own by clicking New for the *Gallery Category* setting and entering a new category name.

5 Select the *Target* browser setting.

When you view the Gallery you can choose to see only those interactions that will work in a 3.0 browser. This setting determines when this interaction appears in the gallery:

6 Enter a name in the *Name* field (up to 20 characters with no spaces) and choose a custom icon to represent the new interaction (optional):

Selecting an icon to represent your custom interaction is optional. If you do, make the icon 80x80 pixels.

Enter the name for your custom interaction here.

7 Click **OK**.

That's it. You've added a custom interaction to the CourseBuilder gallery. If you've created a new category, the category appears in the category list:

If you don't choose a custom image to coincide with your custom interaction, CourseBuilder displays this one.

Deleting Unwanted Templates from the Gallery

Once you have added several custom interactions to the Gallery you may want to delete some of the original interaction templates that come with CourseBuilder.

Before you delete interactions from the Gallery, it is important to understand the file structure behind the Gallery.

The Gallery File Structure

The gallery objects are stored as files in the ... *program files\Dreamweaver 4\CourseBuilder\Gallery* directory. You can usually find this at the root level of your main hard drive using this path:

```
C:\Program Files\Macromedia\Dreamweaver 4\ CourseBuilder\Gallery
```

Within the Gallery directory, each category has its own subdirectory. For example, with the addition of a new category called "My Objects" the list of directories looks like this:

```
└─ CourseBuilder
   ├─ Config
   └─ Gallery
      ├─ 010_Multiple Choice
      ├─ 020_Drag and Drop
      ├─ 030_Explore
      ├─ 040_Button
      ├─ 050_Text Entry
      ├─ 060_Timer
      ├─ 070_Slider
      ├─ 080_Action Manager
      └─ 100_MyObjects
   ├─ Help
   ├─ SupportFiles
   └─ Tutorial
```

Inside each of the category subdirectories are two files for each gallery template. For example, this is a list of the files in the Multiple Choice category subdirectory:

The template file itself is the file with the extension *.agt.* The *.gif* file is the icon that displays in the gallery when you choose that particular template.

Deleting the Files

You may want to delete some of the interactions that you never use from the Gallery to clean up your workspace. This would also prevent team members that might be using the same gallery for a collaborative project from accidentally using an interaction they shouldn't.

To delete the interaction templates that you don't want, simply navigate to the directory where their corresponding files are found, select and delete both the *.agt* and the *.gif* files that correspond to that template.

Tip: To save these interactions, just in case you want to replace them into the Gallery later, Cut and Paste the files into a different directory. That way you have a backup. To restore them, simply Copy and Paste them back into the Gallery subdirectory they were moved from.

Sharing Custom Galleries with Team Members

By now you have probably realized that you could create an entire gallery filled with custom interactions. If you work on an e-learning development team, you may want to share these custom objects with others.

For example, a Development Team Leader might, in conjunction with a graphic artist, the IT department, and an instructional designer, create a series of interaction templates that use custom graphics and style sheets that tie in with the organization's overall website. These templates might also use custom designed feedback to meet the needs of a particular target learning audience. The team leader could then distribute the gallery to the team to use during development.

Distributing the Files

To distribute a custom gallery to other team members, you simply need to understand where the templates are stored on your hard drive, and then distribute the Gallery directory.

Follow these steps to distribute a custom gallery to other team members:

1   Find the Gallery subdirectory on the hard drive of the other team member's machine and rename it (i.e. Gallery_old).

Caution: This is a precautionary measure to backup the gallery of the end user. Your team member may have his or her own custom interactions that would be difficult to replace if overwritten.

2 Find the Gallery subdirectory on your hard drive.

More Information: See *The Gallery File Structure* earlier in the chapter for more details.

3 Copy the Gallery subdirectory and all of its contents onto the team member's machine. Make sure it resides in the same directory as the original gallery directory.

Tip: Uncompressed, the contents of the Gallery are 112 KB in size. If you want to distribute the gallery to team members via email, you may want to use a compression utility to zip the contents of the Gallery directory (see *www.winzip.com*).

That's all there is to it! Isn't that simple?

Summary

You can quickly and easily create custom CourseBuilder interactions and custom galleries that can be distributed to other team members. By doing this, your team members are using the same custom interactions, saving loads of time, and creating interactions that are uniform in appearance and functionality.

Behind the Scenes: Deciphering CourseBuilder's JavaScript

16

If you are like us, you often want to know more than what's on the surface. In fact, there is so much going on behind the scenes (which is why CourseBuilder is so nice to work with), that we could write another book on the subject. Since we can't do that here, in this chapter we introduce you to some of the JavaScript elements that can be useful to understand and manipulate.

In this chapter you will learn:

- The basic anatomy of a CourseBuilder interaction.

- How to reference properties of an interaction or an element of an interaction in a JavaScript function and in other Dreamweaver behaviors.

- How to use interaction properties to score an interaction or a series of interactions.

- How to replace the value of certain interaction properties with a custom value to overcome some of CourseBuilder's scoring limitations.

CourseBuilder Interaction Anatomy 101

Whenever you add a CourseBuilder interaction to a web page, dozens of lines of JavaScript code are added. In this section we will explain some of that code.

External JavaScript Files

Most of the code that is *added* is attached as external JavaScript files. (In other words it isn't actually stored in the document, but gets loaded when the pages loads as if it were stored right in the document.) You can look in the *<head>* tag and find several references to these external files:

```
 2 <head>
 3 <title>Untitled Document</title>
 4 <meta http-equiv="Content-Type" content="text/html; charset=iso-8859-1">
 5 <script language="JavaScript"></script>
 6 <script language="JavaScript" src="scripts/behActions.js"></script>
 7 <script language="JavaScript" src="scripts/behCourseBuilder.js"></script>
 8 <script language="JavaScript" src="scripts/interactionClass.js"></script>
 9 <script language="JavaScript" src="scripts/elemIbtnClass.js"></script>
10 </head>
```

You can find all of these script files located within your site in the *scripts* directory. These external files are part of what gets copied into your site when you first create a CourseBuilder interaction and copy the *support files*.

This table lists the basic purpose of these files and their file sizes:

Script Filename	Purpose	File Size
behActions.js	Contains the functions that get called when you use basic Dreamweaver behaviors such as Call JavaScript, Change Property, and so forth.	6K
behCourseBuilder.js	Contains the functions specific to CourseBuilder such as Judge Interaction, Reset Interaction, and so forth.	3K

Script Filename	Purpose	File Size
behDragLayer.js	Contains a function used to make sure drag and drop layers work in both Netscape and IE.	6K
behTimeLine.js	Contains functions that ensure the Timeline actions work properly.	4K
cmi.js	Contains functions that aid in passing data to a Learning Management System when using the Knowledge Track setting on the General tab.	7K
ElemDragClass.js	Contains functions that create the drag and drop elements of a Drag-and-Drop interaction. These functions also control such things as moving the layer, snapping to the correct spot, or snapping back when incorrect.	11K
ElemHotaClass.js	Contains functions that create and control the hot areas of Explore interactions.	5K
ElembtnClass.js	Contains functions that create and control Button interactions.	6K
ElemInptClass.js	Contains functions that create and control elements of Multiple Choice interactions.	5K
ElemSldrClass.js	Contains functions that create and control elements of Multiple Choice interactions.	8K
ElemTextClass.js	Contains functions that create and control Text Entry (fill-in-the-blank) interaction elements.	6K
ElemTimrClass.js	Contains functions to create and control the elements of the Timer interaction.	8K

Script Filename	Purpose	File Size
InteractionClass.js	Contains numerous functions having to do with many different parts of interactions in general, such as the functions that control how the Action Manager works.	19K

The Interaction Object

In addition to these external script files being inserted into the head of the page, CourseBuilder inserts an *<interaction>* tag in the body of the page.

This tag generally starts with code that looks like this:

```
<interaction name="MultCh_ImageRadios01" object="G01"
template="010_Multiple Choice/030_MultCh_ImageRadios_04.agt"
includesrc="interactionClass.js,elemIbtnClass.js">
```
This code ends with this tag terminator:

```
</interaction>
```
The code that is placed between those lines defines what is known as the *interaction object*.

The interaction object is not a standard HTML object. It is specific to CourseBuilder. The fact that it is an object means that it has properties that come with preset values that can also be set on the fly. It also means that there are *methods* (or pre-built functions) associated with the object that can be called when needed.

When referencing object properties and methods it is important to reference the correct interaction object.

Follow these steps to find out the appropriate reference for any kind of interaction object:

1 In Dreamweaver Design view, place your cursor somewhere in the interaction.

2 Click the *<interaction>* tag selector at the bottom of the screen:

<interaction> ——————— `<body> <interaction> <div> <form>`
tag selector

3 Access Dreamweaver's Code view.

In Code view, the entire code for the *<interaction>* tag is selected.

4   Locate the top of the selected code where it begins with *<interaction...*.

5   Find the word *object*.

6   The text in quotes following the word *object* is the object title:

In this example, this is the G01 interaction object.

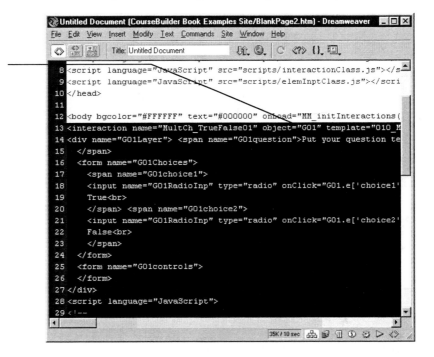

Interaction Object Properties

All interactions have some properties that are common among all interaction types. There are also some properties that are specific to certain interactions.

Here is a list of the different *types* of properties:

- **Select list** –the property is selected from a dropdown list.
- **Boolean** –the property has only one of two values: True or False.
- **Text** –the property is a string of text characters.
- **Numeric** –the property is a number, usually an integer.

More Information: You can get a complete list of CourseBuilder interaction properties by looking for *Properties* in the index of CourseBuilder's Online Help:

Select properties under the CourseBuilder Interaction sub-heading.

Discovering How to Reference a Particular Property

Referencing properties of any object is important to JavaScript programming. Macromedia provides an interesting way for us to find out how to reference interaction properties.

Follow these steps to find out how to reference a particular interaction property:

1   Edit the interaction whose property you want to reference.

2   Click on the Action Manager tab.

3   Add a Condition (it doesn't matter where in the Action Manager because you won't be saving it).

4   In the Condition Editor, choose the interaction and property for which you want the reference syntax.

In this example, we've chosen the *Score* property of the input element *choice1*:

Condition Editor

Condition Name:	OK
	Cancel
Add Delete	Help
Expressions:	Input "choice1" Score equals <incomplete>

Type: Interaction

Interaction: MultCh_TrueFalse01   Input "choice1"

Property: Score

equals

Type: Number

Number:

and

5   Now change the Type from *Interaction* to *JavaScript*.

CourseBuilder displays the equivalent JavaScript code in the JavaScript field:

Type: JavaScript

JavaScript: G01.e['choice1'].score ==

The contents of the **_JavaScript_** field is the code you would use to reference this property in a JavaScript function or in another behavior such as the Call JavaScript behavior.

Note: Notice that the code ends with an equality operator (checks to see if the score is equal to something). The equality operator might be used with an *if* statement or some other kind of conditional JavaScript statement. But you could make it an assignment statement (assign a new score) by changing the equality operator ($==$) to the assignment operator ($=$).

Using this method to discover the syntax you should use to reference interaction properties can be valuable. The Online Help provided with CourseBuilder does not supply JavaScript statements along with the properties they list.

Using Scoring Variables/Properties

Some of the properties keep track of information about the interaction's score: total score, possible correct, and so forth. There are places in the CourseBuilder help files that refer to these properties as variables. While it's true that you can store them in variables, they are really properties of the *interaction* object that get changed as the learner responds to the interaction.

You can use these properties with single interactions, but scores are more likely to be desired when learners are answering several questions in a single round. You can use the Action Manager object to tabulate the score and display it. In this section we'll review what variables CourseBuilder creates and what information is stored there.

More Information: For information on using the Action Manager object to tally several scores on a single page, see *Chapter 14: The Power of the Action Manager Object*.

What is Stored Where

This table contains a list of all of the properties you might use for tracking student scores:

Property Name	Description
score	Contains the total numeric score of the interaction.
totalCorrect	Contains the total number of correct responses the learner made in the interaction. For example, in a *Choose all that apply* type of multiple choice question, this would record the number of correct responses they made.
totalIncorrect	This is the opposite of the *totalCorrect* variable and contains the number of incorrect responses made by the learner.
possCorrect	Contains the total number of elements of the interaction that are labeled as Correct. This is not the possible correct *score* but rather just the number of possible correct elements.

Property Name	Description
possIncorrect	Contains the total number of elements of the interaction labeled Incorrect.
correct	Contains a TRUE if the entire interaction is correctly answered, and FALSE if the entire interaction is incorrect.

On CD: Use our interactive *CourseBuilder Interaction Property Interrogator* on the CD to get a clear understanding of how these properties work. Open *prop_interrogator.htm* in a browser and try out the interaction.

Using "dot syntax" to Work With the Information

You can assign any of these properties to a variable by using the dot syntax shown here:

```
var varname = G01.score + G02.score + G03.score…
```

You can also use any of these properties with the ***Popup Message***, ***Set Text of Frame***, ***Set Text of Layer***, and ***Set Text of Text Field*** actions by using syntax in the ***New HTML*** field similar to this example:

```
You scored a total of {G01.score + G02.score + G03.score} out of
{G01.possCorrect + G02.possCorrect + G03.possCorrect}.
```

Note: Using the *possCorrect* property in this way will only work correctly if every element that has a score has a score no greater than one. This is the case because this property doesn't calculate the possible score of the interaction, just how many elements are designated as *correct*. See the next section, *Tallying the Correct Possible Score*, for a solution. Also remember that you can only add up interaction properties for interactions on the same page. To calculate scores for interactions on multiple pages use the Learning Site extension.

Replacing Property Values With a Custom Value

As you learned in the last section, CourseBuilder supplies you with a *possCorrect* interaction property that counts the number of possible correct responses. What it does ***not*** do is calculate the possible correct score.

You might be asking, "What is the difference?" The difference is that every element in an interaction can contain a different score that has a value other than "1".

Because each element has its own score, problems can occur when you create a multiple-correct question and display the score for that question.

The Problem

To illustrate the problem, take a look at a variation on the multi-question quiz you created in Chapter 14.

On CD: In a browser, open *Sample_16-1.htm* and take the quiz (this exercise was designed for Internet Explorer—you may experience some differences if using another browser).

In this example we've added a *multiple correct* type of multiple choice question. It is worth 6 points while the first question is only worth 1 point. The correct answers are the first, third, and fourth choices. Each choice is worth two points for a total of 6.

The problem here is that even if you get the overall interaction wrong you still get some points for the correct choices you chose:

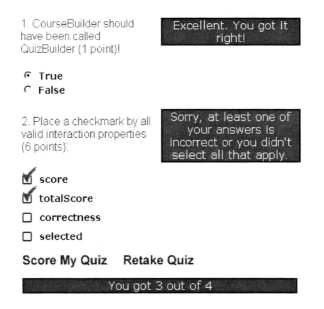

In this example our feedback says we received 3 points (1 point for getting the correct answer on the first question and 2 points for choosing one of the correct choices on the second question) out of 4 points.

There are two problems with this:

- First, the total possible points is really 7 not 4. The reason it thinks it is 4 is because, as we mentioned before, the *possCorrect* property counts how many possible correct responses there are. It doesn't calculate what the possible score is.

- Second, we shouldn't be getting any score at all for the second question since we got it wrong.

The Solution: Part 1

So, how do we solve these problems? Let's tackle the first problem first—the issue of not calculating the correct possible score.

View the Partially Finished Interaction

Before working through this example, take a look at the same quiz with the partial solution in place:

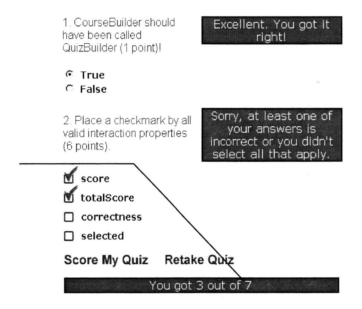

1. CourseBuilder should have been called QuizBuilder (1 point)!

Excellent. You got it right!

⊙ True
○ False

2. Place a checkmark by all valid interaction properties (6 points).

Sorry, at least one of your answers is incorrect or you didn't select all that apply.

Choosing the same responses yields the same total score, but the possible correct is calculated correctly. This time it says "...out of 7."

☑ score
☑ totalScore
☐ correctness
☐ selected

Score My Quiz   Retake Quiz

You got 3 out of 7

On CD: Open *Sample_16-2.htm* in a browser and complete the quiz (this exercise was designed for Internet Explorer—you may experience some differences if using another browser).

Completing Part 1 of the Solution

In this section you'll add a ***Set Interaction Properties*** action that will redefine the *possCorrect* property value for the second interaction. It will calculate the total possible score for the interaction rather than the total possible correct responses and place the result in the possCorrect property.

Follow these steps to make the possCorrect property calculate the total possible score:

1   In Dreamweaver, open *Sample_16-2_Start.htm* (this exercise was designed for Internet Explorer—you may experience some differences if using another browser).

2 Edit the Action Manager object by clicking the small layer in the banner image at the top of the page, selecting the *<interaction>* tag selector, and clicking **Edit** on the Properties panel.

3 Click on the Action Manager tab.

The contents of the Action Manager tab should look like this:

```
-- Judge Question 1
   -- if Answered All Questions
      Judge Interaction
   -- else if question 1 unanswered
      Popup Message
-- Judge Question 2
   -- if Answered All Questions
      Judge Interaction
   -- else if question 2 unanswered
      Popup Message
-- Show Scores
   -- if Answered All Questions
      Set Text of Layer
```

We've already figured out that to reference the *Score* property. For each choice we use this syntax:

```
G02.e['choice1'].score
```

We also know that to reference the total score of an interaction we use this syntax:

```
G02.score
```

More Information: You may want to review the technique described in *Discovering How to Reference a Particular Property* earlier in this chapter.

4 Select *if Answered All Questions* in the *Show Scores* segment:

```
-- Judge Question 1
   -- if Answered All Questions
      Judge Interaction
   -- else if question 1 unanswered
      Popup Message
-- Judge Question 2
   -- if Answered All Questions
      Judge Interaction
   -- else if question 2 unanswered
      Popup Message
-- Show Scores
   -- if Answered All Questions
      Set Text of Layer
```

5 Add a ***Set Interaction Properties*** action.

6 Make changes to the Set Interaction Properties window based on the values in this table:

Setting	Value
Set	Interaction
Interaction	MultCh_ImageChkboxes02
Property	Possible Correct

7   Select *JavaScript* for the Set setting:

CourseBuilder displays the JavaScript field and it is already populated with "*G02.possCorrect=*". This is good because we want to assign the possCorrect property a new value.

8   Complete the expression with this code:

```
G02.possCorrect=(G02.e['choice1'].score +
G02.e['choice2'].score + G02.e['choice3'].score +
G02.e['choice4'].score)
```
This expression adds up all of the potential scores for each element of the interaction and assigns the total to the *possCorrect* property of the interaction.

9   Click **OK** to close the Set Interaction Properties window.

Your Action Manager tab should look like this:

```
-- Judge Question 1
    -- if Answered All Questions
        Judge Interaction
    -- else if question 1 unanswered
        Popup Message
-- Judge Question 2
    -- if Answered All Questions
        Judge Interaction
    -- else if question 2 unanswered
        Popup Message
-- Show Scores
    -- if Answered All Questions
        Set Interaction Properties
        Set Text of Layer
```

10 Click **OK** to close the CourseBuilder Interaction window.

11 Test the interaction in a browser.

The possible score is now correctly calculated.

More Information: For another approach to solving a similar data tracking problem with CourseBuilder and Learning Site, see *Chapter 20: Using Learning Site to Track Learner Data.*

The Solution: Part 2

Now that you have CourseBuilder reporting the correct possible score, you need to change it so it reports a score only when they get the entire interaction correct.

Viewing the Finished Quiz

Before implementing part two of the solution, take a moment and view a sample of the completed quiz so you can understand what you're working towards.

On CD: Open *Sample_16-3.htm* in a browser and complete the quiz (this exercise was designed for Internet Explorer—you may experience some differences if using another browser):

1. CourseBuilder should have been called QuizBuilder (1 point)!

Excellent. You got it right!

◉ True
○ False

2. Place a checkmark by all valid interaction properties (6 points).

Sorry, at least one of your answers is incorrect or you didn't select all that apply.

☑ score
☑ totalScore
☐ correctness
☐ selected

Score My Quiz   Retake Quiz

You got 1 out of 7

This version not only displays the correct possible score but it displays the correct score as well.

Completing Part 2 of the Solution

In this section you'll add a condition and an action to the Action Manager object that will set the second interaction's total score to zero if the *Correctness* property is False (meaning they didn't get the answer right).

Follow these steps to make the interaction's *Score* property set to zero based on a condition:

1   In Dreamweaver, open *Sample_16-3_Start.htm* .

2   Edit the Action Manager object and go to the Action Manager tab.

3   Select *Judge Interaction* in the *Judge Question 2* segment:

```
-- Judge Question 1
   -- if Answered All Questions
         Judge Interaction
   -- else if question 1 unanswered
         Popup Message
-- Judge Question 2
   -- if Answered All Questions
         Judge Interaction
   -- else if question 2 unanswered
         Popup Message
-- Show Scores
   -- if Answered All Questions
         Set Interaction Properties
         Set Text of Layer
```

4   Add a condition and complete the Condition Editor based on the values in this table:

Setting	Value
Name	This interaction is incorrect
Type	Interaction
Interaction	MultCh_ImageChkboxes02
Property	Correct State
Property Operator	Equals
Type (lower)	Select

Setting	Value
Type Value	Incorrect

The Condition Editor should now look like this:

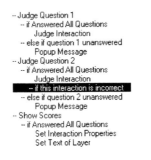

5   Click **OK** to close the Condition Editor.

Your Action Manager tab should look like this:

```
-- Judge Question 1
    -- if Answered All Questions
        Judge Interaction
    -- else if question 1 unanswered
        Popup Message
-- Judge Question 2
    -- if Answered All Questions
        Judge Interaction
    -- if this interaction is incorrect
    -- else if question 2 unanswered
        Popup Message
-- Show Scores
    -- if Answered All Questions
        Set Interaction Properties
        Set Text of Layer
```

If the interaction is incorrect, you're going to set the interaction's total score to zero.

6   With *if this interaction is incorrect* still selected, add a ***Set Interaction Properties*** action and complete it based on the values in this table:

Setting	Value
Set	Interaction
Interaction	MultCh_ImageChkboxes02
Property	Total Score
Type	Number
Number	0

The Set Interactions Properties window should now look like this:

7   Click **OK** to close the Set Interaction Properties window.

The Action Manager tab should look like this:

```
-- Judge Question 1
   -- if Answered All Questions
      Judge Interaction
   -- else if question 1 unanswered
      Popup Message
-- Judge Question 2
   -- if Answered All Questions
      Judge Interaction
      -- if this interaction is incorrect
         Set Interaction Properties
   -- else if question 2 unanswered
      Popup Message
-- Show Scores
   -- if Answered All Questions
      Set Interaction Properties
      Set Text of Layer
```

8   Click **OK** to close the CourseBuilder Interaction window.

9   Test the quiz in a browser:

The correct score and possible score are now displayed:

Summary

In this chapter you've learned how to identify the interaction object. You've also learned how to identify its properties and reference them. Using these skills you completed a tutorial in which you learned how to replace the value of certain interaction properties (such as possCorrect) with a custom value. You need this skill because of the limitations of the possCorrect and Score values with regard to multiple correct interactions.

Section III: Using Learning Site Command for Course Architecture

You've learned to create interactive pages using CourseBuilder. In this section you'll learn how to tie it all together with a user interface and navigation controls provided by Learning Site Command— Macromedia's newest e-learning extension to Dreamweaver.

Getting to Know Learning Site 17

Learning Site, officially known as Learning Site Command on the Macromedia Exchange site, provides several features. These features allow you to assemble a training course that includes a navigational structure, quizzes, and other learning interactions. If you use Learning Site with Dreamweaver UltraDev, you can also track student activities on a server-side database.

In this chapter you will learn:

- About Learning Site and how to use it.
- The potential of Learning Site.
- How to install Learning Site.
- About Learning Site basics.
- How to use the Learning Site Help.
- To use Learning Site and CourseBuilder together.

What is Learning Site?

As you learned in Chapter 1, Learning Site is an extension to Dreamweaver and Dreamweaver UltraDev. It provides features that let you assemble, track and administer a training course online. These features include the following:

- A set of predefined navigational structures that you can use to establish the user interface for your course.
- The ability to add three types of interactive pages to your course.
- The ability to generate a random set of questions from of pool of pages.
- A database and other features for tracking student results across multiple pages. (This feature is only available if you are using UltraDev.)
- Tools to help administer the training course.

The concepts behind Learning Site are quite a bit different than those for CourseBuilder. With Learning Site you are not working on a single HTML page; you are working with an entire Dreamweaver site. You establish certain characteristics about that site, define the types of pages you want to include, determine the course navigation, and decide whether or not you will use student tracking.

After setting up a learning site and the pages that are a part of that site, you then need to add the content to the individual pages. However, you do not need to create the user interface for those pages. Learning Site does that for you.

Learning Site is a tool that will save you a lot of development time. You still must create the meat of the course, but you will not need to deal with all the student tracking issues and the user interface issues.

Exploring Learning Site Possibilities

Now that you know some of what Learning Site can do, let's look at this tool in more detail. We've divided Learning Site features into two sections: Learning Site possibilities using Dreamweaver and Learning Site possibilities using UltraDev.

What You Can Do with Just Dreamweaver

If you choose to use Dreamweaver and not UltraDev, Learning Site still provides several nice features. The features that are not available using just Dreamweaver are the student tracking capabilities. All others are available and are reviewed here.

As you review the features in this section, you may want to view the sample courses we have included on the CD ROM. They are labeled *site_1, site_2, site_3*. Open the *index.htm* files in each folder to begin viewing the site. These sites are very simple examples of what you can do without student tracking.

A Site Tool

Learning Site receives its name because it is a site tool, not a page tool like CourseBuilder. Using the Learning Site command, you can add "learning" features to a Dreamweaver or UltraDev site.

A Planning Tool

When you establish a learning site, you identify, among other things, the types of pages your course includes. Because this is part of setting up the learning site, it can be a great planning tool. You can establish the structure of your course up front and then fill in the content later.

There are some limitations in using Learning Site as a planning tool. It only allows you to identify three page types: Media (such as Macromedia Flash and Shockwave®), CourseBuilder interaction, and blank. You should use blank pages for all content that doesn't fit into the media or CourseBuilder categories. Therefore, a major portion of your course may fall within the "blank pages" category. This can make it difficult to do in-depth planning.

> ### Learning Site is not an Instructional Design Tool
>
> Even though Learning Site helps you establish the structure of a course, it is not an instructional design tool like Designers Edge®. You must still devote time to instructional design during the development of your course.

 Note: Even though you initially add certain number of pages while setting up your site, Learning Site does not limit you to those pages. You can always add or remove pages later.

A User Interface Development Tool

Learning Site provides default user interface designs that can save a good deal of time in user interface development. The navigational structure is already established for you. You simply choose a predefined style or make modifications to a custom style.

Learning Site's default user interface includes basic navigation as shown in this screen shot:

If you want to create a more sophisticated user interface, such as pop-up menus, you will still need to do a lot more development on your own.

Tip: You can use Macromedia Fireworks® to simplify the process of creating pop-up menus. Search for "pop-up menus" in Fireworks Help. Also see http://www.projectseven.com/tutorials/menuing/mcloser/index.htm for a tutorial an alternative way to create popup menus.

What You Can Do with UltraDev

When you couple UltraDev with Dreamweaver, you are able to access more of what Learning Site has to offer. In fact, one of the nicest features of Learning Site is only available when used with UltraDev.

On CD: As you review the features in this section, you may want to view the sample courses included on the CD ROM: site_1, site_2, or site_3. Open the *index.htm* file in each folder. If you have installed Personal Web Server (PWS), you may also view student tracking in site_4_fin and site_5 by defining them first in UltraDev and publishing them to your local machine. See *Chapter 20: Using Learning Site to Track Learner Data* for more information. These are very simple sites that show you what is possible.

A Student Tracking Tool

One of the nicest features about Learning Site is that it simplifies the process of setting up student tracking for an on-line course. Learning Site comes with Active Server Pages (ASP) and a Microsoft Access database already setup for you that you can use to track the results of multiple page interactions. This provides a way for you to track student activities without having to invest in a Learning Management System (LMS).

The tracking database was designed based on Aviation Industry CBT Committee (AICC) guidelines for Computer Managed Instruction (CMI).

More Information: Student tracking is covered in more detail in *Chapter 20: Using Learning Site to Track Learner Data.*

An Administration Tool

When you are tracking student data, you need a tool to maintain the information, view reports and so forth. An LMS normally provides these features. If you use Learning Site with UltraDev, Learning Site provides this functionality for you.

Using the basic student tracking available with Learning Site, you can add, modify, and delete users. You can display a student activities report. This report shows each activity completed, the date, total time, total score, and status. You can also display an activity report. This report shows the average time and average score for each activity. For further analysis you can choose a specific activity that shows information by user ID.

Installing Learning Site

Before you can install Learning Site you must have these three items:

- Dreamweaver or Dreamweaver UltraDev version 4 or higher.
- The Dreamweaver Extensions Manager. (This comes preinstalled with Dreamweaver 4 or higher.)
- The Learning Site Command install file.

Follow these steps to install the Learning Site Command extension:

1   Access the Dreamweaver or UltraDev Exchange site:
     (*http://www.macromedia.com/exchange/dreamweaver/*)
     (*http://www.macromedia.com/exchange/ultradev/*)

What is a Learning Management System?

An LMS helps manage on-line courses. Most systems let students register, select courses, take courses, complete exercises and quizzes, and communicate with instructors and other students. Instructors, administrators and managers can then monitor student participation through reports.

There are numerous LMSs to choose from—at prices ranging from minimal to astronomical. This URL contains an article that provides suggestions for evaluating an LMS as well as a list of sites that publish evaluations: *http://www.e-learninghub.com /Selecting_an_LMS.html.*

LMS standards and guidelines have been created to assist in the transfer of information between the course and the LMS. AICC and SCORM are the two most common standards.

2   Find and download the Learning Site Command package file (.MXP).

To find the extension, choose *Learning* from the Browse Extensions drop down box.

> **What is the Extension Manager?**
>
> The Extension Manager works inside Dreamweaver and helps you install new Dreamweaver extensions and manage your existing extensions. To open the Extension Manager from within Dreamweaver, choose Commands → Manage Extensions. You can also open the Extensions Manager without Dreamweaver by choosing it from the Start menu.

Tip: You may want to save this file to the *Downloaded extensions* folder that is within the Dreamweaver folder.

3   Find the package file you downloaded and double-click it or choose Install Extensions from the File menu in the Extension Manager (File → Install Extensions). This starts the installation program.

4   Accept the disclaimer and the Learning Site Command extension installs.

You should be able to view the extension in the Extension Manager.

When you install Learning Site, you won't notice any significant changes to Dreamweaver. However, if you look in the Site menu you will notice a new menu option: Learning Site.

Besides this change, other files were installed:

- Template files that let you choose a navigational style
- The Learning Site Command extension files
- Access to the Learning Site Help
- Sample files that aid you in setting up tracking with UltraDev
- A menu option that lets you copy the Admin Files. (This menu option is only active if you are using UltraDev.)

Using Learning Site

Learning Site is a fairly easy tool to use. It takes very little effort to learn the basics. In this section we want to show you how easy it is by giving you an overview of the basic process. In the next chapter, we address each of these topics in more detail.

To begin creating a learning site, you can use an existing Dreamweaver site or define a new site.

Choose Create Learning Site from the Learning Site sub-menu (Learning Site → Create Learning Site):

This command displays the Learning Site window:

This window contains four tabs if you are using Dreamweaver: Site, Pages, Style, and Navigation. Three additional tabs are included if you are using UltraDev: Tracking, Login, and Results. By entering information in these tabs you can set up the initial structure for an on-line course.

 More Information: The steps in this section are covered in more detail in *Chapter 18: Defining a Learning Site.*

Step 1: Defining the Site

You define the site in the Site tab. In most cases you do not need to change any of the information on this tab. The navigation file is disabled and shouldn't be changed. This page contains the navigational template for your site. Also, data tracking is disabled unless you are using UltraDev.

From this tab you can define a new Dreamweaver site or edit the existing Dreamweaver site by clicking the **Define** button.

Step 2: Adding the Pages

The pages tab lets you indicate the types of pages and how many of each page type you want to include in the course:

The top portion of the tab lists all of the pages that are included in the site. You add pages by entering a ".htm" file name, a page title, a background color if you wish, and by choosing a page type. These three page types are available:

- **Blank Pages** are for any page you want to include that does not fit under the Media or CourseBuilder Interaction type.

- **Media Pages** are for playing Macromedia Flash files, Macromedia Shockwave files, or a web-packaged Macromedia Authorware® piece.

- **CourseBuilder Interaction** pages are used for CourseBuilder Interactions. When you choose this page type, you must also choose the question type you want to include on the page.

You can set up as many pages as you like and rearrange the order. You can add and delete pages at any time, so even after you are done defining this tab, it does not have to be the final state of the course.

Tip: If you have already created several Coursebuilder pages and would like to add them to the site, click on the folder icon, search for and select those pages.

Step 3: Choosing the Navigation Style

The Style Tab lets you choose the look and feel of the navigational framework:

This navigational framework surrounds your individual pages. The navigation takes place in one frame of a frameset and your content is displayed in another frame.

Navigation file

Content files

When you select a style, Learning Site displays a visual preview of that style to the right.

There are five predefined styles to choose from. You can also choose *Custom* as your style, but this requires that you choose graphic files for each navigational element such as the **Next** and **Previous** buttons.

More Information. Customizing your layout is described in more detail in Chapter 19: *Customizing a Learning Site.*

Step 4: Defining How the Navigation Works

The navigation tab lets you determine exactly how the navigation works.

You can either keep the default settings or change the options to meet the specific needs of your course design:

Once you have defined all the tabs, click **OK**. If you have included CourseBuilder Interaction pages, the system adds the CourseBuilder support files to your site.

Step 5: Adding Student Tracking Features

One of the powerful features of Learning Site is that you can use it to track student results. These features require the use of UltraDev. You set up these features using the Tracking, Login, and Results tab.

The Tracking tab lets you set up an Access® database for tracking student results:

The Login tab allows you to setup the login page for the course:

The Results tab lets you define the results page, which is used to display testing results to the learner:

If you are using student tracking features, you may also want to install the administration files. Learning Site comes with preset administration files. These administration files help you view student results as well as add, modify, and delete users.

More Information: The student tracking features of Learning Site are described in more details in *Chapter 20:Using Learning Site to Track Learner Data*.

Using Learning Site Help

Learning Site comes with basic help. You can access this help from the Learning Site window:

The help is an HTML-based help system like other Macromedia products. However, the Learning Site help is not context sensitive, so you may prefer a printed version.

If you prefer to use a printed version of the help, a .PDF file comes with Learning Site. Search your hard drive for *Using Learning Site.pdf*. This file contains the same basic information as the help files.

Using Learning Site and Coursebuilder Together

You learned in the Learning Site overview, that Coursebuilder is closely tied to this extension. One of the three pages that Learning Site lets you add is a Coursebuilder page. These two extensions were meant to be used in tandem. However, if you aren't planning on including any CourseBuilder interactions in a particular course, then you wouldn't need to choose the Coursebuilder page type.

Learning Site is ideal for creating the navigational structure of your course, while Coursebuilder is ideal for creating quiz questions or other types of interactions on specific pages in your site.

 Note. You must have the Coursebuilder extension installed to add Coursebuilder interactions in Learning Site.

Since Learning Site lets you add a Coursebuilder interaction and choose the type of question you want to include, does that mean that you won't need to do anything in Coursebuilder? No. You still need to open the question in Coursebuilder to define the question and the answers (see Sections I and II of this book for complete instructions and tutorials on setting up CourseBuilder interactions).

If you want to add existing Coursebuilder interactions to a learning site, you can do so on the page tab by browsing for that page and selecting it. In fact this can be done with any type of HTML page. If you are using student tracking, you need to check Knowledge Track on the General tab of the Coursebuilder interaction you added for Learning Site to track the learner's response to that interaction.

Summary

In this chapter you have been introduced to Learning Site. Installation is a simple three-step process. You now understand what Learning Site can do and you have seen an overview of the steps required to define a learning site. This is covered in more detail in the next chapter.

Even though the help for Learning Site is not robust, it provides you with step-by-step instructions if you need them. Finally, we discussed how Coursebuilder is closely tied to Learning Site.

Defining A Learning Site 18

There are two main tasks that you must perform when setting up a Learning Site. First, you must define the site. Second, you must set up student tracking. This chapter focuses on the first task: Setting up a Learning Site. See *Chapter 20: Tracking Learner Data Using Learning Site* for details about how to setup data tracking.

As was mentioned in the last chapter, student tracking is only available with UltraDev. Unless otherwise stated, the settings discussed in this chapter work with either Dreamweaver or UltraDev.

In this chapter you will learn:

- The difference between a Dreamweaver site and a Learning Site.
- How to define a Learning Site.
- How to add activity pages to a Learning Site.
- How to choose a navigational style for a Learning Site.
- How to control navigation.
- How to edit an existing Learning Site.
- How Learning Site's frameset works.
- What files Learning Site adds to your site.

Introduction to Defining a Site

When working with Learning Site, you actually define a site twice. Once as a Dreamweaver site and then again as a Learning Site. As an introduction we discuss how the two tasks differ. We also provide an overview of the steps required to define a Learning Site.

How Does a Dreamweaver Site Differ from a Learning Site?

Defining a Dreamweaver site establishes all the settings that allow you to work with the site and offer it over the web. Defining a Learning Site provides the necessary pieces to turn that site into an on-line training course.

You should already know how to set up a new site in Dreamweaver. Normally, you establish the location on the local drive as well as the HTTP address where the web site exists. There are also other settings you can make if you choose. This process of setting up a new site is called defining a site.

 More Information: See the Dreamweaver manual for more information on defining a site.

Before you can begin creating a Learning Site, you must have defined a site in Dreamweaver. You can either define this before using Learning Site or as a part of the process of setting up a Learning Site.

When you define a Dreamweaver site, you generally do these tasks:

- Enter a site name.
- Specify a folder on the local disk where files will be stored.
- Enter an HTTP address for the web site.
- Build a Cache file.
- Decide how you will work with the files in the site.
- Establish other settings as desired.

When you define a Learning Site, you generally do these tasks:

- Set up a home page that contains a navigation frameset.
- Insert a navigation page.
- Determine a user interface style (i.e. look and feel).

- Identify the pages that are a part of the course (site).
- Determine how the navigation works.
- Determine if you will track student information.
- Add files that provide functionality to the Learning Site.

Overview of Defining a Learning Site

You begin defining your Learning Site within an existing Dreamweaver or UltraDev site where you establish certain settings for the site. Once this is done you add the activity pages to the site. To tie all of your activity pages together into a cohesive course, you select one of the default navigation template styles or choose to create your own. At that point you may also want to change some of the navigation settings.

Once you have finished these steps, you have defined your Learning Site. However, you've only just begun the process of completing your course. You still need to develop all the content pages in the course.

Your navigation (and student tracking if you include it) is ready to go. You may want to come back and add more pages later on, but that is all it takes to set up the navigation.

Creating a Learning Site

If you are using Learning Site with just Dreamweaver, then there are four major tasks you need to complete:

- Define the site
- Add activity pages
- Choose a navigation style

What Does a Normal On-line Course Contain?

Most on-line courses begin with these elements:

- An introduction
- A menu page of all the topics that lets the learner to jump to different areas of the course
- A how-to section that explains how to use the course.

Topics within the course are organized with these components:

- Introduction
- Explain and/or demonstrate the concept.
- Allow the learner to practice (interactive activities and pop-quizzes).
- Learner assessment if needed.

- Set up navigation controls

If you are using UltraDev then you will also want to set up student tracking.

 More Information: The steps necessary to set up student tracking are presented in *Chapter 20: Using Learning Site to Track Learner Data.*

As a part of the step-by-step instructions that are included in the next four sections, you will set up the framework for a sample Learning Site. You will not set up student tracking in this chapter.

Viewing a Finished Site

Before you begin setting up this site, you may want to view the finished example.

 On CD: To view a simple course created with Learning Site, open *site_1/index.htm* in a browser. To view how it is set up in Learning Site, you must first define the folder as a Dreamweaver or UltraDev site.

While viewing this site, try the following:

- Navigate to each page of the course.
- Answer the questions and replay the Macromedia Flash movie.
- What happens when you click **Next** at the end of the course? What happens when you click **Previous** at the beginning of the course?
- What happens when you click **Finish** and **Restart**? Where is this action established?
- Try the **Menu** button.
- Try the **Quit** button.

Defining a Site

When you install Learning Site a new submenu is added to the Site menu. The Learning Site sub-menu provides you with the menu options you need to set up a Learning Site.

To begin defining a site, you should open a Dreamweaver site that you have defined and then choose Create Learning Site from the sub-menu (Site → Learning Site → Create Learning Site):

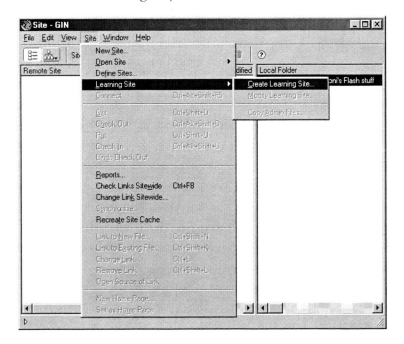

Dreamweaver displays the Learning Site window:

The four tabs you see when using Dreamweaver.

If you are using just Dreamweaver, you will only see four tabs as shown in this sample screen capture. If you are use UltraDev, you will see a total of seven tabs as shown here:

The seven tabs you see when using UltraDev.

In this chapter we discuss the settings for the first four tabs.

Settings on the Site Tab

There are only a few settings on the Site tab. In most cases you do not need to make any changes to these settings. This table describes the purpose of each setting:

Setting	Description
Site	Use the drop down box to choose from a list of all sites currently defined in Dreamweaver or UltraDev. Clicking the **Define** button brings of the Define Sites window and allows you to define a new Dreamweaver site if you wish. If you opened the Dreamweaver site before choosing to create the Learning Site, it is unnecessary to do anything with this setting.

Setting	Description
Frameset File	The Frameset file is an HTML page that contains frames to display the navigation and activity pages together. See the *How Does Learning Site Navigation Work?* Section for more information. Generally you do not want to change this setting.
Set as Home Page	The Set as Home Page check box should be checked. The index.htm file should be your default home page unless you have a reason to change it. The only reason to change the home page is so you can display the site map differently.
Navigation File	The Navigation File field is inactive. This field simply tells you which HTML file contains the navigation images and scripts.
Data Tracking	This checkbox is not enabled unless you are using UltraDev. If you are using UltraDev you have the option of tracking student data.

Defining the Site: Step-by-Step Tutorial

The best approach for setting up a Learning Site is to define a site in Dreamweaver.

Follow these steps to set up a Learning Site:

1   Use the Dreamweaver site menu to define a new site. Place the local site on your hard drive. You don't need to worry about an HTTP address at this point.

More Information: You can get more information about defining a Dreamweaver site in the *Using Dreamweaver* manual that comes with the software or in Dreamweaver's online help.

2   Choose Create Learning Site from the Learning Site submenu (Site → Learning Site → Create Learning Site).

If the existing Dreamweaver site already has files in it, you will receive a warning that some files could possibly be overwritten:

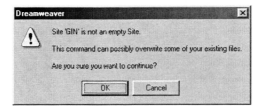

Since Learning Site adds a few HTML pages(some graphic files and some JavaScript files), it overwrites files that have the same name. Some of the most obvious filenames are: *index.htm*, *navigation.htm*, and *menu.htm* (.html if you are using a Mac). You must click **OK** to continue, or you can click **Cancel** and create a new site where files are not overwritten.

If the warning doesn't apply to your site, the Learning Site window displays.

3   For this exercise, don't make any changes to the site tab.

Continue with this tutorial in the next section.

Adding Activity Pages

Activity pages make up the bulk of the e-learning course. Activity pages are added on the Pages tab:

The pages tab allows you to add and define three types of pages:

- **Blank Pages.** Pages that do not fit under the Media or CourseBuilder Interaction type.
- **Media Pages.** Play Macromedia Flash files, Macromedia Shockwave files, or a web-packaged Macromedia Authorware piece.
- **CourseBuilder Interaction.** Used for CourseBuilder Interactions. When you choose this page type, you must also choose the interaction you want to include on the page.

You can set up as many pages as you like and rearrange the order. You can add and delete pages at any time, so even after you are done defining this tab, it does not have to be the final state of the course.

Settings on the Pages Tab

As you add pages, you can establish certain settings for those pages. This table summarizes all the settings on the pages tab:

What are Authorware, Flash, and Shockwave?

Authorware is an e-learning authoring tool created by Macromedia. However, it requires the user to download and install a plugin in order to run it over the web.

Flash is a tool for creating animations and interactivity for the web. Flash requires a plugin, but most web users have already installed the plugin.

Shockwave is a file format for movies created using Macromedia Director Shockwave Studio. Shockwave movies require a plugin. Although this plugin is not as prevalent as the Flash plugin, many users have it.

Form more information visit *www.macromedia.com.*

Setting	Description
Pages	Displays all pages that are part of a Learning Site (course) and the order in which they appear in the course. After creating a new site only one untitled page exists. To add pages, click the **Plus** ⊞ button. Learning Site always adds pages to the end of the page list (a rather annoying limitation in our view). To delete pages, click the **Minus** ⊟ button. To rearrange the order of pages, select a page and click the **Up** ▲ or **Down** ▼ buttons.
Page File	Name a new page.

Setting	Description
Page Title	Give a new page a title. This title is used to identify the page in the menu. Use titles that makes sense to the learner.
Background Color	Set the color of the page background. You can enter either a hexadecimal number or click on the **Color Palette** button ⬛ and select a color. (If you would like to include a graphic, use standard Dreamweaver techniques to add the image.)
Page is	Choose the page type using one of the three radio buttons. Use these settings to establish the type for a new page. You cannot change the page type later, only at the time you define the page.

Note: The order in which the pages appear in the Pages field is the order that the pages appear when the learner navigates through the course.

Tip: If you have already created several Coursebuilder pages and would like to add them to the site, click the **Plus** button, then click on the folder icon, search for and select those pages.

If you choose *Media* as a page type, Learning Site displays several additional settings at the bottom of the tab:

⦿ ◉ Authorware ○ Flash ○ Shockwave

File: [.aam   ] 📁

Width: [320]   Height: [240]

☐ Center Media on Page

This table describes these settings:

Setting	Description
Authorware	Select *Authorware* if the type of media you would like to add to the page is a web-packaged Authorware piece.

Setting	Description
Flash	Select *Flash* if the media you want to add is a Macromedia Flash movie.
Shockwave	Select *Shockwave* if the media you want to add is a Shockwave movie.
File	Click on the folder icon to search for the Authorware, Flash, or Shockwave file. Learning Site provides the default extension for each file type.
Width	Define the width of the media. You may want to enter the original width.
Height	Define the height of the media. You may want to enter the original height.
Center Media on Page	Check this box if you want the media centered on the page.

Note: Right now you can add only one media file to a page using Learning Site.

If you choose CourseBuilder Interaction as the page type, you must also select the type of interaction you want to add:

Treelist of CourseBuilder interactions and templates. Click the plus or minus to expand or contract the list.

Thumbnail of currently chosen interaction.

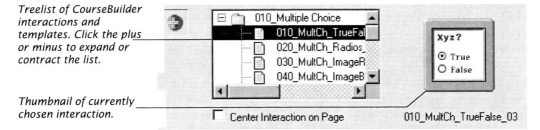

This table describes the settings you can choose:

Setting	Description
Interaction type	Choose the CourseBuilder interaction from the scrolling text box. Every interaction template is available. They are grouped by category. To open a category, click the + symbol. To close a category, click the − symbol. As you select each template, a thumbnail and the name of that interaction is displayed to the right.
Center Interaction on Page	Check this box if you would like the interaction centered on the page. (This does not place the interaction in a movable layer.)

Adding the Pages: Step-by-Step Tutorial

To begin adding activity pages, click on the pages tab. In this section you add four pages to your site: one blank page, one Flash page, and two CourseBuilder interaction pages.

Follow these steps to add pages to the site you started creating in the previous section:

1   Click on the Pages tab.

By default Learning Site adds one page named *Untitled-1.htm*.

Enter a new file name and page title. ——————

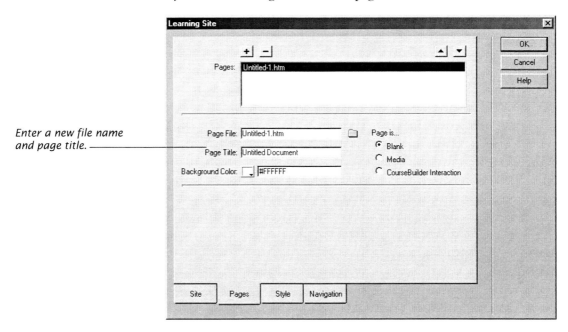

2 Change the name of the page to *four_tabs.htm* by entering the new name in **Page File** field.

3 Change the title of the page by entering *Four Tabs Introduction* in the **Page Title** field.

4 Leave the background white and choose blank as the page type.

5 Click the **Plus** button to add another page and establish the settings as shown in this table.

Option	Setting to Enter
Page File	four_tabs_demo.htm
Page Title	Four Tabs Demo
Page is:	Choose Media for the page type.

Note: Learning Site always adds pages at the end of the page list. To insert a page between pages that already exist, you'll have to use the **up** arrow button to move it to the correct sequential position.

When you click on the media page type, you need to fill out the other options as shown in this table.

Option	Setting to Enter
Media Type	Select *Flash* as the media type.
File	Click on the folder icon and search for and select *samples/site_1/learn_site_tabs.swf.*
Width	618 (The width of the flash file.)
Height	550 (The height of the flash file.)
Center Media on Page	Click this checkbox so that the media is centered on the page.

6 Click the **Plus** button to add another page and establish the settings as shown in this table.

Option	Setting to Enter
Page File	four_tabs_quiz1.htm
Page Title	Four Tabs Quiz1
Page is:	Choose "CourseBuilder Interaction" for the page type.

7 Choose *060_MultCh_ImageChkboxes_04* as the CourseBuilder template and center the interaction on the page.

8 Click the **Plus** button to add the last page and establish the settings as shown in this table.

Option	Setting to Enter
Page File	four_tabs_quiz2.htm
Page Title	Four Tabs Quiz2
Page is:	Choose "CourseBuilder Interaction" for the page type.

9 Choose "010_Text_Singleline_03" as the CourseBuilder template and center the interaction on the page.

The pages tab should now look like this:

Choosing a Navigation Style

Learning Site comes with five different navigation styles and one custom style to choose from. You choose a navigation style from the Style tab:

Choose layout ——
style.

Learning Site	☒

Layout Style: Corporate
Consumer
Educational
Simple
Techno
Custom

previous   next

OK
Cancel
Help

| Site | Pages | Style | Navigation |

As you select each navigation style, a portion of that style appears on the tab. The navigation style appears at the top of the course, while the activity pages you create appear at the bottom.

More Information: For more information on how the navigation style and the pages you create work together, see the *How Does Learning Site Work?* section later in this chapter.

Settings on the Style Tab

The Style tab does not contain many settings. You simply choose the Layout style that you want. The five styles that are available are:

- Corporate
- Consumer
- Educational
- Simple
- Techno

A custom style is also available. If you choose a custom style you need to provide six images to customize the layout.

More Information: For more information on creating your own custom layout see *Chapter 19: Customizing a Learning Site*.

Each navigation style comes with six buttons:

- **Previous button**. Takes the learner to the previous page.
- **Next button**. Takes the learner to the next page in the course (i.e. loads the next page in the page order).
- **Restart button**. Lets the learner restart the course.
- **Finish button**. Lets the learner end the course.
- **Menu button**. Displays a list of all the page titles in the course. When the learner clicks a page name, Learning Site loads that page.
- **Quit button**. Lets the learner quit the course.

Choosing a Style: Step-by-Step Tutorial

In this section you choose a navigation style for the tutorial you started in previous sections.

Follow these steps to choose a navigation style for the site you started creating in the previous sections:

1 Click on the Style tab.

2 Select *Techno* as the **Layout Style**.

Techno style.

Controlling Navigation

Each of the six buttons available in the navigation has a default action. In the case of almost every button, Learning Site allows you to choose another action. The only stipulation with most of these alternative actions is that you need to be using UltraDev.

Navigation Controls are available on the Navigation tab:

Navigation options are presented in this section even though many of them can only be used with UltraDev. If you aren't using UltraDev, the options are grayed out.

Note: If you are using UltraDev and you do not have **_Data Tracking_** selected on the Site tab, the options are grayed out as well.

Settings on the Navigation Tab

On the Navigation tab you can either accept the defaults or choose another action. We also point out any options that are only available in UltraDev.

Previous on First Page. Lets you determine what happens when the learner clicks the **Previous** button while on the first page of the course. There are two options.

- **Display Alert**. Default. The computer beeps and an alert box displays to the learner:

Microsoft Internet Explorer

⚠ You are on page 1.

OK

You can change the default message to any message you would like by editing the field. The default message is: *You are on page 1.*

- **Exit the Quiz and Go to the Login Page**. Available if you are using UltraDev. The login page is the first thing the learner comes to when the course is started. If this option is chosen, the learner is taken back to that point.

Next on Last Page. Lets you determine what happens when the learner clicks the **Next** button while on the last page of the course. There are two options.

- **Display Alert**. Default. The computer beeps and an alert box just like the one used for the **Previous** button displays to the learner. The default message is: *You are on the last page.*

Once again you can change this default message by editing the text field.

- **Exit the Quiz and Go to the Results Page**. Available if you are using UltraDev. The results page displays to learners how they did in the course. Basically it gives them their score. If this option is chosen, the learner is taken to the results page.

On Restart. Lets you determine what happens when the learner clicks the **Restart** button. There are two options:

- **Go to the First Page**. Default option if you are not using UltraDev and available only when using UltraDev. When this option is chosen, the course returns to the first page as defined in Learning Site.

- **Exit the Quiz and Go to the Login Page**. Default option if you are using UltraDev. When this option is chosen, the course returns to the login page.

More Information: For more information about the login and results pages, see *Chapter 20: Using Learning Site to Track Learner Data.*

On Finish. Lets you determine what happens when the learner clicks the **Finish** button. There are two options:

- **Go to the Last Page**. Default option if you are not using UltraDev. When this option is chosen, the course goes to the last page as defined in Learning Site.

- **Exit the Quiz and Go to the Results Page**. Default option if you are using UltraDev and is available only when using UltraDev. When this option is chosen, the course exits the activity and displays the results for quizzes taken.

On Quit. Lets you determine what happens when the learner clicks the **Quit** button. There are three options:

- **Go to the Results Page**. Available if you are using UltraDev. When this option is chosen, the course exits and displays the results for quizzes taken.

- **Go to Page**. Lets you specify the page that a learner is taken to when he quits. You can type in the file name or search for the page by clicking on the folder icon.

- **Close the Browser Window**. Default. When this option is chosen, the browser window closes.

Display Pages in Random Order. Lets you force Learning Site to display the pages in a random order. This option is discussed in more detail in *Chapter 19: Customizing a Learning Site*.

Choosing Navigation Settings: Step-by-Step Tutorial

In this section you choose navigation settings for the tutorial you started in previous sections. In this tutorial we use the default settings.

1   Click on the Navigation tab.

2   Make sure the *Display Pages in Random Order* setting is not checked:

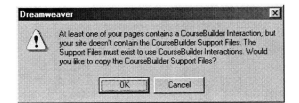

Uncheck this setting. ——————

3   Click **OK**.

Since you have added CourseBuilder pages to the site, Learning Site prompts you if you would like to load the CourseBuilder support files.

4   Click **OK** to load the CourseBuilder support files.

Your site should look similar to this:

Completing Your Course

Once you have defined the settings on the first four tabs, you have done all that Learning Site requires for a course that does not include student tracking. However, you are not finished with your course. You must still complete all of the activity pages and then publish the course to a web site.

One of the first things you will notice as you begin to develop the content pages is that when you open them, the navigation style you chose is nowhere to be seen. That is because the navigation style is not added to each page. The navigation is stored in a separate file and the content and the navigation pages are brought together using a frameset page.

More Information: For more information on how the navigation style is implemented, see the *How Does Learning Site Navigation Work?* section later in this chapter.

Completing the Content Pages

Before your course is finished you must finish developing all of your content pages.

Most likely the blank pages will require the most work. You can turn these pages into anything you would like. Here are some possibilities for the blank pages:

- A list of objectives
- An introduction or transition page
- A static page with text and/or graphic information
- A menu page
- An instructive page that contains interactions not available in CourseBuilder
- Any other type of page you feel your course needs

Your media pages may not require much work. However, you may want to add some instructions or other graphics to this page to help the learner.

You need to open each CourseBuilder page and complete the CourseBuilder interaction. To do this you need to edit the interaction using one of the methods shown in Chapter 2. You can use all the techniques discussed in *Section I: Using CourseBuilder for Interactivity* and *Section II: Extending CourseBuilder* when completing these interactions.

Publish the Course to the Web

Once the course is complete, we recommend thorough testing. You are then ready to place your course on a local intranet or on the Internet. Once this is done, you can provide the URL of the course to those who need the training.

 More Information: If you need more information about publishing a course, refer to the Dreamweaver user manual.

If you place the course on the Internet, the URL consists of your domain name, any subdirectory, and the index.htm file (index.html if you are using a Macintosh). For example, Rapid Intake's domain is rapidintake.com. If we placed a course inside a folder called test, the URL would be:
http://www.rapidintake.com/test/index.htm.

If you place the course on a company intranet, the URL consists of the machine name that is serving the course, any subdirectories and the index.htm file. (In place of the machine name you could use an IP address.)

Completing the Tutorial

If you want to complete the tutorial that you started in the previous section, you must finish developing the four pages that you added to the course. As you follow these steps, you may want to copy information from the sample pages.

Follow these steps to complete the tutorial:

1 Open page *four_tabs.htm* and add the tables and text as shown in the sample page *samples\site_1\four_tabs.htm*.

2 Open page *four_tabs_demo.htm* and add the instructions and the replay button as shown in page *samples\site_1\four_tabs_demo.htm*.

3 Open page *four_tabs_quiz1.htm* and complete the CourseBuilder interaction so it is like the interaction in page *samples\site_1\four_tabs_quiz1.htm*.

4 Open page *four_tabs_quiz2.htm* and complete the CourseBuilder interaction so it is like the interaction in page *samples\site_1\four_tabs_demo.htm*.

5 You can now test the course by opening *index.htm* in a browser.

If this were a real course, you would now need to publish the course to an Internet or intranet site.

Modifying an Existing Learning Site

You will almost always want to make changes to a Learning Site you have created. You may want to add or delete pages, change the navigation style, or change navigation settings. You may also want to make changes to individual pages.

In this section we talk about how to make changes to a Learning Site. We address the best way to make these changes.

Modifying an Existing Learning Site

To make changes to a Learning Site's settings or add and delete pages you must modify the Learning Site.

Follow these steps to modify an existing Learning Site:

1   Open the Dreamweaver site (Site → Open Site → *yoursite*).

2   Choose Modify Learning Site from the Learning Site submenu (Site → Learning Site → Modify Learning Site).

The Learning Site window appears. Now you can make changes to the site.

Adding Pages

Adding pages requires that you modify the Learning Site at some point. There are two approaches to adding pages.

- Add the pages using Learning Site and then develop the pages.
- Create the pages in Dreamweaver with all the content and then add them to Learning Site.

 Caution: If you only add pages to the Dreamweaver site and don't use the Learning Site command, you can't navigate to those pages from within the course.

Follow these steps to add pages using Learning Site first:

1   Open the Learning Site window (Site → Learning Site → Modify Learning Site).

2   Click on the Pages tab:

```
Learning Site                                                    [X]
  ┌───────────────────────────────────────────────┐   ┌─────────┐
  │     +  -                              ▲  ▼      │   │   OK    │
  │ Pages: Untitled-1.htm                          │   ├─────────┤
  │                                                │   │ Cancel  │
  │                                                │   ├─────────┤
  │                                                │   │  Help   │
  │ ─────────────────────────────────────────────  │   └─────────┘
  │  Page File: Untitled-1.htm         ☐   Page is...
  │  Page Title: Untitled Document          ⦿ Blank
  │                                         ○ Media
  │ Background Color: ☐ #FFFFFF             ○ CourseBuilder Interaction
  │ ─────────────────────────────────────────────
  │
  │
  │
  │
  │  Site | Pages | Style | Navigation | Tracking | Login | Results
  └───────────────────────────────────────────────┘
```

3   Click the **Plus** button to add a page.

4   Enter the page file name, page title, and choose a page type.

Note: The page is automatically added to the end of the course. Move the position of the page if necessary.

Follow these steps to add a page to Learning Site after the page has already been created:

1   Create the page using standard Dreamweaver techniques.

2   Open the Learning Site window (Site → Learning Site → Modify Learning Site).

3   Click on the Pages tab.

4   Click the **Plus** button to add a page.

5   Click on the folder icon ☐ and search for and select the page you created earlier.

If the file does not exist in the current site, Learning Sites prompts you to copy the file to the site.

Deleting Pages

If you need to delete pages, do it from the Learning Site window. If you delete the page directly from Dreamweaver, the page is not deleted from the navigation array in the navigation.htm file. Accordingly, as learners use the course and try to navigate to that page they will see an error because the page cannot be found.

More Information: For more information about the navigation array see the *How Does Learning Site Navigation Work?* section later in this chapter.

Follow these steps to delete pages:

1 Open the Learning Site window (Site → Learning Site → Modify Learning Site).

2 Click on the Pages tab.

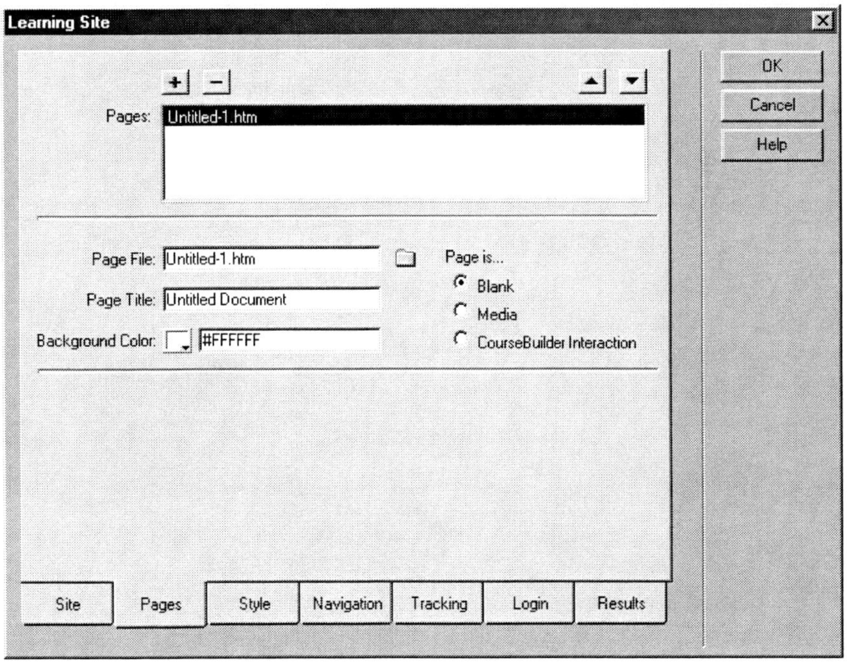

![Learning Site dialog box screenshot showing the Pages tab with buttons +, −, up and down arrows. Pages list shows "Untitled-1.htm". Page File: Untitled-1.htm, Page Title: Untitled Document, Background Color: #FFFFFF. Page is... Blank (selected), Media, CourseBuilder Interaction. Buttons OK, Cancel, Help. Tabs along the bottom: Site, Pages, Style, Navigation, Tracking, Login, Results.]

3 Select the page you want to delete.

4   Click the **Minus** button.

Changing the Navigation Style

Learning Site lets you to change the navigation style at any time. You simply need to select a new style.

Follow these steps to change the navigation style:

1   Open the Learning Site window (Site → Learning Site → Modify Learning Site).

2   Click on the Style tab.

3   Select a new layout style.

Changing Navigation Settings

Learning Site lets you change any of the navigation settings.

Follow these steps to change navigation settings:

1 Open the Learning Site window by modifying the site.

2 Click on the Navigation tab.

3 Change any of the navigation settings.

Difficult to Make Changes

In this section we discuss some changes that can be difficult to make or should only be made from within Learning Site. For example, you learned in a previous section you should only delete pages from within Learning Site.

There are also of few changes that require the use of both Dreamweaver and Learning Site. Here is a list:

- Changing the file name of a page
- Change the title of a page
- Changing the home page of the site

Changing the File Name and the Title of a Page

At some point you may want to change the file name or title of a page. Page titles are important because they are used in conjunction with the **Menu** button to display a list of page titles the learner can use to navigate non-sequentially through the course.

You may have noticed that when you modify an existing Learning Site you cannot make any changes to the pages that already show up on the Pages tab. The radio buttons for the *Type* setting don't even show up and the other fields are grayed out. So how do you change the file name and title? The answer is that you must be very careful about it.

Changing the file name and title requires that you first make those changes within Dreamweaver. For example, enter a new title in the Title field for a page or change the file name in the site window. However, this is not enough. If you stop at this point, the changes are not made in Learning Site and can cause errors or unintended results during navigation.

To make sure the changes are recorded in Learning Site, you must modify the Learning Site and click on the pages tab. If you do not, these problems could occur:

- If you change the page title, the correct page title does not show up in the menu when the learner clicks on it.

- If you change the file name, an error occurs when the learner tries to navigate to that page.

Follow these steps to change the file name and title of a page:

1 Use standard Dreamweaver techniques to change the file name or the title of a page.

2 Open the Learning Site window (Site → Learning Site → Modify Learning Site).

3 Click on the Pages tab.

   You should be able to see the new title or file name.

4 Close the Learning Site window.

Caution: If you have changed the page name and do not click on the Pages tab before closing the Learning Site window, Learning Site creates a new page using the old file name.

Changing the Home Page for a Site

Dreamweaver uses the web page defined as the *home page* to show the top of the site hierarchy when you display the site map:

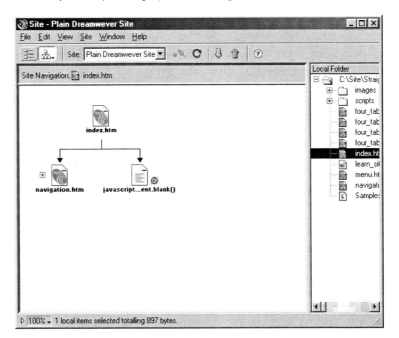

If you would like to change the home page for a Learning Site, you must do it in both Learning Site and Dreamweaver. First, access the Site tab and uncheck the ***Set as Home Page*** check box. Then you can use Dreamweaver to define a new home page.

Caution: If you don't uncheck the check box first, the change made in Dreamweaver does not take affect.

Follow these steps to change the home page:

1   Open the Learning Site window (Site → Learning Site → Modify Learning Site).

2   Click on the Site tab.

3   Click on the ***Set as Home Page*** check box to uncheck it.

4   Close the Learning Site window.

5   Select a new page in the Site window and set it as the home page (Site → Set as Home Page) or, for Macintosh (Site → Site Map View → Set as Home Page).

How Does Learning Site Navigation Work?

When working with Learning Site, it is helpful to understand how the navigation works. In this section we discuss some of the concepts about Learning Site Navigation. These topics help answer these questions:

- How do the pages I create display with the navigation style?
- What default pages are added by Learning Site?
- What do those default pages do?

We address these questions in this section.

How Do the Navigation and Content Pages Display Together?

You have probably noticed that when you open up one of the pages you have created with Learning Site, it doesn't display the navigation bar at the top. However, when you access the index.htm file from a browser and navigate through the course, the navigation appears at the top of every page. How is this done?

The navigation style is stored in its own HTML page. All of the activity pages are HTML pages as well. The two are combined using frames.

More Information: For more information about frames, refer to you Dreamweaver manual.

The *index.htm* page is a frameset page. It has a frame at the top for navigation and one at the bottom for the activity pages as shown here:

The navigation file never changes. However, as the learner navigates through the course, the file that is displayed in the content frame changes.

Because the *index.htm* file is the frameset, it is important that you start the course from that file or you will not see the navigation buttons. Moreover, additional information important to the course is tracked in the navigation frame.

What Default Pages Are Added and What Do They Do?

When you define a Learning Site, three pages are added to the site along with images and scripts. These pages provide the default navigation functions.

- index.htm
- navigation.htm
- menu.htm

 Note: If you are using UltraDev and tracking student data, several more pages are added. See *Chapter 20: Using Learning Site to Track Student Data* for a description of those files.

 Caution: If you are making an existing site a Learning Site, make sure none of your existing pages are named *index.htm, navigation.htm,* or *menu.htm.* If they are, they are overwritten as Learning Site copies in it's default pages.

We have included a description of what each page does in these sections.

The Index.htm File

As we explained earlier, the *index.htm* file is the frameset. You can see both frames if you open *index.htm* in Dreamweaver and display the Frames panel. The top frame is called navFrame and the bottom frame is called mainFrame.

Also, you should see the navigation file in the top frame. The bottom frame isn't currently displaying a page because it uses JavaScript to dynamically load the correct page in when viewed through a browser.

The Navigation.htm File

The *navigation.htm* file contains the navigation framework and images. When you open the *index.htm* frameset, this file displayed in the top frame.

One of the important functions of this file is that it stores all the key navigation information in an array. Since this page is always available, it is the logical place to store that information.

If you are interested you can view the array that controls the navigation.

Follow these steps to view the navigation arrays:

1   Open the *navigation.htm* page.

2   Display the page in Code view (View → Code) or click the **Show Code View** button.

3   Scroll to the top of the page, and you should be able to see an array that looks like this:

```
<script language="JavaScript" name="prismPages">
  var pageURLs = new Array()
  pageURLs[0] = "four_tabs.htm"
  pageURLs[1] = "four_tabs_demo.htm"
  pageURLs[2] = "four_tabs_quiz1.htm"
  pageURLs[3] = "four_tabs_quiz2.htm"
</script>
```

This is the array from the sample site created in this chapter. Notice that all four pages are accounted for in the array. This is the array that is used to determine which page to display next when the learner clicks a navigation button.

You may also notice another array directly below this one. This second array contains a list of all the titles for each page. This array is used for the menu file, which we discuss next.

The Menu.htm File

The menu.htm file is only displayed when the learner clicks the **Menu** button. The **Menu** button opens a new browser window and display the menu.htm file in it. This file contains JavaScript that retrieves the titles of all the pages in the course.

When the learner clicks on one of the titles, that page is loaded into the Content frame and the Menu Browser window is closed.

> **What is an Array?**
>
> In programming an array is just a variable (container) that can hold separate pieces of data under one name. In this case the array contains multiple file names.

Summary

To set up a Learning Site, begin with a standard Dreamweaver site. You then complete these four general steps:

- Define the Learning Site
- Add activity pages
- Choose a navigation style
- Establish navigation settings

Once you have completed these four general steps, you must still open each page and add the content. Then you can publish the page to the Internet or an Intranet.

If you need to you can modify an existing site using the modify command. Some changes should always be made within Learning Site while others must be done both in Dreamweaver and Learning Site.

Learning Site uses a frameset page to display the navigation and content pages together. Three pages are added to a Learning Site when it is defined.

Customizing A Learning Site 19

Learning Site lets you customize a site and include your own creativity within the look and feel of a site. You can also change the way the site works. Some of the customizations that you can do in Learning Site are part of the extension; others must be done from within Dreamweaver or UltraDev.

The changes included in this chapter work whether you are tracking student data or not.

In this chapter you will learn:

- Different methods for customizing a learning site.
- How to remove unwanted navigation buttons.
- How to use custom button and background images.
- How to change a background graphic.
- How to change the orientation of the navigation frameset.
- How to change the browser windows to encourage learners to use Learning Site navigation tools rather than standard browser tools.
- How to generate a random navigational page order.
- How to connect multiple learning sites to provide more flexibility with your training course.

Introduction to Customization

Now that you have learned a new tool, Learning Site, you probably wonder what type of customization is possible. Learning Site customization is not apparent at first look. However, there are several things you can change.

More Information: We discuss some additional customizations that apply to student tracking and UltraDev in *Chapter 20: Using Learning Site to Track Learner Data*.

In this chapter we first discuss several ways to customize the layout of the navigation and the images that are used. We also look at how to control what is included in the browser window. In some courses you may want to limit the controls that are available in the browser window.

At the completion of this chapter, we show you how to have Learning Site generate a random page order. This is sometimes required for on-line quizzes. We also discuss some of the issues associated with connecting multiple sites together.

Customizing the Layout

Learning Site comes with a custom layout. This layout lets you change the graphics that are used for the buttons. However, this is not the only way you can customize the layout. In this section we look at these three methods:

- Removing unwanted navigational buttons
- Choosing custom button and background images
- Changing the orientation of the frameset

Removing Navigation Buttons

Learning Site comes with six default navigation buttons:

- Previous
- Next
- Restart
- Finish
- Menu
- Quit

You may not want to use all these buttons. In fact having so many buttons may confuse some learners. The **Restart** and **Finish** buttons may be logical ones to remove.

Learning Site does not provide an easy way to delete buttons. Therefore, you need to use Dreamweaver for this task. The navigation layout is kept in the *navigation.htm* file. It is this file that you need to open to delete buttons.

To completely delete a button, you must delete the image and any programming associated with the image.

Follow these steps to delete navigational buttons:

1   Open the *navigation.htm* file:

![Navigation (connect1/navigation.htm) - Dreamweaver UltraDev window showing navigation bar with buttons: previous, next, restart, finish, menu, quit]

2   Click on the image of the button you want to delete.

This selects the button.

3   Click on the <a> tag selector at the bottom left of the Dreamweaver screen. It is to the direct left of the <img> tag:

```
<body> <table> <tr> <td> <table> <tr> <td> <a>
```

Selecting the <*a*> tag selects not only the image but also any JavaScript code associated with it.

Note: In the corporate style, there are so many tags that the <img> tag may be too far to the right to see. Also, in this style you may want to select the right-most <td> tag so that an empty table cell isn't left on the page.

4   Press the DELETE key to delete the button and its scripting.

5   You may want to use standard Dreamweaver formatting techniques to rearrange the remaining buttons.

Choosing Custom Buttons and Graphics

As explained in the previous chapter, Learning Site comes with a custom style. This style allows you to change the images that are used for the navigation buttons. This section shows you how to change those images.

You use the Style tab in Learning Site to choose a custom style and include your own button images. There are a total of six buttons if you choose to use them all:

The six buttons you can replace.

As you can see in this graphic, when you choose custom, you are provided with six fields used to identify the custom buttons. Even though Learning Site doesn't display any thumbnails, six default button images are already supplied for you. Here is what those buttons look like:

By default Learning Site provides no background image when you choose the Custom style.

Each button used in Learning Site normally has two states: a normal state and a mouse-over state. Before changing buttons, you may want to create both states for all six buttons or for as many buttons as you plan to use. If you choose to, you can limit your custom buttons to a single, normal state.

If you choose to include a second, mouse-over state, you cannot do that from within Learning Site. That task requires using the Swap Image behavior from the Behavior panel in Dreamweaver. You will go through this process in the hands-on that follows.

In addition to changing the buttons, you will probably want to change the background image as well. The next section shows you how to do this.

To help you understand the process required to include your own custom buttons, we have included the following tutorial. As a part of this tutorial you will be creating a new style. In this first tutorial you'll add custom buttons. In a later tutorial you'll add custom background images to complete the new style.

Viewing the Custom Buttons

Before using the step-by-step instructions to setup a navigation style with custom buttons, take a moment to look at the finished product.

On CD: Open *sample_navigation.htm* in a browser and Dreamweaver to see the navigation style you will create in this step-by-step. Do not click the buttons as this file is not a part of a learning site. To see how the file looks in a learning site, it needs to be displayed in a frame as part of an *index.htm* file.

As you view this file with a browser and in Dreamweaver, consider these items:

- What type of structure is used to layout the navigation.htm file?
- Pass the mouse over each button to see how they change.
- How are the two states of each button achieved?

Assembling Custom Buttons

In this section you create a custom navigation Style that uses custom buttons. The buttons you use in this step-by-step have already been created and placed on the companion CD. The completed buttons will look like this:

Previous   Next   Restart   Finish   Menu   Quit

Note: Even though buttons are provided for this tutorial, it is important to remember that you will need to create buttons yourself for your own custom styles.

Follow these steps to add custom buttons to the navigation style:

1   Define the contents of the *site_3* folder on the CD as a new site.

2   Modify the learning site (Site → Learning Site → Modify Learning Site).

Dreamweaver displays the Learning Site window.

3   Click on the Style tab.

4   Select the Custom style:

Access the Style tab and choose Custom for the Layout Style.

Learning Site			
Layout Style:	Corporate / Consumer / Educational / Simple / Techno / **Custom**		OK / Cancel / Help
Previous:	previous.gif	Width: 40	Height: 40
Next:	next.gif	Width: 40	Height: 40
Restart:	restart.gif	Width: 40	Height: 40
Finish:	finish.gif	Width: 40	Height: 40
Menu:	menu.gif	Width: 40	Height: 40
Quit:	quit.gif	Width: 40	Height: 40

Site | Pages | Style | Navigation

5   Change the images in each of the six fields to match the file shown in this table.

Field	Image File to Select
Previous	Site_3/Images/pPreviousButton_Up.gif
Next	Site_3/Images /pNextButton_Up.gif
Restart	Site_3/Images /pRestartButton_Up.gif

Field	Image File to Select
Finish	Site_3/Images /pFinishButton_Up.gif
Menu	Site_3/Images /pMenuButton_Up.gif
Quit	Site_3/Images /pQuitButton_Up.gif

Note: As you select the new image, the width and height changes automatically.

6   Click **OK**.

The custom buttons are added to the style:

Note: If you wish to include a mouse–over state, additional steps are required. You need to add a *Swap Image* behavior to the **onMouseOver** event.

The remaining steps show you how to create a mouse-over state for the buttons.

7   Open the *site_3/navigation.htm* file.

8   Click on one of the new buttons to select it:

Selected ——

9   Open the Behaviors panel (Window → Behaviors).

Don't worry that there are other actions already showing on the behavior panel.

10 Choose the Swap Image behavior (+ → Swap Image).

The Swap Image window appears.

11 Enter the correct image file name in the ***Set Source to*** field. Use this table to choose the correct image file:

Field	Image File to Select
Previous	Site_3/Images /pPreviousButton_Over.gif
Next	Site_3/Images /pNextButton_Over.gif
Restart	Site_3/Images /pRestartButton_Over.gif
Finish	Site_3/Images /pFinishButton_Over.gif
Menu	Site_3/Images /pMenuButton_Over.gif
Quit	Site_3/Images /pQuitButton_Over.gif

12 Select ***Restore Images onMouseOut*** and ***Preload Images*** if they aren't already selected:

13 Click **OK**.

14 Make sure the event for Swap Image is ***onMouseOver*** and the event for Swap Image Restore is ***onMouseOut***.

The events should be onMouseOut and onMouseOver.

15 Repeat steps 6-12 until all buttons have a mouseOver state.

16 Open the index.htm file in a browser to see how the buttons look.

Currently these buttons do not have a background. You will add the background in the next section.

Changing the Background Graphic

You can also change the background image that is used in a navigation style. However, you cannot do this from within Learning Site. You must open the navigation.htm file in Dreamweaver and make the changes.

To change the background image, you simply need to select a new background image for the table that contains the buttons.

When you choose a custom style, no background image is provided. Therefore, if you use a custom style you need to add that background image. If you choose to you can also replace the existing background image of one of the other styles.

Note: The default styles that come with Learning Site are much more complex. They contain graphics in other cells of the table not just in the background. If you explore a navigation.htm file that uses a standard style, you can see these differences.

Viewing the Finished Product

Before using the step-by-step instructions to change the background graphic, take a moment to look at the finished product.

On CD: Open *sample_navigation2.htm* in a browser and in Dreamweaver to see the navigation style you will create in this step-by-step.

As you view this file with both a browser and in Dreamweaver, consider these items:

- Notice how the graphic is created to blend with the buttons.
- While you have the file opened in Dreamweaver, notice the settings used Property Inspector for the table.

Choosing a Background Image

In these step-by-step instructions you add a background image to the navigation.htm file you worked with in the last tutorial.

Note: Even though a background image is provided for this tutorial, it is important to remember that you will need to create the background yourself for your own custom styles.

Follow these steps to choose a new background image for a navigation style:

1 Open *site_3/navigation.htm* file.

Caution: You should have completed the previous hands-on exercise in order to have the new buttons included in this file.

The navigation file appears:

2   Select the table that contains the navigation buttons.

The best way to select the table is to click on one of the button images to select it and then click the left-most <table> tag selector at the bottom of the screen:

`<body> <table> <tr> <td>`

3   Open the Property Inspector (Window → Properties). (Click the expander arrow to expand the property inspector if necessary.):

Choose a background image for the table.

4   In the *Bg Image* field, click on the folder icon and search for and select *site_4/images/pNavigationBackground.gif*.

Dreamweaver adds the background image to the table. Because the image added to the table is a background image, it may be repeated in the navigation.htm file. If you don't want the image to repeat then you need to limit the size of the table.

In the steps that follow, you will limit the size of the table.

> **Tip**: To make a background image that looks good when it repeats, you generally want to use a solid color. You can then use additional cells in the table to display other graphics over the top of the solid color. See some of the standard styles for examples.

5 In the Property Inspector for the table enter a width of 780 pixels and a height of 100 pixels:

New height and width for table entered in pixels.

		Table Name	Rows	1		W	780	pixels ▾	CellPad	0	Align	Default ▾	⑦
			Cols	1		H	100	pixels ▾	CellSpace	0	Border	0	
					Bg Color						Brdr Color		
					Bg Image	images/pNavigationBackground.gif							

6 View *site_3/index.htm* in a browser to see how the new navigation looks.

Changing the Orientation of the Frameset

As explained in the previous chapter, Learning Site uses a frameset page to display the navigation and the content pages together. That frameset places the navigation at the top of the course as shown here:

This orientation works well for many courses, but you may come across situations were you would like to place the navigation on the left or on the bottom of the page.

Tip: A good rule of thumb in user interface design suggests putting navigational buttons at the bottom right because learners tend to work through a page from left to right and top to bottom.

You can make this change by editing the frameset file.

Follow these steps to change the orientation of the index.htm file:

1 Open the *index.htm* file.

Here is a sample *index.htm* file:

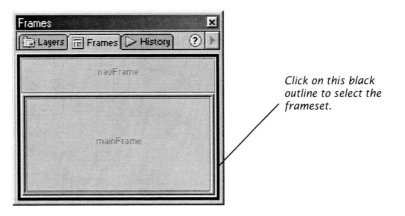

2   Choose Window → Frames to open the Frames panel.

The Frames panel appears:

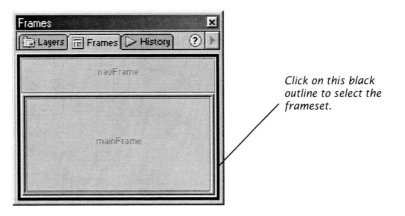

Click on this black outline to select the frameset.

3   Select the frameset by clicking the outside border in the frames panel:

Now you need to add another frame that is positioned either to the left or the bottom depending upon the orientation you want to use.

4 Select the Frames category in the objects panel and insert either a bottom frame or a left frame:

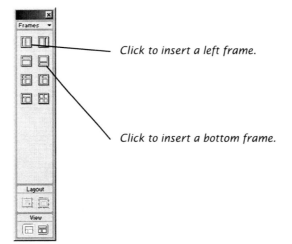

Click to insert a left frame.

Click to insert a bottom frame.

5 Delete the old navFrame frame.

There are a couple of ways to delete the frame. If you have chosen to view frame borders (View → Visual Aids → Frame Borders), you can drag the bottom frame border off the page. You can also select the navFrame frame and delete it.

6 Select the new frame that you have added, using the method shown in step 3, and open the Property Inspector (Window → Properties).

7 Enter navFrame as the *Frame Name* and choose *navigation.htm* as the source:

Enter navFrame as the name.

Enter navigation.htm as the source.

	Frame Name	Src	navigation.htm		Borders	Default
	navFrame	Scroll	No	No Resize	Border Color	
		Margin Width				
		Margin Height				

8 Save the frameset and try it in a browser.

If you choose to create a left frame, you need to make modifications to the navigation.htm page so that it displays correctly in a left frame.

Changing the Browser Window

Delivering e-learning through a browser is a bit different than delivering a typical informational web site. With a standard web site you want the user to be able to move anywhere in the site at will. When designing e-learning you generally want to provide some restrictions, or at least some guidance through the information and activities.

For example, you may want to hide parts of the browser window so that the learner is restricted to using the navigational controls you provide within the course. You can hide these browser window elements:

- Navigation toolbar
- Location toolbar
- Resize handles
- Status bar
- Menu bar

You can also control the size of the window.

This graphic shows you the parts of a browser window that you can hide.

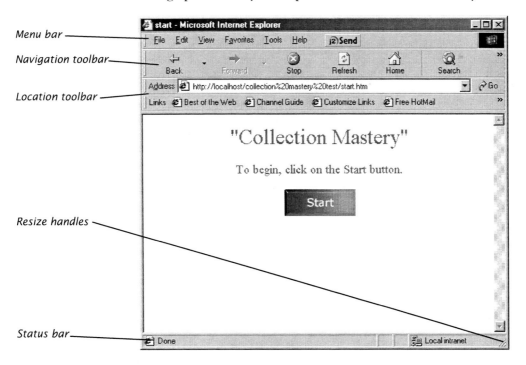

A very simple way to prepare the browser window for training purposes is to begin the course with a start page as shown above. A start page requires the learner to click an image (button) to start the training. When the learner clicks the image two things happen: a new customized browser window opens and the first page of the course loads into that browser window (*index.htm*).

We use the *Open Browser Window* behavior to customize the browser window.

Tip: You could use these same techniques with a text link. For example, you might have several courses that start from one page, listed as links within a table. Each link would use the Open Browser Window behavior but load a different page into the window.

Follow these steps to customize the browser window:

1   Create a start page that contains an image the learner must click to begin the course.

The previous screen shot shows you an example of a start page.

2   Select the clickable image (button).

3   Add an Open Browser Window behavior for ***onMouseDown***, ***onClick***, or ***onMouseUp*** event (generally use ***onClick*** as it requires the learner to push the mouse button down and release it before the event triggers):

4   Choose the settings you think are appropriate in the Open Browser Window window.

These are typical settings:

*Enter index.htm as the
page to display.*

*Enter the size you want
the window to be.*

Open Browser Window

URL to Display: index.htm   Browse...

OK
Cancel
Help

Window Width: 780   Window Height: 520

Attributes: ☐ Navigation Toolbar   ☐ Menu Bar
              ☐ Location Toolbar   ☐ Scrollbars as
                                        Needed
              ☐ Status Bar   ☐ Resize Handles

Window Name:

5 Click the **OK** button

6 Test the page in a browser.

The one downside of this method to change the browser window is that it leaves another browser window open. You could use JavaScript to close the original window, but if it is the main window, which is very likely, then it requires the learner to confirm that they want the window closed. This becomes confusing to the learner. For that reason, we have usually opted to leave the original window open in the courses we have created.

Tip: If you would like to control the size of the browser window and the position, use this JavaScript method: window.open('*url*','*title*','width= 780,height=520,left=5,top=1). In place of URL, enter the URL for the page you want to open. Title is just a name for the window. The left and top parameters specify how far from the left and top of the screen the window is positioned. Experiment with numbers until you obtain the position you want.

Tip: Choose the size of the browser window carefully. In general, learners don't like to scroll through course content. Find out what your user base's minimum screen resolution is and design your course around that. We suggest a 780x520 window for courses that run mostly on 800x600 machines. This leaves enough room for the window's title bar, borders, and the Windows 98/2000/NT taskbar. As a general rule of thumb, you can subtract 20 pixels from the width and 80 pixels from the height of the target machine resolution to give you a nicely sized course window.

Generating Random Pages

Learning Site provides the ability to randomly load pages from your site into the lower frame of the course frameset. This option can be valuable if you are delivering an on-line quiz and you want to make sure each student takes the quiz in a different order. However, remember that all pages in the site are displayed randomly not just quiz pages. For that reason you will only want to use this option for an online quiz that doesn't have instruction as a part of the course. Or you can create two separate sites, one for instruction and one strictly for the quiz, and then combine them.

More Information *:* For more information on how to connect multiple learning sites together, see *Connecting Multiple Sites* in this chapter.

You can also choose to have a specified number of pages loaded at random from a pool of questions. For example, suppose you had 30 questions in your quiz site and you wanted to randomly load 10 questions every time the quiz was taken. This is called "pooling".

Selecting the Random and Pooling Options

To set up the random and pooling options for a learning site, modify the site settings (Site→Learning Site→Modify Learning Site) and access the Navigation tab:

Select this option to display pages randomly

Deselect this option and enter a number to select a certain number of pages from a pool.

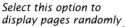

To cause the site to display all of its pages in a random order, you need to select the *Display Pages in Random Order* setting. This forces the site to display all pages randomly. This means that each time you access the course, the pages should appear in a different order.

By default the *Display All Pages* setting is selected. If you would like to have learning site only display a certain number of pages, deselect this option. You must then enter the number of pages you would like displayed in the *Number of Pages to Display (Pooling)* field.

When you choose to use pooling, Learning Site uses all the pages in the site as a part of the pool. It then randomly displays pages until it has displayed the number of pages you have specified. For example, if you have created 15 pages, but you want the quiz to consist of only 10 pages, deselect *Display All Pages* and enter 10 in the Pooling field.

 More Information: When creating quizzes you will most likely want to track scores. See *Chapter 20: Using Learning Site to Track Learner Data* for more information.

Creating a Random Quiz

In this section you will create a quiz that will randomly display three questions from a pool of four questions.

Viewing the Site Before Randomization

Before creating this quiz, view the site before randomization and pooling are enabled.

On CD: Open *site_2\index.htm* to view the four quiz questions without randomization and pooling activated.

As you view the course, take notice of the following:

- Open the course multiple times. Notice that the quiz questions always appear in the same order.
- Notice that four pages are always loaded.

Adding Randomization and Pooling to the Site

You can modify the learning site you just viewed so that it randomizes the pages and displays only three of those pages each time the quiz is taken.

Follow these steps to randomize the pages:

1   Define *site_2* from the CD as your current site (Site → Define Sites).

The Site Definition window appears:

Enter a name and the Local Root Folder where you copied site_2. Other information is optional at this point.

Site Definition for Unnamed Site 3

Category   Local Info

Local Info
Remote Info   Site Name: site 2
Application Server
Design Notes   Local Root Folder: C:\Site\site_2\
Site Map Layout
File View Columns   ☑ Refresh Local File List Automatically

                         HTTP Address: http://

                              This address enables the Link Checker to
                              detect HTTP links that refer to your own
                              site.

                         Cache: ☑ Enable Cache

                              The cache maintains file and asset
                              information in the site. This speeds up the
                              Asset panel, link management, and Site Map
                              features.

                              OK   Cancel   Help

2   Modify the learning site (Site → Learning Site → Modify Learning Site).

3   Click on the Navigation tab.

Learning Site displays the Navigation tab:

Learning Site

Previous on First Page	Next on Last Page	OK
⦿ Display Alert: You are on page 1.	⦿ Display Alert: You are on the last page	Cancel
○ Exit the Quiz and Go to the Login Page	○ Exit the Quiz and Go to the Results Page	Help
On Restart	On Finish	
⦿ Go to the First Page	○ Go to the Last Page	
○ Exit the Quiz and Go to the Login Page	⦿ Exit the Quiz and Go to the Results Page	

On Quit

○ Go to Results Page

○ Go to Page: index.htm

⦿ Close Browser Window

Settings for displaying random pages.

☐ Display Pages in Random Order

Number of Pages to Display (Pooling): 1   Pages, or ☑ Display All Pages

| Site | Pages | Style | Navigation | Tracking | Login | Results |

4 Click the ***Display Pages in Random Order*** setting to select it:

☑ Display Pages in Random Order

5 Click the ***Display All Pages*** setting to deselect it.

6 Enter 3 in the ***Number of Pages to Display*** field:

Number of Pages to Display (Pooling): 3   Pages, or ☐ Display All Pages

7 Test the site by opening *index.htm* in a browser.

If you have successfully completed this task, only three of the quiz questions should display and they should display in a random order.

Caution: If you need to remove random pages and pooling from a site, make sure you select the *Display All Pages* setting after deselecting *Display Pages in Random Order*. If you don't, you will not be able to view all of the pages in the site.

Connecting Multiple Sites

Connecting multiple learning sites together is something you may want to do if you are presenting a quiz with random questions. For example, you may want to include a quiz at the end of a course that is random and uses a pool of questions. However, you don't want the instructional pages presented in a random fashion. A logical way to do this is to create two learning sites and connect them.

You may also want to connect multiple learning sites to make team-based development flow more smoothly. One team member can be working on one lesson, while another team member works on another. When they are finished, connect the sites together so the learner experiences them seamlessly.

There are some difficulties involved in connecting multiple sites. We discuss those first and then present methods for connecting multiple sites.

Limitations to Connecting Multiple Sites

Connecting multiple learning sites is not difficult if you are not including student tracking. If you are including student tracking, there is no easy way to do this. The reason for this is that Learning Site requires the learners to log in each time they access a new learning site that is tracking data. Hopefully, future versions of Learning Site will address this problem, but for now here are some possible solutions:

- Create the instructional portion of your course without data tracking. When it is time to test the learner, connect to another learning site that tracks the data. (The problem with this approach is that the student needs to log in when they access the test.)
- Connect multiple sites together that collect data. (The downside to this approach is that the learners will need to log in each time they access a new learning site.)

In addition to these issues, you also need to consider the problem presented with the **Menu** button and the **Previous** button. When learners click the **Previous** button they are not taken back to an earlier learning site. Also, the menu only displays pages for the current learning site.

Connecting the Sites

If you decide to, there are a few methods you can use to connect sites. Each method is described in more detail in the sections that follow.

- Create a blank page that goes to the new site when it is accessed.
- Create a menu that connects to the new site.
- Create a clickable image (button) that the learner must click to go to the new site.

Using a Blank Page to Connect Sites

If you would like to seamlessly move between sites, use the blank page method. This method requires you to include a blank page at the end of each learning site. The blank page directs you to a new URL when it is loaded.

For this method to work, the second site must be stored in a subdirectory of the main site or you must enter an absolute path to the new site (i.e. *http://www.rapidintake.com/*).

Follow these steps to create a blank page to connect sites:

1 Using Learning Site, add a blank page at the end of the course. You can name it something like "link" so you remember what it is for.

2 Open the "link" page and select the body tag selector at the bottom of the window:

<body>

3 From the behaviors panel, choose *Go To URL*.

Dreamweaver displays the Go To URL window:

4   In the URL field enter the correct URL. If the new site is stored in a subfolder of the main site, you can browse for and choose the index.htm file. If not, you need to enter a full URL (i.e. *http://www.rapidintake.com/site_2/index.htm/*).

5   Click **OK**.

6   Make sure the event is *onLoad*.

Click the down arrow button to change the event.

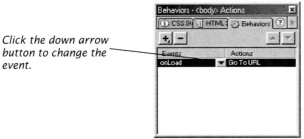

7   Save the file.

When Learning Site loads the page it will automatically go to the new site.

Using a Menu to Connect Sites

If you have more than one site that you are connecting together, you may want to create a menu. This method simply requires you to create a page that contains multiple links. Each link contains an href to the index.htm page of a different learning site. Once you create the menu page, you will probably want the learners to begin the course from that page.

More Information: You may want to have each link open up a course in a separate window. See *Changing the Browser Window* earlier in this chapter.

Using a Clickable Image to Connect Sites

Similar to using a menu, a clickable image (button) simply contains a link to the *index.htm* page of another learning site. This might be the method you want to use if you are connecting multiple sites that track learner data. Once learners have completed one site, you could add an image that they can click to continue to another site.

Note: If you are connecting multiple sites that track student data, you will probably want to use the same database. See *Chapter 20: Using Learning Site to Track Learner Data* for more information on how to do this.

Summary

In this chapter we have discussed several ways to customize Learning Site. You learned how to do these tasks:

- Remove unwanted navigational buttons.
- Change the button and background images.
- Change the orientation of the frameset.
- Determine what controls are visible on the browser window.
- Generate random pages.

We also discussed some of the problems inherent with connecting multiple sites and presented a few solutions. We also presented three methods for connecting multiple sites if you decide to do that.

Section IV:
Tracking Learner Data

There are a lot of Learning Management Systems (LMS) out there that can track student data. Learning Site is not the most robust LMS on the market, but you can't beat the price. In this section you'll learn how to use it and overcome some of its most troublesome shortcomings. You'll also learn about what is required to communicate with another LMS if you choose to go that route.

Using Learning Site 20 to Track Learner Data

One of the nice things about Learning Site is that it lets you track student data with relative ease and little expense. You can pay a lot of money for an LMS to track learner data and Learning Site will do it free.

In this chapter we discuss many issues associated with tracking learner data. We show you how to set up a learning site and look at several enhancements.

In this chapter you will learn:

- The pieces critical to tracking learner data.
- The Learning Site database structure.
- What settings are necessary to track and score questions.
- How tracking is handled and what issues are involved.
- How to set up data tracking for a site.
- How to test and edit a learning site that includes data tracking.
- How to administer and report on information gathered about the learner.
- Several ways to enhance data tracking.
- Some of the ways we think Learning Site can be improved.

Introduction to Data Tracking

In many courses that you develop you will want to keep track of how the learners are doing. Learning Site, using an Microsoft Access database, lets you track how the learners perform on the quizzes that are a part of the course.

More Information: If you need more information about Microsoft Access, visit your local library or bookstore, which should carry several titles on this subject, or visit the Microsoft web site: *http//www.microsoft.com/*.

Learning Site enables you to track this data:

- Activities and whether the learner has completed the activity
- The date and time spent on an activity
- Learners' responses to the questions and whether the responses were Right or Wrong
- Individual scores and total scores
- Basic learner data such as name and email

Learning Site keeps track of learner data by activity. All scores are associated with an activity. In Learning Site, an activity is considered to be one learning site (one course). If you attach more than one learning site (course) to a single database, then you could have multiple activities.

More Information: For more information about using a single database for multiple learning sites, see *Unique Enhancements for Data Tracking* later in this chapter.

For data tracking to occur, there are several pieces that must be in place. In this section we give a quick overview of these pieces.

The Tracking Database

Learning Site provides a pre-built Access database for tracking student data. As a part of the process for setting up student tracking, you need to add the database and create a connection for it. A connection tells the web server how to talk to the database.

You can view data stored in the database using one of two methods:

- Use the administration files and web-based reports provided by Learning Site

- Or, view the database within Access if you own the Access software.

More Information: The tracking database is described in more detail in *Getting to Know the Learning Site Database* later in this chapter.

The ASP Pages

Learning Site comes with several ASP (Active Server Pages) pages. These pages have an *.asp* extension. ASP pages contain special scripting interpreted by the web server. The server then returns an HTML page to display in the learner's browser.

More Information: If you need more information on ASP, visit your local library or bookstore, which should carry several titles on this popular subject.

Learning Site adds these ASP pages to your site:

- studentLogin.asp
- results.asp
- tracking.asp
- adminLogin.asp
- adminMenu.asp

Learning Site uses the *studentLogin.asp* page to log the student into the course. When data tracking is activated, by selecting the Data Tracking setting on the Site tab, the *index.htm* page calls the *studentLogin.asp* page and requires a login. This page checks the user ID and password against the tracking database.

The *results.asp* page displays the results of the quiz to the learner. This page is activated from the **Next** button, the **Finish** button, the **Quit** button or any combination of the three. It depends on your choices on the Navigation tab:

You can set up these three buttons to access the results page.

Learning Site	☒

Previous on First Page
- ⦿ Display Alert: You are on page 1.
- ○ Exit the Quiz and Go to the Login Page

Next on Last Page
- ⦿ Display Alert: You are on the last page
- ○ Exit the Quiz and Go to the Results Page

On Restart
- ○ Go to the First Page
- ⦿ Exit the Quiz and Go to the Login Page

On Finish
- ○ Go to the Last Page
- ⦿ Exit the Quiz and Go to the Results Page

On Quit
- ○ Go to Results Page
- ○ Go to Page: index.htm
- ⦿ Close Browser Window

☐ Display Pages in Random Order
Number of Pages to Display (Pooling): [ ] Pages, or ☑ Display All Pages

OK	Cancel	Help

Site	Pages	Style	Navigation	Tracking	Login	Results

The *tracking.asp* page is used to communicate tracking features to the database such as activity ID and user ID.

The *adminLogin.asp* and *adminMenu.asp* pages are used for site adminstration. These pages allow you to log in as an administrator to print reports and update users.

The Administration Files

The administration files that Learning Site provides allow access to the tracking database through a browser. The user simply needs to know the administration login and password.

Once you have accessed the database, you can add and delete users, and generate reports about the learners.

More Information: For more information on using the administration files, see *Administering Your Course* later in this chapter.

UltraDev and Testing

As we've mentioned before, UltraDev is required to set up data tracking. In addition you should follow some specific guidelines when testing a site.

UltraDev

Initially, UltraDev is required to set up data tracking initially. If UltraDev is not present, Learning Site does not display the three tabs that are used for setting up tracking. Those tabs are Tracking, Login and Results. Also, if you have not selected the Data Tracking setting on the Site tab, the three tabs will not be visible:

Select this setting to track data.

Tip: If you choose, you can set up data tracking using UltraDev and other developers can still work on the individual pages using Dreamweaver. For more information see *Developing in Both Dreamweaver and UltraDev* later in this chapter.

Testing the Site

A site that has been set up for student tracking uses ASP pages, and you need to test its student tracking features from a web server. You can do this using one of three methods:

- Publish the pages to a commercial web server and access them through a browser. The web server must be set up to handle ASP pages.

- Install Internet Information Server (IIS) on your own PC if you are running Windows NT Server or Windows 2000. You can then access the site locally through a browser.

- Install Personal Web Server (PWS) on your own PC if you are running Windows 95, 98, or NT Workstation. You can then access the site locally through a browser.

More Information: Testing is covered in more details in *Testing and Editing Your Course* later in this chapter.

Getting to Know the Learning Site Database

The purpose of the database is to keep track of learner results while taking the course. The default database that is delivered with Learning Site is an Access 97 database. If you don't have Access 97 or even Access at all, it doesn't matter. You can still use the data tracking features. If you do have Access 97 or a later version, you can open and work with the database.

Note: If you plan to deploy a course that requires access from more that 10 concurrent learners, it is strongly recommended that you look at creating a replacement database using a product like Microsoft SQL Server or Oracle.

If you have a later version of Access and you would like to enhance it, you must convert the database first. If you don't convert that database, you can view data but cannot make changes to it.

Note: If you are well-versed at creating ASP pages and you know how to use Access, you can customize the data tracked by Learning Site by editing the ASP pages that come with Learning Site.

In this section you will learn what is necessary to convert the database. Then you will learn about the tables that are contained in the database.

Converting the Database to Access 2000

Converting the database to Access 2000 is a straight-forward matter. When you open the database it prompts you to convert it. You must have Access to receive this prompt and convert the database.

Note: Before you can convert the database, you must first set up data tracking so that the database is present. For more information on setting up data tracking, see section *Setting Up Data Tracking* later in this chapter.

Follow these steps to convert an Access 97 database to Access 2000:

1 Double click on the Access database.

An Access database contains a .mdb extension. The Convert/Open Database dialog box displays:

Default option is to convert the database.

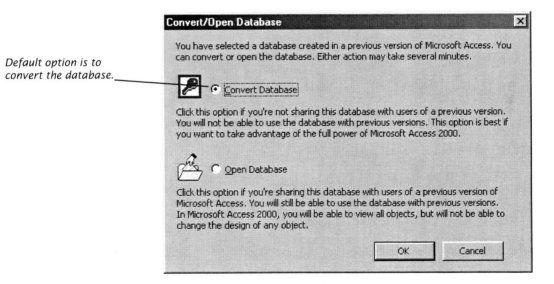

By default the ***Convert Database*** option is selected.

2 Make sure the ***Convert Database*** option is selected and click **OK**.

Access prompts you to name the new database. You must enter a new name. Your Access 97 database name won't work. After entering a new name, old database connections you have created will not work. If you haven't created a connection yet, then you have nothing to worry about.

 More Information: For steps on creating a database connection see *Setting Up Data Tracking* later in this chapter.

3   Enter a name for the converted database.

Access converts and opens the database in Access 2000.

Description of Database Tables

Database tables are designed to follow industry-standard guidelines specified in AICC version 2.0. This standard specifies that these elements should be tracked for each interaction:

- Interaction ID
- Objective ID
- Weighting
- Question Type
- Correct Response
- User Response
- Result
- Date/Time
- Latency

The database consists of six tables. As we describe each of tables you will see where this information is stored.

The Activities Table

The purpose of the Activities table is to store a list of scorable activities. An activity is a course (one learning site) that you have created. The table consists of four fields:

ActivityID	ActivityName	ActivityURL	ActivityDescription
100	Collection%20N	http://localhost/	

Activities : Table

Record: 1 of 1

You assign the ActivityID and the ActivityName on the tracking tab:

The Activity ID and Activity Name are assigned here.

The four fields are described in this table:

Field	Description
ActivityID	Stores identification information for the activity. A single learning site is an activity and consists of an AcitivityID.
ActivityName	Stores a name for the activity.
ActivityURL	Stores the URL that is used to access the activity (learning site course).
ActivityDescription	Store a description of the activity. There is no place to enter this information in Learning Site. If you would like a description, you need to enter it here.

The Activity_Detail Table

This table tracks student scores by user ID and activity. It stores the response, the date and time, the time it took to complete the question, the weight, and other information about each question. This table consists of 13 fields:

First 8 fields

ActivityID	UserID	Question	UserResponse	Result	QuestionTime	QuestionDate	TypeInteract
100	garin	m2q1	{choice6}	c	09:03:21	27/09/2001	c
100	garin	m2q2	choice2	w	09:05:11	27/09/2001	c
100	garin	m2q3	choice1	c	09:05:26	27/09/2001	c
100	garin	m2q4	choice2	c	09:05:37	27/09/2001	c

Record: 1 of 23

Last 5 fields

TypeInteractio	CorrectRespor	ResponseValue	Weight	Latency	ObjectiveID
c	{choice1,choice		1	00:00:45	
c	choice1		1	00:00:12	
c	choice1		1	00:00:08	
c	choice2		1	00:00:05	

Record: 1 of 23

The 13 fields are described in this table:

Field	Description
ActivityID	Identifies the activity.
UserID	Identifies the user.
Question	Stores the Question ID to identify the question. This is entered on the CourseBuilder Tracking tab.
UserResponse	Stores the learners response to that particular question.
Result	Indicates whether the learners response was correct (c), wrong (w), or not judged (n).
QuestionTime	Stores the time the interaction was completed.
QuestionDate	Stores the date the interaction was completed.
TypeInteraction	Stores a code to identify the type of interaction. The codes are: Drag and Drop (m), Button (t), Text (f), all others (c).
CorrectResponse	Stores the correct answer for the interaction.

Field	Description
ResponseValue	The field is not currently used. The early version of the AICC specifications did not include a response value. This was added in version three. This field was added in case CourseBuilder is updated to accommodate a response value.
Weight	Stores the weight assigned to the interaction. The weight is entered on the CourseBuilder Tracking tab.
Latency	Stores the amount of time the learner spent on the interaction.
ObjectiveID	Stores identification for the objective associated with the interaction. This is entered on the CourseBuilder Tracking tab.

The Activity_Status Table

The Activity_Status table tracks information about the learner's status regarding the entire course. There are 8 fields in this table:

This table describes each of the fields:

Field	Description
ActivityID	Stores identification information for the activity. A single learning site is an activity and consists of an AcitivityID.
ActivityName	Stores a name for the activity.
UserID	Identifies the user.
TotalTime	Total amount of time spent on the activity (in the Learning Site course).

Field	Description
ActivityDate	The date the learner started the activity.
Score	The highest score achieved by the learner on the activity (Learning Site course).
Location	Stores the name of the last page accessed last time the learner entered the activity (Learning Site course).
Status	Indicates if the activity is complete (c) or incomplete (i).

The Admin_Data Table

This table stores basic information about the administration logins. You can add more than one administrative login if you like. You can see from the table the type of information that is stored in this table:

Caution: As you can see, it is very easy to find out the user ID and password if you have access to the database. For that reason you may want to include a login and password on the database.

Here is a description of the six fields:

Field	Description
UserID	Identifies the administration user and is used as a part of the login process.
Password	Stores the user's password.
FirstName	Stores the user's first name.
MiddleName	Stores the user's middle name it one is entered.

Field	Description
LastName	Stores the user's last name.
Email	Stores the users email address if one is entered.

The Session_IDs Table

This table contains each user's latest session ID. Each time a learner logs into the course, Learning Site creates a new session ID. For example, if a learner has accessed the course 5 times, the session ID should be 5. There are three fields in this table:

The three fields are described here:

Field	Description
SessionID	Keeps track of the learner while in the course. A new session ID is generated and the old one is deleted each time the learner accesses the course.
UserID	Correlates a session ID with the user.
ActivityID	Identifies the activity accessed for the session ID.

The Student_Data Table

This table is very similar to the Admin_Data table. It stores basic information about the student logins. You can see the type of information that is stored in this table:

UserID	Password	FirstName	MiddleName	LastName	Email
garin	12345	garin		hess	
steve	12345	steve		Hancock	

Record: 2 of 2

Caution: Once again the passwords are not secure.

The six fields are described here:

Field	Description
UserID	Identifies the user and is used as a part of the login process.
Password	Stores the user's password.
FirstName	Stores the user's first name.
MiddleName	Stores the user's middle name it one is entered.
LastName	Stores the user's last name.
Email	Stores the users email address if one is entered.

Tracking and Scoring Interactions

Once you decide to track learner data for a course, there are certain settings that are necessary for each CourseBuilder interaction. You may also want to provide a score to the learner, which requires additional settings. In this section we discuss the settings required to track data and provide a score. Afterwards we take a look at how scoring works in Learning Site.

Setting Up Tracking and Scoring

For Learning Site to track a CourseBuilder interaction, you must establish certain settings. A critical setting is selecting the Knowledge Track option on the General tab:

Select the Knowledge Track setting.

Selecting Knowledge Track sends the learner's response information to the database after the question is answered. This includes the correct response, the learner's response, whether or not the response was correct, when the learner started the interaction, and how long it took.

Note: If you use Learning Site to create the CourseBuilder interactions, then Knowledge Track is automatically selected. However, if you create CourseBuilder interactions before adding them to Learning Site then you need to select Knowledge Track.

Selecting Knowledge Track causes the Tracking tab to appear:

.

On the Tracking tab you can fill in three additional settings:

- **Interaction ID**. Identifies the interaction in the database and the Learning Site reports. It is a good idea to enter an Interaction ID.

- **Objective ID**. Stored along with the question ID. Use an ID that clearly defines the associated objective. This is a great way to keep objectives correlated with interactions. Currently, Learning Site doesn't provide a report that will display the objective ID, but you can make modifications using the techniques described in the *Enhancing Learning Site Reports* section.

- **Weight**. Necessary for scoring. The weight defines the relative importance of an interaction within the overall group. For example, if certain questions are more important and should carry more weight, enter a higher number. If all interactions are similar, you can enter a 1.

Finally, you need to enter a score for each interaction. No individual score is recorded, but the score is used to compute the total score. Refer to *How Scoring Works* later in this chapter to better understand how an individual score is figured into the total score.

Refer to this table for information on how you enter a score for each interaction type:

Interaction Type	Entering a Score
Multiple Choice & True/False	Access the Choices tab and enter a score for each answer.
Drag & Drop	Access the Pairs tab and enter a score for each pair.
Explore	Access the Hot Areas tab and enter a score for each hot area.
Button	Access the General tab and enter a score for the state of the button (e.g. down and up).
Text Entry	Access the Response tab and enter a score for each possible response.
Timer	Access the Triggers tab and assign a score for each trigger.
Slider	Access Ranges tab and assign a score for each range.

Tip: When assigning scores, you normally want to assign incorrect answers a score of 0 and correct answers a positive score. Negative values can cause problems with the scoring.

In summary, follow these steps to set up a CourseBuilder interaction for data tracking:

1   Make sure the Knowledge Track setting is selected on the General tab.

2   Access the Tracking tab:

Enter interaction ID, objective ID and weight here.

> **CourseBuilder Interaction**
>
> Tracking Options
>
> Interaction ID: [   ]
>
> Objective ID: [   ]
>
> Weight: [   ]
>
> OK
> Cancel
> Help
>
> General | Tracking | Choices | Action Mgr

3   Enter an Interaction ID.

4   If you want to correlate objectives with interactions, enter an Objective ID.

5   Assign a weight to the interaction.

6   Access the appropriate tab (depending on the interaction) and enter a score for each possible response. (See the table on the previous page for tab information.)

7   Repeat this for each interaction in the course.

Now the interactions are ready to send data to the database once you establish the correct settings in Learning Site.

More Information: To prepare Learning Site for data tracking, see *Setting up Data Tracking* later in this chapter.

How Scoring Works

Learning site keeps track of a total score for the entire course. It does not keep track of a score for each interaction. So, how does it generate that total score?

When the learner completes a course, Learning Site generates an individual score for each interaction and sums those for the total score.

To completely understand how scoring works in learning site, you must first understand two main concepts:

- How scores are generated for a single CourseBuilder interaction
- How the total score is tracked by Learning Site

How is the Total Score Generated?

When the learner completes a course or wishes to quit, Learning Site may generate a total score for the course. (Learning Site generates a total score each time the results page is displayed. You determine when the results page displays [on the Navigation tab].

 More Information: For more information on the Results page see *Chapter 18: Defining a Learning Site*.

To generate a total score, Learning Site multiplies the score for each correct response by its weight and sums them all. It also multiplies the possible score for each question the learner had a chance to answer by the weight and sums these. The total correct scores is divided by the total possible score and then multiplied by 100 and rounded off. This formula illustrates how the scores are computed.

```
ROUND(((Q1 correct score * Q1 weight) + (Q2 correct score * Q2
weight) + . . .)/ ((Q1 possible score * Q1 weight) + (Q2 possible
score * Q2 weight). . .) * 100)
```

Here are a couple of examples to help explain this concept.

Example 1
In example 1 lets assume there are 5 questions. Each question has a weight of 1 but the scores differ. Therefore, each question is worth a different amount:

Question	Weight	Score	Answer
Q1	1	1	Answered Correct
Q2	1	1	Answered Incorrect

Question	Weight	Score	Answer
Q3	1	2 (1 point for each correct response.)	Answered both correct
Q4	1	2 (1 point for each correct response.)	Answered only 1 correct
Q5	1	4 (1 point for each correct response.)	Answered only 2 correct

The total score generated for this scenario is 60. First add up the score for each correct response multiplied by the weight: (1*1) + (0*1) + (2*1) + (1*1) + (2*1)=6. Then add up each possible score multiplied by the weight: (1*1) + (1*1) + (2*1) + (2*1) + (4*1)=10. Now divide the correct score by the possible score: 6/10=.6. Multiply by 100 and round off: .6 * 100 = 60.

Note: There are several interaction types that may provide more than one correct response: multiple correct, drag and drop, and explore are some examples. When you assign a score to more than one correct response, the total possible score for that question becomes more than the possible score for other questions with a single correct response. If you would like to make a multiple correct type question return only one score and only if every correct response is chosen, see section *Sending a Single Score from a Multiple Correct Question* later in this chapter.

Example 2

In this next example we use a different weight for each question and keep the scores the same.

Note: Assigning a different weight to a question assigns more importance to that question. For example, lets say that one question covers two objectives while another question covers only one. You may want the question that covers 2 objectives to have more weight. Another reason to weight interactions could be based on criticality of the skill.

Question	Weight	Score	Answer
Q1	2	1	Correct

Question	Weight	Score	Answer
Q2	1	1	Incorrect
Q3	2	1	Incorrect
Q4	1	1	Correct
Q5	2	1	Correct

The total score generated for this scenario is 63. First add up the correct score multiplied by the weight: $(1*2) + (0*1) + (0*2) + (1*1) + (1*2)=5$. Then add up each possible score multiplied by the weight: $(1*2) + (1*1) + (1*2) + (1*1) + (1*2)=8$. Now divide the correct score by the possible score: $5/8=.625$. Multiply by 100 and round off: $.625 * 100 = 63$.

As you have probably guessed, it is also possible to have different scores for each question as well as different weights. The least complicated scenario to deal with is to have each question worth 1 point and have a weight of 1 point. These fictional scenarios demonstrate the flexibility that is available in scoring.

How is the Score Tracked by Learning Site?

As we mentioned in previous sections, a total score is generated and stored in the database each time the results page is displayed or whenever the learner quits the course. You determine *when* the results page is displayed by the settings you select on the Navigation tab. You can choose to go to the results page when:

- The learner clicks next on the last page of the course.
- The learner clicks Finish.
- The learner clicks Quit. (Even if you do not take learners to the results page when they quit, a total score is still generated.)

If the learner has already taken part of the course and a score has been recorded, then Learning Site may or may not overwrite the old score. If the new score obtained by the learner is higher than the previous score, then the new score is recorded and the old score is lost. If it is not higher, the score is not recorded.

More Information: For more information about how Learning Site tracks data and scoring, see *Tracking and Scoring Issues*.

Tracking and Scoring Issues

You are now aware of some limitations regarding how Learning Site tracks learner data and scores. Some of these issues may be frustrating to you, so we would also like to provide some quick fixes to some of the problems you might encounter.

 Note: For you to effectively use Learning Site you need to be aware of these issues. You may not feel they are a problem, but if you do, knowing about them allows you to decide if you want to use the quick fix provided or take some other action.

The Tracking and Scoring issues discussed in this section are:

- **Issue 1**. Learning Site generates a total score before the entire course is completed.
- **Issue 2**. Each time a learner logs into the course the individual interaction data is deleted from the database.
- **Issue 3**. You are not allowed to have more than one interaction per page.
- **Issue 4**. Non-judged interactions still have individual data tracked in the database.
- **Issue 5**. There is a few second delay between the time the student answers a question and when the results get recorded.
- **Issue 6**. The scoring of Multiple Correct (all that apply) questions is not always accurate.

You will find a complete description of the issue and possible solutions in this section.

Issue 1: A Total Score is Generated before the Entire Course is Complete

First we describe the problem. Then we present a few simple solutions.

The Problem

A total score is generated for learners each time they quite a Learning Site course. If the Results page is displayed upon quitting the course, then the learner sees the total score. The fact that a total score is generated each time creates a problem. The reason this is a problem is that when Learning Site computes the total score it does not take into account every possible interaction in the course. It only includes the interactions that the learner saw while in the course.

Here is a scenario of how this can cause a problem: Let's say a learner accesses the course and learns the first bit of information. The learner is then presented with a quiz question. The learner answers the quiz and gets it correct. The learner then decides to quit the course and come back to it later. Learning Site generates a score of 100 because the learner saw only one question and answered it correctly. (Remember, by default Learning Site doesn't take into account other questions the learner may not have seen yet.) The total score of 100 is recorded in the database.

To make matters worse, that score of 100 is never overwritten with a new score even if the learner comes back to the course and finishes the other questions. Learning Site only overwrites a score if a follow-up score is larger. For example, if the score were 50, and later the learner got 75, the database would store a 75 as the total score. But if the learner got 45, Learning Site would not store the score.

To us, this is probably the most serious limitation with Learning Site. Therefore, we came up with a few solutions.

The Solutions

We suggest two possible solutions:

- Always record a total score of 0 unless the learners complete the entire course in one sitting.

- Always overwrite the total score with any subsequent scores regardless of whether the score is higher or lower than the previous score.

Both of these solutions require a minimal amount of JavaScript knowledge. Other solutions are possible, but they would require numerous changes and are beyond the scope of this book.

Record a Total Score of 0

You can apply a simple fix by changing the function that calculates the score so that it returns a score of 0 unless the learner has completed the entire course. This means that the learner has completed the entire course during that session (one sitting).

You make this change by modifying the calculateScore function in the *navigation.js* file.

Follow these steps to change Learning Site so that it records a total score of 0 unless the entire course is completed:

1   Open the *navigation.js* file. This file is located in the scripts folder.

2   Locate the *calculateScore()* function.

This function calculates the total score. It is located around line 106:

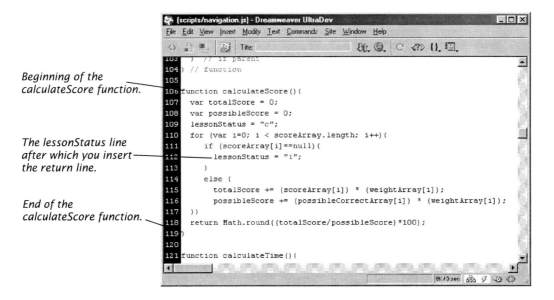

Beginning of the calculateScore function.

The lessonStatus line after which you insert the return line.

End of the calculateScore function.

3   Insert this line of code immediately following the line *lessonStatus = "i"*:

return 0;

Once inserted, the function should look like this.

```
function calculateScore(){
  var totalScore = 0;
  var possibleScore = 0;
  lessonStatus = "c";
  for (var i=0; i < scoreArray.length; i++){
     if (scoreArray[i]==null){
       lessonStatus = "i";
       return 0;
     }
     else {
       totalScore += (scoreArray[i]) * (weightArray[i]);
       possibleScore += (possibleCorrectArray[i]) *
(weightArray[i]);
  }}
  return Math.round((totalScore/possibleScore)*100);
}
```

4   Save the file, publish it (Site → Put) or click the **Put Files** button, and test it by logging in, completing just one question and finding out what your score is.

You should receive a score of 0.

Tip: You can see the score when it is displayed in the results page or by opening the database in Access and opening the Activity_Status table.

Always Overwrite the Total Score

If you like the fact that Learning Site returns a score for only the questions the learner has answered, then you may just want to change Learning Site so that it always writes in the latest score. If not, lower scores are never recorded.

This change requires that you update the tracking.asp page.

Follow these steps to change Learning Site so that every score is recorded even if it isn't larger than a previous score:

1   Open the *tracking.asp* page.

2   Switch to the code view (View → Code).

Locate this if statement.

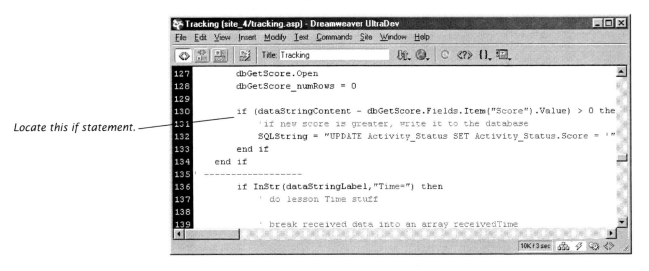

3   Locate the following lines of code around line 130 of the tracking.asp page. (The lines have been truncated so they will display correctly.)

```
if (dataStringContent - dbGetScore.Fields.Item("Sc…
    'if new score is greater, write it to the …
    SQLString = "UPDATE Activity_Status SET Activi…
end if
```

This *if* statement checks to see if the score is greater than the previous score by subtracting the previous score from the current score and testing to see if the results are greater than 0. To make it record every score that is generated, we simply need to turn the *if* statement into comment lines. (Comment lines are not executed. This way we don't delete any of the code. If you every want it back, you can just remove the comment marks.)

This ASP page was written in VBScript, and the comment mark is a single quote.

4 Enter a single quote in front of line the line that reads "*if (dataStringContent*" and a single quote in front of line that reads "*end if*".

The line should gray out when you enter the comment mark:

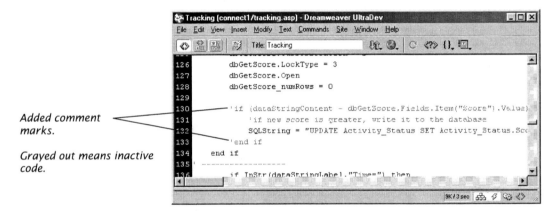

Added comment marks.

Grayed out means inactive code.

5 Save the file, publish it to your site (Site → Put) or click the **Put File(s)** button, and test it by logging in multiple times and see if the score changes each time.

For a complete test, make sure to answer in a way that you receive a score that is less than a previously stored score.

Issue 2: Interaction Data is Deleted at Each Login

Whenever a CourseBuilder interaction is completed, data about that interaction is sent to the tracking database. That data is stored in the Activity_Detail table. When a learner logs into the system, any past information for that learner is deleted. This may not be desirable.

First we describe the problem. Then we present a few simple solutions.

The Problem

This function may not always be a problem. But here is an example where it may cause problems:

Assume that a learner has completed a course and taken all of the quiz questions. The administrator hasn't printed off a detail report of the activity yet. The learner logs back in to review some information. All the previous detail information about each interaction is lost because it is deleted.

The Solution

You can prevent the data from being deleted at the time of login. Doing so causes a lot of data to be kept in the database. A lot of this data could be duplicated as well. (If the learner takes the quiz more than once, another entry for that interaction is made.)

The change is made by modifying the *studentLogin.asp* page.

Follow these steps to prevent Learning Site from deleting interaction data at the time of login:

1   Open the *studentLogin.asp* page.

2   Switch to the Code view (View → Code).

3   At about line 98 find this comment line: '—Delete Activity_Detail:

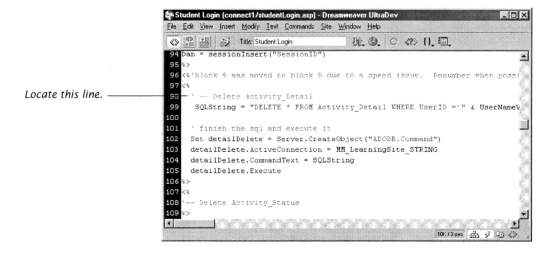

Locate this line.

```
 94 Dan = sessionInsert("SessionID")
 95 %>
 96 <%'block 4 was moved to block 8 due to a speed issue.  Renumber when possi
 97 <%
 98   ' -- Delete Activity_Detail
 99     SQLString = "DELETE * FROM Activity_Detail WHERE UserID ='" & UserNameV
100
101   ' finish the sql and execute it
102     Set detailDelete = Server.CreateObject("ADODB.Command")
103     detailDelete.ActiveConnection = MM_LearningSite_STRING
104     detailDelete.CommandText = SQLString
105     detailDelete.Execute
106 %>
107 <%
108 '-- Delete Activity_Status
109 %>
```

4   Place a comment mark (') in front of the five lines indicated in this table:

Line Begins with . . .
SQLString = "DELETE * FROM Acitivity_Detail
Set detailDelete = Server.CreateObject("ADODB.Comm
detailDelete.ActiveConnection = MM_Learning
detailDelete.CommandText = SQLString
detailDelete.Execute

Note: Comment lines are not executed. In using comment lines you don't delete any of the code. If you ever want it back, you can just remove the comment marks.

5   When you place the comment mark in front of the line, it should turn gray.

6   Save the file, publish it (Site → Put) or click the **Put File(s)** button, and test it by logging in multiple times and checking the Activity Detail report.

More Information: To learn how to check the Activity Detail report see *Administering Your Course*. You can also open the database in Access to see if the data is accumulating like it should.

Issue 3: Only One Interaction per Page is Allowed

Learning Site does not function correctly if you place more than one interaction per page. The reason for this is that the JavaScript files are hard-coded to look for a G01 interaction. This is the object name assigned to the first interaction added to a page. Because it is always looking for G01, any other object name does not work.

This could also cause a problem if you added two interactions to a page and then deleted the first interaction. The remaining interaction still has a G02 reference and is not tracked correctly by Learning Site. If this has happened to you, delete all of the interactions and begin again.

A solution to this interaction would require a lot of coding and is beyond the scope of this book

Issue 4: Data for Non Judged Interactions is Still Tracked

When you add interactions using Learning Site, Learning Site automatically selects the Knowledge Track option on the General tab. This causes data to be sent to the tracking database even if you choose not to judge the interaction.

This can happen when you add a CourseBuilder interaction that you are using for instructional purposes rather than for testing. You may not realize the Knowledge Track setting is selected. To correct this problem simply uncheck the Knowledge Track setting:

Deselect this setting when you are using the interaction for instructional reason and not for testing.

Issue 5: There is a Delay after the Question is Answered

After the learner answers a question, there is a 1- to 2-second delay before the information about that interaction is passed to the database. If the learner quickly clicks the **Next** button before the data is passed to the database, it is lost.

This delay is probably due to the processing time that must take place. We don't have a solution to this issue other then providing instructions for your audience on using the training and making sure that you emphasize that they pause briefly before moving on.

Issue 6: The Scoring of Multiple-Correct Question is not Always Accurate

Multiple-correct (all that apply) questions are not always scored correctly. This can be a multiple choice question with more than one correct answer, or another question type like a Drag-and-Drop.

In this section we look at the problem and then present a possible solution.

 More Information: Also see *Chapter 16: Behind the Scenes: Deciphering CourseBuilder's JavaScript* for another look at this problem and a solution.

The Problem

This problem of multiple-correct questions not scoring correctly manifests itself in three ways:

- The interaction data that is recorded may indicate that the question was answered correctly when it was not.
- A partial correct question receives a partial score. (This may be what you want, and if it is, great, no changes necessary.)
- An incorrect selection is recorded as correct as long as the correct selections are made along with the incorrect selections.

On CD: To see these problem illustrated, take a look at our interactive Interaction Properties Interrogator by opening *prop_interrogator.htm* on the CD ROM.

Interaction Data Recorded Incorrectly
Let's discuss the first problem mentioned. Here is a portion of a sample results page.

Question	User Response	Result	
1-1	choice1	c	
1-2	{choice1}	c	

Question 1-2 is a multiple choice question that has two correct responses. As you can see in the User Response column, the learner chose one response. That response was one of the correct responses, so the Result column contains a "c" for correct.

This question is only scored as half credit, but the results the learner sees shows a different story. Here is a portion of the Student Detail report, which shows the same information:

Question	User Response	Result
1-1	choice1	c
1-2	{choice1}	c

If you look at this information in the database you can see that the correct response consists of more than one answer. The database knows there is more than one answer because the answers are stored in the CorrectResponse field, so the score is correct; however, incorrect information is displayed to the learner:

One way to correct this problem is to communicate to the learner how to read the feedback on the report. If there are curly braces around the UserResponse data it means that the question is a multiple-correct question. In the Result column, Learning Site tells the learner which responses were correct and which were not. If multiple responses are made you see more than one letter. Either a "c" for correct or a "w" for incorrect.

Here is an example when more than one response is made:

Question	User Response	Result
1-2	{choice1,unnamed1,choice2}	c,c,c

Recording a Partial Score

If you set up a multiple-correct question in a standard fashion, you assign a value of 1 to each correct question and a value of 0 to each incorrect response. This allows Learning Site to record a partial score for the interaction.

For example, if the learner gets two of three possible answers correct, the score is two out of a possible three. This means that the multiple-correct question is being counted as three questions worth 1 point each. You score just like getting two of the three questions correct.

This problem is resolved using the solution presented in the next section.

Recording Incorrect Selections as Correct

The last way multiple-correct question problems are made manifest is if all of the correct responses are chosen and some incorrect responses as well. The individual results for the interaction shows that one response was incorrect as shown here:

Question	User Response	Result
1-1	choice1	c
1-2	{choice1,unnamed1,choice2,choice4}	c,c,c,w

Incorrect response is indicated.

However, the total score does not reflect that one of the responses was incorrect. For example, if there are three correct responses that means there is a possible score of three. If three correct reponses are chosen then the learner will get 3 out of 3 because the incorrect reponses do not subtract from the total score.

A Possible Solution

A workable solution for this problem consists of two parts:

- First, you need to communicate to the learner how they should view multiple correct data.

- Second you need to change the way the multiple-correct question is scored.

To change how a multiple correct question is scored, use the Action Manager tab.

Follow these steps to correct the way a multiple correct question is scored:

1 Edit the interaction.

2 Assign a score of 1 to one of the correct responses or one of the correct pairs if it is a drag-and-drop question.

3 Assign a score of 0 to all other responses or pairs.

4 Access the Action Manager tab.

5 Select the *if correct* condition.

Why not use a negative score?

You may ask why not make incorrect responses worth a negative value while the correct responses are worth a positive value. Good idea. But it does not work with the scoring mechanism used by Learning Site.

Giving a question a negative value throws off the possible score. For example, if you have four answers, two correct (1 point) and two incorrect (-1 point), the possible score is 0 because the negative numbers cancel out the positive numbers.

This is true for any question type, not just multiple correct.

6   Choose *Set Interaction Properties* in the ***segment*** drop down.

Choose Set Interaction Properties and click Add.

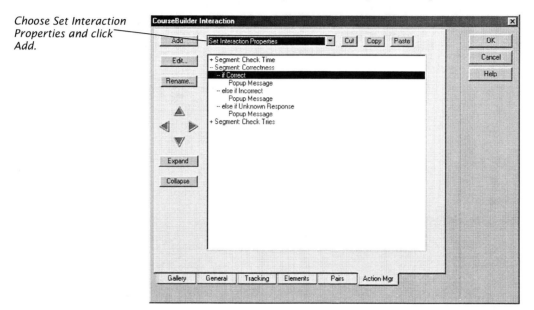

7   Click the **Add** button.

The Set Interaction Properties window displays:

8　Establish the settings shown in this table:

Attribute	Value
Set	Interaction
Interaction	The name of the interaction you are working with.
Property	Total Score
Type	Number
Number	1

This causes the interaction to return a total score of 1 only when the entire interaction is correct.

9　Click **OK**.

CourseBuilder adds the Set Interaction Properties. You can keep any other action under that condition.

10　Add another *Set Interaction Properties* under the *else if incorrect* condition and make the Total Score *0*.

You can keep all other interactions under the *else if incorrect* condition.

11　Click **OK**.

12　Test the interaction in a browser.

This interaction will now score correctly. When the answer is correct, it always returns a value of 1. The possible score is always 1 because only one choice or pair was given a score. If the question is incorrect, it always returns a score of 0.

Tip: If you want your multiple-correct questions to be worth more than other questions in your quiz, increase the weight of the interaction. For example, if you have a multiple-correct question with three responses, and you want it worth three times as much, use a weight of 3 while standard questions use a weight of 1.

More Information: Also see *Chapter 16: Behind the Scenes: Deciphering CourseBuilder's JavaScript* for another look at this problem and a similar but slightly different solution.

Setting Up Data Tracking

Now that you know what data tracking involves and some of the issues associated with data tracking, you are ready to set up a site. There are five main tasks you need to complete to set up your site to include data tracking. These tasks are:

- Setting up the Tracking database
- Setting up the Student Login page
- Setting up the Results page
- Configuring the CourseBuilder interaction pages
- Copying the Administration files

Each of these tasks are addressed in this section. Each main task includes hands-on exercises.

To complete the hands-on exercises included in this section, you need to define *site_4* on the CD as a site in Dreamweaver UltraDev. You are not be able to use Dreamweaver in this section. Continue to use this site in the next main section in this chapter: *Administering Your Course*.

Setting up the Tracking Database

As we have discussed earlier in this chapter, Learning Site provides a Microsoft Access 97 database for the tracking of learner data. To use this database, you must create it and define an ODBC connection.

This section teaches you how to create the tracking database and define a connection to that database. You may want to view the finished site before you begin making any changes.

Viewing the Finished Site

Before setting up the tracking database, you may want to view the settings in a completed site.

On CD: Define site *site_4_fin* from the CD as an UltraDev site. Then you can view the settings using Learning Site. You cannot access this site through a browser unless you have either PWS or IIS installed and have created a Data Source Name (DSN).

Here are some things to look for while you have this site opened:

- What is the name of the DSN? (See the Tracking tab in Learning Site.)
- What name was assigned to the database? (The database should have a .mdb extension.)

Completing the Tracking for the Site

To practice setting up the tracking database for a site, follow this hands-on exercise.

Note: To follow along with these steps, you need to define *site_4* from the CD as an UltraDev site. You must have this site opened.

Follow these steps to set up database tracking:

1 Modify Learning Site (Site → Learning Site → Modify Learning Site).

2 Click on the Tracking tab to access it.

The Tracking tab displays:

Enter an activity name and then create the Access database.

```
Learning Site                                                    [x]
                                                          ┌──────────┐
                                                          │   OK     │
         Activity ID: │100            │  ☑ Include Results Page
                                                          │  Cancel  │
       Activity Name: │site_4         │
                                                          │   Help   │

    Step 1: Create Tracking Database (optional)
         ┌────────────────────────────────────┐
         │  Create Microsoft Access (.mdb) file │
         └────────────────────────────────────┘

    Step 2: Create Data Source Name (optional)
         ┌────────────────────────────────────┐
         │       Open ODBC Control Panel        │
         └────────────────────────────────────┘

    Step 3: Select Data Source Name (required)
         DSN: │              │
     Username: │              │
     Password: │              │

    │ Site │ Pages │ Style │ Navigation │ Tracking │ Login │ Results │
```

The activity ID and Activity Name at the top of the tracking tab are important database information. This information identifies this activity (course created with Learning Site) in all reports.

3 Leave the *Activity ID* as 100.

The *Activity ID* can include up to 50 alpha or numeric characters.

4 Enter *e-Learning Book* as the Activity Name.

The first step in setting up the tracking database is to create it.

5 Click the **Create Microsoft Access (.mdb) file** button.

The Save Tracking Database As window appears:

Save Tracking Database As	? X
Save in: connect1	

- _notes
- connect2
- Connections
- images
- reports
- scripts
- connect1.mdb

File name: Save

Save as type: Microsoft Access Database (*.mdb)   Cancel

Select a location and a name for the database. You can save the tracking database in any location. It does not need to be in the site folder.

6 Enter *handson* as the name of the database. Search for a folder to save the database in. You can save it inside your site folder if you would like.

Note: If you are using a Macintosh, you may want to save the database on the web server you plan to use.

Next, either create or select a DSN so the server can communicate to the database. If the DSN is already created, you can skip to step 3 on the Tracking tab.

The DSN is stored on the machine where it is created. If you transfer a site to another server you need to create a new DSN.

The Creating a DSN option is disabled on a Macintosh. The reason for this is that the Mac cannot act as the server for the site. Therefore you need to create the DSN on the server you will be using.

7   To begin creating a DSN, click the **Open ODBC Control Panel** button.

The ODBC Data Source Administrator window displays:

You can access this window from the Windows Control Panel as well.

8   Click the System DSN tab.

This screen displays all DSNs that have been defined for the current machine:

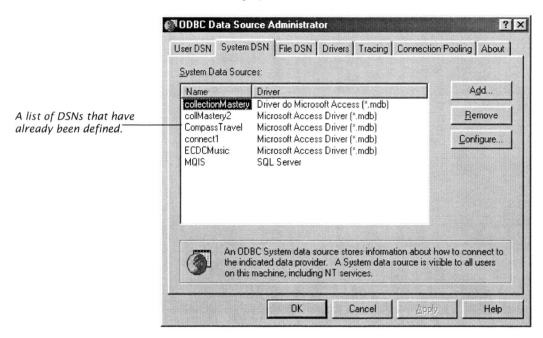

A list of DSNs that have already been defined.

At this point if you see a DSN that has been defined for you, you can cancel and enter the DSN. If not, you can create a new one.

9   To create a new DSN, click the **Add** button.

The Create New Data Source wizard appears:

10 Since we are using the predefined Microsoft Access database, select the Microsoft Access Driver (*.mdb).

Tip: You could create a new database using a database program other than Access if you would like.

11 Click **Finish**.

The ODBC Microsoft Access Setup window appears:

Enter a name, a description, and select the database.

In this window you only need to enter a name, description, and select the database.

12 Enter *handson* as the ***Data Source Name***.

13 Enter *e-learning Book* as the ***Description***.

14 Click the **Select** button to choose a database.

15 Search for and select the *handson.mdb* database that you created earlier.

16 Click the **OK** button on the ODBC Microsoft Access Setup window.

You should now have a new DSN listed in the System DSN tab of the ODBC Data Source Administrator window:

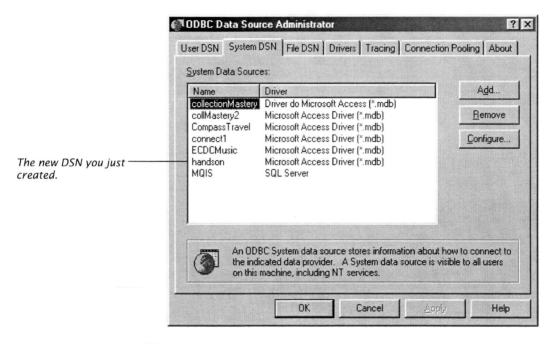

The new DSN you just created.

17 Click **OK**.

Windows returns you to the Tracking tab.

18 Click on the globe icon 🌐 next to the DSN field:

Globe icon ―

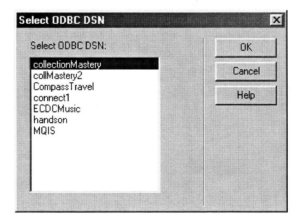

The Select ODBC DSN window displays:

19 From the Select ODBC DSN Window, select the handson DSN and click **OK**. If you are using a Macintosh simply enter the DSN that was set up on the server. Don't click the icon.

If your database requires a user name and password then you can enter that in the Username and Password field. This feature allows learners access the database when they are taking the course. The default Access database is not set up with a username and password.

You have now created the database and the database connection.

Setting Up the Login Page

The next logical step in setting up student tracking is to set up the Login page. This step is done on the Login tab. You can choose a style that matches the navigation style or you can create a custom style.

This section teaches you how to set up the Login page.

Viewing the Finished Site

Before setting up the Login page, you may want to view the settings in a completed site.

On CD: Define site *site_4_fin* from the CD as an UltraDev site. Then you can view the settings using Learning Site. You will not be able to access this site through a browser unless you have either PWS or IIS installed and have created a DSN and published the site.

Here are some things to look for while you have this site opened.

- What style is used for the Login page? (See the Login tab in Learning Site.)
- What ASP page controls the login process? (The page should have an .asp extension.)

Creating the Login Page

To practice creating the Login page for the site, follow this hands-on exercise.

Follow these steps to set up the Login page:

1   Click on the Login tab to access it.

Learning Site displays the Login tab:

On the Login tab you can enter a title for the Login screen, select a background color and choose a logo. You can also change the Login File Name if you want to use a different ASP page.

The only change you will make is to the **_Login Logo_** setting.

2 Since the course is already using the Techno style, select _Techno_ as the **_Login Logo._**

Tip: When you choose Custom as the logo, a new field displays that lets you search for and select a custom graphic you have created.

That is all there is to creating the Login page. When you click **OK**, Learning Site adds this page to the site.

Setting Up the Results Page

The Results page displays the learners' scores when they have completed the course. You determine when the Results page displays by the settings you establish on the Navigation tab.

The Results page is optional. If you don't want to include this page, deselect the Results Page option on the Tracking tab. This disables all settings on the Navigation tab that include the Results page.

This section teaches you how to set up the Results page.

Viewing the Finished Site

Before setting up the Results page, you may want to view the settings in a completed site.

On CD: Define site *site_4_fin* from the CD as an UltraDev site. Then you can view the settings using Learning Site. You will not be able to access this site through a browser unless you have either PWS or IIS installed and have created a DSN and published the site.

Here are some things to look for while you have this site opened:

- What style is used for the Results page? (See the Results tab in Learning Site.)
- What ASP page controls the Results page? (The page should have an .asp extension.)

Creating the Results Page

To practice creating the Results page for the site, follow this hands-on exercise.

Follow these steps to set up the Results page:

1   First make sure that the ***Include the Results Page*** setting is checked on the Tracking tab. If the Results tab is visible, then the setting is checked.

2   Click on the Results tab to access it.

The Results tab displays:

![Learning Site dialog box with Results tab selected. Results File Name: results.asp; Results Title: Student Summary; Background Color: #FFFFFF; Results Logo list showing Blank (no logo), Corporate, Consumer, Educational, Simple, Techno, Custom. Buttons OK, Cancel, Help on right. Tabs at bottom: Site, Pages, Style, Navigation, Tracking, Login, Results.]

On the Results tab you can enter a title for the Results screen, select a background color and choose a logo. You can also change the Results File Name if you want to use a different ASP page.

The only change we will make is to the ***Results Logo*** setting.

3   Since the course is already using the Techno style, select *Techno* as the Results Logo.

Tip: When you choose Custom as the Logo, a new field displays that allows you to search for and select a custom graphic you have created.

That is all there is to creating the Results page. When you click **OK**, Learning Site adds this page to the site.

4   Click **OK** to save all the settings you have established in these three hands-on sections.

When you click OK, Learning Site adds several new files are added to your site: *tracking.asp, results.asp*, and *studentLogin.asp*. These were added because you are now tracking data. You should also have the handson.mdb database saved somewhere. Learning Site inserted additional script files into the scripts folder as well.

Setting Up the CourseBuilder Pages

We discussed in the *Tracking and Scoring Interactions* section the settings that must be established in each CourseBuilder interaction for it to work for data tracking. In this section you go through a hands-on exercise of establishing these settings for our sample course: *site_4*.

Viewing the Finished Site

Before setting up the CourseBuilder interactions, you may want to view the settings in a completed site.

On CD: Define site *site_4_fin* from the CD as an UltraDev site. Then you can view the settings in the individual pages. You cannot access this site through a browser unless you have either PWS or IIS installed and have created a DSN and published the site.

Here are some things to look for while you have this site opened:

- Open and view the settings in these pages: *five-points.htm, quest1.htm, quest2.htm*, and *quest3.htm*.

- How are the settings for the interaction on page *five-points.htm* different than the other pages? Why is this the case?

- Which setting allows data tracking to occur?

Configuring the CourseBuilder Interactions

To practice configuring CourseBuilder interactions for a site that is tracking data, work through this hands-on exercise.

Follow these steps to configure the pages in the sample site:

1 Open file *site_4/quest1.htm*.

2 Edit the CourseBuilder interaction.

3 Make sure that the Tracking tab is visible. This means that the Knowledge Track setting has been selected on the General tab.

4 Click on the Tracking tab to access it.

The Tracking tab displays:

```
CourseBuilder Interaction                                          [×]

                                                                    OK
         Tracking Options
                                                                  Cancel
          Interaction ID: [                              ]
                                                                   Help
           Objective ID: [                              ]

               Weight: [        ]




     [ General ] [ Tracking ] [ Choices ] [ Action Mgr ]
```

5 Enter *Q1* in the ***Interaction ID*** field.

6 Enter a *1* in the ***Weight*** field.

We have not developed any objectives for this sample site, so leave the ***Objectives ID*** field blank.

 More Information: For more information about the weight and scoring, see the *Tracking and Scoring Interactions* section earlier in this chapter.

7 Click on the Choices tab.

8 Enter a Score of *1* for the correct answer.

9 Click **OK**.

10 Repeat steps 1-9 for pages *quest2.htm* and *quest3.htm*. For the ***Question ID*** enter *Q2* and *Q3* respectively.

11 Open page *five-points.htm*.

12 Click the General tab to access it.

13 Deselect the ***Knowledge Track*** setting.

If you leave this setting selected, this interaction records data in the database. We don't want this interaction doing that because we are using it for instructional reasons rather than for testing reasons.

14 Click **OK**.

Now all four interactions are ready for data tracking.

Copying the Administration Files

You must complete one more step to implement data tracking. You must copy the administration files to your site. This step allows you to administer the site and perform such tasks as generating reports and creating users.

In this section you go through a hands-on exercise in which you copy the files for our sample course: *site_4*. You may want to view the files in the finished site before you begin making any changes.

Viewing the Finished Site

Before setting up the CourseBuilder interactions, you may want to view the files in a completed site.

On CD: Define site *site_4_fin* from the CD as an UltraDev site. Then you can view the files in this site.

Here are some things to look for while you have this site opened:

- Can you tell which files are used to control administration functions?
- Which folder exists in this site but doesn't exist in the site you are working on? What could be the purpose of this folder?

Copying the Administration Files to the Sample Site

To practice copying the administration files, follow this hands-on exercise.

Follow these steps to copy the administration files:

1 Select Copy Admin Files from the Learning Site submenu (Site → Learning Site → Copy Admin Files).

The Copy Learning Site Admin Files window appears:

The default DSN that is being used by the site should appear in the DSN field.

2   If the Default DSN doesn't appear, enter it into the field or click on the **Globe** button and select it.

If the database you are using requires a username and password, you can enter that information. If you would like these files to replace Administration files that you copied previously, select the ***Overwrite existing admin files*** option.

3   Click **OK**.

Learning Site copies several files into the site.

Testing and Editing Your Course

One of the tricky things about creating a site that tracks learner data is you can't easily test the site from Dreamweaver. Because the data tracking uses ASP pages, you need to publish the site to a web server and then access it through a browser.

If you are using a Macintosh you need to publish to a web server. If you are using a PC, you can publish to a web server or configure your local machine as a web server and publish to that. This section addresses both issues.

We also discuss some special considerations for editing your course.

Publishing to a Remote Web Server

You or your System Administrator must set up the server to accommodate the site. This includes creating a subfolder where the site files will be located, copying the database, and creating a DSN.

Tip: You can actually store the database on a separate server if you wish. Just make sure the DSN points to the correct server.

Note: If you are using a Macintosh, you must publish to a remote server. If you are using a PC you may choose to use this method as well.

The information necessary to publish to a remote server is established in the Remote Info category of the Site Definition window. You can establish the information when you define the site (Site → Define Sites) or you can edit it later (Site → Define Sites). Here is a sample Site Definition window:

Site Definition for Final Collection Mastery

Category: Local Info / **Remote Info** / Application Server / Design Notes / Site Map Layout / File View Columns

Remote Info

Access: FTP

FTP Host: ftp.rapidintake.com

Host Directory: test

Login: collmast

Password: ******** ☑ Save

☐ Use Passive FTP
☐ Use Firewall (in Preferences)

Check In/Out: ☑ Enable File Check In and Check Out
☑ Check Out Files when Opening

Check Out Name: Steven

Email Address: steveh@rapidintake.com

[OK]   [Cancel]   [Help]

You may also want to configure the *Application Server* category to accommodate ASP pages.

More Information: For more information about configuring your site, refer to your Dreamweaver UltraDev manual.

Using Your Local Machine as a Web Server

If you are running Windows 95, 98 or Windows NT Workstation, you can install Personal Web Server and use your local machine as a web server for testing. If you are running Windows 2000 or Windows NT Server, Internet Information Server

(IIS) may already be installed. This is all you need to use your local machine as a web server on Windows 2000/NT machines.

More Information: For more information about PWS, refer to UltraDev User Manual.

Follow these steps to establish the correct settings on your local machine so it can act as a web server:

1 Access the Site Definition window by either creating a new site or editing an old site.

2 In the *Local Info* category, establish the settings as described in this table:

Field	Description
Site Name	Enter a Site Name.
Local Root Folder	Create or choose a folder on your hard drive to store the local files.
Other Settings	You can establish other settings as you would like.

3 In the *Remote Info* category, choose *Local/Network* as the Access method.

4 Choose or create a folder within the *C:\Inetpub\wwwroot directory*.

Note: The *C:\Inetpub\wwwroot* directory is created when PWS or IIS is installed.

5   You may want to define the Application Server category as shown in this screen capture. However, it isn't necessary for testing:

To define the Application Server, choose a Server Model, a Scripting Language, and a Page Extension. The Access and Remote Folder was already set on the Remote Info category.

6   You can define all other settings and categories as you wish.

7   Click **OK** to save the site definitions.

You are now ready to publish your course and test it.

Publishing and Testing Your Course

Once you feel you are to the point that you need to test your site through a browser, you need to publish your site first. Publishing your site simply means using the Put command to place your files on the web server whether it is remote or local.

Follow these steps to publish your course:

1   To publish your site, select the site directory and click the **Put** 🔼 button (Site → Put).

Dreamweaver prompts you to confirm that you want to put the entire site:

Dreamweaver UltraDev ✕

❓ Are you sure you wish to put the entire site?

OK   Cancel

2 Click **OK**.

Dreamweaver transfers the files.

Now you are ready to begin testing your course. Before you can login into the course to start testing, you need to create a student ID.

More Information: See *Administering Your Course* for information on how to create a new student ID.

Once you have a student ID, you can open a browser and enter the URL to your course. If you are testing the course locally, your URL begins with localhost (e.g. *localhost/site_4/index.htm*). The folder in the *Inetpub/wwwroot/* folder where you put your course goes before the index.htm file. In the example shown in this paragraph, the folder name is *site_4*.

Caution: You should not enter a URL that points to *studentLogin.asp* or any other asp page. Always enter a URL that points to the *index.htm* page.

Editing Your Course

As you begin testing your course, you will undoubtedly find things that you want to change. When that happens, use the techniques discussed in this book to make the changes.

Once the changes are made you need to remember to publish the changed files. If you don't you will not see any of the changes in the course. This is a very common mistake when working with Learning Site because it's easy to forget that your testing site is stored locally but is still served as if from a web server.

Caution: After editing a file in your course, make sure you published all files that have changed before you attempt to access it through a browser again.

If the change you made was to a single page, then you need to publish that page. However, if you had to modify the Learning Site settings, then you need to publish several files. To be completely safe, publish the entire site again. If your server is remote or your site is quite large, then publish these files: *index.htm, navigation.htm, tracking.asp, studentLogin.asp, results.asp, and global.asa.*

Administering Your Course

Administering a Learning Site course consists of two main tasks: maintaining learner information and printing reports. The administration files added to your site allow you to perform both tasks.

Maintaining learner information involves creating, modifying and deleting student IDs. All learners are tracked by a student ID that is created by the administrator. These tasks are discussed in this section.

Generating reports involves creating both Summary and Detail reports about either activities or students. Methods for report generation are covered in this section.

Before you can work with student IDs or generate reports, you must first log into the Learning Site administration function.

To complete the exercises that are included in this section, you need to publish (put) your site to a server. If you are running IIS or PWS locally, you can publish the site to your local machine. For more information see *Testing and Editing Your Site* earlier in the chapter.

Logging into Site Administration

Before you can perform any administration functions, you must first log in. Learning Site provides a default administrator user ID and password for your initial login. After your initial login, you may want to change the password. The default user ID and password is admin and admin.

To begin logging in you must point your browser to the *adminLogin.asp* page (e.g. *http://localhost/site_4/adminLogin.asp*). Once you have logged in, you are presented with the Admin Menu:

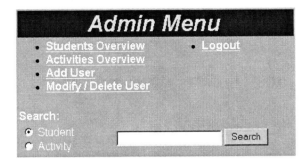

From this menu you can print reports, and add, update and modify users.

Follow these steps to log into site administration:

1   Open a browser.

2   Enter a URL that points to the *adminLogin.asp* page that resides on the web server. This may be remote (e.g. *www.rapidintake.com/site_4/adminLogin.asp*) or local (e.g. *localhost/site_4/adminLogin.asp*).

The login prompt appears:

Records Administration

User ID: [   ]

Password: [   ]

[Reset]   [Login]

3   Enter *admin* for the **User ID** and for the **Password** and click **Login**.

The Admin Menu appears. Now you are ready to work with reports and users.

Maintaining Learner Information

The administrator creates all student IDs used for tracking learner information. When creating student IDs, you enter basic information about the learner such as name and email address. You must also enter the user ID and the password. Once you have created a valid user ID and password, you can inform the learner of the URL and how to log in.

In this section you go through a hands-on exercise in which you create user IDs. To see how the site is different when you complete the exercise, you may want to view the contents of the finished site before proceeding.

Viewing the Finished User Information

Before creating the user information, you may want to view the completed information.

On CD: Define site *site_4_fin* from the CD as an UltraDev site. Publish (put) this site to a web server. Then you can login in to the administration site and view the information.

Here are some things to look for while you have this site opened:

- Notice that only one user has been created.
- Notice how easy it is to make changes to this information.
- Notice that you can also change the administrator information.

Creating a User ID

To practice creating a user ID, follow this hands-on exercise.

Follow these steps to create a user ID:

1   Log into the site administration using the methods discussed in the *Logging into Site Administration* section earlier in this chapter.

2   At the Admin menu click the **Add User** link.

The Add New User page displays:

Add New User
ID:
First Name:
Middle Name:
Last Name:
Password:
Email:
Type: Student ▾
Add User
Return to Admin menu

3 Fill in the fields using the information in this table. Leave *Middle Name* and *Email* blank.

Field	Value
ID	test
First Name	Testing
Middle Name	
Last Name	User
Password	12345
Email	
Type	Student

4 Click the **Add User** button.

You are given the option to add another user or return to the admin menu.

5 Click the **Return to Admin Menu** link.

Let's look at how easy it is to change user information.

6 Click on the **Modify/Delete User** link

You are shown a table for students and admins:

<u>Admin Menu</u> > *Select User*

Students

	UserID	First Name	Middle Name	Last Name	Email
modify / delete	test	Testing		User	

Admins

	UserID	First Name	Middle Name	Last Name	Email
modify / delete	admin	first	middle	last	

7   Click the **Modify** link for the single admin user.

Learning Site displays the Modify User Info screen:

<u>Admin Menu</u> > <u>Select User</u> > **Modify User Info**

ID:	admin
First Name:	first
Middle Name:	middle
Last Name:	last
Password:	admin
Email:	

Cancel   Modify User

8   Enter *12345* as the new password.

9   Click the **Modify User** button.

10 Click the **Admin Menu** link in the upper-left corner to return o the Admin Menu.

11 Click the **Logout** link to exit.

That is all there is to adding and modifying users.

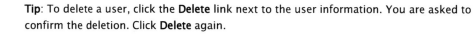

Tip: To delete a user, click the **Delete** link next to the user information. You are asked to confirm the deletion. Click **Delete** again.

Generating Reports

Learning Site comes with a few predefined reports. These reports are categorized under activities or students. There are both Summary and Detail reports. These reports access information directly from the database.

To generate reports, you must login as the administrator. From the Admin Menu you can follow links to each report.

In this section we discuss how to access both Student and Activity reports. We also look at searching for a specific activity or student.

Generating Student Reports

Student reports display how each learner performed in the course. The provide specific information about each interaction.

Follow these steps to access student reports:

1 Log into the Admin Menu using the methods discussed in the *Logging into Site Administration* section earlier in the chapter.

2 Click on the **Students Overview** link.

A list of all the users is provided:

Admin Menu > Students Overview

	UserID	First Name	Last Name	E-mail address
Modify	garin	Garin	Hess	garinh@rapidintake.com

3 To view the student summary information, click on the **User** link that appears in the UserID column for the student whose information you want to see.

Learning Site displays summary information about each activity the learner has participated:

Admin Menu > Students Overview > Student Summary

Garin Hess

Activity ID	Activity Name	Last Date Accessed	Total Time	Total Score	Status
100	Learning Site Test	9/29/01	00:03:03	67	i

4 To view how the learner performed in each interaction, click the activity link that displays in the Activity Name column.

Learning Site displays more detailed information:

Admin Menu > Students Overview > Student Summary > Student Detail

Garin Hess   Total Score: 67
Collection Mastery   Total Time: 00:03:03
Last Attempt: 9/29/01

Question	User Response	Result	Latency
m2q1	{choice1}	c	00:00:03
m2q2	choice2	w	00:00:09
m2q4	choice2	c	00:00:06
m2q1	{choice1,choice5}	c,c	00:00:08

Learning Site displays the learner's total score and total time and how the learner did in each interaction.

5   To return to a previous report or to the Admin menu, click on one of the links in the upper-left corner.

Generating Activity Reports

Activity reports display summary information about each activity. For example, they display information about how each student did in the activity.

Follow these steps to access activity reports:

1   Log into the Admin Menu using the methods discussed in the *Logging into Site Administration* section earlier in this chapter.

2   Click on the **Activities Overview** link.

Learning Site provides a list of all the activities:

Admin Menu > Activities Overview

Activity ID	Activity Name	Activity URL	Average Score
100	Collection Mastery	http://localhost/collection%20mastery%20test/index	67

3   To view more detailed information about a specific activity, click the **Activity** link displayed in the ***Activity Name*** column.

Learning Site displays information about how each learner did. You also get information on average score, high score, and low score. The URL for the activity is part of the display.

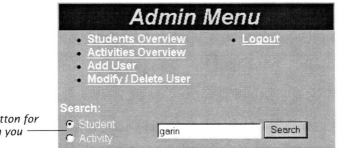

Admin Menu > Activities Overview > Activity Summary

Collection Mastery
ActivityID: 100
Activity URL: http://localhost/collection%20mastery%20test/index
Description:

| | Average Score: 67 |
| High Score: 67 |
| Low Score: 67 |

UserID	First Name	Last Name	Total Time	Score	Status
garin	Garin	Hess	00:03:03	67	

4 From this report you can view specific user information by clicking the user ID listed in the *UserID* column. Or you can return to a previous report or the Admin Menu by clicking the links in the upper-left corner.

Searching for Students or Activities

If you have a large number of students or activities in the database, you search for a specific student or acitivity. In the Admin menu, select the correct radio button, and type in the student ID or name or the activity ID or name and click the **Search** button.

Click the radio button for the type of search you want to conduct.

A list of matches displays, and you can use the links to get further information.

Unique Enhancements for Data Tracking

Now that you know more than you ever wanted to know about data tracking, we are going to provide just a little bit more information. There are a few unique ways you can enhance data tracking.

In this section we discuss these topics:

- Developing in both Dreamweaver and UltraDev
- Attaching Multiple Sites to a Single Database
- Customizing the Login and Results Page
- Customizing Reports

Developing in Both Dreamweaver and UltraDev

The majority of the information contained in this chapter can be done only if you have UltraDev. But what if you have multiple developers working on a single course? Do all of them have to have UltraDev?

The answer is, "not necessarily." If you want, you can assign one developer to be responsible for the data tracking architecture. This developer has UltraDev and sets up the initial site. Once the initial site is established, Dreamweaver developers can access the site to work on individual pages.

If it is necessary to modify the Learning Site, the developer with UltraDev should be responsible for that. If other developers create pages that need to be included in the course, the UltraDev developer adds them to Learning Site.

Tip: It is also possible to develop a Learning Site in Dreamweaver and then later convert it to UltraDev to add the tracking settings.

Caution: If a Dreamweaver developer modifies the Learning Site, critical tracking files and data could be lost. To prevent this, only developer's with UltraDev should modify Learning Site options if you are tracking data. Obviously, if you're not tracking data, Dreamweaver or UltraDev users could make modifications to the Learning Site settings.

Attaching Multiple Sites to a Single Database

It is possible to use a single database for multiple courses. This may make the administration of these courses much easier because there is a single access point.

Here are two important details to make this work correctly:

- Each different learning site must be assigned a different activity ID on the Tracking tab.
- Each different learning site must be assigned the same DSN.

If both of these items are in order, you can track multiple sites by the same database. The learner still needs to log into each site however.

Customizing the Login and Results Page

Throughout this book we have shown a number of ways you can customize pages and objects that are delivered with CourseBuilder and Learning Site. The Login and Results pages are no different. In this section we look at two different enhancements.

First, we make a few changes to the login page to make it look nicer. Second we change the Results page so that it displays more information.

Before making these changes, you may want to view the finished results.

Viewing the Redesigned Login and Results Pages

Before customizing the Login and Results page, take a moment to view the redesigned pages.

On CD: Define site *site_5* from the CD as an UltraDev site. Publish (put) this site to a web server. Then you can login using a user ID of test and a password of 12345.

Here are some things to look for while you have this site opened:

- What changes were made the Login page?
- What additional changes could be made to the Login page?
- What information was added to the Results page?
- What additional information could be added to the Results page?

Customizing the Login and Results Pages

In this section will change the look of the Login page. You also add information to the Results page. First you customize the Login page.

Customizing the Login Page

Follow these steps to customize the Login page:

1 Open the *studentLogin.asp* page for site *site_4*. (This is the site you have been working in throughout this chapter.)

The student login page appears:

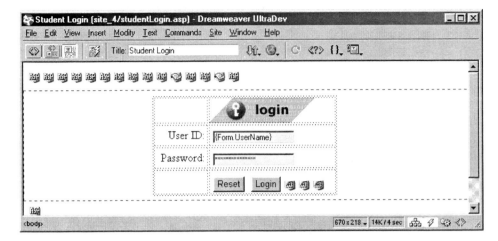

2   Select the table that contains the login form. To do this you can click in a cell and click the *<table>* tag selector at the bottom of the page.

`<body> <form> <table> <tr> <td> <input>`

3   In the property inspector (Window → Properties), enter a *1* in the border field:

Enter a 1 for the border.

4   Select the bottom three rows of the table by dragging the cursor across them.

5   In the Property Inspector, change the background color (Bg) to *#FFCCFF* and the border color (Brdr) to *#CC00FF*.

Enter colors for background and border.

6   Select both cells in the top row by dragging the cursor across them.

7   Merge the cells (Modify → Table → Merge Cells). You can also click the **merge cells** button ⬚ on the Property Inspector.

8   With the cursor in the merged cell, change the horizontal alignment (Horz field in the Property Inspector) to center.

The table should now look like this:

9   Save the changes.

Adding Information to the Results Page

You can now add the correct response to the Results page, so it displays as a part of the results.

Follow these steps to add information to the Results page:

1   Open the *results.asp* page for site *site_4*.

You will add a new column before the Latency column.

2   Click inside one of the cells in the Latency column to place the cursor there.

3   Insert a new column (Modify → Table → Insert Column).

The new column.

4   In the top cell of the new column enter: Correct Response.

5   Format the text so that it is the same as the other columns: (Arial, Helvetica, Sans Serif; bold, and Font Size change of –1).

6   Click inside the bottom cell of the new column.

7   Open the Data Bindings panel (Window → Data Bindings).

The Data Bindings panel displays and shows several recordsets:

Recordsets let you add information from the database.

8 Click the **plus** symbol next the *ActivityDetail* Recordset to open it up.

9 Find the CorrectResponse and drag it to the bottom cell of the new column and let go.

This action inserts a line of data into the new cell:

Correct Response
}	{ActivityDetail.CorrectResponse}

10 Save the file.

11 Now publish (put) both of the files to the web server and login through a browser to test your changes.

You have just made changes to both the Login page and the Results page.

Customizing Reports

Learning Site stores nine ASP pages inside the reports folder. Learning Site uses several of these pages to display the reports discussed earlier in the chapter.

These pages are structured much like the results page. They consist of tables to which you can add additional columns and drag additional data from the Data Bindings panel.

For example, you could modify the *studentDetail.asp* page in much the same way you modified the Results page. It doesn't currently display the correct response. Or you may want to display the objective ID because the objective ID is not included on any report.

Tip: You may want to create a new ASP page that would serve as a new report. If you did this you would need to create a link for this page from one of the existing ASP pages. For more information about creating ASP pages refer to the UltraDev manual.

Our Learning Site Wish List

Before we wind up this chapter, we would like to let you know some of the things we would like to see in future versions of Learning Site. Learning Site is a new product, so there are a lot of ways it could be enhanced.

These items are at the top of our list of enhancements:

- **A bookmarking capability**. Learning Site tracks the last page a learner visited, but there is currently no mechanism for returning to that page.

- **Initial student sign up**. When learners access a course, they cannot log in unless the administrator has created a user ID for them. We think Learning Site should have the flexibility to allow students to self register, if that is what the e-learning designer chooses.

- **Seamless integration of multiple sites**. Being able to connect multiple sites opens up another world for Learning Site. Right now there are too many negatives when connecting multiple sites.

- **A lot more flexibility in tracking and scoring data**. Earlier in the chapter we presented some issues with tracking and scoring. We would like to see a lot more flexibility in this area.

- **The ability to insert new pages at any point in the course**. When you are creating a large course and you want to insert a new page in the middle, it can be very frustrating. Learning Site always puts the new page at the bottom of the list. You must then move it up.

- **Recording of multiple words for Text Entry interactions**. Right now the Learning Site database only records the first word that a learner enters into a Text Entry interaction.

- **Support for other application server technologies such as PHP and JSP**. Right now ASP is the only technology supported.

Summary

Congratulations. You have made it to the end of this very long chapter. We have covered a number of different topics that have to do with data tracking.

You first learned those pieces critical to tracking learner data. One of those pieces is the database, which we described in detail.

You learned how to set up learning site for tracking scoring questions. There are several issues with data tracking, and you learned some solutions for these.

Once you have your data tracking settings established, you are ready for testing. Testing requires publishing (putting) your site files on a web server. You learned a couple of methods for doing this.

You learned about the administration element of data tracking, which involves maintaining user data and printing reports.

You looked at a few ways in which you can enhance data tracking. The last thing covered in the chapter was our wish list of future enhancements for Learning Site.

Although Learning site has some problems, they are not insurmountable. This is a valuable tool that greatly facilitates your development of e-Learning. We expect great things in the future.

Communicating with a Learning Management System 21

In the last chapter you learned how to track learner data using Learning Site. However, it's possible that Learning Site may not meet your needs for tracking learner data. If this is the case, you probably need to begin a search for an LMS. There are numerous LMSs on the market, and finding and configuring an LMS to work with your training course is a project in and of itself.

In this chapter you learn standards and basic information required to communicate with an LMS.

In this chapter you will learn:

- The importance of the AICC and SCORM standards.
- Important issues to consider when searching for an LMS.
- How to setup CourseBuilder interactions to communicate with an LMS.

Introduction to LMS Communication

If you have decided that you need to find an LMS to manage and deliver your training courses, then this chapter can provide you with some basic information to get you started. Purchasing an LMS is no small decision. Therefore, you should be well informed about the different LMSs available and what is entailed in getting CourseBuilder to communicate with an LMS.

In this chapter we try to provide some basic information by defining standards and providing basic setup steps. We also provide some resources for getting additional information.

What is AICC and SCORM?

AICC and SCORM are standards that have been established to facilitate the delivery of computer based courseware. AICC was developed first, so we will discuss it first.

AICC

The Aviation Industry CBT (Computer-Based Training) Committee (AICC) is an international association of training professionals. This organization has developed guidelines for the aviation industry in the development, delivery, and evaluation of CBT.

Although these standards were developed for the aviation industry, they have been widely adopted by other industries and training professionals. Most, if not all, LMSes strive to be AICC compliant.

The term *AICC Compliant* means that a training product complies with one or more of the nine guidelines and recommendations detailed by the AICC. Accordingly, AICC compliance can mean different things for different products. This makes it important that you have your LMS vendor delineate what it can and cannot do.

AICC has developed a certification program for its guidelines and recommendations. If you are looking for specific compliance, you can ask the LMS vendor if the product has been certified and for what.

AICC publishes its guidelines and recommendations in AGRs (AICC Guidelines & Recommendations). You can download AGRs from this URL:
http://www.aicc.org/pages/down-docs-index.htm.

More Information: For more information about AICC, including a list of AICC–certified LMS products, visit *http://www.aicc.org*.

CourseBuilder has the ability to send data to an AICC-compliant LMS, but it is not AICC compliant in and of itself.

SCORM

The Sharable Content Object Reference Model (SCORM) is a set of specifications built upon the work already done by AICC, IMS Global Learning Consortium, Inc., and the Institute of Electrical and Electronics Engineers (IEEE). The purpose of SCORM is to create one content model. These specifications enable the reuse of web-based learning content across multiple environments and products.

The SCORM specifications consist of three main parts:

- An XML-based specification for representing course structure. (This allows courses to be moved from one LMS to another.)
- A set of specifications for the runtime environment of the course.
- A set of specifications for the content of the course.

More Information: For more information about SCORM, visit *http://www.adlnet.org*.

Is CourseBuilder SCORM Compliant?

CourseBuilder interactions, in their current state, are not compliant and do not meet SCORM specifications for interacting with a SCORM-compliant LMS. However, a learning extension is available for Dreamweaver and UltraDev that helps make HTML pages SCORM-compliant. The name of the extension is SCORM RTI Minimal Code. You can download it from the Dreamweaver or UltraDev exchange site *http://www.macromedia.com/exchange/dreamweaver/*.

What Does the SCORM RTI Minimal Code do?

The SCORM RTI Minimal Code extension provides JavaScript and HTML code to address one part of the SCORM specification: navigation issues. As mentioned earlier, there are three main parts to the SCORM specifications, and this extension helps satisfy basic requirements for the runtime specifications. This extension meets this specification by providing the code to call the SCORM Application

Program Interface (API). The API is used by the LMS for communication during runtime.

Also, we should mention that this extension was developed for SCORM 1.1 specifications. SCORM 1.2 specifications are now available.

Another learning extension, Manifest Maker+, creates a course structure that meets the IMS 1.1 specifications. Remember, a set of specifications for the course structure is one of the three main parts for SCORM compliance. The IMS standard that Manifest Maker+ is based on was used as a part of the SCORM standard. However, that does not mean that the resulting file is SCORM compliant.

Why Do We Need All of these Standards?

After reading these short descriptions on AICC and SCORM, you may not want anything to do with standards. However, there is a good reason they were developed.

A standard can ensure that certain things happen, as well as ensure that different training products work together.

When student data tracking started, there were no standards at all. Each person had to either develop their own LMS or retrofit an existing LMS if they wanted it to work with the courseware they created. Standards allow multiple products to work together and in the long run it makes things easier on e-learning professionals.

It is not absolutely necessary that you understand all standards unless you are developing e-learning products. When you are looking for an LMS, you just want a product that meets your needs. Standards help make all this possible.

Finding an LMS

As we have mentioned, finding an LMS that works for you is a big project. In order to accomplish this task effectively, you need access to valuable information. In this section, we provide some information to help in your search for an LMS.

As you are looking for an LMS that is right for you, remember, all LMSs are not created equal. There may be several LMSs out there that contain more functionality then you need. For example, if you are authoring in Dreamweaver and CourseBuilder, you don't want to purchase an LMS with an authoring tool. You just need to make sure it is compatible with what you are developing. Why pay for the extra functionality?

Here are some sources of information:

- For an article that introduces LMSs and provides guidelines on what to look for see *http://www.e-learninghub.com/ Selecting_an_LMS.html.*

- Brandon Hall has recently published a report on 60 different LMSs. You can purchase and download the report at *http://www.rapidintake.com/elearning_products.htm.*

- Brandon Hall has other publications on LMSs. For more information see *http://www.rapidintake.com/elearning_products.htm.*

- You may want to look at each individual LMS. Here are some sites. For more sites, perform a search on Learning Management Systems or see *http://www.aicc.org/pages/cert.htm* for a list of AICC certified LMSes.

  aba: www.saba.com
  Docent: www.docent.com
  Aspen: www.click2learn.com
  Teamscape: www.teamscape.com
  Solstra: www.solstra.com
  Registrar: 194.205.72.130/registrar7/reg7.htm
  TopClass: www.wbtsystems.com
  WebCT: www.webct.com
  LearningSpace: www.ibm.com/mindspan
  Intralearn: www.traineasy.com
  Thinq: www.thinq.com
  Pathlore: www.pathlore.com
  iLearning: http://www.oracle.com/applications/ilearning/index.html
  Theorix: http://www.theorix.com
  Pinnacle: http://www.learnframe.com/solutions/pinnacle/
  Quelsys: http://ww.quelsys.com/
  Pathlore: http://www.pathlore.com/

- Possible courses on Learning Management Systems: *http://cybercentral.berkeley.edu/training.html*

 Note: One LMS that is proven to work well with Dreamweaver and CourseBuilder is IBM LearningSpace®. Macromedia provides documentation in the online help file for the specific steps required to communicate with this LMS.

Setting Up CourseBuilder to Communicate to an LMS

Before CourseBuilder interactions are ready to communicate with an LMS, you must establish certain settings. In this section we discuss the settings required to track data and provide a score. We also look at tracking actions that are available with Knowledge Track.

Using Knowledge Track

To track CourseBuilder interactions on a server running an LMS, you must establish certain settings. The most important setting is selecting the Knowledge Track option on the General tab:

Select the Knowledge Track setting.

The Knowledge Track feature is designed to send data to a server running an LMS.

When you select Knowledge Track, this information is automatically sent to the LMS every time an interaction is judged:

- The current data and time
- The interaction ID (entered on the Tracking tab)
- The objective ID (entered on the Tracking tab)
- The type of interaction
- The correct answer
- The answer given by the learner
- Whether the learner's answer was correct or incorrect
- The weight given to the interaction (entered on the Tracking tab)
- The time it took for the learner to answer the question

Once you have selected the Knowledge Track option, there are two additional tasks you must complete:

- Complete the scoring and tracking tab options
- Create a tracking frameset

 Note: Establishing Tracking an Scoring options for an LMS are very similar to the same task used for Learning Site.

Completing the Tracking Tab and Scoring Options

Selecting Knowledge Track in an interaction causes the Tracking tab to appear:

CourseBuilder Interaction

Tracking Options

Interaction ID:

Objective ID:

Weight:

OK   Cancel   Help

General   Tracking   Choices   Action Mgr

There are three fields on the Tracking tab:

- **Interaction ID**. Identifies the interaction in the LMS. It is a good idea to enter an Interaction ID.
- **Objective ID**. A unique identifier assigned to the interaction to identify its corresponding objective.
- **Weight**. Defines the relative importance of an interaction within the overall group. For example, if certain questions are more important and should carry more weight, enter a higher number. If all interactions are similar, you can enter a 1.

 Note: Some LMSs may ignore the weight setting and use their own settings. IBM LearningSpace is an example of an LMS that does this.

Finally, you need to enter a score for each interaction. Refer to this table for information on how you enter a score for each interaction type.

Interaction Type	Entering a Score
Multiple Choice & True/False	Access the Choices tab and enter a score for each answer.
Drag & Drop	Access the Pairs tab and enter a score for each pair.
Explore	Access the Hot Areas tab and enter a score for each hot area.
Button	Access the General tab and enter a score for the state of the button (e.g. down and up).
Text Entry	Access the Response tab and enter a score for each possible response.
Timer	Access the Triggers tab and assign a score for each trigger.
Slider	Access Ranges tab and assign a score for each range.

In summary, follow these steps to set up a CourseBuilder interaction for data tracking on an LMS:

1   Make sure you've selected the Knowledge Track setting on the General tab:

Select the
Knowledge Track
setting.

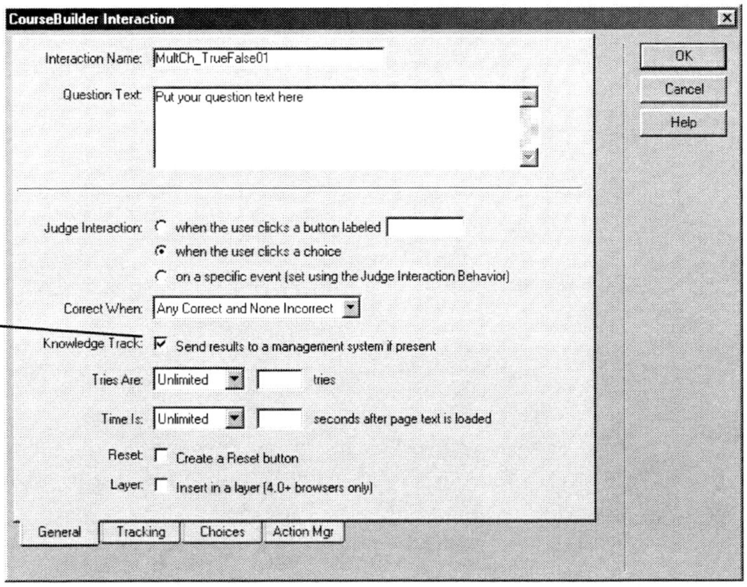

2   Access the Tracking tab:

Enter an Interaction
ID, an Objective ID
if you wish, and a
weight.

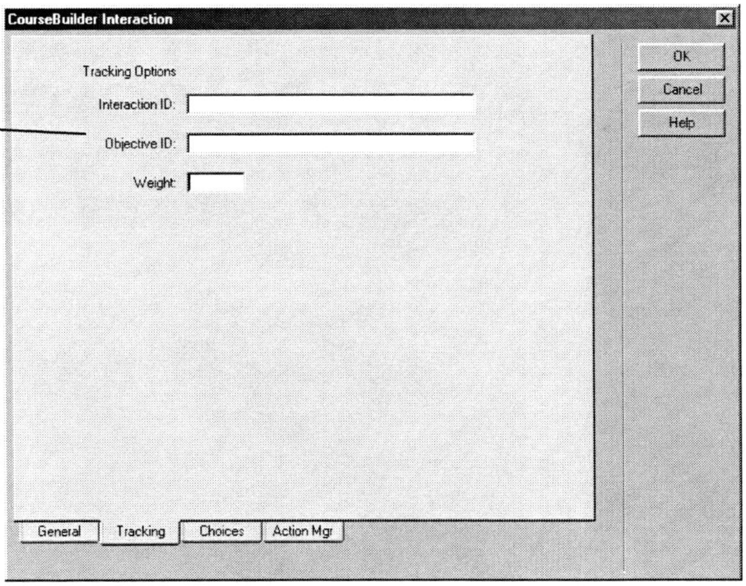

3   Enter an *Interaction ID*.

4   Enter an *Objective ID*.

5   Assign a *Weight* to the interaction.

6   Access the appropriate tab and enter a score for each possible response.

7   Repeat steps 1-6 for each interaction.

Now the interactions are ready to communicate with an LMS. However, there is still work to be done to make the communication happen.

Creating a Tracking Frameset

A frameset is an HTML document with more than one frame. The frameset that is used for communicating with an LMS contains two frames: top and bottom.

The top frame displays the page that contains the CourseBuilder interaction. The bottom frame is hidden and is used so the LMS can communicate to the CourseBuilder interaction.

Follow these steps to create a tracking frameset:

1   Open an HTML page that contains a CourseBuilder interaction.

2   Use the menu command to create the tracking frameset (Modify →
       CourseBuilder → Create Tracking Frameset).

       The Create Tracking Frameset window appears:

Create Tracking Frameset	☒
Frameset File: quiz1-frameset.htm	OK
Results File: results.htm	Cancel
Options: ☑ Overwrite existing files	Help
☐ Display frameset document	

3   Change the *Frameset File* name (if desired) and click **OK**.

       CourseBuilder creates a frameset file as well as a *results.htm* page. The
       results.htm page is used in the hidden bottom frame.

Note: the Create Pathware Frameset option in the CourseBuilder menu is specifically for the
LearningSpace LMS.

Additional Tracking Actions

With Knowledge Track enabled, you can use additional tracking actions in the Action Manager. These actions communicate with the LMS.

This table describes each action:

Action	Description
Send Score	Sends the score to the LMS.
Send Lesson Status	Sets the interaction status as passed, failed, completed, or started.
Send Lesson Time	Sends the amount of time the student spent on the interaction.
Send Objective Information	Sends information about the interaction's objective. The objective ID is identified on the Tracking tab.
Send Interaction Information	Sends information about a specific interaction.

Setting Up the LMS

Now that the CourseBuilder interactions are set up for the LMS, you can get the LMS ready. Each LMS has different setup requirements. Some of these requirements can take some time to set up. Refer to the LMS's documentation and any other sources of help to set up your LMS.

Summary

Deciding which LMS to use can be a difficult decision. It is important to have as much information as necessary to make the correct decision. Having a basic understanding of AICC and SCORM can help in this area. We highly recommend choosing an LMS that complies with AICC standards.

Setting up CourseBuilder Interactions for use with an LMS requires the Knowledge Track setting and a few other settings. More setup must be done in the LMS itself. You need to refer to the LMS's documentation to establish those settings.

Appendices

Here we've added a few extra topics that may be helpful.

Appendix A: Using Page Templates with CourseBuilder

A page template is a document that lets you create multiple pages that share the same layout. Portions of a template are marked as editable others as non-editable. You can change the editable portion. You cannot change non-editable areas except in the template itself. Therefore, templates can help you keep a consistent look and feel while giving you a jump-start on the creation of each page.

More Information: For more information on creating and using templates, see the Dreamweaver user manual.

Some Issues with Templates

If you are not careful, templates can cause numerous problems on CourseBuilder pages.

You may remember that a CourseBuilder page links several JavaScript files in the head tag. The code that links these files look like this:

```
<script language="JavaScript"></script>
<script language="JavaScript" src="scripts/behActions.js"></script>
<script language="JavaScript" src="scripts/behCourseBuilder.js"></script>
<script language="JavaScript" src="scripts/interactionClass.js"></script>
```

If this code is not included on a CourseBuilder page, then the interaction will not function correctly. Also, when a page that contains a CourseBuilder interaction is loaded, the *MM_initInteractions()* function is called. This function initializes the interaction. If this function is not called, the page will not work.

Many times a templates non-editable areas are the exact location where the CourseBuilder code needs to reside. If you apply a template to a CourseBuilder page, it is very likely that the template will remove the code shown above and then the interaction will no longer work.

Caution: Because applying a template to a CourseBuilder page may break it, we recommend that you never apply templates to an existing CourseBuilder page. Instead create a new page based on a template and then add the interaction.

Using Templates Correctly

There are two main ways to use a template in Dreamweaver: create a new page from a template (New → New from Template), or apply a template to an existing page (Modify → Templates → Apply Template to Page).

As we have mentioned, applying a template may cause problems. For example, suppose that your template is set up with the basic JavaScript files attached as shown earlier. You have created a drag-and-drop interaction and you apply the template. Applying the template removes these two lines of code that exist for the Drag-and-Drop interaction:

```
<script language="JavaScript" src="scripts/elemDragClass.js"></script>
<script language="JavaScript" src="scripts/behDragLayer.js"></script>
```

Without these two JavaScript files attached, the Drag-and-Drop interaction does not work correctly.

Now if you create a new page using this template, and the template has been set up correctly (see section *Creating Templates Correctly* later in this chapter), then when you add the Drag-and-Drop interaction these two lines of code are also added. Therefore, this is the preferred method for using templates.

Creating Templates Correctly

Before using a template to create CourseBuilder pages, you should apply the template fix (Modify → CourseBuilder → Add Template Fix).

Note: If you forget to add the template fix, CourseBuilder will prompt you to add the fix the first time you add a CourseBuilder interaction to a page created using the template.

The template fix adds an editable region to your template where CourseBuilder can attach JavaScript files and where the *MM_initInteractions()* function is called. The code for this editable region looks like this:

Identifies an editable region.

```
<!-- #BeginEditable "CourseBuilder" -->
<script language="JavaScript">
<!--
function MM_initInteractions(){}
//-->
</script>
<!-- #EndEditable -->
```

Now when you add a CourseBuilder interaction to a page created from a template with the fix, the JavaScript files are inserted within this editable region as shown here:

```
<!-- #BeginEditable "CourseBuilder" -->
<script language="JavaScript">
<!--
function MM_initInteractions(){}
//-->
</script>
<script language="JavaScript" src="scripts/behActions.js"></script>
<script language="JavaScript"
src="scripts/behCourseBuilder.js"></script>
<script language="JavaScript"
src="scripts/interactionClass.js"></script>
<script language="JavaScript" src="scripts/elemInptClass.js"></script>
<!-- #EndEditable -->
```

Note: Remember that just because the template has the fix does not mean that you can use it to apply to a page that already has a CourseBuilder interaction. If you absolutely need to apply templates to pages, make sure that the template already includes all of the JavaScript files that are used for every interaction or at least the interactions you are using. You can do this by viewing the code for different interactions.

Creating Templates to Use with CourseBuilder

There are two kinds of templates you may want to use with CourseBuilder: a generic template that you can use for any interaction, or a template that is specific to an interaction type. In this section we have included instructions for creating both.

Creating a Generic Template

You can use a generic template to create any CourseBuilder interaction. The important thing to remember when creating a generic template is to apply the template fix.

Follow these steps to create a generic CourseBuilder template:

1   Create the document you want to use as a template using the techniques discussed in Dreamweaver's user manual.

2   Save the page as a template (File → Save As Template).

3   Add a new editable region for the CourseBuilder interactions (Modify → Templates → New Editable Region). Add any other editable regions that you would like.

4   Select the template fix menu option (Modify → CourseBuilder → Add Template Fix).

The Add Template Fix window appears:

5   Click the **Add** button.

Now your template is ready to use.

Creating a Template for a Specific Interaction

You may run into a situation where you want a template that always creates a specific interaction such as Multiple Choice. Then you can use that template to create the page and the interaction with just a few modifications.

Follow these steps to create a template for a specific interaction:

1 Create a page that contains the interaction and the look-and-feel that you want in your template.

2 Save the page as a template (File → Save As Template).

3 Select the interaction by clicking the icon or the tag selector at the bottom of the screen.

4 Change it to an editable region (Modify → Templates → New Editable Region).

The tag selector for the interaction should change to *mm:editable*:

`<body> <mm:editable>`

5 Save the template.

Now you can use this template to create a new page. You can then edit the interaction and make changes as you normally would.

Appendix B: Setting CourseBuilder Preferences

Even though CourseBuilder is only an extension to Dreamweaver, it is really quite a complex piece of software. As you use it you may prefer that it behave a certain way or start with certain defaults.

Macromedia has provided a way to customize how CourseBuilder works. These settings are called *preferences*.

The Preferences File

To set CourseBuilder preferences, open the *preferences.txt* file. You can find this file in the *Config* folder wherever CourseBuilder is installed on your hard drive:

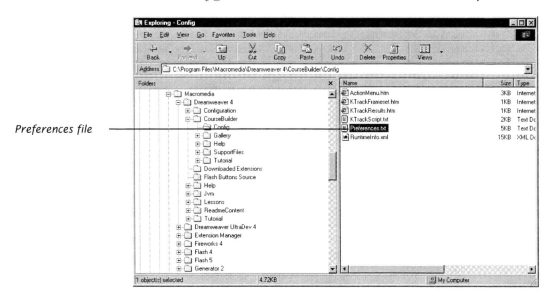

Preferences file

Viewing the Preferences File

The Preferences file is a text file, but it contains JavaScript code. So it is best to view and edit the Preferences file by opening it within Dreamweaver.

When you open it in Dreamweaver it looks like this:

Double forward slashes (//) indicate JavaScript comments. These lines don't do anything, they simply give you instructions on how to set the preference.

"var" indicates that line contains a value that sets a preference.

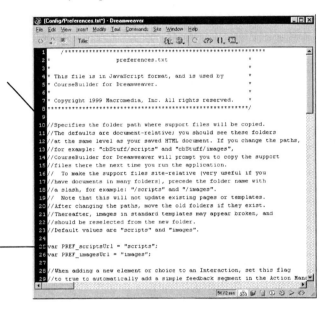

Changing Preferences

Instructions within the *Preferences.txt* file tell you how to change its settings. You can find the instructions for any preference above the *var* line that sets the preference.

Instructions are set off by JavaScript comment lines. Comment lines usually begin with double forward slashes (//):

Instructions for the Judge button preference.

The variable that actually sets the Judge button preference

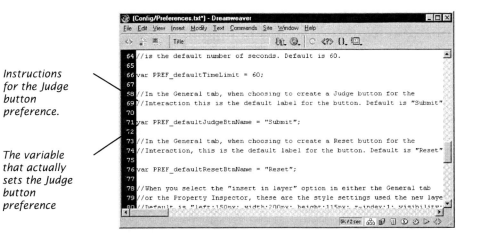

To set a preference, you usually change the value within the quotes on the *var* line. However, make sure to read the instructions for any preference you want to change. For example, to change the default label of the submit button from *submit* to *Am I Right?*, you need to replace the word *Submit* with *Am I Right?*:

This preference has been changed.

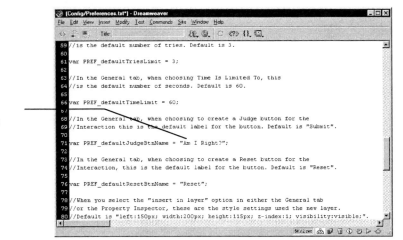

Changing a setting in the Preferences file changes the default for all future CourseBuilder interactions:

The setting change takes effect.

Settings the Preferences File Contains

This table lists the settings that can be changed, provides a brief explanation, and supplies the line number in the Preferences file that contains the setting. (To view line numbers select View→Code View Option→Line Numbers):

Setting	Description	Line Number(s)
CourseBuilder Support Files location	You can set the support files to be document-relative or site-relative. Choose the site-relative option if you have HTML files in different folders in your site and you want to use one set of CourseBuilder support files.	25, 26
Adds response-specific Action Manager segment	Automatically adds a new segment for new elements added to the interaction. Very useful if you want to create response-specific feedback. It will not, however, add Action Manager segments for already existing elements (such as the choices that exist by default in a Multiple Choice interaction).	39

Setting	Description	Line Number(s)
Removes response-specific Action Manager segments	Automatically removes segments in the Action Manager that are associated with an element when you delete the element. You probably want this turned on if you have chosen the setting on line 39.	51
New element default name	Sets the default name for new elements (such as choices in a Multiple Choice interaction).	56
Tries Limit	Sets the default number of tries when choosing *Tries are Limited To* on the General tab.	61
Time Limit	Sets the default number of seconds when choosing the *Time is Limited To* on the General tab.	66
Judge interaction button name	Sets the default name for the button that is created when you choose the *when the user clicks a button labeled* option on the General tab.	71
Reset button name	Sets the default name for the button that is created when you choose the *Reset* option on the General tab.	76
Interaction layer properties	Sets the properties of the layer in which the interaction is placed when you choose the *Layer* option on the General tab.	82
Explore interaction backdrop layer properties	Sets the properties of the layer in which the optional backdrop image is placed in Explore interactions.	88
Image tag attributes	Sets the attributes of the optional images that can be added in Multiple Choice, Drag-and-Drop, and Explore interactions.	95

Setting	Description	Line Number(s)
Maximum condition name length	Sets the maximum length of a condition name in the Action Manager.	100
Segment name	Sets the default name of new segments added in the Action Manager.	105

Appendix C: Cross-Browser Limitations

In this appendix you will find information on using CourseBuilder to create interactions that work within multiple browsers.

CourseBuilder Works With Multiple Browsers

CourseBuilder writes JavaScript that is usually compatible with these browsers:

- Internet Explorer 3 (and higher)
- Netscape Navigator 3 (and higher)

While CourseBuilder interactions are usually compatible with both browsers, you can experience some differences. The following table shows the limitations of different CourseBuilder interactions in four different browsers:

Interaction	Netscape 3	Netscape 4	IE 3 (Win)	IE 4
Multiple Choice with form elements	OK; radio buttons aren't cleared by Reset; both radio buttons and check boxes can be selected even when disabled	OK; radio buttons aren't cleared by Reset; both radio buttons and check boxes can be elected even when disabled	OK; radio buttons aren't cleared by Reset; both radio buttons and check boxes can be selected even when disabled	OK
Multiple Choice with graphic elements	OK; transparency in images may cause redraw problems	OK	Fails without error	OK
Drag and Drop	Fails without error	OK; cannot insert in layer	Fails without error	OK

Interaction	Netscape 3	Netscape 4	IE 3 (Win)	IE 4
Explore	Fails without error	OK; cannot insert in layer	Fails without error	OK
Button	OK; transparency in images may cause redraw problems	OK	Fails without error	OK
Text Entry	OK; accepts text entry even when disabled	OK	OK; accepts text entry even when disabled	OK
Timer	May have only one running on each page	May have only one running on each page	Fails without error	OK
Slider	Fails without error	Only one per page; layers after the slider won't function correctly; setting background color on the slider layer causes a failure without error	Fails without error	OK
Action Manager	OK	OK	OK	OK

The information in this table is found in <u>Using CourseBuilder For Dreamweaver</u>, Macromedia Press, p. 73. Reprinted with permission from Macromedia Inc.. Copyright ©2001 Macromedia, Inc.. All rights reserved. Macromedia is the exclusive Trademark of Macromedia, Inc."

More Information: Also see Tech Note 13985: Browser Issues with CourseBuilder for Dreamweaver on Macromedia's website (*www.macromedia.com/coursebuilder*). You can find Tech Notes under Getting Started.

Our Recommendations

Even though, generally speaking, CourseBuilder works with both Internet Explorer and Netscape browsers, IE comes closer to adhering to DHTML standards than Netscape. Moreover, they both use slightly different versions of JavaScript, with IE again offering a wider array of JavaScript capability for developing interactive web pages. That's why we almost always recommend that online courses be developed in Internet Explorer.

You would be wise to do all you can to narrow the number of browsers you have to develop for. You can do this by encouraging your IT department to do an organizational upgrade to a newer release (IT department often maintain a standard release organization-wide, so you may already have some of your battle taken care of for you).

No need to be discouraged, however, if you need to develop for Netscape. Just make sure you are familiar with which CSS styles work in NS and which don't. You have a more limited array of tools available to use, but you can still create highly interactive training with CourseBuilder using Netscape.

So, what do you do when you need to develop for both? You basically have two options:

- Design each page so it works identically in both browsers. This often requires that you develop for the "lowest common denominator", or in other words, whatever will work well in both browsers (see the chart in the previous section).

- Design separate pages for each browser and check the browser (using the ***Check Browser*** action) before navigating to those pages to make sure that the user will have a successful experience once the page is loaded. Load the page that was designed for the browser the user has.

Whatever route you choose make sure you leave adequate time for cross-browser testing. Cross-browser development can often increase the development and testing time significantly. We've found that this can be a major issue in course development that teams that are new to WBT development frequently overlook.

Appendix D: Using Media with CourseBuilder

There are several ways to use media with CourseBuilder. In this appendix we'll briefly discuss using audio files, Macromedia Flash movies, and streaming video.

Using Audio

Using audio in any web-based application can be tricky. The reason for this is that there are many different audio formats, and even more audio players. This leads to a great deal of unpredictability when it comes to the end-user experience. You never know what audio player the end-user has and how it will play the audio.

Some browsers support integrated audio capabilities. You've probably visited web sites that start playing a MIDI file when the page loads. The MIDI file is played by a default browser plugin.

However, most current browsers launch an external player when a WAV or MP3 file is served from the web server. This creates a very clunky experience for the user and is especially undesirable in a learning application where you want the technology to be as transparent as possible.

This kind of awkward user experience takes place when you use the *Play Sound* action in Dreamweaver. In this section we explain a few more acceptable solutions.

Solution 1: Use Macromedia Flash

We recommend using Macromedia Flash to package your audio for delivery over the web. The Flash Player plugin has penetrated the browser user base sufficiently to give you confidence that the majority of end-users won't have to download or install a plugin to hear your audio. It is also packaged and installed by default with most new major browser releases.

For Flash movies that should play when the page loads and contain only audio (and no animation) we suggest creating a 18x18 pixel-wide flash movie (the smallest size

Flash allows) and placing it in a layer. The Flash movie normally plays automatically when the page loads.

For Flash movies that should play in response to something the learner does, use the *Control Shockwave or Flash* action:

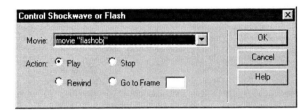

 More Information: For more information on how to use this action, see *Using Macromedia Flash* later in this Appendix.

 On CD: See *Sample_AudioFlash.htm* on the CD ROM for an example of Flash–based audio integrated into a CourseBuilder interaction. You may also want to open *SoundSample.fla* in Macromedia Flash to see how we constructed the flash file.

 More Information: Explaining how to use Macromedia Flash to create audio and animation is outside the scope of this book. Please refer to any of the excellent books on Macromedia Flash available on the market.

Solution 2: Use Beatnik™

Beatnik is a browser plugin that makes "sonification" of web pages completely transparent to the user. Web pages that use it can be a lot of fun and very compelling. However, the plugin is not as widely used as the Macromedia Flash plugin, so your end-users will probably need to install it.

At one time Beatnik provided Dreamweaver behaviors to help integrate the plugin into Dreamweaver pages, but they are no longer found on the web site. When we asked for an explanation, Beatnik responded that instead of the Dreamweaver behaviors, they offer Beatnik's Music Object API.

 More Information: See *www.beatnik.com* for more details about the Beatnik plugin. Also see *www.sonify.org* for tutorials on Beatnik and other web sonification issues.

Using Macromedia Flash®

To use Macromedia Flash movies in CourseBuilder, use the ***Control Shockwave or Flash*** action in the Action Manager.

Follow these steps to insert and play a Macromedia Flash movie from within CourseBuilder:

1   Define a Flash movie by clicking the **Insert Flash** button on Objects panel:

2   Choose the Flash file you want to insert.

Dreamweaver displays this visual placeholder to represent the Flash movie:

3   Open the Properties panel (Windows→Properties):

Name field

ID field

4   Enter a name and an ID:

5   Edit the CourseBuilder interaction and click the Action Manager tab.

6   Choose **Control Shockwave or Flash** from the drop down list at the top of
the tab, to add an **Control Shockwave or Flash** action:

Control Shockwave or Flash	☒
Movie: movie "flashobj" ▾	OK
Action: ⦿ Play ◯ Stop	Cancel
◯ Rewind ◯ Go to Frame [ ]	Help

7   Select the movie from the drop down list in the Control Shockwave or Flash
window.

8   Select *Play* (or one of the other actions: *Rewind*, *Stop*, or *Go to Frame*).

9   Click **OK**.

The Flash movie is now set up to play based on your Action Manager settings.

On CD: For a very simple example of a CourseBuilder Interaction starting a Flash movie, see
Sample_6-2.htm. You may also want to see Samp*le_AudioFlash.htm*.

Tips for Working with Flash Movies

Here are some things we've noticed when working with Flash movies and
Dreamweaver that might make your experience a little easier:

- Flash movies are often set to loop by default. If you only want it to play
  through once, make sure the *.fla* file is set to stop using the stop action in the
  final frame.

- Make sure you name your object and give it an ID in the Properties panel (as
  described above). If you try to use the Control Shockwave or Flash action
  before you take this step you may get unpredictable results.

- Make sure the Flash movie is visible at the time you try to control it with the
  Control Shockwave or Flash action. In other words, if you place it in a layer
  (which we usually do to get it out of the way or position it for good viewing),
  make sure that layer is showing *before* you try to control it.

- For best results, make the name and ID of the Flash movie identical.

Using Streaming Video

There are many formats of streaming video. Discussing the formats, variations of streaming media, and streaming media authoring tools is beyond the scope of this book. However, we want to give you some ideas to get you started.

Here we'll review two potential solutions, one for Real Media and one for Windows Media.

Note: You won't be able to test the streaming video effectively until the page and the media source file are uploaded to a server that can stream the video.

Note: Both of these solutions use third party extensions that help you work with ActiveX controls. For more information about ActiveX controls, see your favorite Dreamweaver reference.

RealMedia®

To embed a Real Media video or other type of Real Networks streaming file into your web page or into a layer, download the RealMedia Suite extension from the Macromedia Exchange for Dreamweaver site:

    http://www.macromedia.com/exchange/dreamweaver/

Once installed, Dreamweaver displays a new option in the Insert menu:

RealMedia submenu —————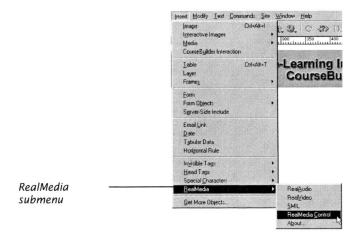

When you choose to insert an object from the RealMedia submenu, the object displays these properties on the Properties panel:

RealMedia	W 375	Control	Basic Control	
	H 100	Src	RealMedia Sample.rr	
		☑ Metafile	Sample_Video Embed.r	

More Information: Choose Insert→RealMedia→About to see RealMedia's online help for their extension.

Windows Media®

To embed a Windows Media format video, you can use the third party extension called Videoembed. Search for and download this extension from the Macromedia Exchange for Dreamweaver:

```
http://www.macromedia.com/exchange/dreamweaver/
```
Once installed you can insert the video into the Dreamweaver page by choosing the Videoembed button from the Media category of the Objects panel (Windows→Objects):

The Videoembed extension displays this window:

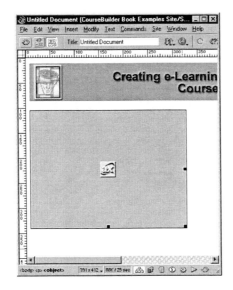

Complete the options and your video is embedded in the web page. A placeholder looks like this displays:

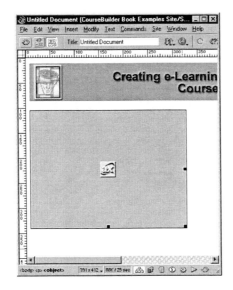

As you can see, embedding video is not terribly hard using these extensions. However, there are many issues including bandwidth, streaming server licensing, and plugin downloading that all make delivering streaming video a little more complicated than it appears on the surface. Both Microsoft (*http://www.microsoft.com/windows/windowsmedia/en/default.asp*) and RealNetworks (*www.realnetworks.com*) have additional information on their sites about streaming technology.

Index

Z